EUROPE
AT THE
MASTERS

BY
Steve Rider

This edition first published in the UK in 2006 by Green Umbrella Publishing
exclusively for:
Sutton Publishing, Phoenix Mill, Thrupp, Stroud, Gloucestershire GL5 2BU

First published in the UK 2006

© Green Umbrella Publishing 2006

British Library Cataloguing in Publication Data.
A catalogue record of this book is available from the British Library.

Printed and bound in China   ISBN 0 7509 4254 1

EUROPE AT THE MASTERS

CONTENTS

FOREWORD

Steve Rider has produced a most fascinating look at golf at The Masters, this time through European eyes. Steve has been part of the BBC golf team for over twenty years and this book helps emphasise how many incidents, moments and strange happenings disappear into the mists of time.

The main reason for this may be that The Masters, apart from the weather, is pretty well always the same, although every year it's different! It has always amazed me how the Club has managed to change the golf course in so many different ways with hardly anybody noticing – a new tee here, a reshaped green there, some extra bunkers on the hill, some tree planting – all manner of things that add to the mystique of Augusta and The Masters.

The Club and its committee are very much their 'own men' but it's obvious that they have a good understanding and rapport with BBC Television, and recently awarded them the longest contract ever bestowed on a television company, including the host broadcasters CBS. Whether it's the style of commentary, the lack of commercials, (although due to their operating style, commercials are cut to an absolute minimum), its content, I know not. We certainly have not been sycophantic over the years and, when we thought the occasion merited, criticisms were voiced, but through it all we remained 'partners.'

Steve Rider has many glorious qualities, not least of which is being a good luck talisman. During the years of covering The Masters he saw a number of British and continental golfers winning the coveted Green Jacket. What excitement, after so many years of being elated if one of our players

merely managed to play all 72 holes. To have winners was a wondrous thing and, I confess, on those occasions we were slightly partisan in OUR particular celebrations at the close of play.

Steve has gone beyond the winners to tell the stories and achievements of the European players who competed from the early years of the event, and he has also managed to capture a lot of the atmosphere of the event. To this I would add the enjoyment of staying together for so many years at the same houses at West Lake just a few miles from the course. The barbecues, the late night chats and the rather randomly organised supermarket shopping, all added to the adventure which I have been pleased to be part of. Although Steve was rather slow in helping lay the dinner table or doing the washing up, he was a glorious companion.

Enjoy.

Too many cooks! Dougie Donnelly, Alex Hay, Ken Brown, myself and Steve toasting European success and a sausage.

CHAPTER 1

A DEFINING MOMENT

CHAPTER 1

To both the spectator and the television viewer, the Augusta National, and in particular the back nine of the Augusta National, is one of the great theatres of sport, witnessing glories to rival not only a Covent Garden finale but also a downfall of Shakespearean proportions. The best tactic is to plant your green folding chair in a prize spot and watch the drama pass. Following the play on foot is for the fit and committed.

But on that afternoon of April 10th 1988, no British spectators, and especially no Scots, were sitting still. The few hundred yards from the 17th green, past the stand of trees to the bunkers that guard the left of the eighteenth fairway, are a congested corner, especially when the last pairing in The Masters was playing this final hole.

Those that were able to push their way towards the gallery rope were just able to see the ball of Sandy Lyle in the first of those bunkers. It was lying well, but the flag on the steeply sloping eighteenth green was 150 yards distant. Lyle was in the form of his life, but those who had managed to get to this second shot vantage point would not have seen his anguished reaction on the tee.

He'd hit a one iron that initially seemed perfect before drifting off left into the sand. His chance of Masters victory seemed to be drifting with the shot, and back on the tee Lyle hopped from one foot to the other in frustration. The best he could really hope for now was the par four that would take him into a sudden death play-off with Mark Calcavecchia. After all, no player had birdied the last hole to win The Masters since Arnold Palmer in 1960.

But even so, this was by far the best British performance in the fifty four year history of this most distinctive of golf's four Majors. Seve Ballesteros had made the breakthrough on behalf of European golf with his two Masters victories in the early eighties. Bernhard Langer was also triumphant: Europe had won the Ryder Cup and successfully defended it in America the year before. Lyle and Nick Faldo had both won the Open Championship Jacklin had won the U.S. Open, but for British golf The Masters remained elusive.

Any British victory here would have a huge impact on the growing strength of European golf. No event outside the Open and the Ryder Cup registered as strongly with British television viewers for whom that special Sunday night in April had meant Fuzzy Zoeller's debut win, the triumphs of Ballesteros and Langer, the chip-in of Larry Mize that denied Greg Norman and the epic win for Jack Nicklaus at forty six years of age.

When Sandy got to his ball in the bunker the frustration that he'd shown on the tee had subsided. He had a chance. Someone in the gallery mentioned that they'd seen Craig Stadler get to the green from this bunker just a short time before, but he wasn't quite this close to the lip, and he didn't need a three to win The Masters.

The seven iron he played needed to be clean, and if it cleared the lip anything was still possible. It would later be named shot of the season and one of the greatest shots Augusta had ever seen. As it soared toward the horizon, caddie Dave Musgrove scrambled to rake the bunker, merely relieved it was out unimpeded.

His boss was on his way, almost running up the deceptively steep eighteenth fairway, desperately anxious to discover the result of what seemed to be the perfect shot. The roar of the gallery told him it had hit the green, and the growing crescendo of noise told him it was still on the move, coming back down the slope and toward the hole.

In the BBC commentary box Peter Alliss urged it closer to the hole; so too did millions of television viewers in the UK, where it was shortly after eleven o'clock at night.

The ball had rolled in a dead straight line back toward the hole, coming to rest just ten feet away. Lyle and Musgrove correctly read the putt as continuing dead straight. For the first time a British golfer had a putt to win The Masters.

It was just a touch to set it on its way. Years later it was the putt that both Phil Mickelson and, in 2005, Tiger Woods would make to secure victory. When it dropped, the brief jig of victory was a happy contrast with the hop of frustration we had seen ten minutes earlier on the

eighteenth tee. But it hardly seemed sufficient celebration for what had been achieved.

At last British golf had broken through at the tournament that British golf fans seemed to covet most. The impact of European golf at Augusta was complete.

A hundred yards away on the balcony of the Augusta National, myself and the rest of the BBC presentation team were doing our best to put the achievement in context. We had the ideal personalities to do that. Tony Jacklin, the inspiration of all the recent Ryder Cup success and Open Champion Nick Faldo, who, a few

Sandy Lyle holes his putt on the 18th green to secure The Masters.

LYLE

weeks later, would be beaten in a play-off for the U.S. Open. But neither had ever threatened at Augusta. They knew the scale of what they had just seen, and they found the perfect words and sentiments to do justice to Lyle's victory.

A few minutes later we were joined live by Sandy's parents Alec and Agnes and then by Dave Musgrove, and after a few breathless comments we watched Sandy in the Butler Cabin receiving the Masters Green Jacket, symbol of so much in golf, from the previous year's winner, Larry Mize.

Any Masters winner will tell you that the next few hours are an absolute whirlwind, but straight from the Butler Cabin, Sandy somehow managed to dodge the bodyguards marching him to the formal prize-giving on the practice putting green, and there he was bounding up the steps to the clubhouse balcony to our own particular reception, broadcast live to our late night audience.

Minutes later we were off the air, an historic night for British sport, and the question lingered: how much more could European golf achieve?

Then up the whitewashed steps came the ominous figure of Jim Armstrong, the General Manager of the Augusta National, the man who runs the Masters, and he clearly was not happy. For any broadcaster The Masters contract hangs by a thread, even CBS who have just clocked up fifty years as host broadcaster at Augusta only get a one year deal, and our performance is constantly monitored.

Mr Armstrong explained that he did not appreciate us interposing ourselves in the new champion's schedule and so delaying the formal prize-giving and the tightly choreographed timetable that follows.

Humble apologies followed, at which point he smiled indulgently and said he appreciated how unique the occasion had been for us and how the opportunity for British golf to celebrate like this at Augusta might not happen again for many, many years.

I grinned, and alongside me so too did Nick Faldo. Augusta and The Masters was going to define the progress of European golf, like no other venue and no other competition.

The Augusta National Clubhouse and gardens.

Nick Faldo on the 1st tee at Augusta, in front of the Butler Cabin.

CHAPTER 2

THE EARLY YEARS

Bobby Jones drives off from the first tee at the Old Course, St. Andrews in the 1927 Open.

Bobby Jones would have approved of what Sandy Lyle achieved. It might have taken European golf a while to figure on The Masters roll of honour, and it might have taken far too long for European faces to be seen in the Champions locker room at the Augusta National, but the influence of Europe on the Augusta National and The Masters was strong from the start.

Jones, a native of Georgia, was the greatest golfer of his generation and, through the Twenties and early Thirties, did as much to promote the popularity of this most distinguished of amateur sports as Arnold Palmer did, as the professional era gathered pace in the Sixties. And like Palmer, Bobby Jones crossed the Atlantic with regularity and enthusiasm.

It was the Old Course at St. Andrews that had the most profound effect on Jones as a player and a personality.

In 1921 he had contested his first Open Championship there, and torn up his card in a fit of immature temper after taking four to get out of a bunker at the eleventh.

And it was at the Old Course at St. Andrews that Jones won the Open in 1927, and then the Amateur Championship in 1930, on his way to winning the Open and Amateur Championships of the United States and Great Britain in a single year. A Grand Slam which will surely never be repeated.

Many years later when Jones, by this time crippled by a rare spinal disease, was invited back to Scotland to receive the Freedom of St. Andrews, he spoke with great emotion of his feelings for the Old Course, 'a wise old lady, whimsically tolerant of my impatience, but ready to reveal the secrets of her complex being, if only I would take the trouble to study and learn. I could take out of my life everything except my experiences at St. Andrews, and I would still have a rich, full life.'

Soon after that Grand Slam, at the age of 28, Jones set about dedicating his life to things other than tournament golf. There was his law practice, there were other business opportunities that his fame had brought, but more than anything there was the dream to build a golf course, as near to perfection as could be produced, where his friends could gather and socialise and play golf in private. All he needed was finance, a location and the best golf course architect he could find.

Slowly the components came together. Jones wanted to build near to his native city of Atlanta. As the Depression began to bite, the resort town of Augusta, with its textile manufacturing and heavy industry, was hit as hard as any. Jones knew the town as a welcoming resort, and was persuaded that the declining hotel businesses in Augusta would profit from the attraction of a new Bobby Jones golf course.

His friendship and association with a mid-western businessman named Clifford Roberts helped source the finance, and the Mayor of Augusta helped identify a

St. Andrews, the home of golf proved to be influential in the design of The Augusta National course.

potential site. It was one that Bobby Jones had glimpsed through the perimeter pine trees on the occasions when he had been playing at the Augusta Country Club.

Fruitlands was an abandoned 365 acre nursery off the Washington Road. It had been set up as the first commercial nursery in the South by a Belgian baron in the mid-nineteenth century. When it was unsuccessfully handed down through his family it fell into disrepair, but even in the early Thirties the raw material was clear.

An old colonial style manor house on top of the hill, and then a vista of rolling slopes full of pine, pear trees, magnolias and azaleas, as well as many rare shrubs and plants. Most of the flowering plants that bloom now at the Augusta National during Masters week are descended from Fruitlands stock.

The oldest part of the property was the access road that connected the Manor House to Washington Road. The magnolias that lined this driveway were planted from seeds

Clifford Roberts (centre) standing with President Dwight D. Eisenhower (left).

before the outbreak of the Civil War. Magnolia Avenue, as it was known then, would later become Magnolia Lane. All the ingredients were there. No wonder Jones gazed out over the slopes for the first time and said, 'To think this ground has been lying here all these years, just waiting for someone to come along and lay a golf course upon it.'

But who would take on the task? Certainly Jones had visions of the character of the course he wanted to build and the kind of holes he wanted to construct. And he had a timetable, having no desire to turn professional, and having long

since made the decision that 1930 would be his last competitive season, no matter what kind of 'Grand Slam' he achieved.

This was where fate took a hand, and where the first formal transatlantic connection was made with what was to become the Augusta National.

In 1929, Bobby Jones, at the height of his glorious powers, went to Pebble Beach in California to contest the U.S. Amateur Championship as overwhelming favourite. He would be defending the title for the third time, having won four of the last five Championships. He was also U.S. Open Champion, and, just like Tiger Woods today, Jones, at 29, had the golfing public speculating about the number of major titles he could go on to win.

But at Pebble Beach the unthinkable happened. In the first round of match play, Jones was drawn against the comparatively little known Johnny Goodman who was the 157th ranked qualifier. Jones was beaten on the final green. The scale of the shock was enormous. For the first time in six years the U.S. Amateur did not have Bobby Jones dominating the event all the way to the final.

By now however, this was a different Bobby Jones to the immature character who stormed petulantly away from St. Andrews in 1921. Other beaten players would take the first train home after such a defeat, but Jones decided to stay on at Pebble Beach to see how the competition progressed, partly because he had never had the opportunity to watch such a major championship as a spectator. Not only that but he also offered his services as a third round referee.

But other spare time he had, as the weekend approached, he spent in conversation with the renowned

British golf course architect Alister Mackenzie who had designed the neighbouring Cypress Point and had been a resident in California since 1927.

Mackenzie was a slightly mysterious personality. Some say he was born in Birmingham, others say he was born in

during World War I. When his enthusiasm for golf later evolved into a passion for golf course design, a subtle use of what he saw as camouflage would become his trademark.

He wrote,' I was a keen golfer, and while studying camouflage defences it struck me that inland golf courses could be vastly improved, not only from the point of view of beauty, but in creating interesting strategic problems by the imitation of the natural features characteristic of the only golf courses which were at that time worthwhile, namely the sand dunes by the sea. I then became one of the pioneers of modern golf course architecture and wrote the first book on the subject.'

Mackenzie clearly had a strong sense of self-worth, but there was nothing overly flamboyant in his philosophy of golf course architecture. He believed in using natural contours and resources, and he believed in avoiding a formulaic, predictable approach. He wanted his courses to have the eccentricity and ability to surprise, that links golf provided.

His style of design could be summarised by an ambition to bring links golf inland. As the consulting architect to St. Andrews he had an intimate understanding of the original form of golf, and it was clear that he had Bobby Jones's support in trying to transfer at least some of the feel and challenge of the home of golf to what would become the Augusta National.

In his foreword to Mackenzie's book, *The Spirit of St. Andrews*, Bobby Jones wrote, 'Like myself, Dr. Mackenzie is a lover of old St. Andrews. Of course, like everyone else, he despairs of producing anything quite so good, but the doctor's experience with camouflage and his innate artistry enable him to convert an inland terrain into something surprisingly like the seaside links land, which is the very best golfing country.'

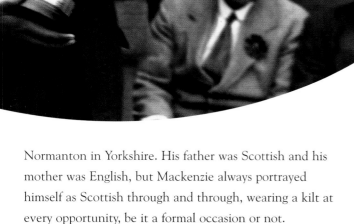

Bobby Jones holding the Open trophy in 1927. He won with a record score of 285.

Normanton in Yorkshire. His father was Scottish and his mother was English, but Mackenzie always portrayed himself as Scottish through and through, wearing a kilt at every opportunity, be it a formal occasion or not.

He trained in medicine and served as a civilian surgeon in the Boer War, where he became a great admirer of the art of camouflage that the Boers had perfected, and he would go on to set up the British School of Camouflage

The partnership seemed to be formed from that meeting in 1929, even though at this stage Jones had not been introduced to the Fruitlands site, and his course and club were still a distant ambition for when his playing days were over, at the end of the following year.

But when the components did come together Mackenzie and Jones were able to go to work with a

Alister Mackenzie poses in his kilt.

relationship built on mutual respect, and an acknowledgement that each was bringing something different to the project. And even though the plan was, in theory, to build the greatest inland course that golf had ever seen, there was no ego on either side.

Mackenzie enjoyed working to a budget, believing that no golf course should take more than a hundred thousand

dollars to design and construct. In theory he should have had no fears of budgetary constraints with the Augusta project. The final bill was a mere $101,000, and astonishingly it was completed within a year.

But this disguised a lot of uncertainty in the decision making in the early stages of the project, and ultimately, Mackenzie would have a lot of trouble getting his final bill paid by the club. America was in the midst of the Depression, and although this gave the club a huge amount of very cheap labour to work on the construction, there was a lot of doubt whether the time was right for a project of this ambition.

The decision to proceed with construction was taken in 1931 with Mackenzie making his first site visit in July, and with Bobby Jones he hacked his way through some pretty dense undergrowth to stake out tees and greens.

Construction began in earnest in February 1932, and even though it involved much felling and removal of trees, the movement of 120,000 cubic yards of soil and the installation of a sophisticated irrigation system, the construction was completed in 124 consecutive calendar days; still believed to be a record for major golf course construction.

The Bermuda grass seed was planted in May. According to reports, mowing began on June 10th and Bobby Jones played his first round on the course in August, and pronounced himself delighted.

But although Jones had at least part of his dream complete, the atmosphere of the time remained bleak. The club's debts mounted at an alarming rate. The blue chip membership that the club craved, remained reluctant to

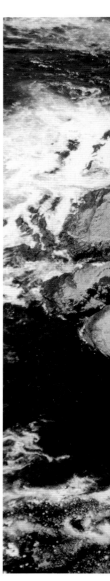

commit in the continuing grip of the Depression; and out in California Dr. Alister Mackenzie's pleas for payment became ever more urgent.

With his wife unwell and his own bills mounting, they had to mortgage their home and live frugally in an attempt to ride out the crisis. But the man whose imagination and design skill provided the template for so much sporting drama to come, would not be part of the Augusta National dream, let alone The Masters.

In January 1934, after a brief illness Dr. Mackenzie died, aged sixty three. He had paid his last visit to Augusta to supervise the seeding in April. He never lived

to see the course completed or golf played upon it. After a funeral service in California his ashes were sent back home to Scotland.

So had Mackenzie and Jones created an imitation of St. Andrews in this Augusta suburb? Certainly the comparisons are not obvious. Windswept links opposed to manicured perfection, and a course that had been ruggedly sculpted by nature instead of planned by the skill of an architect.

The similarity is in the demands that each course would make, and Mackenzie, through his experience at St Andrews, wanted to reproduce the golfing test that the

The mighty Cypress Point Golf Club in California, designed by Alister Mackenzie.

The famous seventeenth at St. Andrews.

Old Course provides. A test that rewards mind over muscle; where strategy is the key and holes which open up the strong possibility of birdies and eagles, also open up the equally strong possibility of something a great deal worse.

Mackenzie was also a strong believer in fairways that were not too rigidly defined, feeling that a formal first and second cut of rough could end up looking like a high street pavement. To this end he also believed that there should be, at times, the option of approaching a hole from an adjoining fairway; something that was also very characteristic of St. Andrews. At Augusta it was a feature that would certainly benefit Seve Ballesteros and Ian Woosnam, as they put together their winning performances in later years.

The reason we are sure that St. Andrews was such a strong influence is from Mackenzie's own writings. In his guide to playing the Augusta National he left no room for doubt:

Number Four, par three. This is a very similar hole to the famous eleventh at St. Andrews.

Number Five, par four. This is a similar type hole to the famous seventeenth at St. Andrews.

Number Seven, par four. This hole is similar in character to the eighteenth hole at St. Andrews.

Number Fourteen, par four. This hole embodies some of the features of the sixth at St. Andrews.

Number Seventeen, par four. The construction of the green is somewhat similar to that famous fourteenth at St. Andrews.

Other courses did get a look-in and it was quite clear that the par three sixteenth at Augusta was based on the seventh at Stoke Poges in Buckinghamshire, one of Mackenzie's favourite courses. In Mackenzie's original Augusta design however, the sixteenth tee was on the right of the fifteenth, and the sixteenth green itself was merely guarded by a small tributary of Raes Creek. It was not until 1947 that Jones proposed moving the tee to its current position, on the left of the fifteenth, and damming the creek to produce a small lake; thus creating one of the most photographed and recognisable holes in golf.

St. Andrews, however, was the defining influence, and the renowned British golf journalist Leonard Crawley wrote, after playing there for the first time in 1947, 'They have not copied one single hole on those maddeningly difficult and infinitely fascinating links. But they built eighteen great holes, every one of which is perfectly fair and provides a problem. It seems to me that each one demands that a player shall firstly and fore-mostly use his brains and not merely his physical, and, in these days, his almost mechanical ability to hit a target from a particular range. It restores the ideas of some of the old original golf links which furnished the world with those great players, upon whose methods and tremendous skill, the modern games is now based.'

In the early stages of construction, Bobby Jones hit hundreds of his elegant iron shots around the site to fine-tune the final design. But one change he made was certainly not fine tuning; it was the equivalent of taking

The first Augusta National Programme Cover from January 1933.

the engine out and sticking it in the boot. Jones decided to reverse the nines from Mackenzie's original plan, so the opening tee shot was the booming drive down what is now the tenth, and what was to become the legendary Amen Corner, was originally the second, third and fourth.

The thinking behind this was unclear, and indeed the first Masters tournament was played with the course in this configuration before the order was reversed back. The reason for the change back was thought to be that the early morning spring frost would clear quicker from the top end of the course, compared to the hollows and shady corners down the hill, allowing more time for play.

In December 1932, the course, immediately known as the Augusta National, was opened for play, and the formal opening of the club, with its membership largely made up of high flyers from the North East and New York, was in January 1933.

The supreme quality of the course was obvious from the outset, and British golf had certainly played its part both in the inspiration and the construction.

Shortly before the Augusta National course opened, an exhibition match was played between Bobby Jones, Dick Metz, Ed Dudley and Ky Lafoon.

CHAPTER 3

THE EARLY CHALLENGERS

CHAPTER 3

The Augusta National, despite its specification, made a faltering start. That 'formal' opening of the club had consisted of the original membership being brought down in a fleet of Pullman cars on the Pennsylvania railroad from New York. There then followed three days of golf in bitterly cold and wet conditions, with the players being sustained, not by the quality of their surroundings, but by liberal measures of corn whiskey taken at regular intervals around the course.

But it was at this gathering that the decision was swiftly taken that this would be no ordinary club run by layers of bureaucracy and committees. Instead, because of the far flung membership, the running of the club would be left entirely in the hands of Bobby Jones and also a New York investment banker named Clifford Roberts.

Roberts, like so many others, had suffered in the Wall Street crash and had spent more and more time in Georgia playing his golf at the Augusta Country Club, where a friendship with Bobby Jones developed. It was this friendship and partnership that would underpin the development of the Augusta National and everything that it became, and the original membership was happy to put the entire responsibility in their hands.

What would help secure the future of the new club would be the opportunity to stage a tournament or championship of significance, maybe even the U.S. Open.

This was a long-held ambition of Bobby Jones, and he was encouraged by some promising overtures by the United States Golf Association who ran the U.S. Open.

In the Thirties, professional tournament golf was a lot more fragmented than it is today, with the modern frameworks that are provided by the likes of the U.S. PGA and the European Tour. Seventy years ago the majority of players on both sides of the Atlantic were locked into responsibilities as club professionals, and building a tournament schedule was not necessarily the number one priority.

So there were only a handful of tournaments in the south eastern corner of the United States in the very early spring, while players looked after their club members, and the U.S. Open itself was locked into being played in the month of June and had never been staged further south than Illinois. Indeed, the other great U.S. GA event, the U.S. Amateur Championship, given new status by the feats of Bobby Jones, had also never travelled south.

This was a geographical bias that Jones was keen to correct by bringing, hopefully, the U.S. Open to the Augusta National. It would also have the significant benefit of attracting attention to the new course which in turn would produce new membership, and maybe a grant from the U.S. GA for some necessary ground improvements. The fledgling Augusta National, despite its pedigree and status, was having the same kind of financial and practical problems as any other new course before or since.

But the obstacles of bringing a championship like the U.S. Open to Georgia were to prove insurmountable. The summer heat in that part of the United States meant that a traditional June date for the U.S. Open was impractical. If the event were to be staged at the Augusta National it would have to be in the more favourable weather conditions of March or April. This would have a knock-on effect for qualifying and also complicate life for the players who had club responsibilities. This was one Bobby Jones dream that was not going to happen.

Instead, the thoughts of Jones and Clifford Roberts started to turn toward the more modest proposal of an

Bobby Jones pictured with the U.S. Open trophy.

Augusta Invitational Tournament to be inserted into the PGA schedule for 1934. It would be a tournament designed, in particular, to attract the players who had been competing in the Florida tournaments and the collection of events in the south east, and were now making their way back up north.

Clifford Roberts, in particular, had been very disappointed with the failure of Augusta to land the U.S. Open, but soon he was starting to feel more and more positive about plans for the new event. He suggested that Augusta did not need the U.S. Open, writing at the time, 'The tournament we are planning will do a great deal more for our club, especially since it would be a regular annual event.'

Horton Smith, the first ever winner of The Masters in 1934.

America for whom Jones still had the audience appeal of a modern day Tiger Woods. Instead, his attitude was, 'how can I invite my friends to a tournament and not take part myself?'

Even though there was great public anticipation for Bobby Jones's return to competition, it seemed as if it was this sociable aspect of the Tournament and the opportunity to return a favour for a few friends, that dictated the shape of the original invitation list. There was not yet any sign of the strict Masters qualification criteria, although this was not too distant in the future.

The invitation list for the inaugural event included the top names of the time such as Horton Smith, the eventual winner, Craig Wood and Walter Hagen. Gene Sarazen was a late withdrawal, having overlooked a prior commercial commitment, but he would make his telling contribution a year later. Jones declared himself 'disappointed' with the international response, although it is unclear precisely what invitations he sent out. Only four overseas players took part in that first year. Canadian C. Ross Somerville was not exactly too far distant. Harry Cooper, officially from England, was actually resident in the United States. C.T. Wilson, a British professional, seems to have disappeared from all record books of the time, and there was an amateur from Sunningdale, C.G. Stevens.

Captain Charles Greville Stevens, late of the 43rd Light Infantry, was a member of the Royal and Ancient and by 1934 he had won the R&A's Bombay medal and Jubilee vase. But it was being a Sunningdale member, where he won the Club Gold medal in 1932, that probably served him best in getting an invitation to Augusta in 1934.

Bobby Jones's feelings for the famous Surrey heath-land course were almost as strong as those for St. Andrews, but it does not seem as if those feelings were completely reciprocated. When, in 1926, Sunningdale staged the Southern Section qualifying rounds for the Open Championship, Jones was in the field, and his opening round of 66, a full six shots inside the existing course record, was seemed to be as close to flawless golf as you could get.

As the inaugural Invitation Tournament, as it was then known, started taking shape, Clifford Roberts's plans for it became grander and grander. He wanted to call it, The Masters, to which Jones objected strongly. Jones also objected to any suggestion that he himself should enter – after all, he had retired from competition four years earlier – but the success and the appeal of the tournament was absolutely dependent on Jones taking part.

Eventually he was persuaded, not officially by the needs of Augusta, nor by the enthusiasm of the PGA of

Those who saw it would never forget it. James Sheridan, who saw just about everything in his fifty-six years as caddie-master at Sunningdale, described it as his supreme golfing memory. Jones himself said, 'It was as perfect a round of golf as I have ever played in my life. Even when I shoot a good round of golf, I doubt that I put six shots exactly where I want, but this was uncanny.' Jones of course would go on to win the Championship itself that year at Royal Lytham.

However, when the suggestion was made at Sunningdale that this superlative performance should be commemorated by a tablet or plaque in the clubhouse, the reply was, 'The Committee does not agree with this suggestion. It does not seem to them appropriate to commemorate by a permanent tablet in the club what, after all, is only an isolated instance of good scoring.'

Hopefully, Jones was ignorant of this debate, but he was only too aware of the head-waiter who barred his way at the Sunningdale clubhouse door and insisted he use the back door that all professionals were compelled to use. No-one cherished amateur status more than Bobby Jones, but none of these slights prevented Captain C.G. Stevens receiving his invitation as the first British amateur to compete at what was to become the U.S. Masters. It would be good to report that he graced the opportunity with a glorious challenge, but after rounds of 82 and 81 left him propping up the field, Stevens withdrew at the halfway stage.

Bobby Jones duly finished that first Augusta Invitational as low amateur, although no-one seemed absolutely sure of the purity of his amateur status, making, as he did, some $100,000 a year from his commercial connections with golf. Horton Smith's victory by one shot over Craig Wood was based on a silky-smooth putting stroke that saw him make a number of telling twenty

Walter Hagen, one of the early competitors in The Masters.

Sunningdale, another favourite of Bobby Jones.

footers, although by all accounts the greens had yet to take on the slick, lightning-fast characteristics we see today.

In most respects the event had been a success and brought in big crowds from far afield, drawn, almost universally, by the prospect of seeing the great Bobby Jones. The press gave it almost the same attention they afforded to the U.S. Open and did not waste any time describing it with a fiddling little title like the Augusta Invitational. Almost from the outset it was described as The Augusta Masters, soon to be abbreviated to simply, The Masters.

The event also set out to establish new standards in spectator facilities, with car parking, draw sheets, scoreboards around the course and paid staff instead of volunteers. As a result, the first Masters tournament, while being a popular success, was not a commercial one and with its $5,000 prize money it sustained a substantial loss. In 1935, with Bobby Jones clearly not the competitive force he once was, and the Depression continuing to grip America, The Masters had to be able to show it could survive in its own right. It needed something or someone, apart from Jones, to create the headlines.

That moment came in the final round of the second Masters Invitational in 1935, when an Augusta caddie nick-named 'Stovepipe' handed Gene Sarazen a four wood for his second shot on fifteen, with the instruction to 'toe it in a little.'

Sarazen had just heard the roar from the eighteenth green on top of the hill that indicated that Craig Wood had birdied to finish with a three shot lead over the rest of the field. In the modest group of spectators following Sarazen was Bobby Jones himself, who had finished with a disappointing final round of 78. Sarazen recalled later how Jones looked up the hill and said, 'That's our winner, I haven't got time to follow you bums any more, I've got a dinner date tonight.'

Whether or not Jones actually saw the four wood that Sarazen played moments later is not clear. Certainly over the years many, many thousands claimed to have seen the shot that just cleared the lake, bounced on the front edge

of the green and disappeared into the cup for an astonishing albatross, or double eagle two. In one stroke the lead of Craig Wood was wiped out. Sarazen would par his way in and go on to win the next day's thirty six hole play off by five shots.

Sarazen was one of the most charismatic figures of the era and his absence at the inaugural Masters was keenly felt. Now he had played the single shot that transformed The Masters from an event, almost wholly reliant on the

representation the previous year had now declined to just Harry Cooper and a couple of Canadians.

At this time it seemed that championship golf was becoming more entrenched on either side of the Atlantic. American players started staying away from the Open Championship. After ten years of American success in the event, largely through Bobby Jones, Walter Hagen and Gene Sarazen, post-Depression USA persuaded them to stay at home rather than make the long sea journey to Europe.

The attitude in Britain seemed to be the same. 1934 was the year that the win by Henry Cotton at Sandwich ended that decade of American dominance. His opening rounds of 67 and 65 marked him out as a player who could take the British game to new and exciting heights, but it would be 1948 before he made the first of his three trips to Augusta. This was the time that the competitive professional circuit was starting to establish itself in Britain. Players were concentrating on that, and an overseas approach to the Royal and Ancient in St. Andrews to try to stage a World Championship of Golf, was met with the terse reply that, 'The Open Championship *is* the World Championship of Golf.'

Craig Wood congratulates Gene Sarazen (left) after his victory.

presence of Jones, to a competition that had been given life and character by one of the most extraordinary shots in golf.

Certainly, Clifford Roberts was aware of the gift that had been bestowed by the four wood of Sarazen and encouraged the Press when they rather melodramatically described it as, 'the shot that was heard around the world.' In actual fact the world had largely ignored the 1935 Masters, and even the modest overseas

CHAPTER 4

THE PRE-WAR YEARS

So Bobby Jones and Clifford Roberts would have to wait a little longer before their Masters tournament became the international jamboree that it is today, but overseas representation had become a lower priority anyway. The club, through its first years, had limped through a number of financial crises, and even though staging their tournament had added to the financial pressures, Roberts still saw The Masters as the salvation of the club and the cornerstone of its reputation.

The participation of Bobby Jones had given the event its initial impetus, but that had now started to fade. The double eagle of Sarazen had given it a further boost, but Roberts saw the long-term future of the event in the quality of its presentation; not just the perfection of the course, but also the first class facilities for spectators, or patrons, as they had already become known. Consideration was given to viewing positions, catering, parking and scoring information, and the players themselves also required an extra bit of pampering to come to an event at an inconvenient time of year, at a comparatively out of the way location.

But amid these struggling formative years, Britain very nearly had its first Masters winner. Harry Cooper came close in 1936, 1937 and 1938. If he had gone on to clinch victory it could hardly be claimed as a huge triumph for British golf, but it would certainly have taken a little bit of the historical gloss off the performances of Sandy Lyle and Nick Faldo, fifty years later.

Harry Cooper was born in Leatherhead, in Surrey, in 1902 and he could hardly have had stronger golfing roots; his father Sid serving as an apprentice under Old Tom Morris at St. Andrews. The family lived at Slough for a year before moving to the Aberdovey Club in Wales where, as a young ten year old, Harry had his first experience of playing the game. The family emigrated to North America in 1912 and the holes that the very young Cooper played at Aberdovey would remain the only time he ever played golf in Britain.

But in all Masters records and all PGA playing records Harry Cooper would be listed as English, and in Al

Barkow's excellent book, *Gettin' to the Dance Floor*, on the early days of American Pro Golf, Harry Cooper said, 'I was born in England and that led to one of my biggest disappointments. You see, all the years I played on the tour I qualified for the U.S. Ryder Cup team, but I wasn't able to play because I wasn't a native born American.' He goes on to make the point that the likes of Tommy Armour and Bobby Cruickshank were ruled out in the same way, but at least they learnt their golf in Britain. Harry Cooper's golf was entirely a product of America.

So if Cooper had won The Masters it would, to this day, be recorded as a British victory. And how close he came, not only in The Masters, but also in the U.S. Open.

In the U.S. Open in 1936, Cooper recalled how the Baltusrol U.S. Open record was 286, and it was a record that had lasted for thirty years. Cooper shot 284, and the record lasted for thirty minutes. In finishing second to

Tony Manero that year, Cooper three putted the last green after waiting ten minutes for his playing partner Les Madison, who had his wallet stolen by a spectator while playing his second shot to the last.

Down the years, Cooper gave himself four opportunities to win the U.S. Open and missed out on each occasion. In an outstanding career in America he won twenty seven tournaments, but he was also twenty eight times runner-up and this misfortune extended to The Masters.

In the 1936 Masters, defending champion Gene Sarazen opened with a 78, and then would force himself back into contention with a second round 67, equalling the best of the week. But it was Cooper who set the pace throughout. On a difficult opening day his round of 70 was good enough to lead the field, and he stayed in front to lead Horton Smith by three shots into the final round. But then as Cooper faltered in rainy final day conditions, Horton Smith

Harry Cooper watches his shot during the first round of the The Masters in 1936.

Harry Cooper (second from right) lines up for a driving contest. Cooper won the event with a drive of 244 yards.

chipped in from fifty feet away at the fourteenth, and birdied the fifteenth as well, to beat the unfortunate Cooper by one shot.

The following year a second round of 69 left Cooper handily placed four shots off the lead, and he would stay in touch until Byron Nelson played the 12th and 13th in three under par to shake off all challengers. Cooper would eventually finish fourth. In 1938 Cooper hit the front in round one with a 68 that remained the best of the week, but the advantage would disappear with a second round 77 and he would finish tied for second, two shots behind Henry Picard.

His record of being consistently among the leaders at Augusta was interrupted in 1939, when Cooper was never

a factor in a tournament won by Ralph Guldahl, by a shot from Sam Snead. Cooper was back in a tie for 33rd. But it was only a brief interruption as the following year Cooper was back up among the first round leaders with a 64. However, he could not live with the form of the eventual winner Jimmy Demaret and would eventually be tied for fourth, his fourth top five finish, and he would add further finishes in the top twenty in 1940 and 1942.

He was known as 'Lighthorse' Harry Cooper because he walked fast and played fast. He got the nickname after winning the Los Angeles Open, completing his final round in two and a half hours, with 5,000 people following. But the man from Aberdovey, by way of Leatherhead and Slough, never won The Masters and never won a major. He said the one lesson he had taken from his career was, 'not to be in such a hurry to play, learn to wait, to be more patient.'

At Augusta, European golf would have to learn to be patient as well.

While Harry Cooper remains officially listed in all Masters records as English, mention must be made of at least two of the many so-called "transplanted Scots" who

Byron Nelson, twice winner of The Masters.

went to America in the early part of the century to try to make progress in the developing professional game. Like so many others, Bobby Cruickshank and Tommy Armour became naturalised Americans but would have brought a lot of reflected glory on Scottish golf if they had achieved Masters success in those early years.

Bobby Cruickshank was born in Grantown-on-Spey and Tommy Armour was born in Edinburgh and their respective golfing careers followed remarkably similar paths but only after they had shared horrifying experiences in the First World War.

Cruickshank saw very active service with the Seaforth Highlanders in the trenches of The Somme and Passchendale, and Armour, a British Officer in the war was seriously injured, eventually losing an eye in a mustard gas attack.

When their golfing lives resumed after the terrible conflict, both were prominent in the amateur game but both had ambitions to develop professional careers in

America; Cruickshank left for the USA in 1921 while Armour followed him in 1924.

It was Cruickshank who was able to take up the invitation for the inaugural Augusta Invitational event, finishing in a tie for 28th, and would go on to make seven Augusta appearances with a fourth place behind winner Horton Smith his best performance in 1936.

When Tommy Armour made his Masters debut in 1935 he was forty years old and had already won the U.S. Open and U.S. PGA Championships as well as The Open at Carnoustie. His transformation from Scottish amateur to American professional had become complete when,in contrast to Harry Cooper, he played for the United States in the 1926 Ryder Cup match. Like Cruickshank he made seven appearances at Augusta without ever threatening victory.

However, in sixth place in that inaugural Augusta event was Aberdeen born Willie McFarlane who had beaten Bobby Jones in a play-off for the 1925 U.S. Open.

The flamboyant
Jimmy Demaret.

CHAPTER 4

Ben Hogan (left) and Byron Nelson are tied with a score of 280 at The Masters in 1942.

Like all the other "transplanted Scots" he was not a direct flag-carrier for the British game but they all paved the way for Sandy Lyle fifty four years later; it was subtle, but the British influence was significant from year one.

The Masters was trying to move on from just being seen as 'The Bobby Jones Event.' Jones might have been the inspiration but sadly he had never been a serious contender at Augusta. Nevertheless, as far as the Press was concerned he was the main headline in the build-up to the Masters, and quite often the main focus of Press attention during the course of the tournament.

Clifford Roberts was swift to appreciate that getting the right things written about The Masters was a vital ingredient in its development, and was concerned that the now, inappropriate amount of attention on Jones, was turning it into more of a ceremonial occasion than a great championship.

He needed the extra breadth that the exploits of Sarazen had given it in 1935 and he certainly got it with the victory of Byron Nelson in 1937, and the arrival of Jimmy Demaret as a champion in 1940. Demaret had become the biggest personality on the tour, with his colourful extrovert clothes, his banter, his wisecracks and his extravagant golfing talent, and he won at Augusta in only his second appearance.

There was a further boost when, in 1942, Byron Nelson defeated Ben Hogan in an outstanding eighteen hole play-off. He overhauled Hogan's early three stroke lead to shoot five under par through the closing five holes, finally identifying this event in Augusta as among the most distinctive and competitive in American golf. Indeed the American game was about to recognise it as that vague but coveted prize, a 'Major.'

It had received the approval of the American golf followers, but it was making no progress in Bobby Jones's ambition for it to be a competition with international appeal. Harry Cooper's British credentials may have been vague, but across the years in which he contended strongly, he was the only professional player who gave European golf any kind of representation at Augusta.

From 1935 until the war, the only British player to compete at The Masters was the Surrey amateur Francis Francis; reinforcing the Sunningdale connection with Bobby Jones. He is described in the Sunningdale records as Frank Francis. He won the Surrey Amateur Championship twice, was Belgian and Dutch Amateur Champion, and runner-up with Leonard Crawley in the 1938 Sunningdale Foursomes. But he never played in the Walker Cup, which was the more formal qualification for a Masters place, so it can only be assumed that it was a special invitation from Bobby Jones that got F. Francis to the 1937 event. He re-paid Jones by beating him by a shot. Finishing a respectable 28th in what would be his only Masters appearance.

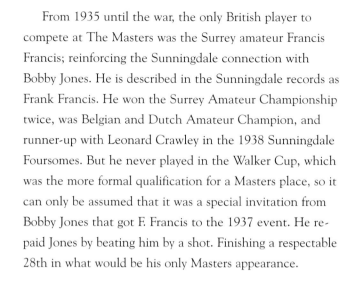

Lieutenant Colonel Bobby Jones receives his rations in a field in Normandy, 1944.

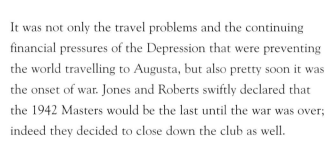

It was not only the travel problems and the continuing financial pressures of the Depression that were preventing the world travelling to Augusta, but also pretty soon it was the onset of war. Jones and Roberts swiftly declared that the 1942 Masters would be the last until the war was over; indeed they decided to close down the club as well.

Jones went into the Ninth Air Corps and at one point was stationed in north west England. Roberts also saw duty in Europe as well. But back at the golf club extraordinary things were happening. Augusta had become a military town with five army installations, and almost ten years after Bobby Jones and Alister Mackenzie had created golfing perfection, the old Fruitlands nursery had effectively become a farm.

Where Sarazen had hit the shot that was heard around the world, there were now two hundred head of steer keeping the grass down, and turkeys scratched and clawed where Byron Nelson had won his epic battle with Ben Hogan just a few weeks earlier. Like everywhere else Augusta had to pay its way in these demanding times, and although the turkeys had not only turned a decent profit but also beat rationing to grace the Christmas tables of members, the cattle had lost money and done a huge amount of damage, destroying turf and bark off the trees, as well as many of the magnificent shrubs with which Augusta was already being identified.

All this could be accepted because there were many in the membership who felt that the play-off win by Nelson

over Hogan would be the last competitive golf ever played at Augusta. But in late 1944 restoration work began, with the course scheduled to re-open in December. The extensive work load was accomplished with the help of forty two German prisoners of war from nearby Camp Gordon.

Along with the restoration of the course, the finances of the club were in much need of refreshment. With the help of a number of philanthropic gifts the property was able to move on to another level, with the construction of much needed extra clubhouse accommodation and two distinctive cottages, one of which would be alongside the tenth tee, for the use of Bobby Jones.

The world had changed. Could Augusta and The Masters resume the progress that they had clearly been making in the pre-war years? After a year of consolidation

and refurbishment the decision was taken that the next Masters would be staged from April 4th-7th, 1946.

When you look back at the records of who did what down the years at Augusta, one of the disappointments and missed opportunities from the point of view of British golf is that The Masters did not see more of Henry Cotton.

Cotton became a professional golfer in 1924, at the age of seventeen, and his Open Championship win at Royal St George's in 1934, that ended a decade of American victories, should ideally have been followed by a more concerted assault on American dominance. Even though he added another Open Championship win in 1937, he saved his Augusta debut until 1948, three months before winning the Open for a third time at Muirfield.

By this time he was 41 years old and the previous November had the dubious privilege of captaining the

Great Britain and Ireland Ryder Cup team as they went down to an overwhelming 11-1 defeat to the United States in Portland, Oregon. The defeat can be blamed partly on the journey: a four day crossing on the Queen Mary, followed by a three and a half day train ride. This also helps underline why more British and European players were not heading for Augusta every April.

But British golf had needed Cotton in his prime at Augusta in the formative years of The Masters, and his absence is more baffling when his career record shows how much he travelled to play the game. He was a copious writer about the sport, and in his book, *This Game of Golf,* he gives a fascinating British perspective on golf in America, especially when writing about his first trip to the USA in 1928.

'I arrived in New York City late in November after a rough crossing on The Aquitania, and went to The Chatham Hotel. Not much golf is played in the New York

Henry Cotton in full swing, 1934.

area in late November, but I could not resist going to see an American course at the first opportunity.

I do not recall the name of the club but I found the greens covered in straw and the ground frozen hard, making real golf out of the question. But I was impressed by the sumptuousness of the club-house and the general rich atmosphere of the club.'

Cotton then went across America to California to play in a selection of events in the American winter tour. But on arrival in San Francisco, instead of preparing for the first event in Sacramento, he immediately went down with flu, called a doctor and was put to bed.

'How miserable I was. I don't think I actually cried but I felt like it; being so far from home and in a strange land, and not knowing a soul. Apparently I was run down a bit and took a while to shake it off. This I did finally with the help of gallons of fresh orange juice, which page-boys in relays from the hotel kept bringing up to me. This health-giving juice so difficult to find in our country, was squeezed

before your eyes at nearly every street corner in America and cost, I think, only five cents a tumbler; tuppence half-penny in those days.'

But Cotton recovered enough to play in the up-coming event in Sacramento, and was surprised to find that the players in the tournament could choose who they played with in their three balls, and within reason and depending on status, could choose their starting time as well. Befriended by U.S. Open Champion, Tommy Armour, Cotton obviously got a good starting time and went on to finish third on his American debut.

Cotton worked his way across the Southern States with the winter tour, getting a lot of experience with the steel shafts that were now legal in the USA, and finding himself particularly impressed with the amount you could practice with them, compared to the traditional hickory shafts that you had to treat with respect and caution.

Other aspects of America and American golfing life he was apparently impressed with. 'I like the weatherproof boxes on the tees, full of cards and pencils. I like the seats on every tee. I like the rakes in bunkers, repairing pitch

Henry Cotton walking to his next shot at The Open in 1934.

marks. I like sandwiches and hamburgers and drinks of all sorts at the ninth hole. I like proper illuminated asphalt car parks and signing for everything at the bar. I like hole by hole score-boards at tournaments and the starter calling players to the tee on a loudspeaker in the bar or locker room.' And eventually he would also be a huge fan of the revolutionary new electric buggies.

But he still chose to wait until 1948 before playing in The Masters, although this wasn't a random choice on his part. 'I returned to America to play in The Masters tournament at Augusta because a number of my senior American golfing friends persuaded me that I could do golf in general a big service at this moment by returning, also I could see that a major golf event outside the National Championships could be run strictly. My criticisms were invited and expected.'

What Cotton meant is that at the previous year's Ryder Cup, criticisms by Cotton and some of his players were suggesting that the United States Professional Golfers Association, despite its undoubted positive influence on the tournament world, was starting to trample over the rules and spirit of the game, as embodied by the United States Golf Association, the principal governing body in North America.

Professional tournament golf had continued through the Second World War in America and it was in this period that commercial interests became more dominant, with tournaments being structured to produce low scoring at all costs, so that sponsors could get maximum publicity. Cotton felt that the rules and spirit of golf were being 'frequently and flagrantly ignored' in order to accommodate these pressures.

So Cotton's presence was particularly desired at the 1948 Masters because the Augusta National Club had, at that time as club officials, the U.S. GA President, Mr. Fielding Wallace, and the U.S. PGA President, Ed Dudley. With Cotton in attendance and with Bobby Jones in the chair a dinner was given to honour the unique club involvement of the two men, at which it was announced by Ed Dudley, 'We will play along with you from now on.

The PGA will support the U.S. GA one hundred per cent in all rules of golf. There should only be one set of rules.'(applause).

After his role as politician and peacemaker, Cotton played respectably enough on his Masters debut, and after three solid days, a final round of 77 left him just outside the top twenty.

But his observations and writings around this time are interesting. He felt it was the understandable inability of British golf to recover quickly after the First World War, that gave the American game the initiative in the Twenties and Thirties and, 'the seven years of the last conflict have done even more damage.' He also felt that the large ball, that was played in America, 'has contributed as much to the improvement in the general standard of American golf as has the steel shaft in the world at large.

This ball that has been so perfected by the manufacturers that its trajectory and performance now resemble that of the small ball, is an ideal ball for all conditions, especially in the south where the coarse bladed grasses provide fairways like thick woollen rugs. This ball sits up well and is easier to pitch with, whilst on the putting green it will run truer, but requires a more delicate stroke.'

He felt that between his visit in 1929 and his return or the 1948 Masters, 'the increase in public demand and the influence of the mighty dollar has meant that courses have been made easier through the whole golfing calendar.'

Sadly his three appearances there were not nearly enough and when he finished thirteenth in 1957, with a final round of 76, it was just a small glimpse of what British golf's biggest star of that era might have been able to achieve.

Henry Cotton in a practise session for The Masters.

CHAPTER 5

THE POST-WAR YEARS

The reluctance of Henry Cotton to risk his reputation in America was an illustration of how much progress American professional tournament golf still had to make in the eyes of British and European players.

The only area in which the development of The Masters tournament had faltered so far was in establishing global appeal, and in 1950 when Jimmy Demaret thrilled American fans by becoming the first three time winner of The Masters, Roberto de Vicenzo of Argentina and Norman von Nida of Australia, represented the entire international entry.

But the pedigree of the event was clear. It had gone from being the Augusta Invitational to simply, The Masters, within the space of the first few months of its life. But the next important promotion from being just a regular tournament to what we now describe as a 'Major,' is harder to pinpoint.

As Charles Price says in his book, *A Golf Story*, 'By the early Fifties it was certainly looked upon as the best run tournament in the world. But it was not spoken of in the same breath as the Open Championships of the United States and Britain or the PGA Championship. They had too much tradition behind them.' It was the years that immediately followed Demaret's 1950 victory that provided the evidence that The Masters should rank alongside the other big three in what we now label the modern Grand Slam.

In 1951 Ben Hogan won for the first time and, as a result, the following year hosted the first of the eve of tournament Champions dinners. A guest that night, Sam Snead, would go on to win his second title that year, only for Hogan to win it back in 1953, breaking the tournament record by five shots. Not only that, but in 1953 Hogan went on to win the U.S. Open, followed by the Open Championship at Carnoustie, the first time this had ever been achieved. Indeed perhaps the first time it had even been thought of.

And as the achievement of The Masters and the two Open Championships was celebrated with a ticker tape

Sam Snead putts on the 16th green at the 1954 Masters.

parade in New York, the concept of the modern Grand Slam was born, and the clash of dates in 1953 that prevented Hogan competing in both the Open Championship and U.S. PGA Championship, was carefully avoided in future years. So it seems that in 1954 the Grand Slam season was set, starting as it has done every year since, with The Masters at Augusta in April. To underline the new-found prestige, Snead beat Hogan in an eighteen hole play-off to win that 1954 Masters, but once again there were no European players in the field.

It would be a few years yet before the European challenge started to muster. As the event started to move from the Hogan-Snead era toward the great years of Palmer, Nicklaus and Player, the British, with the isolated exceptions of Harry Weetman and Dave Thomas, stayed at home.

So Clifford Roberts, a man of traditional values but with a modern marketing brain, attacked the problem from a different direction, and went on a charm offensive with

▲

Ben Hogan at The Masters 7th hole in 1952.

◄ Sam Snead (left), shakes hands with Ben Hogan after Snead won The Masters in 1954.

CHAPTER 5

(From left to right) Ben Hogan, Juan Seguar, Jimmy Demaret and Rorberto de Vicinzo survey the course before a practise round.

the British Press, offering travel and accommodation packages, plus the best working facilities in the sport, if they could come and spread the word of an event and a venue that should have required no extra selling at all. But in the pre-television days the written word was everything and British golf journalists typified down the years by Bernard Darwin, Pat Ward Thomas and Peter Dobereiner, were the most effective messengers in the game.

Pat Ward Thomas recalled how, in the Sixties, he and other British journalists were told, 'If we could get ourselves across the Atlantic the rest of our problems would be solved.' And they were, in remarkable fashion. 'We were told to be at La Guardia airport at a certain time and we would be flown to Augusta in one of the private jets belonging to Jackson T. Stephens, a member of Augusta National. He lived in Arkansas and his aircraft had come all the way from Little Rock to collect us in New York.

'This was privilege indeed. I had not flown in a small jet and taking off gave one the sense of being in a rocket. For several years Jack Stephens sent his aircraft, and on

one occasion Ronald Heager of the Daily Express and I, were the only passengers. As we settled in our seats, a bottle of bourbon between us, we had one common thought, that this was the life. But Augustan hospitality extended to the point where we were housed and fed at no cost to our papers. All this was vastly more than we could have expected, but for a while made the difference to my going or not.'

Pat Ward Thomas then added rather innocently that he 'never discovered the precise reason for this kindness,' but Clifford Roberts, the tournament Chairman and possibly the last great dictator in golf, and Bobby Jones were anxious that The Masters should have an international flavour. To this end many foreign players were invited to compete and coverage by the British Press was welcomed. Furthermore, the club had close associations with the Royal and Ancient, several of whose members are members of Augusta.'

In the late Fifties and early Sixties the British Press did not have a great deal to write home about from the European perspective. The southern hemisphere was

EUROPE AT THE MASTERS

having a spell of domination in the Open Championship through the victories by Bobby Locke, Kel Nagle and in particular Peter Thomson, but even these great players were unable to make any impression on the fortress of American golf that the Augusta National was becoming.

Augusta had a new hero with Arnold Palmer destined to win four titles, claiming victory first of all in 1958 and 1960. But when Palmer hit bunker trouble at the eighteenth and double bogeyed the closing hole of the 1961 Masters, it meant that South African Gary Player had hung on for the victory that at last took the first major of the season overseas.

Palmer won in 1962, with Player finishing second. Then enter Jack Nicklaus with a victory in 1963. Between them this 'big three' would win seven times between 1960 and 1969. What happened through this decade at Augusta would sum up all the drama and adrenalin of golf's golden era. The Masters had not just become a major in America, it had become the sport's favourite major.

The big three, Gary Player, Jack Nicklaus and Arnold Palmer. Seated in front are Bobby Jones and Cliff Roberts.

Arnold Palmer makes his final putt before his Masters victory in 1960.

CHAPTER 6

THE SIXTIES

Even though the reputation and status of The Masters were now complete, the British and European representation into the Sixties remained modest. Of the ten Great Britain and Ireland Ryder Cup players who were beaten by the USA at East Lake in Atlanta in October 1963, only Geoffrey Hunt and Dave Thomas returned six months later for The Masters. Clearly transatlantic travel at this stage was too much of an expense and in some cases, too much of an adventure.

There was however, one other British player in the field for the 1964 Masters and that was the Midlands based Peter Butler. The previous year he had won the British PGA Championship, and his experience showed that The Masters qualification categories so rigidly adhered to these days, were a little more flexible in the Sixties.

'Geoffrey Hunt and myself were sponsored by Cutty Sark whisky to go and play the winter tour in America. We went straight across to the West Coast arriving there just too late for the pre-qualifying in Los Angeles. In those days if you were a Ryder Cup player you were exempt from qualifying, but I wasn't and so missed out and went straight on to San Diego.

There I met up with Wilson Atkins, a nice man who ran the Seniors golf in America. We played a bit together and I stayed with him and played in the San Diego tournament and did well enough to finish eleventh in what was my first event in America. After this he asked me whether I was playing in The Masters. I admitted I didn't know a great deal about the tournament and certainly hadn't been invited anyway. He said "I'll see what I can do", and lo and behold a few days later it arrived, an invitation to play in The Masters at Augusta.'

On the way to Augusta Butler played the rest of the winter tour and added to his experience of American golf at venues from California to Florida. He had no reason to expect that the Augusta National would be much more than just another week of American tournament golf.

'But when I arrived my impression was exactly the same as everyone visiting for the first time nowadays. It was absolutely immaculate, there wasn't a blade of grass out of place and with the shrubs and azaleas in full bloom it was just about the most beautiful golfing venue I'd seen. And of course the greens were faster than anything I'd ever putted on. Geoffrey Hunt and myself took ourselves off to the green-keepers' shed to discover how they got them so fast, and learnt that they took the bottom blades out of the mowers and ground them down in order to cut as close as possible. The only greens I had seen anything like as fast was Birkdale the previous year, where a bad winter had prevented virtually any growth.'

Maybe the Birkdale experience was invaluable because Butler put together two opening rounds of 72 before storming up among the leaders with a third round 69. At one point during the final he was actually lying second,

albeit some way behind Arnold Palmer, who was disappearing from all challengers on his way to a fourth Masters title.

In those days, players did not go out in leader board order as they do on the final day of modern tournament golf, and so Butler was drawn with the American Jim Ferrier in a pairing just ahead of the hard charging Palmer. 'Ferrier was, to put it kindly, a very deliberate player and although there was a vacant slot between us and Palmer in the draw, it wasn't long before Palmer, and the vast and very excited crowds that were following him, had caught up with us.

'So on every shot we were surrounded by noise and movement, and this was something that I had never experienced before on any golf course or in any

Peter Butler –
so near, but so
far, to achieving
Masters glory.

Butler (bottom
row, first left) with
the 1965 Ryder
Cup team.

tournament.' Even forty years on Butler was loath to make excuses, but this atmosphere clearly contributed to his final round of 75 that dropped him back into a tie for 13th. But this was still the best finish, (Lighthorse Harry Cooper apart), that any British or European golfer had achieved at Augusta.

Arnie's Army was in full cry and Augusta was revelling in the rivalry of Palmer, Nicklaus and Player and the astonishing golf they produced through the Sixties. In 1965 it was Nicklaus who dominated, with Palmer in second and Player in third. But Nicklaus set a new tournament record of 17 under par 271 to win by a record margin of nine strokes. Achievements that would not be surpassed until Tiger Woods in 1997.

Peter Butler must have been dreaming of something special when he eagled the second hole in his opening round in 1965, but the dream did not last as he missed the cut with two rounds of 76. Bernard Hunt accompanied his

Jack Nicklaus hits an iron shot at The Masters, watched closely by Arnold Palmer (left) and Gary Player.

brother Geoffrey and finished as the best of the three British players, but Ramón Sota became the first European player to finish in the top ten with his sixth place finish, fifteen shots behind Nicklaus.

Sota in all would make six appearances at Augusta between 1964 and 1972 and during this time was the pre-eminent player in continental Europe. He came up through the caddy ranks at Santander where he kept a sometimes stern eye on the developing talent of his young

nephew Severiano Ballesteros. He and Seve were very different players, Sota being unspectacular and methodical. But what Sota achieved behind Nicklaus in 1965 would provide a fascinating historical echo to Seve's ultimate European breakthrough in 1980 when he left Nicklaus sixteen shots in his wake.

1966 was a breakthrough year for English sport, but three months before England won the World Cup, Peter Butler was at last writing some English headlines at Augusta. The American Press certainly remembered him from two years earlier but hadn't given his thirteenth place finish too many column inches. But now in 1966 he opened with rounds of 72 and 71 in difficult windy conditions to share the halfway lead in The Masters.

The local journalists introduced him to their readers as best they could. The Augusta Chronicle, 'Peter J. Butler sounds like a name that should be that of a professional soccer player, and well it might be had not the sixteen year old Peter J. Butler suffered a knee injury in the game that is England's answer to American football.

The Florida Times Union, 'Butler is a strapping, 34 year old slugger from Birmingham, England's coal center. He has been a pro since 16 and winner of numerous British tournaments. "Peter isn't as good a golfer as some of our others such as Peter Alliss and Neil Coles," a British observer said, "but he has the best disposition of all. The Masters tournament and Arnold Palmer don't faze him at all."

The Augusta Herald, 'Curly haired, ruddy faced Peter Butler looks like the Englishman who always loses the girl in the movie. Never mind that though, because he thinks he has a chance to win this whole bloomin' tournament. He could end up as famous as the Beatles… and he doesn't even take ice in his Coke.'

In the Daily Telegraph Henry Longhurst gave a calmer view of how Butler performed in his second round. 'It was an absolutely model round which could hardly have been more than 71 and might have been less, and he played with an apparent calmness which was beyond praise. This is, in a sense, the great golfing event of the year and

Doug Sanders awaits to play the 18th at Augusta.

everyone feels the unusual pressure.' He went on to describe how Butler had finished by recovering from a greenside bunker at eighteen and holing a tricky downhill putt for a share of the lead.

But in round three all Butler's much praised composure would be tested to the extreme as once again the supposed luck of the draw would put him out amid the most distracting of Augusta's galleries. Even though he had a share of the lead with Paul Harney, he was given a starting time of 1.53, five pairs from last just behind Jack Nicklaus and immediately ahead of Arnold Palmer and Ben Hogan, all of whom were challenging for the lead.

And just as two years earlier, Butler found it difficult as he and playing partner Doug Sanders were sandwiched between the Jack Nicklaus throng moving away and Arnie's Army moving in. Sanders shot 75 and a disconsolate Peter Butler a 79. 'I recall I was so upset that my immediate reaction after that round was to withdraw because I couldn't see this happening twice in three years to be a co-incidence.' But this was simply the challenge of competing at the sharp end of the sport's most high profile event, and even though the experience clearly still irritates close

Henry Longhurst, golf writer and commentator, recognised Butler's efforts.

on forty years later, Butler completed his Masters and did it in fine style, with a 73 that moved him back up to a share of the 13th spot that he'd occupied two years earlier.

In his Daily Telegraph summing up of the 1966 Masters, Henry Longhurst expressed his displeasure at the tedious nature of the eighteen hole play-off that was required on the Monday before Jack Nicklaus earned his third Green Jacket with victory over Tommy Jacobs and Gay Brewer. But he was fulsome in his praise for Peter Butler, 'I do feel that a special word of condolence is due to Peter Butler to once again finish thirteenth in The Masters is no mean achievement. Butler is not by nature a 'we was robbed' character, but I will say it for him, that to a large extent, he was.'

The efforts of Peter Butler came a year too early for British television audiences. It was 1967 when a recording of the final day of The Masters was first shipped across the Atlantic for a delayed transmission on the BBC. Clifford Roberts had first instigated television coverage at Augusta in 1956, a year after BBC TV's first efforts at live coverage of The Open.

Roberts was a visionary when it came to pioneering television coverage of golf. He argued against the players who claimed that the bulky television equipment that

was required at the time was an intrusion and a disturbance to their efforts. Roberts would remind them that, as the audience expanded, television would turn them, 'from poorly paid itinerant players into true professional athletes.'

But right from the outset he tried to take the viewers' point of view when it came to the style of production. For example, he felt it essential to limit the number of commercial interruptions to around two minutes per half hour. The original broadcasters, CBS Television, who still have The Masters contract, were aghast, but it is still a limitation that applies today and substantially increases the appeal of the event to the viewer.

Every Masters broadcast, right from these early days, was also the subject of analysis and a highly critical production review, with the ambition, from the point of view of the club, to make every transmission in some way better than that of the previous year. This attitude continues today even with foreign broadcasters such as the BBC. It creates a certain extra tension but there is no doubt that it produces results in terms of production quality.

British golf, and the style of British golf coverage, had its part to play in these formative years of Masters coverage, and this came via the distinctive voice of the doyen of BBC golf commentators, the aforementioned Henry Longhurst. His golf writings provide an invaluable archive of these times and his commentary provides the soundtrack.

Frank Chirkinian, the legendary CBS Director, would provide his own colourful soundtrack to events within the

CBS truck. He was described in *The Making of The Masters* as, 'a profanity-spewing, chain-smoking, self-promoting vortex of ego, anxiety and nervous energy.' As you would imagine he had an uncomfortable relationship with Clifford Roberts, but it was also hard to imagine his relationship with the urbane Longhurst. 'I just don't know what it is about the guy,' Chirkinian once said, 'He looks like W.C. Fields in drag, but he happens to be the best in the business.'

Others had also recognised the very 'British' quality of Henry Longhurst, who apparently had only learnt he would be on the commentary team at Augusta when he was advised so in a note jointly signed by Bobby Jones and Clifford Roberts. They told Longhurst to inform them immediately if CBS were at all 'niggardly' over the financial arrangements.

And so Henry Longhurst took his place, not only at Augusta, but in particular on the tower behind the par three sixteenth green, looking back across the lake to the tee, with the not insignificant responsibility of describing events on one of the most famous holes in the sport.

Characteristically in his book, *My Life and Soft Times,* Henry did not seem especially weighed down by this

Jack Nicklaus casts a long shadow as he birdie's the 11th hole during a play-off round of The Masters in 1966.

responsibility. Instead he supplies an accurate description of what Masters week was like and, to a certain extent, continues to be like. 'Year by year I have sat on the same chair on the same little balcony upstairs, looking through the wisteria down at the same scene, while the same coloured waiter comes out and says, "you like the same as last year, Sah? Beefeater on the rocks?" Everything is indeed the same and it is only by looking down at the huge scoreboard that you can tell which year it is — a Palmer year or a Nicklaus year or whatever it may be. The same people come, decked out in every colour of the rainbow, ridiculous under the skies of Britain, but exactly right for the spring sunshine of Georgia.

'All the television directors and commentators have to submit to a solemn lecture forbidding mention of any tournaments other than the U.S. and British Opens, Amateur Championships and the American PGA Championship, (other tournaments on the professional tour simply do not exist), and we are especially forbidden to mention prize money in any form.'

But despite the restrictions it was the grandeur of Augusta that held Longhurst enthralled. 'From the side of town on which I am usually billeted, one drives to the

	THRU 16	
WOODS		3
WITTENBERG		4
BJORN		7

	LEA	HOLE	1	2	3	4	5
P R I O R		PAR	4	5	4	3	4
0	RILEY		1	1	1	0	0
0	CEJKA		0	1	2	2	2
0	HOWELL III		0	0	0	0	1
0	LANGER		1	1	0	0	1
0	PRICE N.		0	1	1	0	0
0	ROSE		1	2	2	2	2
0	ELS		0	1	1	1	1
0	DiMARCO		0	0	0	0	0
0	CLARKE		1	1	1	1	1
0	HAAS J.		1	2	2	2	1

course through avenues of elegant houses whose gardens – open to the road as always in America, not hedged in, – are ablaze with azalea, rhododendron and dogwood. On the course itself, two holes stand out and on a really sunny afternoon they take your breath away; the thirteenth, and my hole, the sixteenth. At both holes the water is liable to remain an equally vivid blue, even on a cloudy day, due possibly to the fact that, if you get there early enough, you will see a gang of dusky workers, each with a watering-can full of blue dye.'

If a certain amount of sleight of hand had been employed in keeping the Augusta National as the most scenic backdrop in sport, other practical innovations introduced by Clifford Roberts and his team have been proved to be of long term benefit to tournament golf.

Significant among these was the introduction of giant leader boards and plus or minus scoring against par. Until 1960 golf leader boards just showed hole by hole scores, requiring spectators and also players and journalists to perform some quite complicated mathematics to work out the exact state of a competition. Augusta took away the need for such calculations by red numerals which indicated how much under par a player was, and green numerals signified

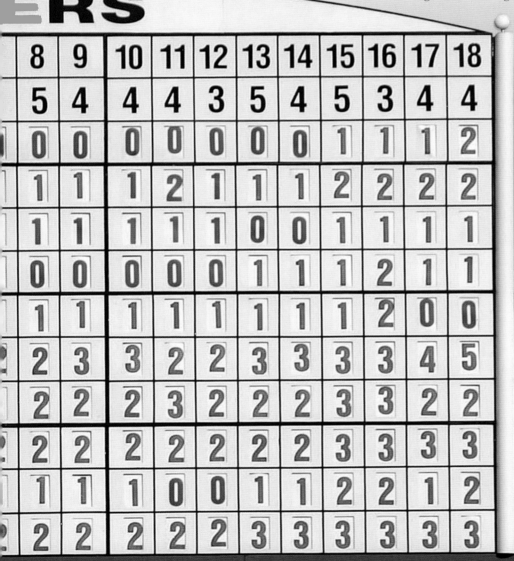

The giant Masters leader board displaying the red and green numerals.
▼

how much over. It was simplicity itself and a model that has been followed worldwide ever since.

But there were still those that criticised. One patron wrote into the club to complain that he was colour-blind and how could he possibly make sense of red and green numerals. Clifford Roberts mischievously replied that any Augusta member out on the course would be happy to interpret the scoring and explain the state of play, and these members could easily be recognised on the course by their green jackets.

The most colour-blind golfer was Jack Nicklaus and in the latter stages of his first Masters victory in 1963 he stared up at the giant scoreboard and anxiously asked his caddie, 'Willie, how many of those numbers are red?' to which the reply came, 'Only you sir, only you.'

Certainly by the mid-Sixties most of the characteristics that we now associate with the modern day Masters were in place. The event had officially taken on The Masters title in 1939. There is no date for The Masters officially becoming one of the big four major Championships, but certainly its status seemed to have become clear by 1954, when Snead beat Hogan in that famous play-off.

In 1949 Snead had been the first recipient of a Champions Green Jacket, another important element of the enduring image of The Masters, conferring on the winner membership of the Augusta National Club and symbolising membership of the most exclusive club of all, The Masters Champions.

Augusta in its early years had also staged another competition, the inaugural PGA Seniors Championship, won in 1937 by Jock Hutchison and in 1938 by Fred McLeod. The

Arnold Palmer receives his Green Jacket from Jack Nicklaus.

The roles are reversed. Jack Nicklaus receives his Green Jacket from Arnold Palmer.

event then moved to Florida and became the foundation of the Seniors Tour. But those two victories by Hutchison and McLeod had given British golf another, albeit distant, Augusta connection.

Hutchison was born in St. Andrews in 1884 and Fred McLeod was born in North Berwick in 1882. Like so many others they emigrated to the United States at an early age and as well as becoming U.S. citizens, McLeod won the U.S. Open in 1908 and Hutchison returned to Royal St. George's to become Open Champion in 1921. But it was their performances in those first Seniors events at Augusta, plus their friendship with Bobby Jones, that earned them an annual ticket back to The Masters to compete in the event and then to act as honorary starters.

So from 1963 to 1973, Hutchison and McLeod would play

nine holes on the opening morning, ahead of the main Masters field. Hutchison dropped out aged eighty eight with a hip condition, McLeod continued until he was ninety three, complaining of his absent playing partner, 'He just got too damn old.' But the two Scots had established the tradition of honorary starters that continued down the years through Gene Sarazen, Byron Nelson and Sam Snead. So Scotland could claim to have had at least some presence at the head of The Masters field. But the efforts of Peter Butler apart, European golf was still conspicuously absent from those magnificent Augusta leader boards.

Jock Hutchinson in action, 1922.

Fred McLeod (second from left) lines up with his fellow competitors in the 1926 Walker Cup.

CHAPTER 7

A CHALLENGER &
A RECORD BREAKER

As the Sixties progressed, there were indications that European golf was capable of producing players who could challenge on the world stage, and the first player to truly commit himself to doing just that was Tony Jacklin.

In Europe there was still no such thing as the full-time tournament professional. It was still a division of time between trying to win titles and fulfilling responsibilities to members as a club pro. And when the principal competitions including three of the majors were in America, the difficulties of trying to compete were clear and seemingly insurmountable.

It was Jacklin who pioneered the change of emphasis that needed to be made, although that pioneering work would not bring him any success at Augusta. Instead the reward would come at the 1969 Open Championship and the following year at the U.S. Open at Hazeltine.

He was the dominant figure in Europe as the Sixties progressed. He proudly identified himself as the first British golfer to make a living from tournament golf, but it was still a brave decision to join the U.S. Tour in 1966. His victory in Jacksonville in 1968, even ahead of the U.S. Open win, meant that he would be the focus of attention for whatever British Press corps that assembled around a U.S. tournament. A role that had its responsibilities and irritations, and as far as Augusta was concerned, its frustrations.

But Jacklin gave hope to European golf. His Jacksonville victory was the first four round PGA Tournament to have been won by a British player. Surely, everyone believed, that even more significant success was not far away. In Jacksonville, Jacklin had been in the final pairing with Arnold Palmer and held his cool as the great man drew level. Jacklin would eventually claim victory by a two shot margin.

And the win had echoes of his first appearance at Augusta which came in 1967 and seemed to have the inspirational effect on Jacklin that it has had for so many players. 'At the beginning of the week no-one knew who I was, they thought I was an amateur. At the end of the week I had made my mark.'

Jacklin recalled that he had played with Bobby Nichols in the first two rounds and Nichols had come away convinced that the British player was going to win on his debut. He had rarely seen a player in such inspired form. In round three Jacklin would get his first experience of not only playing with Palmer, but also playing with Palmer in front of his admiring Augusta army; the same intimidating atmosphere that had upset the composure of Peter Butler. But Palmer shot 77 while Jacklin shot 69, and at one stage held the lead in The Masters. However, the lack of experience would do its damage and Jacklin came in with a final round of 77, to finish 16th behind the eventual winner Gary Brewer and runner-up Bobby Nichols.

But Jacklin looks back on that third round at Augusta as being the one that gave him the belief that he could compete and contend at the highest level, and said that he saw it at that stage as his finest achievement in the sport. The British sport waited patiently every year for Jacklin's

Augusta challenge to really materialise, but he would never finish in the top ten at The Masters. The celebration came instead at Hazeltine.

There were others who carried British and European hopes in the Sixties. Certainly my BBC colleague Peter Alliss was expected to perform better at Augusta than he actually did; two appearances, missing the cut by some margin on both occasions. Peter arrived at Augusta as a winner and a champion of some pedigree, but he left as a serious casualty. Peter had won the British PGA Championship on three occasions. He had won the Open Championships of Spain, Italy and Portugal and had been through the whole range of emotions that Ryder Cup competition can provide. In theory at least, he should have been equal to the demands of The Masters.

This extract from the first volume of his wide-ranging autobiographies tells its own sad story. 'As a member of the Ryder Cup teams I had had plenty of invitations to

Tony Jacklin in full swing in the late sixties.

Tony Jacklin and Jack Nicklaus walk together at the Open played at St. Andrews in 1970.

CHAPTER 7

Augusta. My first appearance was in 1966 and it was a total disaster. I have never felt so tiny, so insignificant, so alone. The way people cheered, the stands, the noise, the bustle, the colours, the blinding sunshine, the sheer 'Americanness' of the whole thing. I just felt completely out of it, a very small fish in an enormous ocean. It was like playing in four Cup Finals on successive days. My putting was creaky. I played one round with Gene Littler and took five putts from six feet at the eleventh hole. Shattering. Ever since then I have had the most tremendous admiration for players who go out there for the first time and do well, or even do well there at any time. It takes a very special sort of person to go out there, put it all together and play well.'

That tribute cannot in all honesty be paid to Clive Clark when he made his Masters debut with an opening

round of 81 in 1968. His talent held exciting possibilities as far as the British game was concerned. He had concluded a fine amateur career by holing a 33 foot putt to ensure the Walker Cup match in Baltimore ended as a tie, eleven points apiece. His burgeoning professional career included a top three finish in the Open Championship at Hoylake in 1967, when he was beaten only by Jack Nicklaus and Roberto de Vicenzo. However his opening round at Augusta was not covering him in glory.

Peter Alliss demonstrates his driving skills.

▼

Tony Jacklin in action during The Masters, 1970.

That was until he came to the par three sixteenth, pulled out a two iron and sent the ball soaring over the lake and into the hole, some one hundred and ninety yards distant. It was the first Masters hole in one by a British player, and remained the only one until Padraig Harrington holed his tee shot, also at the sixteenth, in 2004. His two iron is still the longest club ever to find the hole for an ace in The Masters and his reward was a Crystal trophy and the invitation to take over from Henry Longhurst in the CBS TV commentary booth at sixteen, having established himself as such an authority on how to play the hole. But he only played it twice in anger, having missed the cut by seven shots, even despite that day one bonus. As far as golfing achievement at Augusta was concerned, British golf was still living on scraps.

In 1969, Peter Townsend made the cut on his one and only appearance. Maurice Bembridge also played all four days on his debut in 1970, the year that Tony Jacklin had his best ever Masters finish – tied for twelfth – having

come back to Augusta as Open Champion, a few weeks before taking the U.S. Open title at Hazeltine.

But by the 1973 Masters, Jacklin was a more confused figure. He had withdrawn from the weekly grind of the American tour but now was finding it difficult to make his anticipated impact in Europe. When he came to Augusta it was only to shoot rounds of 77 and 75 that saw him miss the cut by three shots. So it was a good thing that British golf fans had a new talent that they could burden with their Masters hopes.

For three straight years Peter Oosterhuis, a tall 26 year old Londoner, had been European golf's most consistent player. He had won the Order of Merit for the last two years and in 1973 would compile five tournament victories around the world; a real threat to the supremacy of Jacklin. He had made his Masters debut in 1971, making the cut the following year. But it was in the 1973 Masters that Oosterhuis made his most significant impact on the world scene.

CHAPTER 7

Peter Oosterhuis
lines up his putt. ▶

Oosterhuis, soon to be abbreviated worldwide as simply, Oosty, knew he had progress to make in this respect. 'Out in America they all regarded me as that Dutch guy or Peter Ustinov but I knew by the time The Masters came around in '73 that I had the ability to surprise them. Over the previous couple of years I felt I had learnt the important lessons of Augusta. I had learnt the need to be patient round Augusta.'

In round one in 1973, Oosterhuis was paired with the American Tommy Aaron. It was observed rather obscurely that this had to be the first time in Masters history that two players were paired together whose surnames began with double letters. Both players set about making more significant Masters history. Aaron birdied the first two holes, went out in 32 and his eventual 68 was good enough for the first round lead. Oosterhuis was back in the pack after a pretty solid opening round of 73.

In round two Aaron faltered, but so too, most significantly, did his closest challenger Jack Nicklaus. Aaron's round of 73 still would leave him in a four way tie for the lead, while Oosterhuis helped by holing his second shot at the par four third hole would finish with a 70 to move to within two of the top of a leader board that seemed packed with the less familiar names and unexpected contenders.

Peter Oosterhuis
makes full use
of his height in
a very smooth
swing. ▶

Torrential rain wiped out almost all of Saturday's third round play, making a Monday finish inevitable. But Oosterhuis at least took the opportunity to become the first British player to charge through the field and head the leader board at the end of Masters Sunday, and he had

done it in brilliant fashion. A round of 68 at Augusta is always outstanding, but on that Sunday, as the storms and the torrential rain moved away, the British star was the only player to shoot in the sixties, and only one player in the field got within two shots of him.

As in most rounds at Augusta it had its moments of fortune and its moments of regret. Fortune came at the

second when he holed an eagle putt of such monstrous proportions that it would only be surpassed by Nick Faldo's hundred foot effort that would set up his breakthrough win sixteen years later. But this, at the time, did not seem to have created any breakthrough for Oosterhuis as he threw away what had been gained with bogeys at the fourth and the fifth. He got back under par again at the eighth but then after a fine drive at the ninth, put his second shot into a bunker and another bogey followed. 'I felt pretty annoyed at that point because I had put myself in such a good position on the hole, I felt I was playing better than my scoring reflected, and that bit of anger maybe was the key to what happened over the next few holes.'

What he produced was a barrage of brilliant golf as he headed down into Amen Corner. At ten he put his approach to five feet and made the birdie. After a par at eleven he hit his tee shot stiff at twelve and got to two under par. Although he settled for a five at the thirteenth, he had come through one of the most notorious stretches of holes in golf at two under par and had moved to the head of The Masters field. At fifteen, sixteen and seventeen he made three testing putts for birdie, par and birdie. Back in 32 for his 68 and into the final round, Oosterhuis would be leading The Masters by three clear shots at five under par.

But before that final round the British player had to provide the American Press with all the quotes that would

help them write their, 'Ooster-who?', stories.
Not that Peter himself had any doubts about his
credentials for leading The Masters. 'I suppose I felt
nervous, I suppose I felt a responsibility for British golf,
who were so keen for a breakthrough at Augusta after
Jacklin's win at Hazeltine. But I just had to look at my
Order of Merit wins the previous two years to believe
there was absolutely no reason why I shouldn't win The
Masters, especially with a three shot lead.'

One of the favourite questions of the American Press
was how this seemingly inexperienced player would sleep
before taking the chance of a lifetime in the final round of
one of the most famous events in golf. 'The answer is I
slept pretty well or at least I tried to. The Saturday had
been my father's birthday and there had been a few phone
calls back and forth and I suppose with the rain-out people
got a bit out of synch. A very good friend rang me in the
small hours of Monday morning to ask how I got on. I
hope I didn't sound too abrupt but I said I'd got on just
fine and I was now trying to get a good night's sleep before
going out and winning The Masters the next day.'

Britain indeed was only slowly waking up to the
prospect of at last having a Masters Champion. Journalists
were re-booking flights and accommodation and BBC
television schedules were being re-organised to carry
coverage of what could be Oosty's march to victory. But by
the time Oosterhuis teed off with J.C. Sneed in the final
pairing at 1.32, The Masters picture had changed
significantly and there would be scant coverage of Britain's
big hope in the afternoon's broadcast to come.

Nicklaus had played himself back into contention as
he was always likely to, but most significantly, Tommy
Aaron, anxious to lose his reputation of getting close on
regular occasions without nailing down a big win, had
birdied the first three holes. 'Looking back I have to say it
was a huge blow losing the three shot lead before I'd even
finished the opening hole. The way Tommy Aaron started
just changed everything.'

But even though Aaron went out in 32 he was not able
to dominate what became a fascinating final day, and

Oosterhuis, to his credit, would play his full part. J.C. Snead briefly took the lead before dropping two shots at the twelfth. Nicklaus, with a spectacular birdie at eighteen, had set a stern clubhouse target of three under, and when Oosterhuis and Snead came to the par five fifteenth they were at four under one behind Aaron who was playing the eighteenth.

The par five fifteenth with its second shot that tempts the longer players to take on the lake in front of the green, is the last realistic chance for birdie at Augusta. It has been the big moment of attack in many challenges for the Green Jacket. Equally many challenges have disappeared quietly surrounded by ripples of water. Neither fate awaited Oosterhuis or Snead, but they could both look back on the fifteenth as the moment the title went to Aaron.

'Whether or not we psyched ourselves out of it I don't know, but Tommy ended up making an ordinary par and I was just too far back off the tee, tried to go for the green, after not being completely sure what to hit, and ended up carving my shot way right, bogeyed the hole and that was it.'

And that was the end also for Britain's most realistic challenge for Masters glory so far. Oosterhuis would finish two shots back in a tie for third with Jack Nicklaus. Two years later as Oosty continued to search for the major

Jack Nicklaus on the comeback trail.

The eventual winner of The Masters in 1973 Tommy Aaron, receives his jacket from Jack Nicklaus.

Peter Oosterhuis towers over Gary Player as they are pictured together in 1974.

success his talent certainly deserved, he was two shots from glory again, finishing alone in second behind Gary Player at the Open Championship at Royal Lytham.

His association with The Masters however, remains a long and fruitful one, with television's rules of succession requiring him to take over from Clive Clarke as the British commentary voice on the American CBS coverage. And with a cruel sense of irony his American employers have on occasions put him on the tower at the fifteenth gazing at the famous hole that proved his undoing.

'Yes I do think about it but I'm not a great one for staring up the fifteenth and thinking what might have been. I'm just proud of being a strong contender and for that year at least gave myself a great chance of Masters victory.'

The European breakthrough felt imminent, but would it be Oosterhuis, would it be Jacklin or would the winner Champion emerge from the burgeoning ranks of talent in continental Europe? Oosterhuis was strongly fancied in 1974 but never recovered from an opening round seventy nine, but did very well to make the cut with a sixty eight

A portrait of Peter Oosterhuis while working for CBS Television.

in round two. There was no way back for Jacklin who disappointed again, missing the cut with a first round eighty one.

Both were somewhat overshadowed by Trevor Homer attempting to become the first British amateur to make the cut and failing by just one shot, and the entire field was overshadowed on the final day by an extraordinary performance by the unheralded Maurice Bembridge. On his second appearance at Augusta he would not be close to winning, but no-one in the history of the event had produced a better round of golf.

In the forty year history of The Masters only two players had shot sixty four: Lloyd Mangrum when he finished second in 1940 and Jack Nicklaus when he won by nine shots in 1965. To that illustrious company was added a twenty nine year old from Worksop whose reward would be $3,900, a share of ninth, a crystal vase and a place in golfing history.

Maurice Bembridge, despite a solid professional career, had never threatened to hijack a place in the history books in quite this fashion. Like Peter Butler he was a grafting player who travelled the world to play tournament golf. And through this dedication came highlights and rewards.

Lloyd Mangrum with the Ryder Cup in 1953. He shot a sixty four at Augusta in 1940.

In the Open Championship at Carnoustie in 1968 he took fifth place and was the top British finisher on a leader board packed with major championship winners. One of those was Jack Nicklaus and in the 1973 Ryder Cup at Muirfield, Bembridge had the dubious privilege of facing Nicklaus in both the morning and afternoon singles. In the morning Bembridge came back from two down with two to play to salvage a notable half, and in the afternoon he once again took Nicklaus to the final green before conceding defeat. Earlier in the competition Bembridge

Maurice Bembridge in Ryder Cup action, 1973.

had twice been paired against Nicklaus and Palmer in foursomes and fourballs, winning one and losing one, and at the end of the whole competition a battle weary Nicklaus would confront the diminutive Bembridge and exclaim, 'Hey you sonofabitch, you can play this game!'

Of that there was no doubt and along the way he had picked up enough titles to make him a significant presence in the European game. Titles like the last British Professional Match Play Championship in 1969 and the Dunlop Masters at St. Pierre in 1971. But there was nothing in his record that prepared the golfing world for what he did at Augusta on the afternoon of April 14, 1974.

He had made his Masters debut in 1970. Three seventy fives and a promising seventy one in the second round were good enough to make the cut. His next appearance was four years later and as Dave Stockton and Gary Player set the pace, Bembridge was right on the cut limit, but made it with his second round of seventy four.

A third round of seventy two left only a faint veneer of respectability so Bembridge was among the earlier final round starters and whatever excitement he could produce, it would be a long time before Player and Stockton battled it out for the title.

'There were definitely no expectations of any kind before that round,' said Bembridge, 'in fact the expectations were very modest for the tournament. I had been playing badly coming in to Augusta. I had been globetrotting for the previous six months which left very little time for constructive practice, or to work on my game. I seemed to be hitting everything off the toe or the heel, but the Australian Graham Marsh had also made the cut and took a quick look at me on the Augusta practice

Arnold Palmer playing in the Ryder Cup, 1973.

ground and helped me square up the clubface a bit more, and that seemed to transform my game.'

The start, four straight pars, although solid, was not threatening any record books, but at the fifth a superb three iron pulled up four feet short of the hole and Bembridge was on the way with his first birdie. His tee shot at the par three sixth finished seven feet away and the man from Little Aston holed the putt. He had other opportunities on the rest of the front nine, a decent chance for a four just slid past the hole on the eighth and as Bembridge walked down the ninth he shrugged at the small but loyal British Press contingent as if to say, 'it's good but it could be absolutely anything.'

But all the possibilities and potential of the first nine were realised in a fabulous second nine. One member of that British Press corps following faithfully, was Dai Davies now of *The Guardian*. 'I remember from the start of the round he was hitting the ball beautifully, every shot was perfectly struck and seemed to be finding the narrowest part of the greens, and although the pin positions that day were at their most severe at least three other birdie putts slipped just by. You felt that if he could just hole a few, this round could turn into something really special.'

So it proved. At the tenth off a hanging lie, a three iron covered the flag all the way and the putt was holed for birdie from around fifteen feet. The eleventh was even more impressive, an indifferent drive and then a three wood could only finish some seventy five feet from the hole, but Bembridge sank it for one of the most spectacular birdies ever seen at the start of Amen Corner.

There was no indecision off the twelfth tee. As the wind swirled, Bembridge took a four iron and the six foot putt he was left with was duly holed, and now he was to join the select group of players to birdie their way through the first four holes of the back nine of the Augusta National on final round afternoon. He did it by playing the thirteenth in conservative but accurate fashion, chipping to seven feet and sinking the birdie putt.

All these fireworks were still not enough to have a significant effect on the leader board. Bembridge was still outside the top ten, but word of what he was doing was starting to spread around the course. His gallery was noticeably bigger on the fourteenth, and down the hill had come a few more writers and journalists, especially British journalists, aware that Bembridge was doing them all a favour by giving them a good, strong, early, final day story.

They watched him rifle another pinpoint seven iron into the fourteenth, and as he walked on to the green he looked at their assembled company and smiled and shrugged his shoulders as if sharing their disbelief at what was happening. But reality intervened on that fourteenth hole as Bembridge could only manage a two putt par and any premature thoughts of course records were now being swiftly dispelled.

He tackled the fifteenth in the same cautious manner as the thirteenth. He was not a player of prodigious length, and laying up short of the lake was the only real option, but he could do it with confidence in the knowledge that his short game on that miraculous afternoon had never been better. He duly pitched to six feet from the hole and the putter did the rest, finding the cup for the fifth birdie on the back nine.

The response of the gallery around the fifteenth and those craning their necks from the neighbouring sixteenth told him that for the next half hour the attention of the Augusta National would move away from

the Player-Weiskopf-Nicklaus battle for the title, to see whether Worksop's finest could complete one of the best rounds The Masters had ever seen.

Standing on the sixteenth tee Bembridge seemed aware for the first time that this was not only a good round but also possibly a life-changing experience. 'It felt as if I couldn't even see the green from the tee, all I could see was sand and water, water and sand. For the first time in the last couple of hours, a shot felt difficult.'

He tried to play what he described as a 'safe' four iron to the heart of the green but instead found the sand and was faced with one of the most difficult pressure shots on the course: a bunker shot down the super-slick green with the water waiting for any clumsiness in execution. Instead he played it to perfection and left himself with an eight foot putt which was duly holed; his sixth single putt of this amazing back nine.

The walk from the sixteenth green to the seventeenth tee would take him past the drinking fountain installed on the twenty fifth anniversary of The Masters, upon which were inscribed the names of The Masters winners and also the progression of the course record. One more birdie and the name of Maurice Bembridge could be inscribed forever alongside Jack Nicklaus and Lloyd Mangrum, but more realistically in his sights would be the two pars that would give him a sixty five, the best round so far by an overseas player at Augusta.

The first of those pars was salvaged with another courageous single putt of around fifteen feet across the seventeenth green, and now another record presented itself, not only a birdie up the last to tie the course record sixty four, but a birdie up the last to come back in thirty.

Bembridge says he wasn't conscious of the record as he stood on the eighteenth tee but he must have been conscious of something because the final hole was lined with spectators as if they were greeting the new Champion two hours later. Once again caution was the key as he played a three wood short of the bunkers.

The six iron approach was accompanied by the kind of adrenalin normally reserved for Championship winning

Maurice Bembridge makes his way up the fairway on his Masters debut in 1970.

Maurice Bembridge (third from right) pictured with the 1971 Ryder Cup Team.

moments, and in the circumstances it was understandable that it was not his best effort of the day. It found the green but still some thirty feet from the hole just clinging to the edge of the upper tier.

Bembridge got a standing ovation as he headed up the hill, leaving him a little confused as to what they were applauding for. 'Maybe they think that they are applauding the lowest round of the day, it seemed unlikely that they were applauding the prospect of a course record, but whatever, I enjoyed it nevertheless.' Having smiled and waved and taken the applause, Bembridge got to the green and probably wrote off any prospect of getting the birdie for a record equalling sixty four. The putt was fast and across the slope, desperately difficult to read and a three putt seemed the most likely outcome.

He took a few moments to study what was required and probably because the putt was so difficult the tension was eased, the record breaking potential of the moment significantly reduced. Bembridge allowed for eighteen inches of break and struck it with confidence. He reflected that it felt perfect and looked perfect the moment it left the putter face and the sight of his ball taking the borrow and trickling without any further deviation straight into the centre of the cup, is the enduring image from a career that had many fine moments, but none more exultant than this.

It was not a victory, but to Bembridge and everyone who saw it, that putt seemed like the ultimate golfing triumph. Immediately absolute pandemonium broke out, Bembridge wandered around the green in a complete daze his arms spread wide, unable to absorb what he had just

done. Up in the Press stand Dai Davies remembered that everyone was on their feet and American journalists were hugging any British writer they could find.

Down on the green Bembridge recovered himself enough to pluck the ball out of the hole and throw it into the crowd, prompting a rather unseemly scrabble before one of two rather large American ladies claimed it. After all it was a ball that had performed astonishing deeds especially on the back nine. Bembridge had come back in thirty shots, requiring just ten putts on the back nine and the round of sixty four would equal the course record, putting his name alongside those of Mangrum and Nicklaus on the commemorative fountain.

For Bembridge it meant instant, although fairly temporary world recognition. Offers flooded in from Australia, Japan and New Zealand as well as America, and he was able to travel even more, encouraging the Press to identify him as Britain's answer to Gary Player, and of course his tie for ninth meant an invitation back which he made full use of the following year, producing a final round sixty nine to be Britain's best finisher once again.

The year after that with a kind of proud inevitability, Augusta put the upstart Bembridge in his place. His second round of eighty six that followed an opening seventy eight was a full twenty two shots behind his proud performance of 1974, but he had left his indelible mark on the commemorative fountain and the history books. His sixty four was equalled by Hale Irwin in 1975 and then the course record would become overseas property with Nick Price of Zimbabwe setting the new mark of sixty three in 1986 and Greg Norman matching him in the opening round ten years later.

CHAPTER 8

THE AMATEURS AND THE GROWTH OF THE EUROPEAN TOUR

CHAPTER 8

Michael Bonallack chips out of the rough, watched by an avid spectator.

The Seventies were proud years for The Masters, maybe the greatest years of The Masters as Player, Watson and Nicklaus traded the title, sometimes in the most thrilling of circumstances. Europe had little to celebrate but, perhaps without knowing it, plenty to look forward to with a young Severiano Ballesteros making his first appearance at Augusta in 1977.

European golf was struggling to make a breakthrough in another area. The Amateur Champion of Britain had always been an automatic invitee to The Masters, acknowledging the warm associations Bobby Jones had with the British game and his affinity with the amateur game in particular. Today the reward of a place in The Masters is one of the most valued aspects of success in the Amateur Championship.

Frank Stranahan drives from the tee.

No amateur of any nationality has ever won The Masters although Frank Stranahan, Charlie Coe and Ken Venturi all finished as runners-up, and, most famously in 1954, Billie Joe Patton was leading with six holes to go and then took seven at the thirteenth. All valiant efforts, but until 1978 no British amateur had even made the cut.

Britain's finest amateur player Sir Michael Bonallack played at The Masters three times between 1966 and 1970 and still treasures the memory of playing alongside Ben Hogan in the first round in 1966, as one of his greatest experiences in golf. 'But the problem for British amateurs at that time,' he says, 'was that for obvious reasons, work and weather, we were not playing much during the winter, and then a letter would arrive saying come and play in The Masters and virtually your first competitive round of the season would be teeing it up alongside Ben Hogan at Augusta.'

His memory of Hogan at Augusta in 1966 is still vivid. The 1953 Champion was at the end of his career but

would always enjoy legendary status in the game. 'I knew that I was to play with Hogan and was trying to quietly prepare myself for the moment as best I could. I was at what I thought was the quiet end of the practice ground, when I sensed a huge crowd moving in unison to where I was. I realised it was Hogan and he was coming to practice more or less alongside me. Not only that but with him was the golf writer Pat Ward Thomas who was a mutual friend of us both, and Pat made a big performance of introducing me. Then to add to my discomfort, Pat produced a camera and insisted that we all had our photograph taken with each other. In the middle of all that he ran out of film and his very choice language could be heard all over the practice ground.'

'When all that had died down it was time for Hogan to practice. This was what the crowd had come for and I stood back and watched. In those days, it seems extraordinary now, no practice balls were provided; each player had to bring his own. So Hogan's caddie emptied the balls out of his bag and headed down the practice ground, empty bag in hand. At about a hundred and twenty yards he stopped, held out the bag and Hogan started hitting wedges. Every shot went one bounce into the bag with the caddie hardly having to move. He would then move back twenty yards, Hogan went down a club and the same thing would happen, every ball into the bag. When Hogan started hitting the driver he might have taken the odd step left or right to catch the shot, but it was the most amazing exhibition I had seen. Hogan left the practice ground to a standing ovation.'

'Our round together was just as much of an experience, the galleries being enormous, and Hogan being far from the shy, uncommunicative figure I had expected. We talked a lot especially when we were delayed on the fourth tee; he would talk about his Open Championship experiences, Carnoustie in particular.' Hogan shot seventy four and eventually finished in a tie for thirteenth, Bonallack came in with a seventy nine and would go on to miss the cut by two. In fact Sir Michael that year was playing in the largest amateur field ever to contest

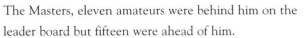

The Masters, eleven amateurs were behind him on the leader board but fifteen were ahead of him.

The player who eventually made the breakthrough and became the first British amateur to make the cut at

Augusta was Peter McEvoy in 1978. Like Sir Michael Bonallack his memories are as much about the Augusta experience as his own personal achievement.

'I was a student at the time, had no problems getting time off and so wanted to make as much use of the Augusta invitation as I could. So I went to the course a week early to practice, as the amateurs were invited to do and just immersed myself in the whole place. Other amateurs like Fred Ridley and Jay Sigel were there. We played thirty six holes a day, eventually setting up little scenarios pretending we were winning The Masters. We stayed in the Crows Nest,' (the very basic but very atmospheric accommodation for amateur players at the top

of the clubhouse), 'and got to meet and play with Sam Snead. The whole thing just had these great echoes of the Thirties which for a student of the game and lover of the history of the game was a wonderful experience.'

The experience was to get better because when the U.S. Amateur Champion John Cook withdrew, McEvoy was moved up the order to play with the defending Champion and Open Champion Tom Watson. 'Luckily I was able to draw on what I had learnt from playing with Jack Nicklaus and Gary Player in the Open Championship at Turnberry the year before, otherwise the whole thing could have become completely overwhelming.' In fact McEvoy did himself proud by matching the opening round seventy three of his illustrious playing partner.

There was more historical resonance for the British Amateur Champion in round two where he was paired with Lee Elder who had become the first coloured player to compete in The Masters. But by this time it was starting to dawn on McEvoy that he might just make the cut. 'I looked as if I would make it quite comfortably but then put my ball in the water at fifteen and it all became a bit tense.'

But McEvoy made it; another modest breakthrough for British golf at Augusta. A third round of seventy seven meant that he wasn't able to climb up the weekend leader board but at least he still had the thrill of playing in the final day of The Masters to come, although this was to turn out to be the one big disappointment of a great two weeks.

Peter McEvoy captain of the GB & Ireland Walker Cup team, lifts the trophy in 2001.

'I was paired with another amateur who had made the cut, Dick Siderowf, and even for the loyal patrons of Augusta this must have been an incredibly unattractive pairing. There were no stands around the course so the whole round became a bit eerie. Down in Amen Corner in particular, nobody had bothered to wander down the hill that early in the morning so the place was just empty, and with no stands it felt more like the monthly medal than the final round of The Masters.' Even if there was no ovation McEvoy had shown what was possible for a British Amateur Champion, and in the years that have followed each and every one of them has been thrilled by being at The Masters though few have followed him into Masters weekend.

Gary Wolstenholme, a member of a succession of Walker Cup winning sides had the luxury of a couple of attempts and only managed to match par on one occasion, emphasising that however deft the short game was, and Wolstenholme was among the best, if a player were not

also driving the ball huge distances the modern Augusta would take its toll.

Philip Parkin, the 1983 Amateur Champion was such a player and was hitting the ball so far that he became quite an attraction on the practice ground as he revelled in his Augusta debut by launching ball after ball high into the green netting, some two hundred and fifty yards away. His big hitting exploits, especially when a couple of drives dropped on to Washington Road, also drew the attention of Jack Nicklaus and Gary Player as they warmed up just down the range.

I watched from the stands as they stopped what they were doing to concentrate on the exploits of this upstart Welsh prodigy. Perhaps for them it was an unsettling glimpse into the future priorities of the game, but they were smug in the knowledge that the Augusta National still had plenty in its armoury to sort out young Parkin.

'I suppose I was a bit of a hooligan but I certainly got a buzz out of banging balls down the practice ground,' said

playing back to back Masters but could only miss the cut on twelve over par on both occasions.

Gordon Sherry came to The Masters with plenty of experience of not only winning the Amateur Championship, but also, still as an amateur, finishing fourth in the 1995 Scottish Open at Carnoustie and then shining alongside the greats in the game at the Open at St. Andrews. In practice rounds at the Open he impressed the likes of Nicklaus and Watson and then in the Championship, although the honours as low amateur went to Steve Webster, Sherry made the cut and finished ahead of another notable amateur, Tiger Woods.

Garth McGimpsey plays out of a bunker at Augusta.

Gordon Sherry tees from the 2nd hole at the 1996 Masters.

Parkin. 'In the tournament itself, the British amateur always got a prestige partner and for me, to play with Arnold Palmer was the greatest thrill of my life. I started well but then came to grief on the greens as most first time players seem to. But at the end of it all Mr. Palmer shook my hand and said "Good luck in your career, I saw a lot of myself in you out there today." If only that were true, but what a wonderful experience for a young player.'

Experience was the one thing the amateur was not able to bring to Augusta and was not able to develop it to any consistent degree. Garth McGimpsey had the luxury of

It all added a rare bit of spice to the amateur contest at the 1996 Masters which was seen as a head to head between the tall, rangy Sherry and Tiger Woods, the player who was tipped to dominate the future of world golf. The contest never really got going; Tiger on his second visit to Augusta as U.S. Amateur Champion failed to make the cut and Sherry was five shots behind him. 'It's been a good experience,' said Sherry, but reflecting on his problems with the inscrutable Augusta greens, 'it has also been the worst experience I've had on a golf course.' As he came off the eighteenth, his mother Anne was waiting for him with

Tiger Woods in action during the 1996 Masters.

the greeting, 'Welcome to your professional career!' From then on the fortunes of Sherry and Woods diverged dramatically; Sherry into a sad obscurity while a year later Woods was winning The Masters by the astonishing margin of twelve shots. The predictions had been correct, Tiger Woods was changing the whole profile of world golf.

One of the many pieces of history that Tiger created in 1997 was to join the list of Masters Champions who first competed at Augusta as an amateur, a list that also included José María Olazábal, who would take two titles after his 1985 debut as an amateur. The second time he won in 1999 he was able to shake hands in the Butler Cabin with his compatriot Sergio García who had at last given European golf its first low amateur at Augusta.

Some say the presence of the amateurs, along with some of the more senior past Champions tends to dilute the field at The Masters but it keeps faith with the Bobby Jones tradition and adds opportunity and also a sense of perspective of what it takes to conquer Augusta and challenge at The Masters.

Quite simply, Augusta had become the most competitive annual arena for professional golf, and as the Seventies drew to a close the ever progressing European Tour was going to adopt this pristine corner of Georgia as the showcase for its talent and strength.

The architect of the modern European Tour, and the man who enabled European golf to compete so strongly in the majors through the rest of the century, was Ken Schofield CBE. When he was appointed Executive Director in 1975 the European Tour had just seventeen

Sergio García plays his tee shot in front of an expectant Augusta crowd.

Ken Schofield – architect of the European Tour.

tournaments with total prize money of little more than £420,000. When he left the post thirty years later, the European Tour had forty five events and prize money of over £73million. In 1980 European Tour members had a total of six places in The Masters, U.S. Open and U.S. PGA Championships; in 2004 there were one hundred and two European Tour members (although not necessarily European players) in these events.

As far as The Masters was concerned, Schofield had the task first of all of trying to convince Hord Hardin of

the need for Augusta to open its doors wider to European players. Hardin had taken over as Vice Chairman of the Augusta National in 1977, taking full responsibility in 1980. Schofield says, 'I always felt with Hord that deep down he felt that The Masters was an American tournament for American players. Invitations were issued overseas, but for European players to compete there with confidence they needed to feel that they were there as of right.'

That feeling was a while away, so too was the feeling that European players could actually play their way into Masters qualification; indeed it was 1987 before Ken Schofield himself got to go to The Masters. Then in 1991 Jack Stephens took over and the atmosphere eased. 'I got on with both of them but they were different characters,' Schofield recalls. 'The best way of describing it would be that I reckon Hord's ideal playing partner would be Sam

Snead whereas Jack Stephens would be very much a Bobby Jones man.'

Slowly they chipped away at the barriers and as the European successes came, their numbers swelled, usually with players who were swift to acknowledge that The Masters was special and The Masters was different. 'But occasionally there was a Tour member who didn't quite get the message. I remember there was one European who decided he wasn't going to go to the International dinner because he didn't do that kind of thing and anyway he hadn't brought a jacket and tie. We put him straight and marched him off to the local store to get him kitted out.' The Masters needed to be treated with respect, and it deserved respect.

In 1999 The Masters finally fell into line with the rest of world golf by acknowledging the world rankings as the principal means of qualification. It meant that all players by their worldwide performances could feel themselves inching toward the all important Masters qualification, and in turn it helped the tournament present itself as being genuinely representative as the best in the world game. Sixteen European players teed it up in 1999, José María Olazábal won it, but it was ironic that this breakthrough year of European qualification has so far represented the final year of European success. Lee Westwood has led, Darren Clarke has led, Justin Rose has led through thirty six holes, but so far no European player has been able to add to the extraordinary catalogue of success that was enjoyed through the Eighties and Nineties.

So in the next part of this history we will concentrate on those heroic performers who shaped the modern perception of European golf, certainly as far as the Augusta National was concerned.

Justin Rose plays from a bunker at the 6th hole, Augusta.

Lee Westwood can't believe he missed his putt on the 11th hole at Augusta.

CHAPTER 9

THE EUROPEAN CHAMPIONS

SEVERIANO BALLESTEROS

MASTERS CHAMPION: 1980 AND 1983

I t must have been a Bobby Jones moment when the young Spaniard first made the journey down Magnolia Lane to gaze out over the Augusta National. Just as the immediate reaction of Jones was, 'that this is a place crying out for a golf course to be laid upon it,' the reaction of Severiano Ballesteros must have been, 'this is a place where I can win.'

Bobby Jones and Alister Mackenzie must have had Seve in mind when they decided against any rough, and laid out the wide open spaces. They must have had Seve in mind as they plotted the perils of every single shot and the tactical decisions that needed to be made on every hole.

When Ballesteros came to Augusta in 1980 for what was to be his fourth Masters, just about the last thing to be mentioned was his age. No-one as young as 23 had ever won the Green Jacket but with Seve that was irrelevant.

At age 19 he'd finished second behind Johnny Miller in the Open Championship at Royal Birkdale, playing the kind of instinctive golf that identified him as the most exciting talent in the sport.

Two years later on his second trip to America he'd won the Greater Greensboro Open, and then the following year realised his inevitable destiny with victory in the Open at Royal Lytham, hitting two fairways and one car park, in the progress of an extraordinary final round that saw him win by three strokes from Jack Nicklaus and Ben Crenshaw. He drove the ball further than anyone else in the game and no-one could match his touch on the greens. He was not only capable of winning at age 23, but he was also expected to win. That was certainly the mood back in Britain where Ballesteros had hero status after his Open Championship exploits, and golf was now officially European, after the previous year's re-configured Ryder

Ballesteros in one of his many awkward situations, 1976.

Ballesteros escapes the crowd at the 18th hole on his way to victory at Royal Lytham.

Job done! Ballesteros holds the Open trophy in 1979.

Cup competition. Ballesteros was one of two Spaniards to be called up into the new European team that was still abjectly beaten at The Greenbrier.

In America they felt differently. Tom Watson had won in 1977 and probably should have won the two years after that. In 1980 Watson was in his absolute prime and America reckoned he was ready for Seve.

But Seve was making sure he was ready for Augusta, not to overwhelm it with power and self-belief, but for the first time he had been persuaded to tailor his game and to harness his power in readiness for the very specific demands of Augusta. It was a conversation with Tony Jacklin that helped bring about this change of attitude.

Jacklin himself had been driven to exasperation at The Masters and knew that this was a course that Seve could not muscle his way round. He told him if he hit it in the wrong places at Augusta, he would not last. He would not be in a position to produce the miracle shot or the great escape. He would not be challenging for anything at Augusta unless he exerted more control over his power, and if that meant playing the game at ninety per cent instead of a hundred and ten, so be it.

So in the months leading up to Augusta, Ballesteros, through hours of practice back home in northern Spain, perfected a shortened, almost three quarter swing, less distance but more control. And when the tide had just left the beach at Pedreña he would be there with his putter, practicing on sand that for a few minutes at least had taken on the pace of Augusta's notorious greens.

But his most important lesson had come at Augusta two years earlier when playing with Gary Player in the final round. He watched and learnt from one of the greatest competitors in golf. Player, that day seemingly out of it, had seven birdies in the last ten holes to overhaul the leaders, Tom Watson among them, and take the title for the third time, his ninth and last Major title.

On the thirteenth fairway Player pointed at the galleries and confided in Ballesteros, 'look at all these people, none of them think I can win. You watch, I'll show them.' The lesson that the young Seve seemed to absorb was a kind of siege mentality. Like Player, he enjoyed thinking people were against him because it made him try harder. In the book by Dudley Doust, *The Young Champion,* Seve says, 'I'm like that, the more against you are the crowd, the more you want to prove something.' There was evidence of that in the very first time that Ballesteros played in The Masters. The young prodigy was paired with Jack Nicklaus in one of those distinctive combinations that are a trademark of The Masters and are meant as a tribute to the achievements of particularly outstanding players.

On this occasion it was a tribute to the Spaniard's position as the number one player in Europe and the great new talent in the world game. Ballesteros did not see it

that way however. 'The Augusta people are trying to test me, they want to see how I can take pressure,' which of course was not the situation at all, but no doubt Ballesteros was able to darken his mood accordingly and use it to his advantage.

Seve hugs Gary Player, after learning all he can from him at Augusta.

Ballesteros was in good company at The Masters, as he rubs shoulders with Tom Watson, Lee Trevino and Jack Nicklaus in 1980.

He finished that debut making the cut, and was fifteen strokes behind the eventual winner Tom Watson. Then came 1978, the learning experience alongside Gary Player, before his twelfth place finish in 1979 convinced him he was ready to win at Augusta. That year Fuzzy Zoeller proved that it is possible to win The Masters on your debut, but he remains the last player to do it. By contrast the apprenticeship of Ballesteros had been thorough.

So he came to Augusta in 1980 as just about the first European player to challenge for The Masters, in expectation as much as hope. Even Oosterhuis, Jacklin, Cotton and, way back, Harry Cooper, never approached the event with the justified belief of Ballesteros that he could win it. He brought with him a game tailored for the requirements of Augusta. The aggression would be toned down and when required, patience and tactics would take over from instinct. That at least was the plan.

And as the 1980 Masters got under way in warm and sultry conditions, it was a plan that worked. Seven birdies in a round of 66, good enough to share the lead with David Graham, and even now it rates as one of the best rounds of his illustrious career. Never before had Seve prepared so meticulously for eighteen holes of golf. He plotted the ideal position from which every approach shot should be played, adopting the Nicklaus tactic of working out, from the green back to the tee, how a hole should ideally be played; essential at Augusta. He worked out his own distances, his Augusta caddie, Marion Herrington, having dutifully provided them in yards. But Seve worked in metres. Off he went notebook in hand. The only thing that did not work was the white cap that he wore on to the first tee. The plan was it would shield him from the glare of the white sand in the bunkers and isolate him from the supposed hostile galleries. It didn't become a long-lasting fashion statement.

If Thursday's excellent start had been built on patience and planning, then patience ran out on Friday and the old Seve returned to trample over all the theories that tactics and safety have any place in golf, especially at Augusta. He covered the first nine in level par but required scything

recoveries from flower beds and pines after a succession of flailing, all or nothing drives.

On the back nine this tactic, if you can describe it as such, extraordinarily started to pay off. Birdies came at the tenth, eleventh and thirteenth. He hit the par five fifteenth with a driver and three iron to move three clear of David Graham who was on the par three sixth.

On the tee of the 190 yard sixteenth, Seve called for an eight iron. Marion Herrington insisted it was an easy seven iron. Seve took his advice and sent the easy seven way past the flag, from where he faced a long and impossible putt. The bogey came a few minutes after the roars from the nearby sixth green indicated that Graham had made a birdie two. Seve's lead was down to just one.

Herrington was horrified and apologised over and over. Seve did his best to be uncharacteristically magnanimous, 'No, no it was my fault for listening to you', but he was still seething when he snap hooked his drive off the seventeenth and the ball went an astonishing distance left, way past the pines and Eisenhower's tree, on to the neighbouring seventh fairway, where it took a big hop short of the seventh green and ran up to within comfortable one putt distance from the flag.

The bemused two ball on the green was Andy Bean and Seve's closest challenger David Graham. Both expressed no surprise when they learnt the errant ball belonged to Ballesteros. There have been many reported versions of the subsequent conversation that took place. The accepted version has David Graham saying, 'nice drive,' Seve replying 'I am driving the ball good. This is the first time I hit the seventh green today, I missed it the first time.'

Ballesteros declined Graham's offer to play through, and when the two players had putted out, he took a drop by the side of the green and announced to the hugely entertained gallery that he was still going to make a birdie. At which point he flushed a seven iron back over the trees to the distant, invisible seventeenth green. The resultant tumultuous applause was for the ball not only finding the target but rolling fifteen feet from the hole from where, with a sense of inevitability, Ballesteros holed in the putt.

CHAPTER 9

David Graham of Australia, one of Seve's challengers.

It was an incident that deserved to replace the Lytham car park shot as the stuff of golfing legend, and if Gene Sarazen's double eagle a few hundred yards away, forty five years earlier, was the shot heard around the world, Seve's recovery at seventeen was the shot heard across Europe, announcing that surely, at long last, a Masters Green Jacket would be heading across the Atlantic.

His round of 69 put him four shots clear of David Graham and Rex Caldwell at the halfway stage. The challenge of Jack Nicklaus had not materialised and Tom Watson was seven shots back. Only Herman Keiser, Jack Nicklaus and Ray Floyd had held bigger thirty-six hole leads in The Masters and they had each gone on to win.

He had certainly set the target but did he have the ability to intimidate and dominate as Nicklaus could? His escapology on seventeen suggested that Augusta could still have its revenge, and the young Spaniard was heading for at least one big score. And when he sent his opening tee shot carving into the trees alongside the ninth, it looked as if the big score was going to come in round three.

He bogeyed the first and the third but birdied the second to underline how well he had played the par fives all week. His tee shot at the fifth soared left towards the sixth green. The recovery he made was comparable in scale to what he had done the afternoon before, but it was still the third dropped shot of his opening five holes, only two ahead of his playing partner David Graham.

It was not so much his calmness and composure that helped Seve halt the crisis, as much as his fierce competitive instinct. His tee shot on the par three sixth was almost in the hole. He made the putt. On the par five eighth, as Tom Watson was dropping shots on the back nine, Ballesteros hit an arrow-straight three iron to six feet from the hole, and sank it for an eagle. His imperious form had returned and took him through the back nine in 33 for a round of 68, thirteen under par. A seemingly unbeatable lead of seven shots over his nearest challenger.

It is safe to assume that with a lead of that size, and being the personality he was, Seve did not spend the Saturday night consumed by doubt or negative thoughts. In fact he invited a group of Spanish friends to his rented house on Brookwood Drive about a mile from the course. The one stipulation of a very sociable evening was that there was to be no talk of golf, and especially no talk of Seve's sore back, which even at this early stage in his career seemed a threat to his future domination of the game. Dinner was beef stroganoff, noodles, peas and fresh fruit salad. After dinner it was *Saturday Night Fever* on the television, with John Travolta offering the kind of image Seve could present the next day. Then it was bed by ten, and the last voice Seve would hear would be the inspirational words of his

EUROPE AT THE MASTERS

Barcelona sports psychologist on the earpiece of his cassette player.

If there were dreams then they could have been about Masters records as much as Masters Green Jackets. Seve was poised to become the youngest player to win The Masters, joining only Nicklaus, Bobby Jones and Francis Ouimet: the only players to win two major titles by the time they were twenty three. Could he also win The Masters by a bigger margin than the nine stroke win of Nicklaus in 1965?

Through the front nine on a perfect Augusta Sunday afternoon, all those records were within his grasp. He had birdied the opening hole and picked up further shots at the third and the fifth. By the time he came off the ninth he was an amazing ten shots clear of the field. Everyone knew it was all over, and in the clubhouse the Augusta Club manager was briefing Seve's manager on the protocol of the Green Jacket ceremony and the respect which this symbol of golfing prowess must be accorded; and by the way, he was a 42 regular wasn't he?

Seve checks the lie of his ball at the 13th.

Everyone knows, and tradition dictates, that the back nine at The Masters on a Sunday afternoon is a very special examination of technique and temperament. The strongest challenges have foundered around Amen Corner, the finest champions have succumbed to the unbearable tension at fifteen and sixteen. The best defence against everything that lies ahead is a ten shot lead, and even this might not be enough.

At the tenth came the first dropped shot as Seve three putted across the slickest of greens. Jack Newton, his playing partner and closest challenger, then birdied eleven, so the lead was eight shots. On the tee at twelve the hitherto supremely confident Spaniard suffered his first indecision and a blocked tee shot ran off the bank and into the creek. He took a drop, double bogeyed, and when

The pressure mounts for Ballesteros at Augusta.

Newton got his two the ten shot lead had been halved in the space of just three holes.

His composure seemed to have returned with a long, perfectly struck tee shot at the par five thirteenth, but was his second shot a four iron or an easy three? Again there was indecision and eventually Ballesteros failed to fully commit to the three iron, and there was the agonising sight of the ball trickling back into Raes Creek. Another drop was taken, another bogie on the card and with Newton making his third birdie in succession, the lead was now three shots, and Ballesteros was in crisis.

Up the fourteenth he again missed the fairway and the recovery he made for par was essential because Gibby Gilbert playing the fifteenth had also moved to within four of the lead. It was on the fourteenth that Seve's concentration was disturbed by a spectator yelling, 'come on Jack,' clearly urging on Newton, but Ballesteros felt they were taunting him with Nicklaus, and all the lessons he learnt from Gary Player on the thirteenth two years earlier started to strengthen his resolve.

The feeling was that all these spectators were against him, none of them thought he could win. Even the referee, who Ballesteros felt gave him a pedantic ruling on the drop on thirteen, was against him. 'The crowd, the referee, and now this guy. I didn't know whether people were against me or not, but that was how it

felt, and let me tell you, it helped. I am like Gary Player, the more the crowd is against me, the more I want to prove something.'

He needed all the resolve he could muster. He was now trying to avoid records, in particular the unwanted record of blowing the biggest lead in Masters history. From the fifteenth green came news that Gilbert had also moved to within just three shots of the lead, but by that time Ballesteros was striding down the fifteenth fairway having hit the ideal tee shot down the par five hole.

The hole represented the last big hurdle. Survive here and he could surely coast in. But if he faltered again it could all be snatched away, as Seve was to experience standing over this same second shot, six years later. Just as in 1986, a roar from the sixteenth green added further tension to an already supremely demanding moment. Gilbert had birdied and was now within two. Newton's second shot at fifteen had made the green and he had the chance of an eagle. Any thoughts of laying up were dispelled. Seve had to go for the green and try to make the four that would restore at least some comfort for the last three holes. The four iron was not perfectly struck but had the perfect result, landing inside Newton's ball some twenty feet from the hole.

Newton put his putt eight feet past and could only make par. Ballesteros rolled his to four feet and made the birdie. The crisis was passed, especially when Ballesteros hit a six iron to the heart of the sixteenth green and made par to lead by three shots, with just the two closing par fours remaining. He was confident enough to say to his caddie as he left the sixteenth green, 'It's finished, the tournament is ours.'

And so it was with two closing pars for a 72 and a four round total of thirteen under par 275, that Europe had its first Masters champion, a four shot win over Gilbert and Newton. And Seve had his records; at 23 years old he was the youngest winner, and his total of 23 birdies during the four days of the event is a record that still stands today.

With his victories in the Open and at Augusta, Ballesteros had ushered in a golden age for European golf,

Seve's caddie is the first to congratulate him on the first European to win The Masters.

and what was to come, especially in The Masters and the Ryder Cup, can be traced back to what he did at this time, although the full impact was slow to be recognised. The Daily Telegraph reported that Spain's national radio began their news bulletin with details of a new Spanish swimming record. No mention was made of their Spanish winner at Augusta.

Certainly the significance was felt throughout the whole of the rest of the world of golf. Ken Schofield, European Tour Executive Director said, 'Seve winning first at Lytham and then at Augusta was the equivalent of what Tony Jacklin had achieved four years earlier winning the Open at Lytham and then the U.S. Open at Hazeltine. The difference this time was the level of television coverage and world attention that was focused on Augusta, and with a young Spanish winner like Seve, everyone could see that world golf had entered a new era.'

Arnold Palmer came away from Augusta in 1980 with the definite impression that the balance of power had shifted. The era of himself, Nicklaus and Player seemed to be over. Even the dominance of Tom Watson was going to be undermined by this Spaniard with so much natural talent and so many years ahead of him.

All that could stop him was his own temperament, and over the next couple of seasons that seemed to be the case. His attitude that the world was against him might have been productive on the golf course, but behind the scenes it was an ingredient in a bitter battle with the fast-growing European Tour, which was keen to flex its muscles over the subject of appearance money.

As a result, in controversial circumstances, he was not called up to the Ryder Cup team that went down to a heavy defeat at Walton Heath. His absence was seemingly political, but anyway Ballesteros, his head spinning with all the conflicts and arguments, was ill-prepared throughout the 1981 season. His defence at Augusta was a reflection of his isolated mood and he would miss the cut by six shots.

But he was still able to produce wins in 1981, notably in the latter half of the season, in the World Match Play at

Wentworth, and through 1982 the recovery process, in terms of his relationship with the European Tour, was under way. He was a factor at Augusta, again briefly hitting the front during the second round until the setback of a double bogey at the fifteenth. His three birdies in the last four holes on Sunday left him one shot away from the play-off between Craig Stadler and Dan Pohl, which Stadler won.

Seve was ready to win another major and seemed to be in the perfect frame of mind for his Masters challenge in 1983. There was a faltering start with a dropped shot at

Seve in full flight as he hits an approach shot at Augusta, 1983.

the first and a scrambled par at the second, but the round would then contain six birdies and his 68 would put him just one shot behind the first round leaders.

Overnight and the next day a deluge of rain hit the course. No play was possible on the Friday and then further delays through the weekend meant that a Monday finish was going to be inevitable. In Saturday's second round, on a soft course, Augusta's defences may have been down but no-one was able to take particular advantage. It was a 70 for Ballesteros, one shot off Gil Morgan's lead. Similarly in round three, the drying greens were hard to

read and the putts failed to drop, but his 73 still left him in second place, one shot behind Ray Floyd and the defending Champion Craig Stadler.

Monday afternoon, at last sunshine, and at last the final round of the 1983 Masters. It would be Ballesteros and Tom Watson in the penultimate pairing teeing off at 1.17. Even before Stadler and Floyd got under way eight minutes later, Seve had set about taking a firm grip on the contest.

After a good drive at the opening hole, a crisp seven iron to eight feet gave Seve the birdie he needed to tie for the lead. Then at the second, Ballesteros hit the shot of the week; a four wood from a downhill lie that carried the bunker in front of the green and settled just fifteen feet from the hole. Tom Kite later commented that he could not even hit a wedge that close, let alone a 255 yard four wood. Watson almost matched the shot, but failed to match the Ballesteros eagle putt that saw him go two ahead of Floyd and Stadler. A 20 footer for birdie from Seve at the third almost dropped before he hit a glorious two iron stone dead at the par three fourth. Ballesteros was three clear and his challengers were in shock.

Even though Ballesteros made only one further birdie in that final round, the damage was done. Every attempt that Watson, Floyd and Stadler made to get within striking

Tom Watson can only watch from behind, as Ballesteros salutes the crowd making his way up to the 18th.

distance seemed doomed to failure. Watson seemed to have a chance at 12, but with both players finding the green off the tee, Watson three-putted, while Ballesteros made birdie. It was a resolute, ruthless performance and a striking contrast to the manner in which Seve had almost let that ten shot lead slip away on the back nine, three years earlier.

He was not going to let his four shot lead disappear at the closing hole, although there was a gasp from the gallery when his approach shot flew over the back of the green and his miscued chip failed to make the putting surface. He promptly stepped up to the ball and with the same club knocked his fourth shot straight into the hole. Tom Watson remarked at the press conference that if that shot had not hit the flag and dropped in it would have

Seve celebrates clinching his second Masters title.

Seve accepts his Green Jacket from previous winner Craig Stadler.

been straight off the front of the green. Seve seemed to take it as another example of everyone being against him, and his performance not getting its due credit.

This was one event however, where Seve had shown total self-control and control of the contest, due in no small degree to his caddie, Nick DePaul. 1983 was the year that Augusta had lifted its ban on the compulsory use of local caddies and DePaul had just become the first white man to caddie for The Masters Champion. A dominant champion, not needing to get angry to produce his best. From Seve the main observation was a chilling one for those who would have to try to stop him over the next ten years. He felt that he hadn't played well all week and had only hit one decent shot across all four rounds. He became the tenth player to win the title twice and only Jack

CHAPTER 9

Seve in good spirits as he wins the Open in 1984. ▶

Nicklaus at age 25 had been younger. European golf sat back in anticipation of what more the Eighties would bring.

In 1984 as Ben Crenshaw was holding off the challenge of Tom Watson to win his first major, and Nick Faldo was finishing in the top fifteen for the first time at Augusta, Ballesteros was once again following up his victory by missing the cut as defending Champion. But 1984 was also the year of Seve's glorious Open Championship win at St. Andrews and it was safely assumed that he would still have many years of being a contender at Augusta.

But not necessarily a winner. Entering the final round in 1985 he was tied for second with fellow European, Bernhard Langer, but they had had a tense relationship ever since Seve's arguments with the European Tour, four years earlier. The events of that final day are described in the next chapter but it had been assumed that it would be Ballesteros who would get the better of Langer and overhaul the leader Ray Floyd for his third Green Jacket. Seve would finish frustrated in a tie for second, but the real agony came a year later.

The moment that he arrived at his ball on the fifteenth fairway in the 1986 Masters it recalled the crisis that he'd faced on his way to victory six years earlier. To go for the green in two, to take on one of the most mentally demanding shots in golf, in the knowledge that the man on a charge just a hole ahead was not Gibby Gilbert but Jack Nicklaus. The other crises that he was facing in his life at that time were many and various.

His arguments with the European Tour had now been replaced by a dispute with the U.S. Tour. Indeed, five months before The Masters his membership of the U.S. Tour had been revoked by the Policy Board. They and Commissioner Dean Beman taking the action because Seve had played only nine tournaments instead of the required fifteen, and felt a stance needed to be taken against European players supposedly coming across the Atlantic and 'cherry-picking' the big events. At this time Seve's father was in the last stages of his battle against cancer and would die a few weeks before Augusta, but his preoccupation with his father's condition was never put forward as a defence to the Tour Commissioner.

As a result Seve had arrived at Augusta in 1986, bitter, sad, distracted and desperately short of competitive practice, and in no mood to communicate with Press or Television.

I know to my cost because the request had come from BBC TV that for our coverage they wanted a series of quotes from the top players on how it would feel to arrive at the 72nd hole, needing a four to win The Masters. By Tuesday afternoon we had just about all of them, Nicklaus, Watson, Player and Floyd, as well as the defending Champion Crenshaw. We needed Seve, and at around four o'clock he was hitting balls, on his own, at one end of the emptying practice ground.

A sudden rainstorm forced him to take shelter on the clubhouse verandah. He knew of our requirements but did not want to take the opportunity of getting the quick quote done. 'First of all I must go putt.' And go putt he did, for half an hour, forty five minutes, an hour. It was 6.30 and in exasperation my cameraman, who had less need to preserve cordial relationships than I did, walked on to the practice putting green and held a light meter a few feet from Seve's head. Fifteen minutes later when he

Ballesteros and Jack Nicklaus when paired in 1984, walk up the 7th fairway flanked by the crowds.

Seve tees off from the fifteenth, victory within his grasp.

Seve in front of the fifteenth, his second shot having landed in the water, enables Jack Nicklaus to win the 1986 Masters.

was confident there was no light left, a smiling Ballesteros made himself available for the quote. I asked the standard question, 'What might your feelings be if you come to the final hole needing a four for The Masters?' He replied, 'I no worry about the eighteenth, I win this tournament by the sixteenth on the final day,' and with that he was off.

Unfortunately a few members of the local Augusta Press, who had spent the last three days feeding off scraps, as far as Seve was concerned, were eavesdropping the conversation and had the story. Seve had offered a short, wry, ironic quote for the BBC but 'arrogant' Ballesteros was all over the morning papers.

When he was forced to wait over his second shot on the fifteenth, maybe this casual quote and the screaming headlines were coming back to haunt him. He thought he had the tournament won half an hour earlier when he eagled the thirteenth but

However, he would still end the season with tournament successes to celebrate, and he was once again number one in Europe. When he was asked at the World Match Play Championship whether he would like to beat Nicklaus after what happened at Augusta he said, 'there is nothing to avenge. Jack Nicklaus is a great champion. I will take revenge from the golf course, especially the fifteenth.'

He birdied the fifteenth the following year. He needed to do that and he also needed to get up and down from the bunker at the eighteenth to get into the sudden death play-off for the title with Greg Norman and Larry Mize.

Down the tenth they went. They each hit the green in two but Seve was the only one to three putt, missing the return after sending his first putt four feet

Nicklaus had three straight birdies from the ninth, picked up another shot at the thirteenth, eagled the fifteenth, and now had hit it just a couple of feet away at the sixteenth. When he holed the putt to move within a shot of Ballesteros at the top of the leader board, Augusta was in a tumult, and the thunderous applause rolled back up the hill to Ballesteros waiting to compose himself over his second shot into the fifteenth.

A shot that was now asking the Spaniard one of the biggest questions of his career.

The four iron he eventually struck was short on commitment, a shot full of uncertainty, and the ripples it produced on the lake in front of the green spread far and wide. They meant that at age 46, Nicklaus would be Masters Champion for a sixth time, on one of Augusta's most astonishing afternoons. The ripples also seemed to confirm the fallibility of Ballesteros and although there would be one more major title in his career it seemed that the peak had been passed.

past. As Norman and Mize went on, Ballesteros walked back up the hill to the clubhouse clearly distraught.

Lauren St. John in her biography of Ballesteros says, 'During that long, tortuous walk up the tenth hole, away from the gay crowds and the duel for The Masters Championship, Ballesteros was inconsolable. Head bowed and shoulders slumped, he wept for everything he had loved and lost, especially for his father, whom he had promised before he died that he would win The Masters at Augusta. For that one moment in time there was no sadder, more lonely man in all the world than Severiano Ballesteros.'

From my presentation position on the clubhouse balcony, I watched the last hundred yards of that lonely walk. Then just as the clubhouse door slammed, the most astonishing roar rolled up the valley from Amen Corner. Larry Mize had just holed his outrageous pitch to deny Greg Norman in the cruellest fashion.

Augusta National is the most extraordinary place.

BERNHARD LANGER

MASTERS CHAMPION: 1985 AND 1993

With his wins in 1980 and 1983 Seve had opened the door for European golf, but who would stride through? Nick Faldo had made his Masters debut in 1979 and played all four rounds, but would not return until 1984. Sandy Lyle was starting to compile Augusta experience, Oosterhuis played on, but in general the European involvement was still modest and, Ballesteros apart, rarely threatening.

In 1982 Bernhard Langer became the first player from Germany to contest The Masters. Germany had never produced a player of international class, indeed the game in Germany had a very modest appeal, even minority status.

Langer was born in Augsburg in southern Germany in 1957. His father Erwin had escaped from a prisoner of war train bound for Siberia in 1945 and so was able to continue to build a life in the tough conditions of post-war Germany. Life was still hard twenty years later and the young Bernhard took a job caddying at the local Augsburg Golf Club out of financial necessity rather than enthusiasm for the sport.

But that enthusiasm soon came and so did the obvious talent, even though it was demonstrated with rudimentary cast-off clubs, his only coaching aid being a series of photographs of Jack Nicklaus's swing torn from a magazine. So much of his early years in the sport can draw comparison with Ballesteros, but as a player the comparison ends.

Where Seve was swashbuckling passion and invention, Langer was science, percentages and patience. It would be too easy to suggest their styles and personalities simply followed national stereotypes because for Langer, beneath the calm exterior lay demons that had to be overcome more than once during an illustrious career.

The dreaded putting yips did not actually start with Langer (ask Peter Alliss), but Langer, in the first part of his professional life, contracted a particularly savage version. The potential that he had shown by winning the World Under 23 Championship in 1979 was being brought to a grinding halt by the spasm in his putting stroke that golfers of all abilities know so well and fear so much.

In Langer's case the problem possibly came from trying to make the transition from the lush courses of Germany and northern Europe to the lightning-fast greens of Spain and Portugal on the European Tour. In his autobiography he tried to describe what the yips actually were, 'It is the putter not doing what you want it to do. It is an involuntary and uncontrollable movement of the muscles, resulting in a fast, jerky, uncontrolled putting stroke. It's like a muscle spasm; you hold the putter this way or that way, it doesn't matter, and sometimes you can't take it back. You freeze, you totally freeze, or you just jerk.'

Strength of character and the confident knowledge of the quality of his ball striking saw Langer through, but it took around two years of struggle. It also took twenty different putters, constant advice and a variety of grips before Langer established himself as a serious tournament winner in the early Eighties.

Langer lines up his putt at the World Matchplay in 1981.

In 1981 he had finished number one in Europe, winning the German Open and The Bob Hope Classic, and finishing second in the Open at Royal St. George's, four shots behind the winner, Bill Rogers. Then came the putting crisis, but by 1984 the recovery seemed to be complete and he seemed ready to chase Seve once again for the principal European honours.

He won titles in Holland, Ireland, France and Spain and challenged strongly for the Open at St. Andrews

Bernard Langer stands alongside Nick Faldo at the 1985 Masters.

finishing in a tie for second with Tom Watson, two shots behind Ballesteros. In 1985 he was certainly ready to win a major, but as a recovering 'yipper' and with his game held together by the scar tissue from his battle against the affliction, the slick precise greens of Augusta did not seem to be the ideal location for the breakthrough.

The greens were especially fast in 1985 to the extent that players like Nicklaus and Watson were expressing their concerns about the combination of speed and pin positions that looked set to humble even the most composed player, let alone Langer, back from the brink of his biggest putting nightmare. But the statistics show that

The master tactician had swapped the calculator for the dice and this would be the key for his final day challenge.

At the end of round three Langer was well placed: two shots off the lead held by Ray Floyd. In second was Curtis Strange who was putting together an extraordinary Masters, opening with a round of 80, and then fighting back with a 65 and a 68 to head Langer and Ballesteros who would be paired together on the final day.

But there was an almost eerie self-assurance about Langer as that weekend progressed. He had dinner with a German journalist on the Friday evening who was surprised to hear the normally reserved Langer say that not only had he started the tournament well, but that he was going on to win it. I had a similar experience the following evening when our request for an interview was rather forlorn because we could not move out of the Channel Four television complex that was about three quarters of a mile away. Hearing of our plight, Langer commandeered a buggy, drove himself across the par three course to the television compound and talked to me about how hugely confident he was about landing his first major title.

The principal obstacle in his way seemed to be his final round pairing. In recent years, apart from the major Championships, Langer had outperformed the great star of the European game, Ballesteros. But in head to head competition Seve had the edge. The Spaniard had beaten Langer on three occasions in World Match Play competition. When he won the Open it was Langer who finished two behind. 'It seemed the more we played against each other, the more I lost. But I told myself at Augusta, "I must play my own game. If he practices putting on the green I will tell him to go away. If he annoys me I will tell him and I will not be upset if he doesn't say anything.'

Actually Seve hadn't said anything much to Langer since 1981 when he perceived Langer to be involved in the decision that excluded Ballesteros from that year's European Ryder Cup team. He also took offence to Langer's observations in the Press that Seve intimidated his opponents on the golf course. A truce was called in 1984 but this was still the uneasy background against

Langer gets in some putting practice between rounds, with his coach Willi Hoffmann.

on that glorious week in 1985 this was one of the most solid departments of Langer's game as he three putted only once in the seventy two holes.

It was a quiet start for Langer with opening rounds of 72 and 74 just putting him in the hunt. Tied for fourteenth he was in a similar position to the year before, but now in his third Masters he had that extra bit of Augusta experience that might enable him to make better progress. It seems he had the confidence as well and in the third round demonstrated that confidence with a 225 yard three wood across Raes Creek in front of the thirteenth hole. The ball hopped over the water and Langer made eagle.

which they teed up together on this demanding afternoon at Augusta.

Langer and Ballesteros on the first tee of the Augusta National; it should have been a pivotal moment for European golf at The Masters. Europe's finest out to make a significant point to the great heroes of American golf at the very place where that reputation was most sensitive. Instead there was a distinct chill as they shook hands, and Langer would remark later that the words of good luck they exchanged on the first tee, would be the last words they would exchange until the seventeenth hole.

Langer vowed to play the final round without looking at a leader board, in actual fact his subconscious was probably telling him to outscore his nemesis Ballesteros and the rest would take care of itself. Maybe Ballesteros was feeling the same, but while they were doing this Curtis Strange continued his unlikely challenge.

The man who shot 80 in the opening round moved four clear of the field with nine holes to play. Langer at this point abandoned his plan, looked at the leader-board and decided that the only worthwhile tactic was to attack without any of the caution that he had shown through the first nine. It was Ballesteros who had begun the stronger getting a birdie at the second where Langer dropped a shot. Seve then holed nothing whereupon Langer seemed to convert every scant opportunity that came his way. Even so, when Langer, Ballesteros and Gary Hallberg reached the tenth tied for second, The Masters that year was for Curtis Strange to win or lose.

Langer's new found aggressive attitude would see him through Amen Corner in two under par, and when he was on the fourteenth he became aware of the news, through a spectator not through a leader board, that Strange had hit big problems. A three putt on the tenth was followed by a second shot into Raes Creek at the thirteenth. He had tried to extricate himself but with another bogey his lead was down to one and his momentum and composure were shattered.

Langer parred the fourteenth and duly took the opportunity on offer at fifteen with the birdie that tied the lead. It was helpful to play the short sixteenth without any knowledge that he led The Masters. That came as he walked off with his par three to hear the gasps from the adjacent fifteenth. Curtis Strange had dropped a shot. Langer led for the first time. Ballesteros knew the importance of the moment, and when his great chip at sixteen narrowly failed to drop, he flung himself to the ground in exasperation knowing that his last real chance had gone.

He knew that for sure when he dropped a shot at seventeen and Langer birdied. That was when the first communication came since the handshake on the first tee. Ballesteros tapped Langer on the back, 'Well done,' he said, 'this is your week.'

Maybe this was merely yet another bit of psychological intimidation from Ballesteros because Langer put his four iron second shot at eighteen into the greenside bunker, came out to six feet but still made only his second bogey of

Langer purposely strides up to the 15th hole of The Masters final day, 1985.

Langer nervously chips from the bunker at the 18th hole.

the day, and suddenly there was tension in the air again. If Curtis Strange could birdie either of the last two holes it would be a play-off, but instead he dropped a shot at the closing hole. It was Langer by two from Ballesteros, Strange and Floyd.

In the Butler Cabin Langer was able to absorb the moment with his American born wife Vicky while on the CBS Television talkback their director was bemoaning the potential clash between Langer's red trousers and the Green Jacket in equally colourful language.

Everything seemed to happen very quickly in Langer's life in the hours and days that followed. His long-time coach and mentor Willi Hoffman had been heading to Augusta airport midway through the final round, but got

Langer can't believe that he has just bogeyed the last hole. He must now await his fate in the Butler Cabin.

LEADERS

	HOLE	1	2	3	4	5	6	7	8	9	10	11	12	13	14	15	16	17
	PAR	4	5	4	3	4	3	4	5	4	4	4	3	5	4	5	4	3
4	FLOYD	4	4	4	4	4	3	3	3	2	3	3	2	2				
3	STRANGE	3	4	4	5	5	5	6	7	7	6	6	7	6				
2	LANGER	2	1	1	2	3	3	3	3	3	3	3	3	3				
2	BALLESTEROS	2	3	3	3	4	4	3	3	3	3	3	3	3				
1	TREVINO	1	1	0	0	1	1	0	1	2	2	2	1	1	1			
1	NICKLAUS	1	0	0	0	0	0	1	1	1	1	1	1	2	2	2	2	
1	WATSON. T.	1	2	1	1	1	1	1	1	1	1	1	1	2	2	2	2	
0	HALLBERG	0	1	1	2	3	3	2	3	3	4	4	2	2	2	3	1	
2	HAAS. J.	2	1	0	0	0	0	1	1	2	1	1	1	2	2	2	2	
0	LIETZKE	0	1	1	1	1	1	1	1	1	1	1	2	2	2	2	2	

THRU 14

LANGER 5
BALLESTEROS 3

BALLESTEROS

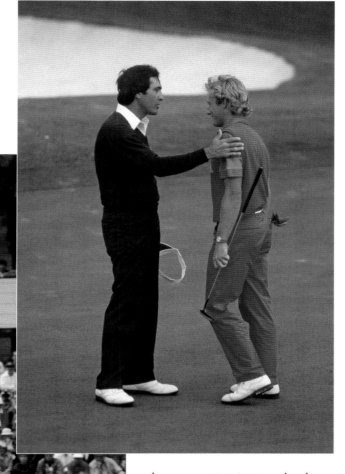

The next day came the drive south to Florida to play in the Heritage Classic at Hilton Head and Langer would admit to a feeling of anti-climax. In his autobiography he wrote, 'I had achieved another of the milestones I had set myself. Great commercial opportunities would open up to me. But underneath it all there was a nagging question – is that it? Is that all there is? I had scaled the mountain but somehow the summit did not seem as exciting when I reached it as I had expected. There was an emptiness within me, saying there must be more to life than this.'

He went on to relate how he then played a practice round with Bobby Clampett the next day who invited him to join other players and their wives at the tour Bible study group the following evening. For Langer it was the start of a very swift journey of discovery that, from then on, would make religion the most powerful driving force in his life. A few days later he went on to win the Hilton Head Tournament, The Sea Pines Heritage Classic.

The Green Jacket, The Heritage and God. A week in the life of Bernhard Langer.

Differences aside – Ballesteros knew it was Langer's week, as he congratulates him on a fine day's play.

The Green Jacket says it all. Bernard Langer shakes hands with Ben Crenshaw as he is crowned the 1985 Masters Champion.

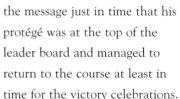

the message just in time that his protégé was at the top of the leader board and managed to return to the course at least in time for the victory celebrations.

Those celebrations, after the formalities of the Press and the similar formalities of the club dinner, included a trip to join Langer's friends Frank Williams and David Inglis who run the Australian Masters. They had the foresight and confidence to stake $3,000 dollars on a Langer victory and their winnings of $100,000 were not far short of the $126,000 dollars Masters first prize.

CHAPTER 9

Langer plays his second shot to the 13th at The Masters 1993.

Eight years separated Langer's two victories at Augusta, during which time a great deal had happened to consolidate the prestige of the European Tour. There was Ryder Cup success both at home and in America, Open Championship success for Lyle and Faldo, and when Langer won his second Masters it would be the eighth victory in the event by a European Tour player in fourteen years and the fifth win in six years.

Maybe not as much had happened to Langer in this period as had been expected or at least he had achieved, without creating the screaming headlines. When the Sony Rankings were first created in 1986 he was the first number one. Seven years later he was still in the top three. Through 1993 he had won in Europe for fifteen consecutive years but the next major title was proving elusive. Two top three finishes in the Open Championship had been followed by another putting crisis which he endured and survived with his now legendary resolve. The putting form that he emerged with had been sorely tested

at Kiawah Island in 1991 when he tried and failed to sink the putt that would retain the Ryder Cup for Europe. If anything he was a stronger player for that experience and certainly by 1993 he was overdue his second major Championship win. Many expected it to be The Open at Royal St. George's where he finished close behind Sandy Lyle in 1985. Others subscribed to the view that Green Jackets come in pairs.

The Masters had begun in 1993 with no thoughts that the title would go abroad yet again. Instead it all began with the impossible dream of Nicklaus and Palmer going head to head once more. Arnold Palmer at the age of 63 opened with three straight birdies before confronting reality. Nicklaus responded with an astonishing round of 67 to share the first round lead with four others. Few noticed Langer, perfectly placed, just a shot behind. He was still in touch when, early on the Saturday morning, he completed a rain delayed second round, a shot behind the halfway leader Jeff Maggert.

Later that day as the wind got up around the Augusta National, Langer was setting the pace himself with a round that he described in this solemn fashion in his autobiography, 'I had an excellent round of 69 on the Saturday in windy conditions and that gave me a four shot lead going into the final round. I had never been in that position in a major before.'

What Bernhard Langer actually produced that day was one of the great rounds of his career. Just as in 1985 any fragility in his putting form was not evident on these notorious greens. He holed from fifteen feet for birdie on the second and other long birdie putts found the target on the fifth and the eighth. And then at the eleventh while all around him were faltering, Langer holed from off the green in a manner reminiscent of Larry Mize and even a couple of dropped shots on the way in after that did not seem to matter. Only Langer and Craig Stadler had broken seventy on this demanding day, and Langer's resultant four shot lead seemed to have put the destination of the title beyond doubt.

Langer of course would not be assuming anything and protested that the tournament was a long way from being won. He would have been mindful of the large lead that Ballesteros almost frittered away in 1980, and his caution was also anticipating the final day collapse of Greg Norman in 1996. True to form, in 1993 the final day of The Masters would produce surprises and controversy.

The first surprise came at the opening hole where Langer missed the green with a straightforward nine iron approach and dropped a shot. He got it back at the par five second and after that it was business as usual, not making any big putts like the day before, but not dropping shots either. The challenge would come from Dan Forsman who picked up three shots on the front nine and was just one behind Langer when he came to the tee at the par three twelfth.

What followed was one of those pieces of golfing drama that only an amphitheatre like Amen Corner can play host to. Stage left on the eleventh green, Langer was under pressure surviving a heart-stopping moment as his

Langers creates a sand storm, as he plays out of a bunker at Augusta.

approach to the eleventh clung to the fringe of the back of green just avoiding rolling into the creek. Langer salvaged another par and then threw a glance across the manicured hollow to stage right: Forsman short of the twelfth green.

Actually it was more than a glance from Langer who claimed he had not looked at a leader board until the tenth but now knew the full significance of Forsman's challenge. What he saw was the American taking a drop short of the water at the twelfth, and then taking another. Forsman's tee shot had been a seven iron and he knew it was in the water short of the green as soon as he had hit it. His third shot from the drop zone hit the bank and it, too, rolled into the water. It would eventually be a quadruple bogey seven for Forsman and his challenge was gone.

An eagle at the 13th hole for Langer, on the final round at Augusta.

Now the only threat to Langer seemed to be his playing partner Chip Beck two shots behind, and he met the threat with his only true piece of aggression in a solid final round. After a perfect drive around the corner at the par three thirteenth, Langer and his caddie Pete Coleman stood in earnest discussion over the risks and merits of the second shot to come. Coleman's view was that Langer had to go for it if he were to maintain the strength of his position. Chip Beck would certainly attack the green with his second shot, and duly did so successfully. History told Langer that this was the place to be bold, but history also told him of those who had tried to be bold and failed. Billy Joe Patton fell at the thirteenth when it looked as if he could become the first amateur winner of the title in 1954, and when Curtis Strange found Raes Creek with his second shot in 1985 it gave Langer the opportunity for his first Augusta win.

A mistake now by Langer could give Chip Beck that same opportunity. Instead his three iron found the heart of the green and finished about twenty feet from the hole.

Beck two putted for birdie but Langer sank his eagle putt and his grip on the tournament had become strong again. He led by three, and was still three shots clear when they came to the par five fifteenth. For right or wrong, this is the hole for which this particular Masters contest will be remembered.

Just like the thirteenth, the fifteenth combines choice, opportunity and risk. Just like the thirteenth it has produced heroes like Gene Sarazen and those that have suffered like Ballesteros. Chip Beck fell into neither category and was unfairly vilified in America as the man who dodged the challenge.

Three shots behind and seemingly secure in second, Beck who was not one of the longest hitters in the game had put his tee shot slightly down the left but into that zone of uncertainty between going for the green and having no option but to lay-up. On the other side of the fairway Langer and his caddie Pete Coleman felt his only option, if he were going to hang on to any hope of the

Langer drives for victory.

Langer celebrates his birdie on the 15th hole.

CHAPTER 9

Champion for a second time – Langer duly receives the applause from the gallery at the 18th.

title, was to go for it in two. But maybe Beck had already abandoned that prospect, and that is what prompted the torrent of criticism when he eventually nudged his ball down short of the water.

Beck was the hapless victim of the frustration that seemed to be building in America at Europe's prolonged domination of this most prestigious of all events. You got the feeling that the success was not exactly begrudged, but at the very least it needed to be challenged. Lyle was made to battle, so too Woosnam and certainly Faldo in surviving two play-offs. Beck however was seen to have shirked the responsibility and to have chosen to protect his card at the expense of the last faint hope of victory.

All would have been forgiven of course if he had made a birdie and closed the gap on Langer, but instead it was Langer who got up and down for his four and when Beck bogeyed the sixteenth the lead was five and the contest was over. Through the last couple of holes that secured another great triumph for European golf there was that rare feeling for a Masters Sunday, a sense of anti-climax. Langer was a great Champion but he wasn't quite the Champion that the Augusta faithful had in mind. I sensed the same sort of mood when Olazábal won for a second time and when Vijay Singh was victorious in 2000. The winner would be greeted with honour and respect but if the challenge to the Champion had not been worthy of

to get at the Butler Cabin presentation to correct an indiscretion from eight years earlier that had always made him feel uncomfortable. When he won in 1985 he was asked at the Green Jacket presentation whether he had looked at a leader board, and whether he knew what was going on in the tournament. He replied, 'I was trying not to look but I saw it for the first time at the ninth and I thought Jesus Christ I am playing well and I'm still four shots behind.'

You will recall it was still a week before Christianity and religion came into his life with such force. When he got home he was deeply affected by the letters he received and the indignant reaction to using the name of Jesus Christ so casually. Now he was being given a chance to correct the mistake, and he did it at the Butler Cabin presentation with some impact. The first question he was asked was how his second Masters win compared with the first and he answered, 'It's a great honour to win the greatest tournament in the world, and especially on Easter Sunday, the day my Lord was resurrected.'"

European golf, plus possibly Dan Forsman and Chip Beck, would certainly say 'Amen' to that.

Fred Couples, the previous winner puts the Green Jacket on Bernard Langer.

the traditions of Nicklaus, Palmer and Snead, even the fever pitch atmosphere of Augusta can fall flat.

Not that European golf had any regrets. Sensing the chill descend on the Augusta galleries was the golfing equivalent of silencing the Kop or winning the respect of the Sydney Hill and for Bernhard Langer on this Easter Sunday, a victory of this authority completed the recovery process from Kiawah Island, although Langer would always say that the missed putt that gave the Ryder Cup to the USA required no recovery on his part whatsoever.

As he played out the seventeenth and eighteenth he may have spared himself a quick Kiawah thought, but he was also thinking about an opportunity that he was about

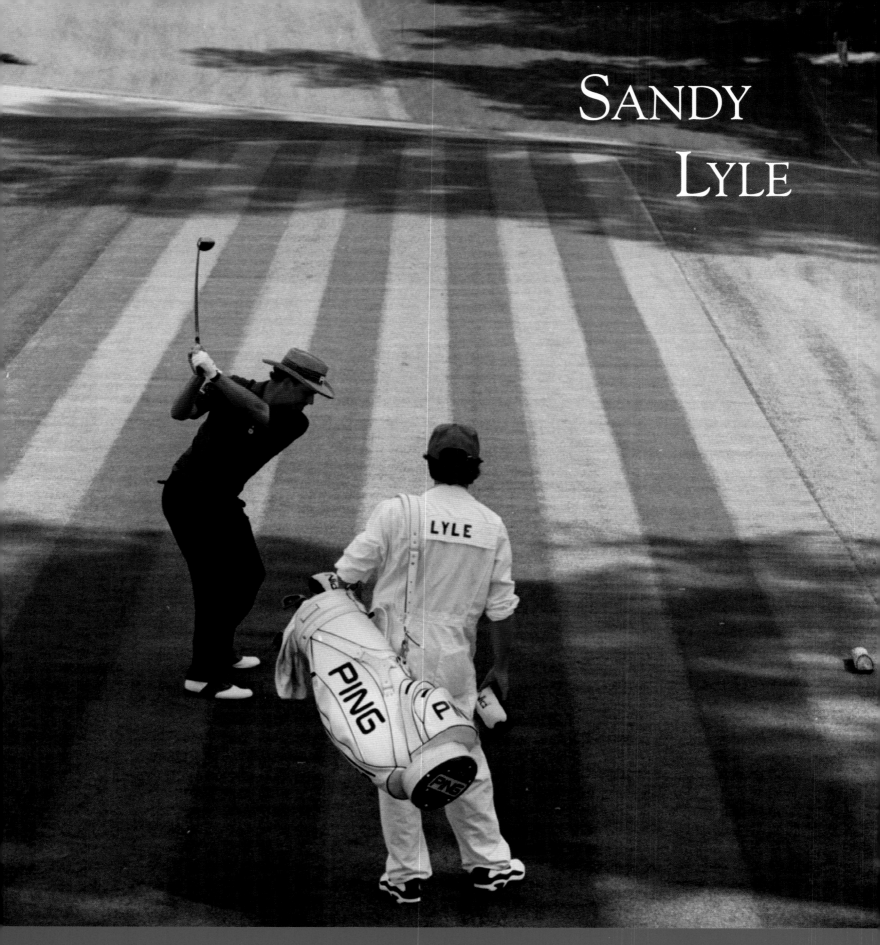

SANDY
LYLE

MASTERS CHAMPION: 1988

Lyle chips to the green at the 1982 Open.

to pick a winner for the following weekend – who failed to rate him in the top thirty five.

Lyle's 1988 form should not have come as a surprise. After all, he was Open Champion three years before, had an earlier win at the Greater Greensboro and the previous year he won the TPC, which even then was rated in significance only just behind the Majors.

As an amateur he played in the Walker Cup in 1977. When he turned professional he was leading money winner in Europe in only his second season and was never out of the top five through the next six years. His Open Championship win at Sandwich in 1985, the first by a British player since Tony Jacklin, gave European golf the extra bit of confidence that helped secure the historic Ryder Cup win at the Belfry.

Lyle kisses the Open trophy after his victory in 1985.

S eve Ballesteros would get angry to get even. Langer would get his inspiration from on high. It was hard to pinpoint what motivated Sandy Lyle, if indeed any artificial motivation was required. Whereas the name of Nicklaus or Ballesteros on a leader board would intimidate the opposition, Sandy Lyle, despite his sublime talents, was a player with an almost eerie lack of presence.

In the days building up to the 1988 Masters we were waiting for Sandy to arrive for a pre-arranged interview under the tree in front of the clubhouse, and it was a few minutes before we realised that Sandy had already arrived and was standing alongside the crew. He arrived at the course on Monday evening in similar fashion. He was leading money winner in the United States. He had won the Phoenix Open and drove to Augusta straight from another win at the Greater Greensboro Open. Yet no-one seemed to notice him arrive, especially the pundits – trying

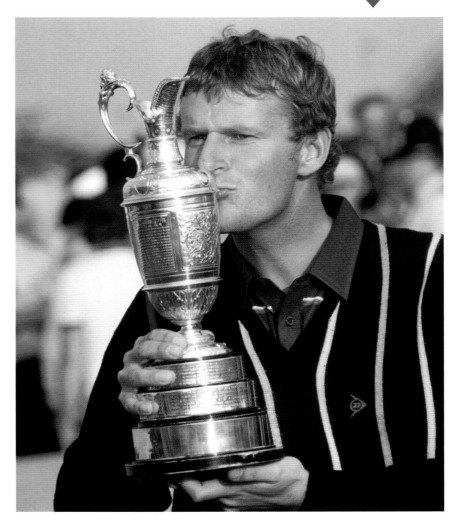

Now in 1988 European golf was oozing self-belief. The Ryder Cup had been successfully defended at Muirfield Village and in his *World of Professional Golf* review of the 1988 season, Mark McCormack wrote that in Masters week one of the many sporting wagers made on the eve of play was Americans v Foreigners. 'Years ago the prospect

Sandy Lyle assists Bernhard Langer on their way to Ryder Cup glory in 1987.

of a foreigner winning at Augusta ranked just above an amateur. Gary Player stood alone. But then came Ballesteros and Bernhard Langer and the successive Ryder Cup victories and now it is a close call. A betting man could take foreigners in all four majors and feel most comfortable. Lyle, Langer, Ballesteros and Nick Faldo have all won majors. The top U.S. fivesome on the 1987 money list would give you Curtis Strange, Paul Azinger, Ben Crenshaw, Scott Simpson and Tom Watson. One vote for the foreigners.'

Wise words, because eight nationalities would finish in the top twenty on Sunday evening. But plenty of players would get blown out of contention as early as day one, as the strong winds of Thursday presented the Augusta National at its most challenging. One of those was Ian Woosnam, making a somewhat belated Masters debut. Four putts on the sixteenth was his welcome to one of the most famous holes in golf as Woosie stumbled to an 81.

Lyle also had his problems in the first round but was able to overcome them with his strength off the tee that put him amongst the longest hitters in the game. He birdied three of the par fives but there were plenty of dropped shots as well, and a missed three footer on the last meant a round of one under par 71, but this was still good enough for a share of third.

Friday by contrast was a perfect Georgia day. The wind had dropped, the spring sunshine illuminated Augusta looking its absolute best, but the problem of the lightning-fast greens remained. Many of the top players joined a chorus of criticism about the speed, which they felt took the

skill advantage away from the best putters in the game and replaced it with mere luck. Even Arnold Palmer said, 'I'm tired of seeing ten foot putts roll forty feet past, they need to redesign some of the bent grass or go back to Bermuda.'

Lyle, after the bogey at eighteen on the first evening, was now among the earlier starters and immediately bogeyed his opening hole of the second round. But that was just about his only mistake as he stormed toward the top of the leader board.

At the ninth, where no less than nine players would four putt during the course of the day, Lyle rolled in his fourth birdie of the round and headed the field. His caddie, Dave Musgrove, reflected later that Lyle had only just started the ball rolling and had he missed the cup on the ninth, his ball would have rolled straight off the green. But it was in and Lyle was in front. In his book, *Life with Lyle,* Musgrove says, 'We literally sat down on the tenth tee and it's rather like living in a glasshouse with just your underpants on. You know everybody in the world is looking at you and at everything you do. You're under a microscope and there's a long way to go. You can't avoid the feeling of being scrutinized. Everybody knows what the stakes are and where the pitfalls are. You get used to it after a bit but I said to myself, it's going to be bloody hard for the rest of the week.'

Lyle was feeling it as well. The responsibility of trying to become the first British player to win the title was just adding to all the expectations. But the composure that had been a characteristic throughout his playing career and the putting form that had been the feature of his great season so far, stayed with him through the back. No dropped shots and the birdies on the par five thirteenth and fifteenth that were always on offer with his distance off the tee. His round of 67 left him at six under par, two shots clear of Mark Calcavecchia and four clear of Fuzzy Zoeller and Gary Hallberg.

His progress was not quite so serene at the post-round press conference, when this seemingly one dimensional character gave the local writers precisely what they wanted with his rather disingenuous stories of how girlfriend

Lyle looks concerned after missing a putt at The Masters, 1988.

CHAPTER 9

The observing gallery watch a tentative Lyle on the green.

Jolanda, a former physiotherapist on the European Tour, was administering foot massages at night in order to help Sandy with problems of nasal congestion. Forget his outstanding performances on the golf course; Lyle, as far as the golfing public was concerned, had at last given himself a profile and a personality they could relate to, and by accident he had given himself a great deal of extra support for the weekend to come.

Lyle in full swing as he goes into the final round leading by two shots.

For the halfway leader in any tournament the third round is the day that the threats and the challenges start to emerge. That was not the case in 1988 although the course did seem to present some opportunities. Ken Brown, like Ian Woosnam, making his Masters debut in 1988, came in with a fine round of 69 after just making the cut at seven over. 'I was proud of that round but it was such a difficult place and such a difficult experience. It was my only Masters but I will never forget the greens; they took on a kind of threatening grey appearance, evil to look at and evil to putt on.'

Lyle plays out of a bunker at Augusta. A much more important bunker shot was yet to come.

No problems for Lyle, the only challenge that was strengthening was his own. He continued his assault on the par fives with a birdie at the second, picked up another shot at the third, where his playing partner Mark Calcavecchia bogeyed, and at that point led The Masters

by four. And his four shot lead remained through to the thirteenth tee. There was a delay, the field had piled up through Amen Corner. Dave Musgrove said, 'He was held up for so long you could see his concentration and his patience had gone and he just hammered it.' Lyle's version was, 'Maybe I was too casual, I'd gotten through number 12 and felt good. I took too much of a gamble trying to get around the corner and I paid the penalty.'

The penalty was a dropped shot as Lyle's hooked drive caught the trees, and his lead over Calcavecchia was briefly back to three. But then the American three putted the fourteenth. On the fifteenth, Lyle would have expected birdie but was too ambitious with his approach, was through the back and could only manage a par. Calcavecchia flirted with the water but sank a twelve footer for eagle. The lead was halved.

After the sixteenth the lead was just one. His tee shot missed the green and settled in the fringe. Lyle chose to putt, describing his effort as, 'very nearly perfect,' but it stayed in the long grass and he took two more to get down. Calcavecchia bogeyed again at the seventeenth, so at the end of round three, Lyle, with a 72, had not only managed to preserve the two shot lead he had at the start of the day, but had now managed to stay in front for twenty

seven holes. But things had changed as Musgrove pointed out, 'all the names you never want to see if you're leading had come on to the leader board: Crenshaw, Norman, Ballesteros, Stadler, Watson. Six of the past eight champions were within six shots of the lead.' And a six shot lead historically provided scant protection in the final round of The Masters.

On the practice ground early the next afternoon, Sandy looked every inch the new Champion, hitting a succession of towering iron shots off his short, punchy, back swing, and shot after shot finished high on the green netting two hundred and fifty yards away. His caddie Dave Musgrove had been with us in the morning recording interviews for use in the BBC transmission. His insights into the caddies' role would be useful material to

Lyle crosses Hogan's Bridge at the 12th hole, final round.

supplement the coverage, which we hoped was about to tell the story of the first British winner of The Masters. He told us how despite appearances, Sandy feels the tension of occasions such as this as much or even possibly more than others. A final round pairing is all important and he would enjoy the company of Ben Crenshaw this afternoon in the same way he had felt at ease with Christy O'Connor Jr. in the final round of The Open at Royal St. George's.

We shared Dave Musgrove's relief when Lyle cleared the bunker at the elbow of the first with his opening tee shot and went on to make a solid par. He then got his fourth birdie of the week at the second, and even though Crenshaw chipped in at the second he was struggling to keep up. These were the days when The Masters authorities were coy about how much live transmission we could show of the front nine of the final round and were

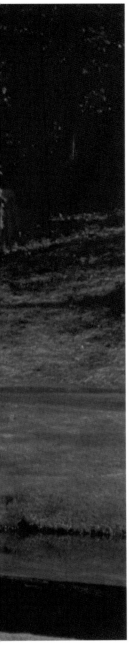

never really able to go live with any confidence until about the eighth. Up until that point we would grab random shots from cameras around the course to give a summary of developments when we came on air.

In 1988 how we would have loved to have been live to see Lyle come to the fourth, where he put a huge five iron into the kind of position beyond the green from which a bogey is just about inevitable. Instead Lyle took his sand iron and flopped the perfect recovery on to the green, twenty feet across the putting surface and straight into the cup. He dropped his first shot of the round when he three putted the sixth, and then survived a big crisis on seven when a poor tee shot left him needing to get up and down from the greenside bunker for par.

Then, as one of BBC Television's biggest golf audiences tuned in for live coverage, Sandy was back on track and millions of viewers immediately saw him take a strong grip on the battle. A birdie putt lipped out at the eighth, but there was no mistake at the ninth, where a brilliant seven iron approach finished a foot from the hole, and with nine holes left to play Lyle was four shots clear of Mark Calcavecchia and three clear of the 1983 winner Craig Stadler.

This was clearly set to be the breakthrough for which British golf had waited for so long, but as the last pairing teed off the tenth, Peter Alliss in the commentary box urged caution, and reminded the audience of the many perils that lay ahead. Certainly a four shot lead was handy and Peter was even tempted to suggest it was encouraging,

but there is no such thing as a comfort zone entering the back nine at Augusta on Masters Sunday.

Sandy Lyle was about to experience the kind of back nine crisis that had blighted the challenge of so many great players before him. First of all at the eleventh he was too strong with his seven iron approach and took three to get down from off the green. It was an unsettling moment and as he made his way from the eleventh green to receive the leaders ovation from the huge terrace of spectators behind the twelfth tee, he needed a clear head and total confidence because he faced one of the most psychologically demanding shots in major Championship golf.

It was a hundred and sixty yards to the frighteningly narrow strip of green that lay beyond the water. Lyle judged it to be perfect eight iron distance but hit the shot thin. The ball hit just short of the green and rolled back, and the ripples it sent out indicated that Amen Corner had claimed another illustrious victim. Lyle's anger, frustration and bewilderment was clearly evident as he marched down the slope to take his penalty drop. Michael

Lyle enters the green at the 12th.

Lyle displays authority in his swing, as he drives onward to the last few holes.

Bonallack, the rules official on the hole, indicated the line he could drop on, the question was the distance. This was where caddie Dave Musgrove really earned his money. 'He was muttering about what a terrible shot it had been. My only thought was I hope we make five. I had no thoughts of a four because I know how difficult the next shot is. I was trying to measure from the tee to wherever he was going to drop, but at the same time I'm trying to calm him down. I'm doing two jobs at once. I had to keep stopping, remember the number I'd reached and say to him, "let's just play the shot" and then start counting again. He went back sixty yards from the flag and then he went five yards nearer. I thought he would be better off going further back, making it a shot of a hundred yards to help him stop the ball easier. The hardest shot in the world is the third shot to that green.'

Despite the maelstrom in his head, Sandy made the shot look easy. It ran up to the back of the green and two putts later he had the double bogey five that Musgrove happily settled for. His four shot advantage had disappeared, he was now back into a tie with Calcavecchia, but there were still the two par fives to come, and with a huge brave drive off the thirteenth tee, Lyle put himself within birdie range at the first of them. But his slightly pulled approach found the bunker at the back of the green. A difficult bunker shot was followed by two putts for a par, it felt like a shot gone. What had gone was his share of the lead. For the first time since the ninth hole of the second round Lyle was not at the front.

He had to fight back. His birdie putt at fourteen stopped on the lip, and it looked as if his last big chance was gone when he failed to make his birdie at fifteen. But neither did Calcavecchia, who also only just stayed in front when he salvaged par on the sixteenth. When Lyle got to the par three he pulled out his seven iron and put it to fifteen feet. The ultra-fast downhill putt was gathering speed when it hit the centre of the hole and dropped.

It was now a battle to get the one more priceless birdie that could secure the title. Calcavecchia almost made it on seventeen and then was mightily relieved to chip and putt for his par on the closing hole. Stadler almost made the birdie on eighteen that would have made it a three way tie for the lead, but then after a routine par on seventeen in these far from routine circumstances, Lyle was left as the only man who could win the title in regulation play.

Back on the eighteenth his dilemma was whether to attack or defend. No player had made a birdie on the closing hole to win The Masters since Arnold Palmer in 1960, but this was the task before Lyle now. Even history was suggesting that maybe the better option would be to try and guarantee himself the four that would take this already absorbing contest into extra holes.

His choice on the eighteenth tee was a one iron and seemed to have hit the perfect defensive positional tee shot. But he'd pulled it just a fraction and watched in horror as the ball stayed left and was swallowed up by the first of the big bunkers on the left of the fairway. The tension and the emotion showed as Lyle hopped from one foot to another in a kind of jig of frustration. The bunker was some 140 yards from the flag and seemed to rule out any prospect of the winning birdie he required, but his actual position in the sand was all important and Lyle was encouraged when he arrived at his ball.

It was far enough back from the lip of the bunker to make a decent recovery possible and the ball was on an upslope providing a kind of launching pad for the shot he would require into the green. It was 142 yards, with the flag another eight yards on. Normally it would be eight iron distance but coming out of sand from an uphill lie to an uphill target would require an extra club, so Lyle would turn once again to the seven iron that had already served him so well during the course of this final round.

The shot needed to be crisp, precise and accurate and after Lyle planted his feet in the sand, the shot he delivered was exactly that. It cleared the lip of the bunker. Musgrove knew it was good as he went for the rake, Lyle knew it was good as he leapt out of the sand and went half-running, half-jumping up the hill. He would not be

Lyle plays his remarkable second shot from the bunker at the 18th.

Lyle signals to the crowd in gratitude as his bunker shot hits the green.

Lyle receives a hug from caddie Dave Musgrove after clinching The Masters, 1988.

able to see it land but it was on line and he could hear that it was good. The roar of approval as it landed twenty feet above the hole, became a crescendo of encouragement as the ball wandered back down the slope to finish just ten feet away, and it was encouragement that was echoed in the BBC commentary box and in living rooms right across the UK.

His playing partner Ben Crenshaw knew the significance of the moment and offered to putt out first which he duly did with a single stroke. When the crowd settled again, Musgrove and Lyle surveyed what was required. 'We both walked around Sandy's putt and he said it looked straight. What struck me was that the grass was pretty green round there and if there was going to be any grain it would influence the putt left to right. I then moved to the left of the green, halfway between him and the hole. Apparently the line is right to left normally but it was held up by the grain, so it ended up a straight putt.

A straight putt for victory, and a straight putt for a place in history as the first British winner of The Masters. The almost overwhelming significance of the shot did not appear to intrude on Lyle. The putt was a mere waft, enough simply to get the ball restarted on the line it had already followed down the hill. The weight of the shot was enough, the weight of the ball did the rest. It never deviated from the centre of the target and when it dropped Britain had its first Masters Champion.

Lyle's swiftly stifled victory jig was a rather happier version of what we had seen fifteen minutes earlier on the eighteenth tee, and amid all the pandemonium that followed Sandy later recalled he walked to the scorers tent just wondering, 'what have I done, what have I done?' When he emerged to give his first reactions to well-wishers and the world's Press, Dave Musgrove had already climbed the last hundred yards to the clubhouse on top of the hill, dispensing balls, pencils and towels as he went. Within minutes he'd got his first beer in his hand and climbed to the balcony to join myself, Nick Faldo and Tony Jacklin to start the analysis of what had been achieved and what it all meant, and with hindsight it was ironic to hear Nick Faldo say that the victory was going to open the door to yet more British success at Augusta.

By the time the Champion joined us, his parents were on the balcony as well and there were thoughts on how this astonishing success might change Sandy. The answer, of course, was not at all and there was evidence of that within forty eight hours. Ken Brown, whose Masters debut had finished with a disappointing

Larry Mize presents Sandy Lyle with his Green Jacket.

final round, recalls that he met up with Sandy on the practice ground at Hilton Head the following Tuesday afternoon. Ken gave his congratulations but it was clear that Sandy did not want a prolonged conversation on the subject. Instead, Ken asked for a bit of advice on the way he was hitting it and Sandy gave his full attention to an hour long clinic on Ken's game. A great champion but still a gracious and unchanged man.

1988 was as good as it got for Sandy Lyle. His performance at Augusta had helped him into the U.S. golf history books, repeating the Greater Greensboro-Masters double of Sam Snead and becoming the first back to back winner in America for three years. The last man to achieve that was of course Bernhard Langer with his Masters-Heritage double. For Sandy that season, there were further wins in the British Masters and the World Match Play to go with his three wins in America, the most important of which, as far as British golf was concerned, was the long awaited breakthrough at Augusta. But it can also be a cruel place and after his starring role Sandy would miss the cut at The Masters the next three years.

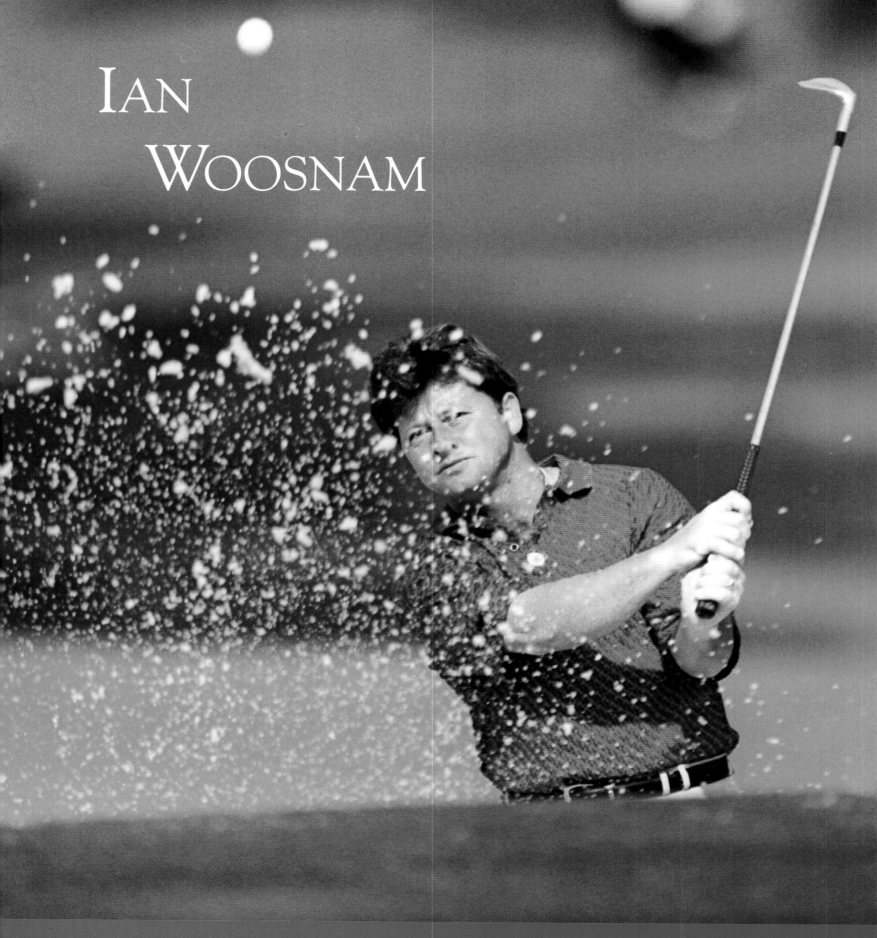

IAN
WOOSNAM

MASTERS CHAMPION: 1991

When Ian Woosnam made his Masters debut in 1988, he made it known, and was supported by many others, that he felt the invitation was a little overdue. The reputation of the battling little character from the Welsh borders had been growing throughout the world of golf. It was not significantly enhanced when he missed the cut in 1988. He improved to a tie for fourteenth the following year but finished with a 76 in 1990, just hanging on to a top thirty place, but his Augusta apprenticeship was complete.

For Ken Schofield, Executive Director of the European Tour, who worked so tirelessly, not only to advance the prosperity of the European Tour, but also the recognition of its players on the world stage, Augusta, at this time, was a place of celebration but also frustration. 'Despite the victories by European players I would still sit down each year with the chairman, Hord Hardin, or other members of The Masters committee, and get the distinct impression that this was first and foremost an American tournament with international invitees, and those invitations were limited. It was not until the rules were changed in 1999 to bring in all players from the top fifty of the world rankings instead of U.S. Tour tournament winners, that European golf got anything like its correct representation.'

Woosnam in action at Wentworth, 1987.

By 1991 Ian Woosnam had not only completed his Augusta apprenticeship, but he had also been through all the trials and tribulations that a career in professional golf can provide. Golf had been his route out from what seemed likely to be a life in farming in rural Shropshire. Long nights and long journeys in camper vans going from event to event were producing slow rewards, but from his first tour victory in 1982 every season got better and better. In 1987 he became the first British player to win the World Match Play Championship. In 1988 it was the

PGA Championship and 'The Million Dollar Challenge' and by 1991 he had won over twenty five tournaments and was recognised as one of the best players in the game.

His priorities for the 1991 season were to win a major and get to number one in the world rankings. He started the season by successfully defending his title at the Mediterranean Open at Estoril and then at English Turn in New Orleans he beat Jim Hallett at the second extra hole of USF and G Classic for his first ever victory in America. Pretty soon the Sony Rankings announced not only

Nick Faldo and Ian Woosnam with similar expressions at the World Matchplay tournament, 1989.

EUROPE AT THE MASTERS

Woosnam at number one but José María Olazábal at number two and Nick Faldo at number three. Two weeks later at Augusta, Ken Schofield was arguing the case for European golf from a position of some strength.

But Woosnam found himself having to defend rankings that had him and Olazábal as the best players in the world, but without a major title between them, and ahead of a player who had won two Opens and was about to attempt the history making feat of a third straight Masters Green Jacket. Woosnam himself had challenged strongly in two

Open Championships and finished only a shot behind the winner, Curtis Strange, in the 1989 U.S. Open. But there was only one way to end this irritating argument for good, and his irritation deepened with every reminder in Masters week that no-one had ever won at Augusta while being ranked number one in the world.

Ian Woosnam, the European PGA champion of 1988.

There were only three Americans near the top of those world rankings and Faldo drew some frosty headlines when he suggested that American players were motivated more by prize money than by prestige major titles like The Masters. The build-up to 1991 centred more on the international intrusion into the Champions locker room than any other issue. Could European golf respond by making it six European wins in nine events?

Given all the rhetoric in the days ahead of the event, the opening round in perfect conditions was almost an

anti-climax, at least from the European point of view. There was a strong 68 from José María Olazábal that left him one off the lead shared by Lanny Wadkins, Mark McCumber and Jim Gallagher, but for Faldo and Woosnam there were unspectacular rounds of 72. From Woosnam it had been a round full of opportunities, few of which had been converted by the putter that had been glowing hot in New Orleans two weeks earlier. He headed out to the practice putting green and after an exhaustive three hour session, decided to abandon the putter and go back to a shorter Tad Moore Maxfli version that he had taken delivery of earlier that week. Woosnam felt it worked better for him with the three footers which in turn helped make him more aggressive from long range, because he had more confidence with the awkward putts coming back.

So much of this game is psychology and so much at Augusta is about being in the right frame of mind. That one change of club seemed to completely change Woosnam's fortunes. He was an early starter in murky overcast conditions in Friday's second round, knowing he had to do something special to get back in the hunt, and he also had to do something positive to make sure of making the cut.

There should have been no concerns because Woosnam emerged with confidence flowing through every department of his game. Birdies on the second, fourth and sixth, a dropped shot on the ninth and then another stunning iron shot to ten feet at the eleventh and Woosnam was flying at three under par. In particular he was playing the par fives brilliantly and a huge drive at the thirteenth left him just a five iron into the green. He put it to ten feet and holed the putt for eagle. He nearly picked up another shot at fourteen, then got to six under at the fifteenth and parred the last three holes for a round of 66 that at the end of the day would give him a share of second place. But the day was far from over.

As Woosnam tells it, 'My putting was massively improved and although it had started to rain, I felt much happier as I drove back to our rented house to watch the rest of the day's play on television. With my feet up and with my daughter Rebecca on my knee I watched an amazing sequence of events unfold on what the Augusta Chronicle later described as the most dramatic Friday in Masters history.'

It is easier just to try to list the bizarre happenings of that afternoon. 1. Lanny Wadkins missed a short putt, then tried to backhand the ball in, and missed again. 2. McCumber's putt at 16 just lipped out and his anguished caddie stepped backwards and fell into the bunker. 3. Jack Nicklaus, to the astonishment of everyone, suffered his first ever quadruple bogey at The Masters, putting two balls into the water at the twelfth. 4. Nicklaus recovered in indignant fashion with birdies at the thirteenth, fourteenth, fifteenth and sixteenth. 5. José María Olazábal took three attempts to recover from a difficult position alongside the sixth, took a quadruple bogey seven, and as television viewer Woosnam pointed out, seemed to walk to the seventh tee with tears in his eyes. At the end of it all Tom Watson had the halfway lead but Woosnam was in a

four way tie for second two shots behind, and Olazábal, despite his tribulations at the sixth, would be handily placed with Bernhard Langer, three shots back.

Day three under overcast skies might have produced less extreme moments but it was still the day when Ian Woosnam underlined his credentials for taking the title. At the same time Nick Faldo regained some respect after drifting off the pace in the first few days, and José María Olazábal forced himself into contention as well.

Augusta was softened by rain and wide open for someone to attack and shoot a really low score. Woosnam by his own admission started cautiously, picking up two birdies on the front nine, but when he holed from just off the green at the twelfth, where the overnight leader Watson bogeyed, Woosnam had the lead. As he described it, the birdie relaxed him, others would guess that the birdie inspired him. At the thirteenth he played a courageous draw two hundred and fifteen yards round the corner and two putted for another birdie. Then at the fourteenth it was a twenty five footer that sank for his third birdie in succession. A moment of controversy at the

Woosnam tees off at the 1991 Masters.

The rain soaked crowd make their way around Augusta.

Woosnam and his
caddie 'Wobbly'
take a well
deserved rest.

Woosnam and his caddie 'Wobbly' take a well deserved rest.

fifteenth where his eagle putt hovered agonisingly on the lip of the hole. Woosnam took his time before tapping it in and his playing partner Tom Watson was seen to say something to him as he holed out. Some commentators suggested that Watson took objection to Woosnam not marking and there was an argument. Woosnam was able to say that the sporting Watson was telling him to be careful because the ball could move at any time.

A dropped shot at the eighteenth meant that it was a round of sixty seven and Woosnam had the third round lead by a shot from Watson. Europe was ahead again,

much to the consternation of the American fans. Not only that but Olazábal, with a run of five straight birdies around the turn, had a share of third with Lanny Wadkins, three shots back.

Right through the build up to this event Woosnam had exuded belief and confidence, now as he led The Masters on that Saturday night there was a particular confidence coming from the Woosnam household.

Ian recalls how the main family discussion that evening was what he should wear, what was clean and what was washable, and what might go best with a Masters Green

Jacket. 'We finally decided I would wear a dark blue Tacchini shirt with red, lightly checked trousers. People would eventually say these trousers were tartan, but those were probably the same people who thought Wales was part of Scotland. In reality, they were a pair of Tacchini's best checks. They might have clashed with The Masters green but they would have to do.'

Amid all this bravado was the thought that Woosnam was going into new territory with all the legendary demands and unpredictability of the final round of The Masters. History was not exactly on his side. In the 57 years of The Masters no player had ever come through to win from as far back as the thirty first position that Woosnam held at the end of round one. 'On the driving range and around the practice green, I started to sense the overwhelming support of the international players. The history of European success at The Masters, combined with recent Ryder Cup history, seemed to have polarised everyone at Augusta and I was caught in the middle. While the handful of Europeans regarded me as the gutsy wee Welshman out to upset the odds, the massed ranks of Americans saw me as an upstart foreigner trying to deny their much loved Tom Watson a third Masters title.'

Woosnam started the third round as if he were burdened by these thoughts. The confidence and belief of the last two days were missing. He traded birdies and bogeys and was needing to make putts of challenging length just to salvage par. It was a tribute to his battling spirit that after seven holes he was still at eleven under par where he had started the day. Watson had fallen two shots behind but the challenge was coming from Olazábal who had picked up three shots through the first seven holes, and when the last of those birdies found the hole, he had got alongside Woosnam at the top of the leader board. One of the most enthralling final rounds in Masters history was set to become a battle between these three. Lanny Wadkins was also up amongst the leaders but would

Tom Watson was one of Woosnam's nearest rivals in the final round.

struggle to press home a challenge, but another player to make his presence felt among the leaders was Steve Pate who had gone round in sixty five and set a decent clubhouse target of eight under.

It was around this time that Nick Faldo came to our presentation position on the clubhouse balcony. He had played himself into the fringe of contention with a third round sixty seven but knew he had to abandon all caution if he were going to make any impact on the outcome. In the end his final round of seventy would be only good enough for a share of twelfth place, his dream of a third consecutive Masters triumph was gone. But all that was swiftly forgotten, he now settled back to perform the analysis and cheerleading role for European golf that

Woosnam had fulfilled so ably a year before. He fancied Woosie to come through but did not expect that Augusta would have the right size Green Jacket in stock.

Just as Faldo was easing himself into his role, Olazábal suffered a crisis. His approach play suddenly became fragile and vulnerable. He missed the greens at eight, nine and ten, and ended up dropping a shot at each of them going from a share of the lead back to eight under par.

It could all change of course through Amen Corner and once again the famous stretch of three holes at the bottom of the course played havoc with the leader board. It started off looking great for Woosnam as Tom Watson, now one behind and his closest challenger, dropped a shot at the eleventh and then put his tee shot in the water at

twelve; three shots gone in two holes and now four shots off the lead.

Even though up ahead Olazábal was recovering his momentum with a birdie on the thirteenth hole, Woosnam, with some justification, was standing on the thirteenth tee thinking that The Masters was his for the taking. However that thought had a long time to prey on his mind as he and Watson waited the best part of twenty minutes for the thirteenth fairway to clear. In the previous round Woosnam had been rewarded for the risk he had taken on the par five, but now the thirteenth would fight back. It was a high hooking shot that crashed into the trees on the left of the fairway and dropped into the murky waters of Raes Creek. The result was greeted by some uncharacteristic cheering and applause from the Augusta

faithful whose support for Watson so far had been total. They saw this as an indication that the contest was far from over.

Augusta correctly prides itself on the sporting behaviour of its galleries and the spectators are encouraged in this by a printed reminder of etiquette from Bobby Jones himself on every course guide and draw-sheet. But the final round in 1991 was an occasion where the fans' desperation for one of their heroes to halt the European tide got the better of them, and no-one was more embarrassed than Watson himself. As the inappropriate applause and comments from the galleries got more and more intrusive, Watson offered apologies and even, as they headed to the thirteenth green, some advice on how best to handle the hecklers.

Woosnam himself was taking the Ballesteros approach of 'the more they are against me, the better I play,' but he

The normally well behaved galleries at Augusta, seen here on the 12th, were slightly biased towards the U.S. contingent in 1991.

Woosnam makes his way up the course at Augusta.

Lanny Wadkins, well placed in the field – but not quite a contender for the title.

certainly appreciated the attitude of Watson. 'His sportsmanship during this round confirmed his status, in my mind, as one of the great gentlemen of our sport. Under intense pressure he had shown great compassion and understanding towards his closest rival, and further enriched the game of golf.'

But the compassion and understanding would not extend to the golf, and at the thirteenth, Watson, who had told himself he needed to eagle thirteen and fifteen, hit a one hundred and ninety five yard five iron on to the green and holed the putt, while Woosnam bogeyed. Three shots gained in just one hole.

Although Lanny Wadkins was well placed on the leader board he was struggling to make progress and the spectators, newly inspired by what their man had done at thirteen, now saw Watson as the man to halt the European challenge. And it had become a double challenge because while Watson and Woosnam were making their par fours at the fourteenth, Olazábal put a three iron just through the back of fifteen but chipped and putted for a third consecutive

birdie that repaired all the damage that he had suffered around the turn and sent him past Woosnam and into the lead on his own.

Ever since Gene Sarazen holed that second shot for his albatross, the fifteenth has always been the pivot of the action at The Masters, but it had never provided quite the level of excitement as we saw in 1991. Watson and Woosnam both saw it as their last reliable chance to pick up a shot and they simply had to take the opportunity. Woosnam hit a four iron to the back of the green, lagged his putt and made the four he was looking for. Watson who had promised himself two eagles on the back nine hit a sensational approach from two hundred and five yards to about eight feet and when he holed the putt, the crowd was ignited again and we knew that we were seeing one of the best ever final round battles.

All three challengers would par sixteen and seventeen, so they came to the eighteenth tied for the lead at eleven under. Olazábal in the penultimate pairing would go first, surveying the tee shot down that narrow chute of trees. There are so many options at this classic closing hole. It could be played with power, it could be played with precision. It had to be played with fade, but there was not enough fade in the shot that Olazábal struck.

It stayed straight and found the first of the bunkers at the corner of the dogleg. Bunkers that, until Sandy Lyle performed his miracle amid the pressure of 1988, almost certainly meant a shot dropped. When Olazábal got to his ball he knew that he did not have the possibilities that Sandy was able to exploit three years earlier. The ball had rolled too close to the face, he had to take an eight iron as opposed to Sandy's seven, and the recovery, although it cleared the lip, would only find the greenside

bunker. From there he was not able to get up and down and he knew that the bogey meant that any real prospect of victory had gone.

Up on the balcony Nick Faldo was fulsome in his praise of the challenge that the Spaniard had put together and gave the opinion that he was ready to become the new major championship hero of European golf. Every player who comes so close to a title like this looks back with one particular regret, but when Olazábal dropped those four shots at the sixth in the second round and Woosnam spotted the hint of a tear in his eye, maybe he was anticipating how desperate the consequences would be. We watched him storm across the clubhouse lawn, and the subsequent sound of locker room doors being slammed beneath us, indicated that this was a man of passion who was determined to one day get his reward at Augusta.

Back on the tee the title now seemed to lie between Watson and Woosnam. The American was first to go by virtue of his eagle at the fifteenth. He had surely been aware of Olazábal's bunker trouble. He was certainly aware of the penalties those fairway bunkers could extract. He took the cautious route…too cautious. The ideal line down eighteen is long, and as close to the trees on the right as you can, but Watson pushed his tee shot into the trees. Playable, but any chance of reaching the green in two seemed to have gone, and his big chance of a third Masters title seemed to have gone as well.

Woosnam certainly knew what had happened to Olazábal and he had just seen Watson put himself in trouble. He could hardly believe that a par at the last was likely to win him the Championship. He had come to the eighteenth with a plan to beat the hole with power. Any temptation to suddenly become defensive was discarded. After all, his two closest rivals had gone for caution and finesse, and found only problems.

Woosnam's idea was to blast the ball clear over the notorious fairway bunkers on to the clear open, spectator area beyond. There would be no trouble lurking there, it was a wide expanse used as a members' practice area, and although the line of approach up the hill to the green would

Woosnam urges
his putt home on
the 18th.

had occupied for many hours in anticipation of this dramatic finale. A task that took the best part of fifteen minutes.

Eventually Woosie could see a route through, even if he could only confirm a line to the flag by jumping high for the best possible view. Coming across the green he had to be careful of the problems short of the green and the bunker beyond, but he sent a cautious eight iron over the rise and on to the left fringe of the lower tier about fifty feet from the hole. Watson meantime had found a line out of the trees but only managed to put it in the bunker where Olazábal had struggled earlier.

It was Watson who played first. For one heart-stopping moment it looked as if he might have sent it straight into the hole, but it ran past some twenty five feet. Woosnam putted up from the fringe and looked to have judged it to perfection, but it drifted away and finished six feet from the hole. Then Watson tried with his putt to deny Woosnam, and at worst take it into a play off. It slid past four feet.

Woosnam took another deep breath. 'I had been up, I had been down. I had been furious, I had been happy and all that was in only the past hour and a half. It was simple now, I had a six foot putt to win The Masters.

"A putt to win The Masters." How many times had I said those words before? Probably a thousand and one times, as a scraggly lad stooping over my ball on the deserted, windswept eighteenth green at Llanymynech Golf Club. Now on 14 April 1991, this was the putt of my wildest dreams. Everything had come true. Here I was on the eighteenth green at Augusta, with the crowd hushed, with millions around the world watching live on television and with my parents following the action from their living room in Oswestry.'

not be ideal, if he hit his tee shot as planned, all the serious problems would have been taken out of the equation.

But those fairway bunkers were 260 yards away and there were not many players in the game who would take on the carry, let alone one who stood only five foot four and weighed barely a hundred and sixty pounds.

He said he was pumped up beyond words as he sent the ball soaring precisely where he intended, with a carry that was later measured at two hundred and eighty six yards. Up on the balcony Nick Faldo was astonished by what he had just seen: the power, the execution and the strength of character to stick with such a brave, unconventional tactic in such a pressure situation.

But Woosnam's route up the eighteenth was posing other problems. He was now outside the galleries, well below the level of the green, with no real sight of the flag, and he and caddie Phil Morbey had the task of persuading spectators to move from their highly prized positions they

None of his army of fans should have had any doubts. The courage that had been with him throughout the round stayed with him through that life-changing moment. The putt was solid, just outside the right lip, eighteen inches away. He knew it was in and sank down

on one knee punching the air in exultation and relief. Phil Morbey lifted him off the ground in celebrations that had to be swiftly curtailed because Tom Watson, who had played his dignified part in the afternoon's drama, still had a putt that sadly he slid by the hole to leave José María Olazábal alone in second.

A European one two to reinforce the astonishing dominance of the previous three years. Nick Faldo had left our position on the balcony to head down to the Butler Cabin for another of those all British Green Jacket ceremonies, right in his assumption that Woosie's determination would see him through, and also right in his assumption that Augusta would struggle for the right sized jacket.

Woosnam left Augusta as Masters Champion and World number one. So much seemingly lay ahead, but just like Sandy Lyle, three years earlier, it was to prove the pinnacle of his career. As for the American Press, they were left to reflect that even the American challengers in 1991 were getting into the twilight of their careers. The Augusta bandwagon of European golf was rolling on and many were already pencilling in the name of José María Olazábal for 1992.

Masters glory, as an ecstatic Woosnam celebrates his victory.

One European Champion to another – Nick Faldo places the Green Jacket on Ian Woosnam.

José María Olazábal

THE EUROPEAN CHAMPIONS: JOSÉ MARÍA OLAZÁBAL

It looked as if the great new Spanish hope, surely the next to be swathed in Masters green, was going to let us all down. 1992 came and went and the European succession at Augusta had been interrupted by Fred Couples. To the great relief of the American fans it felt a lot more like the domestic tournament that some clearly assumed it should be. Couples, his tee shot defying gravity on the bank in front of the twelfth green, beat Ray Floyd by a shot, and lo and behold there was not a European player in the top ten. This foreign domination stuff had clearly been a flash in the pan. Then along came Bernhard Langer in 1995.

But throughout this period the career of José María Olazábal had gone backwards. In 1992 at Augusta he barely made the cut after an opening round of 76. In 1993 a strong final round saw him force his way into the top ten, but there was little to celebrate as the Spaniard's career stuttered and stalled. The locker room door that we heard him slamming in 1991, could well have been the door slamming on his major championship career. He had spent two years without a win and in that time dropped from number four in the world to number fifteen.

But this was a player with too much natural talent to disappear from view. He had a unique amateur record, winning the British Boys, Youths and Amateur titles as well as the Open Championship Silver Medal. He started his Masters career in 1985 as a result of winning the Amateur Championship at Nairn and missed the cut with two instructive rounds of 81 and 76. But as a professional came the inspirational Ryder Cup partnership with Seve Ballesteros and astonishing victories like the twelve shot win in the World Series at Firestone, and he reached £3 million in earnings on the European Tour in a mere nine years. This was a player who was not just going to fade away.

His problems through those comparatively lean years of 1992 and 1993 were the same problems of an errant driver that would haunt him later on his career. Fine tuning from John Jacobs, one of the best teachers in the game, gave him renewed hope at the start of 1994 that he could pick up the momentum of his career once again. Those hopes

Partners in crime – Olazábal and Ballesteros celebrate victory in the 1987 Ryder Cup.

were boosted by his first win in two years. It came in the same event that had produced his previous win, the Turespaña Mediterranean Open. At Villamartín the win might have come courtesy of a play-off against Paul McGinley, but it was a win, and he was leading money winner in Europe and that did wonders for his frame of mind as he headed to America to prepare for The Masters.

The last stage of that preparation was at the Freeport-McMoRan Classic at English Turn in New Orleans, where Woosnam had won in such significant fashion in 1991. José María opened with a 63 and then finished with back to back birdies, holing a bunker shot at the last to beat Sam Torrance to second place. The magic seemed to be back, Olazábal was ready for The Masters.

Once again though it seemed that American golf was struggling to be ready for the challenge of Augusta. There were absentees: Paul Azinger recovering from cancer and Phil Mickelson with leg injuries from a skiing accident. The international challenge was already strong with Greg Norman and Nick Price in some of their best form and it was further reinforced by the arrival of two rookies making their Masters debuts, Ernie Els and Vijay Singh.

There were many that lost their way in the breezy first round conditions attacking the devilish pin positions on the lightning-fast greens and eights, nines and even a ten was recorded on the fifteenth that was playing the toughest of all. Seve Ballesteros had his own distinctive way of tackling the challenge. His seemingly solid start of seventy belied a round in which he had missed all the par

threes, single putted nine of the first ten holes and birdied all the par fives, and as playing partner Ray Floyd recalled, 'had the greatest par he had ever seen,' at the fourth. Ballesteros had missed the green to the right, and opened the blade of his sand wedge, sending a high parachute shot over a bunker to stop five feet from the hole, on a lightning-fast green that was sloping away from him.

His compatriot Olazábal was keen to avoid such dramas but in so doing ended up four shots behind Seve at the end of the first round. There was a dropped shot at the opening hole and others went at the twelfth, fourteenth and sixteenth. But he also produced two birdies in the closing four holes, otherwise his promising challenge could have been over before it started. As it was he finished back in 24th, six shots behind the first round leader, Larry Mize.

The conditions remained as challenging for day two but Olazábal emerged as a man transformed to shoot the only bogey free round of the day. At the end of it the smile

Olazábal and Ballesteros in Ryder Cup action, 1989

Olazábal tees off at The Masters, 1994.

was broad because he knew he had made a huge move on the rest of the challengers and his sixty seven left him beautifully placed just two shots behind the halfway lead that was still held by Larry Mize. After five straight pars it was significant that his first birdie came at the sixth: the beautiful par three hole in the valley behind the sixteenth green, where players drive off the elevated tee and, given the severity of the pin positions, have a fiendishly small target if they are to have any hope of making a birdie.

It was here in 1991 that Olazábal had missed the green. Two pitch shots came rolling back to him and when he finally got one to stay on the putting surface it took three more to get down. The devastating seven he took there haunted him all the way to the clubhouse on Sunday evening where he conceded the one shot defeat to Ian Woosnam, and probably haunted him a great deal longer. But the saying goes at Augusta that to win The Masters you first have to have experience of losing The Masters,

and the birdie he made that Friday afternoon was an indication that the experience had been absorbed. It was immediately followed by another twelve footer holed for birdie on seven and more long putts found the target on the eleventh, the fifteenth and the seventeenth.

At the end of the round he spoke boldly about his chances of challenging for victory two days later. It was one of those rare Augusta leader boards with comparatively little winning pedigree. Larry Mize was up there and so too the man he denied in such cruel fashion in 1987, Greg Norman. Ernie Els had started his Masters career well and was two shots back with Olazábal. Also on that mark was the perennial Tom Watson, fighting back after a triple bogey eight at the fifteenth on the opening day. It was also a leader board that showed Olazábal to be the one surviving standard carrier for European golf. Seve Ballesteros predictably enough had dropped back with a seventy six after his escapology of the day before.

and American Ryder Cup captain, but back then he was just a big guy from Minnesota who had a final round sixty eight to grab a share of third place behind Bernhard Langer on his Masters debut in 1993. But apart from that he had rarely threatened to build on the four victories he had achieved on the Hogan mini-tour.

He shot a sixty seven in round three to take the lead on his own, but on a day of even stronger winds and greater frustration for the players, Olazábal would match him to stay just one shot back. Around the turn, Olazábal had the lead, inspired by a brilliant eagle at the eighth where he hit a 218 yard three iron to six feet and holed the putt, and then a birdie at ten, where his six iron approach almost went into the hole. But as so often happens, as soon as a player hits the front, Amen Corner bites back. Birdie chances on eleven and twelve both failed to drop and his bogey at thirteen, where he put his approach into the creek, was his first dropped shot in almost two days.

That was the cue for Lehman to string the birdies together on the back nine, including an outrageous putt on the sixteenth measured at fifty feet with around twenty feet of break, although he found the three footer on the next hole a little harder to read and the resulting bogey meant it would be a one shot lead over Olazábal with Larry Mize further shot back in third. Norman and Watson both lost ground but both were still capable of making an impact on the final day. Most American hopes, however, rested with Lehman. 'There were times today when I almost had

Olazábal chips out of a bunker at Augusta.

Woosnam, Lyle, Langer and Faldo had all survived the cut but were way back. Europe was looking to Olazábal.

The Spaniard might have feared Greg Norman the most, but against expectations it was the little known Tom Lehman who forged his way to the top of the leader board in round three. We know him now as an Open Champion

tears in my eyes. Who would think a kid from Minnesota could be leading The Masters,' he said. Behind him a twenty eight year old from Fuenterrabía was determined that the lead would be short-lived.

José María admitted to a sleepless night, and he struggled to eat as well. He arrived at the course late on Sunday morning in the knowledge that this was his best opportunity to win the title that he had missed by the

narrowest of margins in 1991. His composure was not helped by his knowledge of how cruel and unpredictable the final round of The Masters can be. When he got to his locker there was a note from Seve Ballesteros who down the years had been through every emotion that can be imagined on Masters Sunday. 'Be patient,' it said, 'you know exactly how to play this course. You are the greatest golfer in the world. Good luck.' The support of his great Ryder Cup partner was timely and appreciated and it sent him to the first tee in a more positive mood for what was to come.

Olazábal checks the line of the green for his next putt.

He might have feared a charge from one of the great names just a few shots back, but as he prepared to set out with Lehman in the final pairing, they were both reassured that those challenges were not emerging. The main excitement had not affected the leader board at all, Jeff Maggert holing his second shot down at the thirteenth, a two hundred and twenty two yard three iron for only the third double eagle in the history of The Masters. Elsewhere, Norman was stumbling his way to a seventy seven, Watson would make seventy four, and Tom Kite was making no progress in his challenge for a long overdue Masters title. It looked as if it would be a three way battle between Olazábal, Lehman and Mize.

With eight holes played, the battle was really joined, Lehman having birdied the second but Olazábal and Mize picking up two shots and three shots respectively, to make it a three way tie at eight under par. Mize had a crisis at the twelfth making bogey from the back of the green but immediately got the shot back at thirteen as the tension grew. Next it was Lehman through the back of the twelfth and he too dropped a shot, and when Mize three putted the fourteenth, Olazábal was where he wanted to be, alone at the head of the field.

His golf was solid, conservative and controlled. He would not make a birdie at the thirteenth and safely made par at fourteen. It was almost as if he were waiting for the crisis to come because no-one wins The Masters without some kind of a notable drama. Equally it may be a miracle moment that defines and identifies the Champion, and the headlines were about to be written as his second shot took flight across the lake at the par five fifteenth. Even as he watched it in the air Olazábal was concerned that he might suffer the same fate as Ballesteros, but this looked to have the distance. However, it bounced near the top of the slope in front of the green and started to roll back towards the water.

In the commentary box Peter Alliss had spent years watching shots at the fifteenth come up short and gather speed down a slope that was as slippery as a wet tiled roof.

He had been very critical of it as too extreme a penalty for shots that sometimes were just a fraction short of perfect. But the penalty was always imposed, if a ball was moving on that slope, it would never stop.

Except that the ball did stop. It clung to just about the last blade of grass a foot from the edge of the water. 'When you see things like that happen you think maybe it is your time to win,' said Olazábal humbly. Lehman was equally astonished. 'When it gets on that grass it just has to go in the water.' The American recovered his composure and

Olazábal putts for his par and his first Masters title in 1994.

the green at seventeen and recording only his second bogey of the weekend. Suddenly it became like that epic battle of 1991, a par at the closing hole would surely be enough.

This time it was Olazábal who found the fairway, and Lehman, with the adrenalin pumping, who put a one iron close to the face of the first of the fairway bunkers. He was able to take a seven iron to it but not able to reproduce what Sandy Lyle had done and left it some thirty yards short of the green. From there it was a chip and two putts for bogey.

Even in his now, even more comfortable position, José María Olazábal was staggering to the finish line. He put his own approach in the gallery above the hole, but the quality of his short game prevented him suffering the ignominy of winning The Masters with a bogey. Instead it was par for a sixty nine and a win by two shots.

His victory had not been completed amid scenes of Nicklaus-like hysteria. Instead there was the polite resigned gloom that we were becoming familiar with as the ultimate tribute to the prestige of European golf, Bernhard Langer, made the presentation of The Masters Green

Olazábal shakes hands with his caddie, as being Champion sinks in.

Bernhard Langer places the Green Jacket on Olazábal, as European success continues.

played the correct shot for the hole, a six iron about fifteen feet above the cup, and walked on to the green, putter in hand, expecting justice to be done.

Instead, as a demonstration of how short and slick the grass was, Olazábal took a putter from the bank, thirty feet away from the flag and stroked it into the centre of the hole. The unfortunate Lehman now had to hole his putt merely to stay within one shot. He hit it dead on line but it stopped, hovered on the lip and would not drop. In the most fortunate of circumstances, Olazábal had got the two shot cushion he would need over the closing three holes.

Lehman would have another chance, missing a short putt for birdie at the sixteenth hole that had served him so well the day before. And then Olazábal prolonged the tension by going through

CHAPTER 9

Jacket, and however much Ollie felt like celebrating with a bit of Ryder Cup style disco-dancing on the eighteenth green, he remained restrained.

Nevertheless it was now an astonishing six European Masters win in the last seven years. In the first forty five years of the tournament Gary Player was the only non-American to win, now it was becoming something of an annual prestige benefit for the European tour, and Olazábal had served notice that a whole new generation of European players were ready to keep the winning run going.

The win was a testament to his character, coming through what was by his standards a slump, to deliver the major victory that everyone knew he was capable of. But instead of building on that success, the next few seasons were going to further test his character to a degree that no-one could imagine.

But before that, The Masters win, as it had done for other European players before, seemed to spur Olazábal on to superlative new heights. Barely a month later he was at Wentworth, winning the Volvo PGA Championship with a brilliant final round of 65. He overwhelmed leader Ernie

Olazábal, 1994 Volvo PGA Champion.

Els with a barrage of birdies on the back nine, taking the lead for the first time on the seventeenth, and completing The Masters-PGA Championship double that had previously been achieved by Ballesteros, Faldo and Langer.

But even during the course of that glorious victory, Olazábal could be seen occasionally limping, taking every opportunity to sit down and ease the apparent discomfort in his right leg. The symptoms became more evident as the season progressed but the Spaniard battled on and even won a second World Series victory at Firestone to leave him ranked sixth in America. However, when Olazábal returned to Wentworth in October he could barely walk to the end of the first eighteen holes of his World Match Play semi-final with Ernie Els. The ailing foot was regularly propped up on his golf bag, and it was only a lunchtime pain killing injection that got him out for an afternoon session in which Els came from behind to win.

There was concern throughout the winter. Tests were conducted and treatment offered for what seemed to be a form of rheumatoid arthritis, and an operation was carried out to have one of his big toes shortened. He was back at

Augusta to defend his Masters title and he did it with distinction despite clearly being in a lot of discomfort. He shared the first round lead after a sixty six, eventually finishing in a tie for fourteenth, but he was still the leading European behind the emotional winner, Ben Crenshaw.

Despite that, the problem remained and the problem was getting worse. Teaming up with Ballesteros for a victory in Paris was a rare boost, but by the second half of the season he was starting to dismantle his season, pulling out of events, most notably the Ryder Cup, where he had been selected by European captain Bernard Gallagher as a wildcard team member.

He would not play again until the spring of 1997. The depths of despair he reached through the next twelve months are hardly imaginable. At his lowest point virtually marooned at his home in Spain, he could barely crawl from one room to the other. He had virtually conceded that his golfing career was over. As the cause of the problem remained elusive it seemed Olazábal was now fighting a battle to avoid spending the rest of his life in a wheelchair.

Always a private person, Olazábal put the barriers up even more, and rumours about his condition became ever more lurid and speculative, but most of golf seemed sadly resigned to the fact that a great player would not be back.

One man who did not give up on him was his good friend Greg Norman who sent regular hand-written letters of encouragement on Great White Shark headed notepaper. These were greatly appreciated by José María who later described one of the loneliest moments as watching Norman collapse in the final round in 1996. It just compounded his own sense of isolation of not being in golf, and not being in Augusta for The Masters.

He suffered through to the end of the year as time and again theories and treatments ended up in a cul-de-sac of despair. It was virtually the last chance when he was referred to the Munich clinic of Dr Hans-Wilhelm Mueller-Wohlfahrt, a man with experience of treating

Olazábal back to defend his title in 1995, lines up his putt alongside Jack Nicklaus.

Olazábal went on to finish the highest European player in the 1995 Masters, playing through the pain-barrier.

sports injuries for the likes of Steffi Graf and Boris Becker. Olazábal, at his lowest ebb, took some persuading to go. He had seen specialists across Spain and America who had all diagnosed a form of rheumatoid arthritis but in Munich he got a different diagnosis. Mueller-Wohlfahrt treated his lower back instead of his feet, pinpointing a herniated disc as the problem. The improvement was immediate.

Olazábal now embarked on an intense period of physiotherapy and rehabilitation, much of it in the chill waters of the Basque coast, but he was happy to do it because his life was no longer on hold. He could see the way back. He was hungry to play golf again and was in action virtually from the start of the 1997 season. His form, and the quality of golf he was playing, showed no evidence of the previous two years of torment.

In his first tournament back, the Dubai Desert Classic, a third round sixty five helped him to a share of twelfth, and just two tournaments later, at the Turespaña Masters in the Canary Islands, he was a winner again, appreciating life and appreciating golf as never before.

Greg Norman became a true friend to Olazábal, offering support when he was at his lowest ebb.

Augusta could not come quickly enough and once again it was a respectable performance that saw him finish in a tie for twelfth. But the mood around The Masters had changed and even in twelfth place Olazábal found himself seventeen shots behind the astonishing winner Tiger Woods, shattering records as he went. Woods, at twenty one years old, had become the youngest winner in the history of the event. The Masters was entering a new era, maybe an era in which European golf or indeed any other nation in the world was not going to get much of a look-in.

Olazábal battled to retain his solid form through the rest of the season and was the slightly controversial captain's pick of Seve Ballesteros for the Ryder Cup at Valderrama. It was here that his comeback was completed

as he took a vital two and a half points in a dramatic European victory. Amid all the rain soaked celebrations at the end of the match no-one was more emotional than Olazábal. Our interview alongside the eighteenth green consisted of just the one faltering line… 'I just thought I would never walk again.'

The following year there was the further encouragement of another big win, this time at the Dubai Desert Classic, and at The Masters another solid tie for twelfth. His last twenty three rounds at Augusta had all fallen in the consistent span between a low sixty six and a high seventy four; that contrasted with Nick Faldo who missed his second straight Masters cut. Mark O'Meara was the 1998 winner proving that his good friend Tiger Woods was not going to dominate everything, and tied for second

second cut, but it re-defined a lot of the fairways and meant that the big hitters had to stop and think just a little bit more.

Olazábal was correct in thinking that the changes favoured his type of game more than Woods and Duval, and that was Augusta's intention. He was still erratic when trying to match the power of others off the tee and was at his best with a more strategic approach that put the emphasis back on his exquisite short game.

There were other changes. Jack Nicklaus, who had surgery for a hip replacement, was missing his first Masters in 41 years, but Gene Sarazen was there. At ninety seven years old he took some persuasion to hit the ceremonial first tee shot. He was desperately nervous of missing it altogether, but instead he sent his last ever golf shot at Augusta neatly down the centre of the fairway. Two months later the man who put The Masters on the map with his double eagle in 1935, died at his home in Florida.

For Olazábal it would be another of those steady opening rounds of seventy, matched by the European

Olazábal had a lot to celebrate in 1997 – winning the Ryder Cup and getting back to form after his wilderness years.

Tiger Woods and David Duval, the favourites for the 1999 Masters.

was another emerging player out to prove the new long term strength of American golf, David Duval.

Most of the talk when the golf world gathered for the 1999 Masters was of the potential Woods-Duval battle and rivalry, given extra strength by the form of Duval who had won on four occasions during the American season so far. The rest of the build-up debate concerned the course which had more changes than Augusta had ever attempted in a single year, all designed to defend the course from the growing distance achieved by the big hitters in the game.

Tees were set back, trees were planted especially on the par fives and, in its biggest concession to the changing character of the game, for the first time rough was introduced. Compared to what is experienced on a British links or a U.S. Open course it was more of a manicured

number one, Colin Montgomerie, who was making his best ever start to The Masters. It was all a sad contrast with the continued bad form of Nick Faldo who would not be able to recover from his opening round of eighty. The 1996 Champion would miss his third straight Masters cut.

But as at least one European stalwart of the past was faltering another was emerging, and another Spaniard at that. The exciting young Sergio García had won the Amateur Championship and at Augusta was joining one of the most talented amateur fields in years. He was enjoying the competition against the likes of Trevor Immelman and Matt Kuchar and was right up among the big names of the game with his opening round of seventy two.

The intense battle between David Duval and Tiger Woods was yet to get started. Duval had a seventy one and Woods was a shot worse off after hitting into the trees at the eighth and taking a triple bogey. The leaders at three under par were Davis Love, Scott McCarron, Nick Price and The Masters rookie Brandel Chamblee.

It was in the second round five years earlier that Olazábal made his most decisive move with a bogey free round of sixty seven. In 1999 it would be another Friday afternoon charge from the Spaniard. For a brief moment it looked as if it might be Montgomerie making the pace as he holed a ninety yard sand wedge at the third for his first ever eagle at Augusta, to head The Masters field for the

Olazábal inspects how the ball is lying in the rough, on the 1st hole of The Masters, 1999.

first time. But then it was Olazábal taking over with brilliant approach play and impeccable putting in dry blustery conditions.

Just as in 1994 it was a second round without a bogey on his card. He had a five footer for birdie at the second, a difficult downhill par save at the fifth and a tee shot to six feet for a birdie at the sixth hole that still held so many tough memories. At the eleventh he was five feet away with a driver and four iron and made his third birdie of the day. Another one came at thirteen and a long range chip of stunning precision at the fifteenth moved him further under par. A nine iron approach to ten feet at the closing hole moved him to eight under par, a shot clear of Scott McCarron and three shots clear of Greg Norman and Lee Janzen. It was a round that confirmed he was back as a major challenger.

Tiger Woods needed three late birdies on the back nine just to make the cut and was eight off the lead at the halfway stage. David Duval was a further shot back after taking an eight at the fifteenth. The battle that was meant to dominate this Masters was actually taking place in comparative obscurity in the middle of the field.

Not far behind them were the amateurs. A total of four made the cut, the best total in fourteen years, and they were still headed by Sergio García who added a seventy five to his first round seventy two, to become the first British Amateur Champion to make the cut since Peter McEvoy in 1978. Spain was leading the main event and the contest for amateur honours as well. The mantle had passed on but the man who started it all for Spain and Europe, Seve Ballesteros, left Augusta that night

Olazábal plays through the trees towards the 18th.

comparatively unnoticed. He had missed his third straight cut and was now ranked a lowly and miserable 472nd in the world.

Round two had seen spectacular pace-setting, round three was a day for consolidation and in the case of Olazábal it was not entirely convincing. His one over par round of 73 was not especially damaging but it did allow the man who had emerged as the sentimental favourite of the crowd to mount his challenge again. Certainly the Olazábal story of everything he had overcome in the previous years had been told many times in Masters week, but that did not stop Greg Norman becoming the player most people felt deserved the win more than any other. I

am sure that if Olazábal had not been leading the way himself, he would have been out there urging on the man who had provided the Spaniard with so much generous support when it was needed most.

Norman himself, barely recovered from serious shoulder surgery a few months earlier, moved to within one shot of Olazábal with his round of seventy one. It was a round that included a tee shot into the bank behind the twelfth that was never found. Norman limited the damage to just one dropped shot which said that the fighting spirit was there as strong as ever. The birdie that Norman made on eighteen when he holed a ten foot putt guaranteed that Norman would play with Olazábal in the final pairing the

A chip from the bunker at the 12th for Olazábal, on the final round.

Olazábal, watched by the gallery makes his way toward the back nine.

next day. Forget looking for sentimental winners, this was a sentimental pairing and guaranteed a final day of high emotion.

Barely had the leaders teed off before some significant names came roaring through the field. David Duval picked up four shots on the leaders and got within two before the momentum left him and he double bogeyed the eleventh, and English golf, looking for a Masters successor to Nick Faldo, was suddenly aware of the progress of Lee Westwood. He had shown steady qualities in each of his two previous Masters appearances, but it was only in the previous day's third round that he had shot his first round below seventy. Now with the leaders faltering behind him on the course, Lee produced some of his third round form on the front nine, having gone out in thirty three, no less than seven shots better than his playing partner Tiger Woods. And suddenly when he reached the tenth tee that Sunday afternoon he found himself leading The Masters.

His total of eighteen victories worldwide, including America, showed that Westwood knew exactly how to nail down a win and through his experience in Ryder Cup competition he knew how to handle pressure. 'I had heard so much about Augusta on a Sunday afternoon. How the competition doesn't begin until the back nine in the last round and how great the pressure is on the leader, but I wasn't up there long enough to really know how I handled the pressure, but certainly I would love to get the chance to be up there again.'

Westwood would bogey the tenth and then drop two more at the eleventh and in the space of two holes his chance was gone and he would eventually finish in a tie for sixth.

Olazábal had made the kind of start that had a lot of people writing off his chances, dropping shots at the third, the fourth and the fifth. History at Augusta has a kind of symmetry and the hole that turned his fortunes around was the par three sixth, the hole that had destroyed him in 1991. Even with the notoriously difficult final day pin position, a somewhat rattled Olazábal hit a six iron ten feet from the hole, and the putt dropped.

The seventh, eighth and ninth were safely parred and then at the tenth where Westwood had suffered a short time earlier, he was cautious off the tee, hit a fantastic eight iron approach, and the birdie put him back in front. The crisis seemed to be over. But Greg Norman was still the one shot back that he had been at the start of the round. And at eleven, where Larry Mize had dealt him the cruellest blow of his career, Norman holed a big putt and was tied for the lead as they entered the most famous arena in golf. Was it to be Norman at last?

But immediately the advantage went back to Olazábal, when Norman took four at the twelfth. Then came the par five thirteenth, scene of so much Masters drama in the past, and in 1999 this famous hole had the adrenalin pumping again. Norman, needing to attack, went for the green in two and felt a special kind of confidence standing over the twenty five foot putt. It had a lot of break in it, a lot of speed, but Norman dropped it straight into the centre of the hole for eagle, and at that point the lead on his own.

But Olazábal had been cautious laying up short of the creek. His pitch to twenty feet was not especially

promising, but the Spaniard responded to the moment by holing his putt for birdie. The lead was shared again. As they left the green they grinned at each other, they pointed at each other, they almost exchanged high-fives. But what they were saying to each other in unspoken words amounted to, 'This is what it's all about, this is what we play the game for. We both know what each other has been through, let's have fun.'

Norman in the Augusta reckoning once again would have loved to have had fun, or at the very least to enjoy himself for a couple more holes, but instead he three putted the fourteenth and failed to get up and down from a greenside bunker for his five at the fifteenth. After all the thrilling drama at the thirteenth, Olazábal had taken a two shot lead simply by making two solid pars.

A hole ahead, and with Greg Norman in a tie for second, was Davis Love. The manner in which he played the sixteenth has become part of Augusta legend. The final day pin position, back left and at the bottom of the slope, offers potential for a great deal of creative shot making and in particular rewards Augusta experience and

all the hard lessons that have been learnt. Davis Love in his seventh Masters experience was high on the list of those overdue success at Augusta. He knew that when his tee shot flew through the back of the sixteenth there was no chance of trying to aim a recovery direct at the flag. Instead he aimed high up on the slope, playing the shot almost with his back to the hole. The ball reached the summit of its long and ambitious journey and turned back toward the hole, and, when unbelievably it dropped, Love leapt in the air knowing that he had pulled off one of Augusta's great shots, and, at one back with two to play, was right back in the hunt.

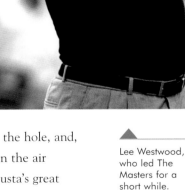

Lee Westwood, who led The Masters for a short while.

Olazábal realises
that he has won
The Masters a
second time.

Back on the tee Olazábal knew that he could not afford any mistakes but he met the challenge with the same apparent relish as he had countered Norman's eagle three holes earlier. The tee shot might have been to barely three feet, but it was still a fiendishly difficult putt: lightning-fast and across the slope. If the putt was not made with total conviction and confidence Olazábal could well struggle for the par he needed to keep him in the lead. Instead it was holed in the manner of a true champion, and with a two shot lead restored, and Norman managing only par, it seemed to be the winning moment.

But Olazábal still had one more crisis to survive. His tee shot at seventeen was pulled left and clattered into the Eisenhower tree some two hundred yards from the green.

An emotional
Olazábal is
congratulated by
his caddie.

Hindered by the branches he needed to manufacture a low recovery, and it looked as if an inevitable bogey was going to leave him with a very tense final hole. But his punched five iron was one of his bravest shots of the week. It ran up on to around forty feet from the hole on one of the toughest greens on the course. Fast, undulating and almost rock hard, the seventeenth green had already been described by Davis Love as, 'virtually unplayable.' The approach putt to seven feet was as good as he could have hoped for, and once again his nerve held. Greg Norman, by now a spectator in the battle for the title, described the five footer that Olazábal made to salvage his par as, 'the best putt he made all day,' and the 1994 Champion knew at that point that the title was his once more.

EUROPE AT THE MASTERS

taken there were going to be strong emotions at the finish. Even Davis Love, who took second, was trying to win at a venue where his late father had been a strong contender in 1964. But it was Olazábal who had won the miracle Masters, and European golf reigned supreme again.

So Olazábal had won a Masters that Lee Westwood had briefly led. Langer and Montgomerie were just outside the top ten, and there was further evidence that the future was bright for European golf when Olazábal got to the Butler Cabin for the Green Jacket ceremony. Mark O'Meara was there to make the presentation and so too was his compatriot Sergio García to receive the medal for low amateur. Just nineteen years old, his final round of 73 gave him the success by a two shot margin. There was every reason to think that Garcia was going to become the next great Spanish champion, maybe the next great world superstar. An opinion that was certainly endorsed by his playing partner through the first two days, Tiger Woods.

American golf resigned itself to further overseas success at this most famous of venues. Vijay Singh delivered precisely that the following year and Canada would take the credit for the victory by Mike Weir in 2003, but in major Championship terms the new century has produced no victory for Europe to celebrate as yet, at Augusta or any other venue.

Sergio García alongside Olazábal receives his prize for low amateur.

Three years on from watching Norman's defeat by Faldo, propped up in bed fighting tears of frustration, fearing he might never walk again, Olazábal took the victory walk for the second time at Augusta. This time it was his job and not the responsibility of Nick Faldo to struggle to find the words of consolation for Norman on the eighteenth green. Whichever twist the story had

Olazábal is crowned 1999 Champion by Mark O'Meara.

NICK
FALDO

MASTERS CHAMPION: 1989, 1990 AND 1996

When I first started presenting The Masters, first for ITV and then for Channel Four before the BBC took over, there was an accepted method of going on the air. We would put all the great American contenders in an opening sequence, hopefully trail a strong charge from Seve, and then before going to live coverage and the battle for the title, swiftly update the audience on what happened to the British challengers.

Sometimes this only took a few seconds, as in 1982 when Peter Oosterhuis was the only British player in the entire field and finished in a tie for twenty fourth, but in subsequent years this little opening sequence became a little more refined, 'Before showing you the battle for the Green Jacket let's just update you on Nick Faldo.'

Other British contenders may have been short on the ground but with Nick, especially at Augusta, there was that nagging feeling of destiny that all European winners seemed to have. With Nick it was because early on in his career he had made everyone familiar with how accidentally switching on Masters TV coverage in 1971, had turned him on to golf. In his autobiography *Life Swings*

he made the point that if the coverage had been black and white and not colour, he was sure The Masters would not have made such an impression. 'Switching through the channels on the Sunday evening of the last round, after an afternoon fishing with Dad, I was entranced not only by the beauty of the place, the flowers, lakes and lush green fairways, but also by the power and personality of Jack Nicklaus. A lot of people wrongly think I was inspired by the sight of Nicklaus pulling on the Green Jacket, but it was the little known Charles Coody who actually won that year, although I only had eyes for the "Golden Bear". I never fail to marvel that this patch of golfing heaven came to gain such a special place in my heart in later years.'

The next day he was down at Welwyn Garden City Golf Club, enrolling for his first lessons, and his almost obsessive commitment was immediately evident. After a fine but brief amateur career, he turned pro in 1976, won his first tournament in 1977 and when he won the Colgate PGA Championship in 1978, he was heading for Augusta.

Nick Faldo made his Masters debut in 1979 and it was respectable enough, making the cut before falling away with a third round seventy nine. At this time he was the

A youthful looking Faldo poses with his clubs in 1978.

Faldo, showing a lot of promise in the early eighties.

Faldo demonstrates his driving under the watchful eye of David Leadbetter.

produce the most unconvincing of final rounds that would barely see him finish in the top fifteen.

We gave him the big build-up at the start of the Channel Four coverage but he would have been wiped off our screens entirely if he had not been playing alongside the eventual winner Ben Crenshaw, and just like Sandy Lyle playing with Jack Nicklaus two years later, it might not have seemed the greatest experience at the time, but it was all part of the learning process that most champions have to go through. The lesson that Faldo learnt watching

most exciting young talent emerging on the European scene and had started out on a run of three wins in the prestigious PGA Championship in four years.

When he returned to Augusta in 1983 he was only three shots behind the halfway leader Gil Morgan, and although he would eventually finish in a tie for twentieth he was starting to show the first hints of what was to come. But it was in 1984 that Nick Faldo got us excited at Augusta for the first time.

In all honesty, when he briefly headed the final round of the Open Championship at Royal Birkdale the previous year only to drop rather tamely away, we, and the rest of the British golfing media were not yet convinced that the young Faldo was made of stern enough stuff to become a genuine major championship challenger. Indeed at Augusta in 1984 he was well placed just two shots behind the third round leader Tom Kite only to once again

Crenshaw surge to victory was a simple one, 'To win The Masters you have to hole everything, it's as simple as that.'

The reaction was cruel, giving the tabloid Press the chance to resurrect the unimaginative 'Nick Foldo' headlines that they had invented the previous summer. For Faldo the response was immediate and within a week he would channel any frustrations he felt and any lessons he learnt into completing victory at The Heritage Classic at Hilton Head, and the impression was that the career, with all its potential, was back on track. However, after winning again at Moortown a few weeks later Faldo would not enjoy victory again for another three years.

Faldo was still number one in Europe but he and a large part of the rest of the golfing world were recognising that there was something fundamentally wrong that was preventing him moving on to the next level.

A less single-minded character may well have left it at that; acknowledging that even with his limitations he had still gone higher, and achieved more than the majority of tournament players can aspire to. And one day maybe the golfing gods would ignore his shortcomings and gift him the major title that he wanted more than anything else; or maybe not.

Faldo was not going to take that risk and he was not going to endure the continuous criticism that came with getting in winning positions and not claiming victory. It was all down, he felt, to a willowy swing with too many disjointed components, each of which could break down at any time especially under pressure.

It is now the stuff of golfing legend, how, with coach David Leadbetter, Faldo took himself away and dedicated himself to completely rebuilding his swing and his technical approach to the sport, instead of just papering over the cracks. The sacrifice was enormous and the risks were clear; he could easily have come back befuddled and confused, a shadow of the former elegant player, and disappear off the radar and the rankings like so many before him; or he could come back a Champion.

What Faldo achieved during those wilderness years was as great a victory as any that would come later, not least because he was trying to make the changes while still playing a competitive schedule. So with his hands raw from the practice ground and his nerves raw from the frustrations of another uncompetitive round, Faldo had to politely endure the questions, not least from myself: 'How are the changes going?…Do you think you're making progress?…What is it exactly you're trying to do?…' For him the honest answer to all those questions must have been, 'I don't bloody know,' but I thank him for his patience at the time.

He has written and talked very honestly and eloquently about that period, when a painful and costly divorce was another ingredient in his turmoil. There were many low points, but the psychological depths came when he made little impression on the Open Championship at Sandwich in 1985, and Sandy Lyle won an historic victory to emphasis how far their careers seemed to be moving apart. Later that year he was part of the European Ryder

Nick Faldo's Coach and golf guru David Leadbetter.

Cup team that achieved the breakthrough win at The Belfry but his contribution was played two, lost two and he struggled to enter into the spirit of the celebrations.

There was the occasional hopeful week such as a top five finish in the Open Championship at Turnberry in 1986, but in general the task of putting four decent rounds together to sustain a challenge seemed beyond him.

For two years he was absent from Augusta, and it was ironic that the breakthrough, when it came, should be in Masters week and in circumstances that starkly highlighted how he had dropped out of the golfing big time. The Deposit Guaranty Classic at Hattiesburg is an event as Faldo describes, 'for all those lost souls who have not been invited to compete in The Masters.' Atlanta airport on the Monday of Masters week in 1987 was the first uncomfortable reminder for Faldo that he was no longer part of the elite. 'I went through the airport at precisely the same time that the plane carrying a number of European players plus the British Press contingent touched down. Thus, while they took a right turn to Augusta, we turned left to catch our connecting flight to the boondocks of Mississippi. The golfing world was assembling for The Masters and I was heading for a tumbleweed town in the woods somewhere; I felt grievously humiliated.'

Faldo on his way to winning the Open in 1987.

Humiliation can be a powerful motivation. I remember at Augusta, that even among the tumult of the Larry Mize victory we were reading the small print in the local paper that told that Faldo had shot four rock-solid rounds of sixty seven to finish a shot behind the winner David Ogrin. Even after so many false dawns Faldo felt that his long practice ground journey was over and he was re-born as a player who could fulfil all his seemingly distant potential.

And so it proved. He returned to Europe and promptly finished in the top four in the Madrid and Italian Opens before ending the three year wait for victory at the Spanish Open at Las Brisas, the kind of course that will expose any frailties in form or technique. Faldo now had no question marks about his ability, and the final convincing proof came at the 1987 Open Championship at Muirfield when his famous victory, built on eighteen straight pars in the final round, removed any thoughts about his ability

And he was up among the contenders in the U.S. PGA Championship as well, finishing tied for fourth behind the winner Jeff Sluman.

An elated Faldo is awarded the Open at Muirfield.

With this record in the most recent majors it was a little surprising that he came to Augusta the following April perplexed about his form and, most worryingly, once again doubting his ability to string four good rounds together, let alone 'hole everything in sight' which he now knew was the essential requirement of winning at Augusta. The biggest question mark over his form was his putting, and a final round of seventy six the previous week in Texas had only increased the doubts.

The course set-up that week would help his recovery. The rock hard greens of the previous year had been replaced by putting surfaces which were, by Augusta standards, almost receptive. Certainly the fear factor had been removed and Faldo prospered in the opening round. His opening round of sixty eight left him just one shot off the lead and it came after he had abandoned his Ping putter of five years and replaced it with a Bullseye that he had not used since his amateur days. The end product was three birdies and an eagle and a new mood of confidence and optimism.

For the whole of the field, second round day was not a day for optimism. The temperature dropped, the wind blew, the rain fell and everyone struggled. Sandy Lyle missed the cut and it would be three years before he made another one at Augusta. Faldo was three clear of the field after nine holes, only to limp home in thirty nine shots to tie the lead with Lee Trevino ahead of the rest.

If the weather had taken its toll on Friday it was even worse for round three and in the dank gloom a heavy rainstorm mid-afternoon forced a suspension of play of close on two hours. The conditions put paid to the challenge of Trevino; his third round of eighty one meant that his new found love affair with a course and a tournament he historically had no affection for, was a short lived thing.

to compete when the pressure was at its most intense. In three tough years he had transformed himself from Nick Faldo under-achiever to Nick Faldo major Champion, and of course he was back at Augusta.

In 1988 at The Masters, he was not exactly mounting the strong challenge he might have anticipated, but instead having to swallow a bit of pride as Sandy Lyle, having beaten him to the Open Championship, now beat him to the Green Jacket as well. If he was jealous he did not show it, instead he was gracious, enthusiastic and supportive as he joined in the television presentation and urged Sandy to victory. There was grunted acknowledgment when I politely suggested that the next year it would be him, but deep down he was even more determined that it would be.

The rest of 1988 provided ample proof that he would be among the strongest of challengers at Augusta. At the U.S. Open at Brookline he finished tied with Curtis Strange and was then beaten in the eighteen hole play-off the following day. At Royal Lytham he put up a strong defence of his Open title but Ballesteros was irresistible with his final round sixty five, and Faldo finished third.

Faldo started in dreadful fashion with a double bogey at the first, and then at the second his third shot just about clung to the far edge of the green, a full one hundred feet from the hole, just about the longest putt on the course. It was early on in our transmission, the pictures on the monitors on the balcony were a little indistinct but surely we just saw that putt from three or even four putt territory drop straight into the hole? Indeed it had, for unofficially the longest putt in Masters history and for Faldo, the significance of that good fortune would become clearer, twenty four hours later.

It was a huge bonus but one that hardly transformed the round and when play was abandoned for the day with Faldo on the thirteenth it was now Ben Crenshaw in the lead. But Faldo was still two under, just two shots behind and hoping to profit from the resumption in calm conditions on the Sunday morning.

The weather at 8 a.m. was damp, misty and still. With no live television commitments we were out on the course to put together a recorded package that we assumed would enable us to go on the air with a strong story of how Faldo had played himself strongly into title contention. Instead it

looked like being the old-fashioned approach of, 'Before we see the battle for the title this is what happened to Nick Faldo…' He had left himself overnight with a sixty yard wedge across the creek into the thirteenth green, and although he played that to six feet, he missed the birdie and from then on went into what he described as a 'downward spiral of bogeys.' Instead of reasserting his position at the top of the leader board Faldo had shot a seventy seven. He had played the first twenty seven holes in six under and the next twenty seven in nine over and was now a distant five shots behind the leader, Ben Crenshaw. It was a straightforward decision not to round off the morning highlights package with an interview, indeed as Faldo walked past us behind the eighteenth green there were tears in his eyes. It was barely nine forty five in the morning and at this stage it did not feel anything like an historic day.

He knew what needed to be done and minutes later we saw him heading to the practice putting green with a selection of putters, and it seems he made a swift decision to abandon the Bullseye, despite the fact it found the centre of the target from a hundred feet range the day

Faldo drives off the tee at The Masters, 1989.

before. Instead he selected a club that he felt allowed him to be a bit more aggressive on the greens and he headed off from the practice green to re-group for the afternoon with a feeling that he still had a great chance in this final round.

The change of putter, the decision taken when spirits were low and composure was scrambled, has become part of Faldo legend. He came out in the final round and holed from thirty feet for birdie at the first, twelve feet at the second, fifteen feet at the fourth and twenty feet at the seventh. He was right back in it. Unfortunately, even though leader Crenshaw was starting to go backwards, others, like Faldo were finding form. In particular there was Ballesteros out in thirty one with four birdies in the first five holes that put him in the lead. But as he missed opportunities Mike Reid took over the lead and then Scott Hoch. Greg Norman had a great chance as well but behind them there was always Faldo, surging on.

He was still three behind at the fourteenth but then birdied the fifteenth and at the next hole sank what he still regards as one of the best putts of his life. 'The ball was approximately fifteen feet from the hole, but – and this is no exaggeration – with ten feet of break to take into account, meaning I was putting almost sideways.' Another candidate for the best putt he has ever holed came at the seventeenth. 'It was a vicious left to right thirty five foot putt up and over the infamous ridge, which would have been daunting on the practice green, let alone the seventy first hole in The Masters. I hit it a tad hard, and if you saw it on TV you might have seen a look of total disbelief on my face. Scott Hoch later said that if it hadn't dropped I'd have finished fourth. But it dropped and I was tied for the lead.'

On the eighteenth in rain and conditions that were rapidly darkening, the hole was not quite so receptive and the birdie putt that Faldo felt might have been enough to win it just pulled up short. But he had set the target, he had shot an outstanding round of seven under par sixty

five and now had the luxury of waiting in the Butler Cabin to see who would falter, who would pass him or who would join him in a play-off.

Norman for the second time in four years bogeyed the eighteenth when a play-off beckoned. Crenshaw failed to get up and down from the greenside bunker at eighteen and he was gone. Hoch had a great chance to win it at seventeen but failed to make the birdie putt and when he got his four at eighteen, the man who had looked the most likely winner through most of the afternoon now joined Faldo in a sudden death play-off.

Faldo on the 18th, just misses his birdie putt.

Scott Hoch, The Masters slipping from his grasp.

Up in the BBC position on the clubhouse balcony was Sandy Lyle who had missed the cut but was obliged to stay on to put the Green Jacket on the shoulders of the new Champion. But in the circumstances he would have probably chosen to stay on anyway. When Faldo had sunk his remarkable putt on the sixteenth, Lyle had pointed out that it was from virtually exactly the same position from which he had holed his big putt the year before, a putt that set up victory. Sandy could sense yet another kind of destiny about Faldo's progress through the day.

He had to leave to make his way to the Butler Cabin to await whichever winner the play-off would produce. Our eyes had not left the TV monitors for about two hours, and as he turned to leave we were amazed to look behind us and see that the light had virtually gone. It was a murky late evening and surely not much more than twenty minutes play was going to be possible. This sudden death play-off had to be sudden.

The tee shot down the first play-off hole the tenth required a powerful high draw. Faldo hit it high but without the distance to get it all the way down the hill and he would have an awkward second shot from a sloping lie of around two hundred yards. The iron was well struck but the ball just caught the bunker on the right of the green. With Hoch hitting his second shot to around twenty five feet, the American seemed to have the advantage. The advantage seemed to become almost decisive when Faldo could only put his bunker shot fifteen feet from the hole and Hoch's lagged putt finished a mere two feet from the hole.

It was a surprise when Hoch chose not to immediately walk up and roll the ball. Instead he marked the ball, stepped away and studied the task that confronted him. Suddenly a straightforward putt that he would surely have holed with a single reflex movement became a difficult read with a strong left to right break, and when Faldo

As the light was fading fast, Faldo gleams with delight – Masters champion 1989.

missed his putt it then became a difficult two footer with a left to right break for the Masters title.

Pace was everything and Hoch, no doubt with adrenalin pumping, struck it too hard. The ball missed on the high side and went two feet past. Almost without breaking his stride Hoch rolled in the return putt, precisely the unfussy approach he should have used with his putt for the title. This of course is the wisdom of hindsight, and Hoch has had to endure a great deal of hindsight over

what happened. He said later that it was just as well he didn't carry a gun as he would have used it on himself. He was hard on himself, too hard, feeling that he'd let down himself, his family and American golf, but probably it is fair to say that he has never fully recovered from that agonising moment in the gloom of the tenth green sixteen years ago.

For Faldo it was a reprieve, the second reprieve that Hoch had granted him within the space of an hour. Now on the eleventh he was going to inherit nothing, he was going to win The Masters in the style of the Champion he was. His tee shot down the eleventh was down the right hand side of the fairway and perfect, but it was an illustration of the deteriorating conditions that he had to take relief from casual water for his second shot. On this day of outstanding golf Faldo then hit what he felt was one of the best long irons of his career: two hundred yards, a three iron, with feel being the important ingredient because he would lose sight of it in the gloom almost immediately it came off the clubface. Faldo was fifteen feet from the hole, Hoch had missed the green and from the swale on the right had failed to produce a Larry Mize miracle so he was eight feet away having played three.

So at last Faldo had a putt for the title, and a putt to prove, once and for all, that there were few stronger and more resolute competitors in the game. But as he settled over the ball, up on the balcony, hunched over the monitors, we were trying to disregard the thought that a week ago his putting form was at its lowest ebb for a long time. A change of putter had brought only a

temporary reprieve, and it was only ten hours earlier that he was fighting back tears of frustration as he went for yet another new putter for this final round. Now he was lining up a fifteen footer for the title.

Despite all the doubts and desperation that had gone before, he cleared his head and concentrated on the basics of routine, repetition and relaxation. The left hand takes the club back, the right hand takes it through, as easy as that. The ball left the clubface, unerringly took the break and sped into the dead centre of the hole. The look of disbelief was back on Faldo's face, the arms spread wide, the white sweater piercing the darkness in Amen Corner; one of the greatest images that European golf has been able to enjoy. The first man across the eleventh green to congratulate him was Sir Michael Bonallack, the secretary of the R&A who had been officiating on the hole. A few minutes later it would be congratulations from Sandy Lyle in a scene that would have been beyond imagination half a dozen years earlier: a British golfer helping another British golfer into The Masters Green Jacket, although Sandy did it with the less than historic words, 'Sorry Nick it's a bit short in the sleeves.'

Sandy Lyle is pictured with Nick Faldo, shortly after presenting the Green Jacket.

For us a long day was about to get a great deal longer as the phone lines from London brought requests for extra review programmes and highlights programmes, all of which were being swiftly shoe-horned into the schedules. Wary of our indiscretion the year before, we politely waited an hour or so before Nick was able to join us in front of the cameras on the balcony, and it was around midnight before we headed down Magnolia Lane and out of the course. We had seen history, the first ever back to back overseas winners at The Masters, the first ever British winner at Augusta, had immediately been followed by the second. Unbelievable.

One of Nick Faldo's favourite memories of the few hours that followed his 1989 success, was a conversation with The Masters Chairman Hord Hardin in his traditional Sunday night dinner with the Champion, in which Mr Hardin was clearly confusing Nick with Sandy.

If the rest of the Augusta faithful were struggling to come to terms with this multitude of European winners, the confusion had cleared by Masters week 1990 where it seemed that Faldo, despite his position as defending Champion, was judged to be only in the ranks of possible contenders as the form was discussed on the eve of the action.

Greg Norman was reckoned to be the favourite and it was hard to disagree that a man who had finished in the top five of the last four Masters and was so cruelly robbed by Larry Mize in 1987 deserved to join the ranks of

Ray Floyd was having a great Masters in 1990.

Augusta Champions. Those Champions assembled in the clubhouse for dinner on the Tuesday evening, with Faldo the host; of their number, only Jack Nicklaus had hosted the dinner and gone on to win the event later in the week, supposedly another reason for disregarding the claims of Faldo.

After being named BBC Sports Personality of the Year for his Augusta performance, Faldo had formed a new partnership with caddie Fanny Sunesson and had made a quiet but solid start to the new season. There still seemed to be a feeling around Augusta that he was Masters Champion by default, that it was only the failings of Scott Hoch that handed him the title and the American was resigned to the inevitable press conference grilling that went over it all again. 'People constantly reminding me how much that putt cost me in fame and money made it tough. The more you look at it that way, the more it hurts, but after a while you develop a thick skin.'

Hoch, like Faldo began with an unspectacular opening round of seventy one, which left them both a full seven shots off the lead. Mike Donald had made an astonishing Augusta debut; his first round in The Masters was a sixty four, just one outside the record, but the chasing pack had no need to be alarmed; Donald would follow it up with an eighty two and dropped to twenty fifth. No Masters leader had ever fallen so far.

Among a big group of players with a first round two under par seventy was Ray Floyd. He was The Masters Champion in 1976 but was now forty seven years old and had not had a tournament victory for fourteen years. This is if you disregard the eve of Masters par three tournament which historically precludes the winner from success in that year's main event. But Floyd was challenging again

Faldo walks towards the next green at the 1990 Masters with caddie Fanny Sunesson.

and was high up on the first round leader board despite dropping two shots in the final three holes.

In the second round he was even more like the Floyd of old, reeling off three straight birdies from the thirteenth. In all he was five under for the par fives, helped by an eagle at the eighth, and was close to the pace that he set in 1976 when he equalled The Masters record of 271. Faldo lost a little more ground with a level par seventy two and, with Bernhard Langer, was five shots off Floyd's halfway lead.

The two Europeans were paired together in the third round when the competition really took shape with Faldo making the most emphatic move, showing his intent at the very first hole where a glorious five iron left him with a straightforward putt for birdie, and he picked up further shots at the seventh and the eighth.

The same form continued through the back nine and when he holed a testing putt for par at the eighteenth it was a round of sixty six, and three shots off the lead, the possibility of a successful defence of The Masters title had become a strong one.

Ahead of Faldo was John Huston and still Ray Floyd who came in with another round of sixty eight, and the assumptions that his new found form might prove a little fragile were starting to be revised. It looked as if it was all slipping away during a rather sloppy front nine, but Floyd came back in thirty one to get everyone thinking that Augusta might be about to produce its oldest Champion.

Clear, crisp conditions for the final round with its added ingredients of tension and expectation especially for the front runners. Down the years Floyd had proved himself strong in that department, and now Faldo it

Faldo weighs up his next shot in The Masters final round.

Stuck in a bunker on the 12th, Faldo chips onto the green observed by a TV camera in the balcony above.

seemed had at last convinced even the British tabloid Press, that he was made of stern stuff as well, and only five shots off the lead was Jack Nicklaus in his fiftieth year. The final round in 1990 had some fascinating ingredients.

It looked as if Faldo would not be an ingredient for very long when he put his opening tee shot into the bunker and would double bogey to drop five shots behind Floyd before the leader had even got on to the course. It looked as if he were set for a further setback when he was well short of the second green in two, but not before time the fighting spirit kicked in and he chipped and putted for birdie.

Then the challenge was on and Faldo got a sense of that all important final round momentum. Birdies at the seventh and ninth moved him to within two of Floyd who had made an unconvincing start. Nicklaus playing with Faldo had looked a threat but then started struggling on the greens. Faldo looked the challenger best equipped for all the demands of the back nine.

But just like the play-off with Hoch the year before, Faldo rather miscued his tee shot on ten and would bogey. Every champion it seems needs to survive a crisis on the back nine and Faldo would have his at the twelfth. His tee shot overshot the green and the ball buried itself in the bunker. A shot was required that would be way beyond

mere mortals and most professionals, and even Faldo was by no means convinced that he could not only get it out but avoid ending up in the water on the other side of the green. He played what he called 'the deftest little thump' which stopped on the far fringe of the green. His putt it seemed would surely finish short but it reached the hole with its very last oscillation, and dropped. His challenge was still alive but minutes later Floyd came to the twelfth and from just off the green holed his birdie putt to increase his lead to four and seemingly take a firm grip on the title.

But Faldo was relentless and would test Floyd's ageing nerves to the extreme with birdies at the thirteenth and the fifteenth; and then at the sixteenth, where he and Sandy Lyle had both produced heroic putts as part of their previous charges to victory, Faldo produced another one, this time from twenty five feet. Destiny.

If Floyd were going to win it he would need all his experience and all his nerve.

As Faldo was climbing the hill to the eighteenth green the news was flashed on to the giant scoreboard that Floyd had dropped that all important shot at the seventeenth. He had left himself with the tough task of trying to two putt from around seventy feet; now he and Faldo were tied. Faldo made his par on eighteen, Floyd's nerve was tested one more time at eighteen. He drove into the bunker from the tee and then had to get up and down from the greenside bunker for his par. To his credit he made it, and for the second year The Masters had gone to a play-off. For the second year it featured Faldo.

Up on the balcony we were ready for it all once again. This time Ian Woosnam was with us. Despite his disappointment at a closing round seventy six, he insisted he wanted to contribute and wanted to be a part of maybe another piece of European golfing history. But it was all taking a toll on him; he'd been perched on a bar stool alongside me for the best part of two hours. It wasn't as dark as a year before but it was colder. Ian was going numb and we wrapped him in a canvas camera cover to keep him warm. We hoped the play-off would be swift and we desperately hoped it would be Faldo.

Yet again it was far from an ideal tee shot from Faldo at the tenth, yet again he found himself in the same greenside bunker from which he had almost conceded the title to Hoch a year before. Floyd, also like Hoch, had put his second shot to within birdie range. The pressure was on the Champion. This time he responded with a great bunker shot to five feet and would make the putt. Floyd missed his fifteen footer. On to the eleventh, on to the scene of the triumph a year before.

Both players found the fairway but Faldo recalls that his opponent took a swift diversion for a comfort break just off the eleventh tee and had to hurry to catch up after that. The second shot into eleven is a daunting one. There is a lot of room to play safe, but you take on the lake if you go for the heart of the green. Floyd was thirty yards behind Faldo but seemed to have a clear line to the flag. He might have had an awkward lie on a slight slope but it is impossible to resist the thought that at the most crucial moment of all, his nerve failed him. The second he hit the shot he knew it was pulled and he was finished. Faldo, along with everyone else watched in disbelief as it dropped softly and tamely into the lake.

Even then the competitive edge did not leave Faldo. He assumed Floyd would make five and with a cautious eight iron approach gave himself two putts for the title, and took them both. It was not an epic finish, but it was a victory that had so much historical significance. Faldo became the only other player apart from Nicklaus to successfully defend the title and had extended European golf's proud new record at Augusta.

On the way back to the Butler Cabin, even Faldo was wondering about the protocol from his point. Surely he could not present the Green Jacket to himself and if he had a choice, it would be a privilege to receive it from Jack Nicklaus. Sadly that did not prove possible,

CHAPTER 9

Faldo has done it again, Masters Champion for a second time. ▶

Hord Hardin made the presentation, got the name right and the jacket fitted.

Up on the balcony we were very aware of what an extraordinary achievement we had seen, and how the huge late night audience back home would have been thrilled by it. There was also the sense that it surely could not get any better than this from the point of view of European golf. However we politely suggested that it could be Woosie next year, and still wrapped in the camera cover he climbed off the studio bar stool, but had no feeling in his legs and fell flat on the floor.

It is a burden for Nick Faldo, though one he is content to bear, that he is perceived as the player who wins The Masters when others lose it. He knows the truth. His final round of sixty five in 1989 was among the finest The Masters had seen, but it was still The Masters that Scott Hoch lost. In 1990 he played the last six holes as well as any other previous Champion apart from Art Wall in 1959,

Sunesson gives Faldo a victory hug, as Ray Floyd shakes hands with the officials. ▼

who birdied five of the last six, but it was still The Masters that Ray Floyd lost. It was all experience that served to prepare him for what happened in 1996.

Of all The Masters I have had the privilege of attending, of all the fifty major Championships I have presented for network television, this is the one that people want to talk about, because it unfolded like some kind of personal drama rather than a sporting event. It was the mental strain of The Masters at its most cruel and a golf tournament that became some weird sort of reality TV that gripped everyone who started watching it.

With respect to the great names who make up The Masters field, this had a cast list of only two, one of whom did not really make his entrance until act three.

Right from the start this was The Masters that Greg Norman was going to win. He was going to put history straight and correct one of golf's great injustices. Not only that but he was going to do it in style. That was clear from round one when his putt for birdie hung on the lip of the hole to deny him the outright course record of sixty two. Nevertheless he became the first player to shoot two rounds of sixty three in the majors (the other being when he won the Open at Turnberry in 1963) and he had the satisfaction of making his best start at The Masters by a full six shots. He was dominating the event already but for the record, Phil Mickelson also had a fine round of sixty five and Nick Faldo was six shots back after a sixty nine. In the five years since his back to back Masters wins, Faldo had been a consistent performer but never a challenger for a third Green Jacket and 1996 had started off looking as if it were going to be no different.

In round two Norman set about stretching and consolidating his lead which, in gusting conditions, was no easy task, but the firm fairways and fast greens were suiting his game and at long last Augusta was giving him some

good fortune as well at the twelfth, where a succession of players were running up big scores. Norman's tee shot clung to the bank in front of the green in the manner of Fred Couples in 1992 and he made his par; all part of a satisfactory second round of sixty nine.

But out of the pack came Faldo putting all his canny Augusta experience to good use to prosper when others were struggling. In the first round, paired with John Daly, he must have felt intimidated playing every shot some sixty yards behind his playing partner. In the second round he recalled that he took every opportunity that Augusta was offering, making six one putt birdies, in a round of sixty seven. Faldo was into second place, but Norman was ahead by four.

People look back on 1996 for what happened in the final round but really the contest between Greg Norman and Nick Faldo took place over thirty six holes of that memorable weekend. There were echoes, distant echoes, of their confrontation in the Open Championship at St. Andrews in 1990. On that occasion Faldo outscored Norman by a demoralising nine shots in the third round and went on to romp to the title. This was the first time they had been paired together since then; a chance for Norman to get even, and get even with Augusta as well.

In the third round, wind was a strong factor again. Faldo's game plan had to be to at least outscore Norman to give himself a manageable deficit to attack on the final day, but through the front nine with mistakes and successes on both sides the

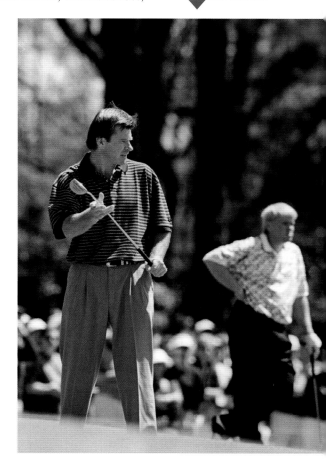

Nick Faldo in the first round of The Masters, 1996 paired with John Daly.

Worlds apart –
Greg Norman
and Nick Faldo
walk up to the
1st hole in the
final round of
The Masters.

gap remained the same. Faldo sensed an opportunity at the twelfth to make giant inroads when Norman put his tee shot into the water, but he sent his own tee shot over the back of the green and the potential two shot swing simply became a bogey apiece.

Whereas on the previous day he had converted every birdie opportunity he was presented with, in round three they all passed him by, and in his interview afterwards he especially regretted putts on twelve, thirteen, fourteen, fifteen and sixteen, all of which should have been holed and would have set up a very different final day to the one we had in prospect now. For Norman's nondescript round of seventy one was two shots better than Faldo and he would take a lead of six shots into day four. The consolation for Faldo was a birdie putt at the last that guaranteed that he, and not third placed Phil Mickelson would be in the last pairing with Norman. At least he could keep an eye on the man to catch, even if it were a distant eye.

He recalled in his autobiography, 'In the Press tent I put on my usual brave face. "Of course I can still win I'm only six shots back," I told them, and as I was talking, I actually began to believe the apparent nonsense coming out of my own mouth. "You know what?" I muttered inwardly, "I'm right. Six back isn't anything at Augusta. If I

can get three back on the front nine. A three shot lead on the back nine is absolutely nothing." I woke up on the Sunday morning fully refreshed and relaxed, placed a call to my parents, which I seldom do before a final round, and became so engrossed in a NASCAR motor-race on television, I did not have time for my usual hour and a half warm-up.'

This apparent failing by a normally meticulous player was in fact, a huge advantage. Norman had arrived early to constant attention. For him it was like the build-up to a victory parade instead of a potentially demanding final round. Faldo was relaxed; he was tense. The sub-text to the day was 'Surely he can't blow this one.' With notable perception columnist Roland Green wrote in that morning's *Charlotte Observer*, 'Greg Norman won The Masters on Saturday. Now if he can only keep from losing it.'

In the half hour before we went on air we watched CBS Television going through their rehearsals. They would not be live until around the eighth hole but they were still confident enough to devote their first fifteen minutes to the life and times of Greg Norman, his trials and tribulations, but at last it was going to be a Masters Green Jacket for the world number one.

Faldo in a
bunker on the
2nd hole,
as Norman
looks on.

We went on the air with a rather different story. Norman receiving a huge ovation on the first tee and then pulling his opening tee shot into the edge of the trees on the left. He was blocked out and bogeyed; the lead was down to five. His approach to the second was also off target, but he recovered brilliantly, almost made it for eagle and was able to match Faldo's birdie.

He was still five ahead at the sixth when Faldo aimed his seven iron at the tiny plateau target on the sixth green and made the birdie putt. The lead was down to four. The body language of Norman, normally so positive and aggressive, now started to reveal his discomfort. Faldo noticed how he was taking longer over every shot, and was starting to grip and re-grip his club on every shot. 'For my part I made a conscious effort to stand taller, walk more purposefully, to show no reaction whatsoever to any wayward shot. That is all you can do in golf. You cannot physically beat up the other guy, and I would never dream of trying to psyche someone out with a patronising remark or a throwaway line. But with my stride, my bearing, my expression, I wanted to remind my opponent, "Hey, I don't know about you, but I'm all right, mate."'

Norman pulled his approach shot into the trees on the left of the eighth at just about the time that CBS Television were going on the air with their 'Greg Norman Masters Champion elect' opening. He would drop a shot there and then suffer further agony at the ninth when his approach spun off the elevated green. Faldo had exceeded his front nine target of trimming the lead by three and had now moved to within just two shots of the shell-shocked Norman.

Faldo thinks about his next shot at the 13th hole.

Faldo and Norman both frown in anticipation for what may lie ahead.

CHAPTER 9

▲ Faldo chips into Norman's fragile lead.

sliding off the slope in front of the green and into the water. He made a double bogey five; Faldo led by two.

On the American networks the glorious Greg Norman programme opening was long forgotten and they were now proclaiming it as the biggest collapse in golfing history. Walking up the thirteenth Nick simply turned to Fanny and said, 'Bloody hell!'

The cameras dwelt on the partnership as they seemingly agonised over Faldo's second shot into thirteen. Clubs were selected and clubs were put back in the bag. The galleries started to jeer. It was all adding to the drama and possibly adding to the discomfort of Greg Norman as well, but Faldo is clear there was no indecision, 'I knew if I nailed a two iron the ball would easily make the front edge and even if it did roll over the green I could still get up and down for my birdie four. With the pendulum having swung in my direction I knew one more fantastic shot would send out even more forcibly the "I'm alright" message. The visualisation complete, I executed one of the very best shots of my life, the ball soaring as if laser-guided into the heart of the green.' Both players made birdie, Faldo's two shot lead remained.

Up in the BBC presentation position which had been moved from the clubhouse balcony to the garden behind the Butler Cabin we were trying to make sense of what we were seeing and in particular we were trying to make the emphasis of the story Faldo's success as much as Norman's demise. But we were thwarted in this by a succession of guests who came to the studio and would instead bombard us with questions. I remember in particular Bernhard Langer, Ernie Els and Frank Nobilo all transfixed by the coverage and demanding to know how could this happen?…what's gone wrong?…how could he lose it? Underlying it all was the golfers' unspoken acknowledgment that 'There but for the grace of God go us all.'

But there was still time for Norman to salvage it. At the fifteenth his chip for eagle did everything but go in the hole and Norman dropped to the floor, rolling on to his back like a boxer absorbing the final knockout blow. That

At the tenth the Australian missed the green on the left and hit a poor chip and at the next he three putted from fifteen feet and within just eleven holes all of that seemingly decisive six shot lead had disappeared.

Faldo then drew on all his match play experience to do what was required at the par three twelfth: hit the green. When his tee shot finished fifteen feet from the flag there was a kind of inevitability about Norman's seven iron

came at the sixteenth when Norman, understandably, felt the need to attack the flag, and pulled his six iron left into the lake.

It was all over except that Faldo still needed the composure to complete the victory in an atmosphere that was stunned rather than exultant. In his two previous victories he had been denied the privilege of completing his success in front of the galleries on the final green. He took the opportunity like a Champion, spurning the luxury of the three or four putts that would still give him a comfortable victory, but instead holing a fifteen footer across the green for an outstanding Champion's final round of sixty seven, a six shot deficit had been turned into an unbelievable five shot win.

The two players hugged, words were exchanged. There was much speculation as to what Faldo said to Norman at that moment; it turned out to be the less than memorable, 'I don't know what to say, don't let the bastards get you down over this.'

It was a genuine sentiment. Minutes later I was with Faldo in the Butler Cabin. Ben Crenshaw had just given him the Green Jacket, CBS had just come off the air, and it was a few seconds before we went live for the BBC. There was a brief moment to offer Nick my congratulations. 'Thanks,' he said, but he still looked distracted. 'I just hope Greg will be OK.'

Down the years Augusta had identified not only British golf's greatest player, but also one of British golf's nicest guys.

Nick Faldo salutes the crowd as he becomes Masters Champion 1996.

Faldo finally gets his victory on the 18th green, in front of the packed galleries.

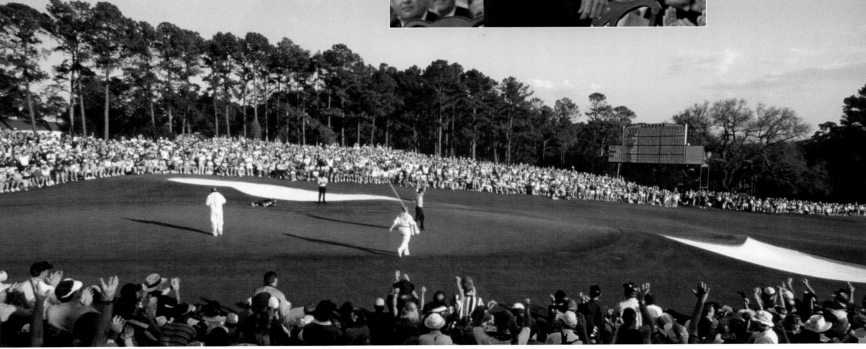

FAREWELL
TO AUGUSTA

The first time I had the opportunity to present Masters coverage for a British audience was 1982 for ITV, a time when satellite communications and technological support were not as sophisticated as they are today. Linking the programme from a London studio, a problem with the satellite booking meant that we lost all pictures and coverage from the course on the stroke of midnight.

This was at exactly the time that Craig Stadler was teeing off on the final hole, and he would eventually complete his victory by defeating Dan Pohl on the first hole of sudden death around thirty minutes later, by which time ITV had long gone. Unfortunately the absence of any kind of communications meant that we came off the air after filling for as long as we could, without knowing the outcome of the 1982 Masters. I remember that Ian Wooldridge wrote in the Daily Mail the following day that, 'ITV should never again be entrusted with a major sporting event.' It was not a great start to my association with The Masters.

So it is ironic that for me, twenty four years on, a return to ITV where, for the time being, I will concentrate on motor sport and Formula One, means that I will miss the opportunity to present a twenty fifth consecutive Masters this coming April. So while this final chapter was meant to be an anticipation of further European success at Augusta, it would be better as a final thank you to those who have given me particular support down the years.

Top of the list would be the seemingly unchanging staff and administration at the tournament, in particular general manager Jim Armstrong and Will Jones with his particular responsibility for the foreign broadcasters.

No event safeguards the quality and integrity of television coverage to quite the same degree as Augusta. The viewer benefits from the results every year, and the BBC gets a great deal of satisfaction from trying to push back the boundaries, with the approval of a rights holder who, you know, has watched every second of your transmission.

Secondly, particular thanks to Renton Laidlaw who helped me fill those agonising minutes in the London Weekend Studio in 1982 and also to BBC Head of Sport at that time, Jonathan Martin, who somehow saw potential in the panic-stricken presenter that night, and gave me a ticket to The Masters for the next quarter of a century.

Masters coverage moved from ITV to Channel Four and then on to BBC TV in 1986 and I was fortunate enough to move with it and work with producers and editors of great quality including Alistair Scott, John Shrewsbury and in latter years Paul Davies and Barbara Slater. It was the energy and insistence of Barbara that has helped expand the coverage, getting it up to around seven hours on the rain delayed final day in 2005, a large part of which was shoe-horned into the schedule at about an hour's notice.

Other excellent producers have helped put the BBC gloss on Masters coverage. Kate McKeag in particular has made sure that all the new technology has been used to its

Pictured here with me are the BBC team at the 1998 Masters.

maximum potential; as a result the days when European players were hardly seen in the coverage are long gone.

So much of the enjoyment of watching television coverage of The Masters is the scenic beauty combined with the knowledge of what has taken place there down the years. The producer on our team who has conveyed that to best effect is Jo McCusker who combined with brilliant VT editors Ross Archer and Lee Eynon to produce glorious award winning features and preview programmes that showed a great feel for history, location and atmosphere. This was precisely the kind of television that sets an event apart from the rest. Jo and her team have probably done more than anyone else to create the 'image' of Augusta in British viewers' minds.

I must not forget one particular American cameraman, HB Hough who has been virtually ever present in manning the BBC studio camera. He has been great company and I thank him for his patience, respect and constant good

manners as a succession of triumphant European heroes have been paraded before his lens through the last twenty years. Our ever present american technical assistant has been under similar pressures down the years and thanks should also go to our engineering chief Peter Wright, for making all this magnificent technology work. Also in the BBC studio in recent years floor manager Chris White has coped with every crisis that Augusta can provide from lightning and torrential storms to collapsing furniture and a badly parked sewage truck which was threatening to spoil our backdrop of Masters perfection. After all this he would further exceed his ill defined job description by cooking magnificently for around thirty people a night, helping to make sure that the BBC's week at The Masters was always special.

Hopefully The Masters will always be special for the BBC viewers. We all know the story of how a young Nick Faldo was inspired to try this strange sport by watching

Well... you can't have come here after all these years without having a go... can you?

I must also mention the late Dave Marr, a wonderful colleague with a fund of memories and stories and a way with words that was colourful homespun Texan. Dave was able to put current events in the context of his own memories of Hogan, Snead, Bobby Jones and the development of professional golf in America. He was a brilliant, economical commentator and an essential link with all the epic past events at Augusta.

More than anyone else, however, there has been Peter Alliss who has added the final gloss, humour and sense of occasion to everything that has happened over the past twenty years. In his kind introduction to this book he was keen to make the point that he has not been blind to what he feels are the occasional imperfections at Augusta either in course set-up, or the way the event is run. His thoughts have always been acknowledged with the greatest respect by all at Augusta; a measure of the reputation and standing of Peter Alliss in the game of golf.

If Peter comes to Augusta a little less starry eyed than the rest of us, it may be due to the travails he endured on the course in his competitive appearances there. However much he suffered at Augusta as a player he has more than made up for it as a commentator and there has been no-one more thrilled and excited by European success at Augusta than Peter.

So to the future, and Europe needs to start winning again at this great arena. Last year Luke Donald with his top three finish showed that the raw material is there for Europe to challenge again, and that challenge may yet come from any one of the new generation, or a back to form Colin Montgomerie or Darren Clarke who blows hot and cold around Augusta.

Good luck to them all, and good luck and thanks to the BBC team at Augusta, may they bring home many more European winners in years to come.

television coverage of Jack Nicklaus at Augusta, and we have been flattered that a number of Faldo's young successors have also acknowledged the impression that watching Sunday night at The Masters made on their development and interest in the game. Just this last year David Howell and Luke Donald both said that coming to be interviewed in the BBC Studio that they had seen so many times on TV was an integral part of their Masters experience.

Completing that experience are the outstanding commentators that BBC television has been blessed with through the Augusta years: notably Alex Hay and Bruce Critchley and especially Wayne Grady whose insights underline that The Masters is now established as the crown jewel of international golf, not merely golf in America. Together with Sam Torrance they have also added greatly to the very important social aspect of a week at The Masters.

EUROPE AT THE MASTERS YEAR BY YEAR

1934 WINNER Horton Smith 70, 72, 70, 72
Leading European C.T. Wilson 80, 83, 80, 79 59th

1935 WINNER Gene Sarazen 68, 71, 73, 70
Only European Harry Cooper 73, 76, 74, 74 25th

1936 WINNER Horton Smith 74, 71, 68, 72
Only European Harry Cooper 70, 69, 71, 76 2nd

1937 WINNER Byron Nelson 66, 72, 75, 70
Leading European Harry Cooper 73, 69, 71, 74 4th

1938 WINNER Henry Picard 71, 72, 72, 70
Leading European Harry Cooper 68, 77, 71, 71 2nd

1939 WINNER Ralph Guldahl 72, 68, 70, 69
Only European Harry Cooper 76, 77, 73, 78 T33

1940 WINNER Jimmy Demaret 67, 72, 70, 71
Only European Harry Cooper 69, 75, 73, 70 T4

1941 WINNER Craig Wood 66, 71, 71, 72
Only European Harry Cooper 72, 73, 75, 73 T14

1942 WINNER Byron Nelson 68, 67, 72, 73
Only European Harry Cooper 74, 72, 79, 74 T18

1946 WINNER Herman Keiser 69, 68, 71, 74
No European players

1947 WINNER Jimmy Demaret 69, 71, 70, 71
No European players

1948 WINNER Claude Harmon 70, 70, 69, 70
Only European Henry Cotton 72, 73, 75, 77 T25

1949 WINNER Sam Snead 73, 75, 67, 67
Only European John De Bendern (A) 81, 86, 81 (w/drew)

1950 WINNER Jimmy Demaret 70, 72, 72, 69
No European players

1951 WINNER Ben Hogan 70, 72, 70, 68
No European players

1952 WINNER Sam Snead 70, 67, 77, 72
Only European Albert Pelissier (Fr.) 78, 80 (w/drew)

1953 WINNER Ben Hogan 70, 69, 66, 69
Only European John De Bendern (A) 80, 77, 75, 80 61st

1954 WINNER Sam Snead 74, 73, 70, 72
No European players

1955 WINNER Cary Middlecoff 72, 65, 72, 70
No European players

1956 WINNER Jack Burke Jr. 72, 71, 75, 71
Only European Henry Cotton 77, 83, 81, 80 T68

1957 WINNER Doug Ford 72, 73, 72, 66
Only European Harry Weetman 79, 77 missed cut

1958 WINNER Arnold Palmer 70, 73, 68, 73
Leading European Flory Van Donck (Bel) 70, 74, 75, 79 T32

1959 WINNER Art Wall Jr 73, 74, 71, 66
Leading European Angel Miguel (Sp) 72, 72, 76, 74 T25

1960 WINNER Arnold Palmer 67, 73, 72, 70
Leading European Harry Weetman 70, 78, 74, 78 T34

1961 WINNER Gary Player (SA) 69, 68, 69, 74
Leading European Angel Miguel 75, 75 missed cut

1962 WINNER Arnold Palmer 70, 66, 69, 75
Leading European Gerry De Wit 76, 74 missed cut

1963 WINNER Jack Nicklaus 74, 66, 74, 72
Leading European Angel Miguel (Spain) 78, 79 missed cut

1964 WINNER Arnold Palmer 69, 68, 69, 70
Leading European Peter Butler 72, 72 69, 75

1965 WINNER Jack Nicklaus 67, 71, 6, 69
Leading European Ramón Sota (Spain) 71, 73, 70, 72 T6

1966 WINNER Jack Nicklaus 68, 76, 72, 72
Leading European Peter Butler 72, 71, 79, 73 T13

1967 WINNER Gay Brewer 73, 68, 72, 67
Leading European Tony Jacklin 71, 70, 74, 77 T16

1968 WINNER Bob Goalby 70, 70, 71, 66
Leading European Tony Jacklin 69, 73, 74, 72

1969 WINNER George Archer 67, 73, 69, 72
Leading European Roberto Bernardini (It) 76, 71, 72, 75 T29

1970 WINNER Billy Casper 72, 68, 68, 71
Leading European Tony Jacklin 73, 74, 70, 71 T12

1971 WINNER Charles Coody 66, 73, 70, 70
Leading European Tony Jacklin 73, 76, 76, 72 T36

1972 WINNER Jack Nicklaus 68, 71, 73, 74
Leading European Tony Jacklin 72, 76, 75, 74 T27

1973 WINNER Tommy Aaron 68, 73, 74, 68
Leading European Peter Oosterhuis 73, 70, 68, 74 T3

1974 WINNER Gary Player (SA) 71, 71, 66, 70
Leading European Maurice Bembridge 73, 74, 72, 64 T9

1975 WINNER Jack Nicklaus 68, 67, 73, 68
Leading European Maurice Bembridge 74, 72, 72, 73 T26

1976 WINNER Raymond Floyd 65, 66, 70, 70
Leading European Peter Oosterhuis 76, 74, 75, 68 T23

1977 WINNER Tom Watson 70, 69, 70, 67
Leading European Seve Ballesteros 74, 75, 70, 72 T33

1978 WINNER Gary Player (SA) 72, 72, 69, 64
Leading European Peter Oosterhuis 74, 70, 70, 71 T14

1979 WINNER Fuzzy Zoeller 70, 71, 69, 70
Leading European Seve Ballesteros 72, 68, 73, 74 T12

1980 WINNER Seve Ballesteros 66, 69, 68, 72
Next European Sandy Lyle 76, 70, 70, 78 48th

1981 WINNER Tom Watson 71, 68, 70, 71
Leading European Sandy Lyle 73, 70, 76, 73

1982 WINNER Craig Stadler 75, 69, 67, 73
Leading European Seve Ballesteros 73, 73, 68, 71

1983 WINNER Seve Ballesteros 68, 70, 73, 69
Leading European Nick Faldo 70, 70, 76, 76

1984 WINNER Ben Crenshaw 67, 72, 70, 68
Leading European Nick Faldo 70, 69, 70, 76 T15

1985 WINNER Bernhard Langer 72, 74, 68, 68
Next European Seve Ballesteros 72, 71, 71, 70 T2

1986 WINNER Jack Nicklaus 74, 71, 69, 65
Leading European Seve Ballesteros 71, 68, 72, 70 4th

1987 WINNER Larry Mize 70, 72, 72, 71
Leading European Seve Ballesteros 73, 71, 70, 71 T2nd
(after play-off with Mize and Norman)

1988 WINNER Sandy Lyle 71, 67, 72, 71
Next European Bernhard Langer 71, 72, 71, 73 T9

1989 WINNER Nick Faldo 68, 73, 77, 65
(after play-off with Hoch)
Next European Seve Ballesteros 71, 72, 73, 69 5th

1990 WINNER Nick Faldo 71, 72, 66, 69
(after play-off with Floyd)
Next European Seve Ballesteros 74, 73, 68, 71 T7

1991 WINNER Ian Woosnam 72, 66, 67, 72
Next European José Maria Olazábal 68, 71, 69, 70 2nd

1992 WINNER Fred Couples 69, 67, 69, 70
Best European Nick Faldo 71, 72, 68, 71 T13

1993 WINNER Bernhard Langer 68, 70, 69, 70
Next European José María Olazábal 70, 72, 74, 68 T7

1994 WINNER José María Olazábal 74, 67, 69, 69
Next European Seve Ballesteros 70, 76, 75, 71 T18

1995 WINNER Ben Crenshaw 70, 67, 69, 68
Best European José María Olazábal 66, 74, 72, 72 T14

1996 WINNER Nick Faldo 69, 67, 73, 67
Next European Ian Woosnam 72, 69, 73, 80 T29

1997 WINNER Tiger Woods 70, 66, 65, 69
Best European Costantino Rocca 71, 69, 70, 75 T5

1998 WINNER Mark O'Meara 74, 70, 68, 67
Best Europeans Darren Clarke 76, 73, 67, 69 T8
Colin Montgomerie 71, 75, 69, 70 T8

1999 WINNER José María Olazábal 70, 66, 73, 71
Next European Lee Westwood 75, 71, 68, 71 T6

2000 WINNER Vijay Singh (Fiji) 72, 67, 70, 69
Best Europeans Padraig Harrington 76, 69, 75, 71 T19
Colin Montgomerie 76, 69, 77, 69 T19

2001 WINNER Tiger Woods 70, 66, 68, 68
Best European Bernhard Langer 73, 69, 68, 69 T6

2002 WINNER Tiger Woods 70, 69, 66, 71
Best European José María Olazábal 70, 69, 71, 71

2003 WINNER Mike Weir (Canada) 70, 68, 75, 68
(after play-off with Mattiace)
Best European José María Olazábal 73, 71, 71, 73

2004 WINNER Phil Mickelson 72, 69, 69, 69
Best Europeans Bernhard Langer 71, 73, 69, 72 T4
Sergio García 72, 72, 75, 66 T4

2005 WINNER Tiger Woods 74, 66, 65, 71
(after play off with DiMarco)
Best European Luke Donald 68, 77, 69, 69 T3rd

IMAGES SUPPLIED COURTESY OF:

GETTY IMAGES
101 Bayham Street, London NW10AG

EMPICS
www.empics.com

PHIL SHELDON GOLF PICTURE LIBRARY
40 Manor Way, Barnet, Hertfordshire EN5 2JQ

DESIGN, ARTWORK & IMAGE RESEARCH:
Kevin Gardner

PROJECT EDITORS:
Vanessa Gardner, Jules Gammond & Tim Exell

SPECIAL THANKS:
Gill Sheldon and Jane Pamenter

WRITTEN BY:
Steve Rider

ACKNOWLEDGMENTS:

Thanks are due for their help in compiling this history to:

Peter Alliss, Maurice Bembridge, Sir Michael Bonallack, Ken Brown, Peter Butler, Peter McEvoy, Peter Oosterhuis,
Ken Schofield, plus all the European winners at Augusta and members of the European tour who have provided insights and
observations for me, recently and down the years.

Thanks also to Lizzie Hazlehurst and Peter Lewis at the British Golf Museum at St. Andrews and David Hill and all at the
R & A. Catherine Lewis was a great help at the Atlanta History Centre and so too the sports staff at the Augusta Chronicle.
At the Augusta National Robin S. Parker and Glenn Greenspan have provided useful contacts and information and I am
grateful to Tony Geer for trying to pursue some of the more elusive historical information.

BIBLIOGRAPHY:

Augusta. Home of The Masters Tournament, Steve Eubanks; Rutledge Hill. The Masters, Dick Schaap, Cassell,
The Best of Henry Longhurst, Collins; Getting to the Dance Floor, Al Barkow, Heinemann Kingswood;
This Game of Golf, Henry Cotton, Country Life; My Golfing Album, Henry Cotton, Country Life;
The Spirit of St. Andrews, Alister Mackenzie, Sleeping Bear Press; The World of Golf, BBC Publications;
The Shell International Encyclopaedia of Golf, Ebury Press/Pelham Books; The Making of The Masters, David Owen,
Simon & Schuster; Golf, Henry Longhurst, The Sportsmans Book Club;
Fun and Games with Alistair Cooke, Pavilion; A Round with Darwin, Souvenir Press; Peter Alliss, An Autobiography, Collins;
Every Idle Dream, Bernard Darwin, Collins; Not Only Golf, Pat Ward Thomas, Hodder and Stoughton;
Golf Architecture, Dr. A. Mackenzie, Classics of Golf; A Golf Story, Charles Price, Atheneum;
Seve: The Young Champion, Dudley Doust, Hodder and Stoughton; Seve, Lauren St. John, Partridge Press;
Tony Jacklin, The Price of Success, Liz Kahn, Hamlyn; Bernhard Langer, Hodder and Stoughton;
While the Iron is Hot, Bernhard Langer, Stanley Paul; The Golden Era of Golf, Al Barkow, Thomas Dunne Books, St. Martins
Press; Life With Lyle, Dave Musgrove with John Hopkins, Heinemann Kingswood; Nick Faldo, Life Swings, Headline;
Ian Woosnam, Collins Willow; Henry Longhurst, My Life and Soft Times, Cassell;
The Lay of The Land, Pat Ward Thomas, The Classics of Golf; Dick Miller, Triumphant Journey, Robert Hale;
plus numerous editions of The World of Professional Golf, Mark H McCormack's Golf Annual, Collins/Collins
Willow/Watchword/Springwood/Chapmans and IMG Publishing.

vintage
handbags

To Glenys Hollingsworth

Design and special photography
copyright © Carlton Books Limited 2009
Text © Marnie Fogg
Foreword © Anya Hindmarch

This edition published
by Carlton Books Limited
20 Mortimer Street
London W1T 3JW

10 9 8 7 6 5 4 3 2 1

ISBN 978 1 84732 300 2

Printed and bound in Dubai

Senior Executive Editor: Lisa Dyer
Managing Art Director: Lucy Coley
Designer: Barbara Zuñiga
Illustrations: Adam Wright
Copy Editors: Jenny McIntyre and Nicky Gyopari
Picture Researcher: Jenny Meredith
Production: Kate Pimm
Special Photography: Russell Porter

RIGHT Two elegantly
dressed women stroll
through the ornate gateway
of a large garden in 1960.
They wear coordinated
pale blue outfits, one in a
sleeveless dress and the
other in a dress suit, both
accessorized with gloves,
hats and handbags.

PAGE 4 American style in
the 1950s. A classic suit
by Alvin Handmacher,
with back-belted
jacket and straight
skirt, is accessorized
with a bamboo and
plastic handbag by the
Philadelphia company
Ingber in 1953. The felt
John-Frederics Charmer hat
is faced with leopard-print.

vintage handbags

Collecting and wearing
twentieth-century
designer handbags

Marnie Fogg

CARLTON
BOOKS

Contents

Foreword

'Why handbags?' This was what my parents asked me when I told them that I knew what I wanted to do, aged 18, rather than go to university, although I had really been designing handbags since I was four. I used to make them out of paper and sellotape and use them to compartmentalize and organize all my (at the time) very important things. I watch my daughter do the same. She puts all her little bits and bobs into small purses and drawers and boxes. I think it is a very 'girly' thing to want to do this and also to want to travel with all these important things with you. I hate the idea of being without something when I am out.

I also remember a defining moment for me, when my mother gave me one of her old Gucci handbags. I was 16 and I remember how this bag made me feel: glamorous and powerful and proud. I think the organizing and how a bag can make you feel are two things that still drive me when I design a bag today.

I think that fashion is a mixture of art (breaking new ground) and flattery/function. A design can work with just one of these aspects but if you can design something that has them all, then you have a real winner. In the early days, I used to make bags that were more about art… bags like little chests-of-drawers and

little evening bags hand-beaded to look like English sweet packets. As I developed my work, I tried to do new things, like working with Old English walking stick manufacturers to create handles but to use them with bags that were easy and light. I am obsessed with finding craftsmen who can do something interesting – with trades that are fading out. I once found a man in London who used to curl all the ceremonial feathers over a naked flame. I made many bags with these feathers and they gave me real pleasure.

I have always had an obsession with bespoke products. I hate the concept of an 'It' bag. I can't see anything luxurious or interesting about being on a waiting list for the same bag as everybody else. When I started my first little shop in Walton Street in Chelsea we offered services to have your monogram embroidered onto the bag, have a handle length to suit you, have your name and address embossed onto the leather, and so on. This is what still excites me as a customer. I used to make many bags for the Princess of Wales to match her outfits and I used to monogram them with a 'D'. She called them her cleavage bags, as she used them as a modesty shield when she got out of the car.

CLOCKWISE FROM FAR LEFT
Anya Hindmarch in her
design studio, a calfskin
Jackson bag, the Lautner
bag in naplak leather, the
Maud in monogrammed
satin and a green crocodile
Bespoke Ebury bag.

I love to give personalized gifts. These are the
pieces that you hand down to your grandchildren and
talk about for years. I think the Bespoke Ebury bag is
our best example of that. It is a handbag that I designed
when I was 20. I still love it and it is still one of our bestselling bags. Because it has your name embossed onto
the pocket, you will always know who it was made for,
and it then has a personal message from the donor in
that person's own handwriting, embossed inside the
bag onto the leather.

So the answer to 'Why handbags?' was simple for
me. It was because it has given me years of pleasure
and even now, I still get a buzz when I am alone in my
design room with a pencil and a blank piece of paper
– at the idea of creating something that can make your
heart skip when you take the tissue paper out and put
all your belongings inside!

Anya Hindmarch

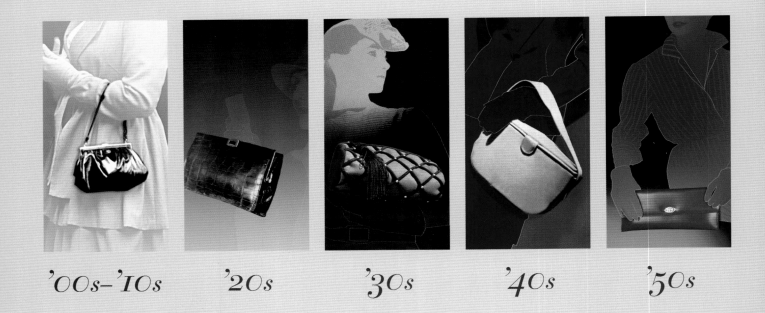

'00s–'10s   '20s   '30s   '40s   '50s

Introduction

A vintage handbag most thrillingly reveals the secrets of past lives. These reside in the lingering scent of patchouli from a 1960s psychedelic velvet tangerine leather bag by Pucci, or in the faded rose petals inside the pocket of a Jamin Puech wristlet. Every vintage bag has a story to tell.

Vintage handbags are the alternative to the homogenized high street and the latest 'It' bag. When brands get bland, sourcing something vintage is a way to develop a unique personal style that requires effort rather than money. Vintage bags are not marketed; there is no waiting list, no formula, and no magazines with lists of stockists. It is not a passive buying into of current trends but an opportunity to make an individual choice. Buying vintage is more than a reaction to design overkill and mainstream fashionability, it is a creative act.

Handbags are a vital accessory to every woman's life, but their practical purpose is secondary to what they say about the wearer's sense of style. Whether it's a classic Kate Spade, a conservative Coach or a freewheeling Falchi Buffalo slouch, the vintage bag represents the wearer's personality, not her bank balance. When cutting-edge fashion becomes available to all, and the time span between the designer handbag and the high street version in the shop becomes so compressed, the uniqueness and rarity of a vintage handbag makes it a desirable commodity.

This book starts with the birth of the bag, when the provenance of the handbag as we know it today lay in the craft of luggage-makers such as Prada and Louis Vuitton, and with the saddler's artisanal skills as in the case of Hermès and Gucci. As women became more independent and their lives less centred on the hearth and home, a handbag was an indispensable adjunct to a life in the outside world. It was a survival kit, a portable boudoir and a mobile office. The burgeoning need for this vital accessory meant that handbags began to be produced by a workforce of anonymous unnamed designers working for the handbag manufacturers. It was not until after the First World War, however, that handbags came into their own, and were subject to the whims of fashion.

'60s   '70s   '80s   '90s–'00s

Handbags then became a vital conduit of style, streamlined and modern in the 1920s, subject to Surrealist fantasies in the 1930s, utilitarian in the 1940s, ladylike in the 1950s and swung from the shoulder of every liberated woman in the 1960s and '70s. The excesses of the 1980s saw the emergence of label and logo mania, fuelled by the sexing up of the originally staid Chanel 2.55 'quilt and gilt bag' by Karl Lagerfeld, who took over as Chanel's design director in 1983. He exaggerated the interlocking double C logo and placed it where it couldn't be missed, on the front of the inflated oversized bag, which became part of the uniform for the newly emergent office glamazon. Handbags became big business, a commodity that drove the lucrative luxury goods market as well as financially upholding a couture label. The litany of must-haves that followed the 2.55 included the Lady Dior in 1994, the Vuitton Graffiti in 1999 and the Prada Bowling bag in 2000.

The celebrity-led frenzy for the latest 'It' bag is now on the wane. Conspicuous consumption is no longer fashionable, or even an option for many. There is now a return to favour of the bespoke, blue-chip classics such as the Kelly and the Birkin, bags that allow you to buy into the look of perennial style icons such as Audrey Hepburn or Grace Kelly. These bags are timeless, and will always hold their value. However, not every bag has to have an important label; there are many unsigned but interesting and good-quality bags of superior construction and materials available for those whose budget is limited. Better to buy good-quality vintage than modern mass-produced mediocrity. Buying a brand-new bag is like buying a brand-new car, on leaving the shop there is instant depreciation. Vintage bags don't date; they belong in the moment, representing the spirit of the age in which they were produced. Whether you prefer the geometric appliquéd colour of a Cubist-inspired clutch from the 1930s or the whimsical rhinestone-studded Lucite box bag of the 1950s, there is a vintage handbag out there waiting to be discovered by you!

1900–19:
The Birth of the Bag

The nine years during which Edward VII reigned in Britain (1901–10) are bathed in a golden glow of retrospective glamour. Caught between the restraints of Victorian society and the cataclysm of the First World War, members of the rich and privileged upper classes lived a life of extravagance and luxury, enjoying a hedonistic social round that included lavish weekend house parties and glittering society balls. It was a time of conspicuous consumption, not least in the fashions of the day. Consuelo Vanderbilt Balsan, who was Duchess of Marlborough during Edward's reign, wrote in her autobiography of the enormous demands made upon her wardrobe by a house party at Blenheim Palace:

> To begin with, even breakfast, which was served at 9.30 in the dining room, demanded an elegant costume of velvet or silk … We next changed into tweeds to join the guns for luncheon, which was served in the High Lodge or in a tent. An elaborate tea gown was donned for tea, after which we played cards or listened to a Viennese band or to the organ until time to dress for dinner, when again we adorned ourselves in satin, or brocade, with a great display of jewels. All these changes necessitated a tremendous outlay, since one was not supposed to wear the same gown twice. That meant sixteen dresses for four days.

Constrained in a corset that pushed out the bosom and flattened the stomach to produce the definitive S-shaped curve, and high lace collars boned or wired to keep the head upright, the upper-class Edwardian woman had little choice but to live a life of leisurely pursuits and negligible activity. Perceived as a symbol of her husband's financial and social status, clothed by couturiers such as Jacques Doucet and Jeanne Paquin, tended to by a lady's maid, and chauffeured from door to door, the highest demands on her time and expertise were merely to exercise choices of taste and recreation.

The Edwardian Lady

For the Edwardian lady, routines were serviced by an army of servants, both in the house and out in the world. Even the middle-class woman, whose role as 'angel of the house' was to oversee its upkeep and the welfare of its inhabitants, had servants for the everyday tasks of cleaning and cooking. Deliveries were made to the house by the local butcher and the greengrocer, so she rarely had to venture beyond the front door for anything other than pleasure, and she did not even need to carry house keys on these excursions, because a servant would always be at home to let her in.

When she did go forth, the ideal Edwardian female was clothed from head to toe, from the hat veil that covered her chin to the sweeping hem of her dress. The tightly draped flat front of the skirt around the corset allowed no room for pockets, so the ensemble required a simple receptacle for her journey's necessities, such as they were. When the well-to-do Edwardian woman ventured out of the house, she required very little to hand: visiting cards, a handkerchief, a small notebook and a pencil. These could easily be accommodated in a reticule, a small pouch-shaped bag fastened with a drawstring. Reticules initially referred to the small net bags carried by women in Roman times, the name derived from the Latin word *reticulum* (*rete* meaning

PAGE 10 Actress Estelle Winwood as she appeared in the play *Too Many Husbands* in 1919. She is wearing a crepe de chine dress with matching cape and carrying an embroidered cloth bag on a metal frame, a design developed from the eighteenth-century reticule.

LEFT The Edwardian woman required few necessities on her excursions away from the home. These comprised a small case containing visiting cards, a handkerchief and smelling salts, all carried in a bag similar to this beaded and tasselled Dorothy pouch from 1905.

RIGHT The chatelaine was the precursor of the handbag and attached to the woman's belt by a series of short chains. The bag was worn indoors and used for carrying household necessities such as needle and thread, scissors and keys. This one is from 1899.

OPPOSITE LEFT As the century progressed, the fashion silhouette became simpler, allowing for more ornate and complex bags, as with this embroidered and tasselled Dorothy bag, dating from 1917.

OPPOSITE RIGHT A cloth reticule dating from 1918 with beaded fringing is worn with the longer, leaner silhouette of 1918. The tubular dress, Louis heel boots with spats, and extravagant hat are typical daywear of the period.

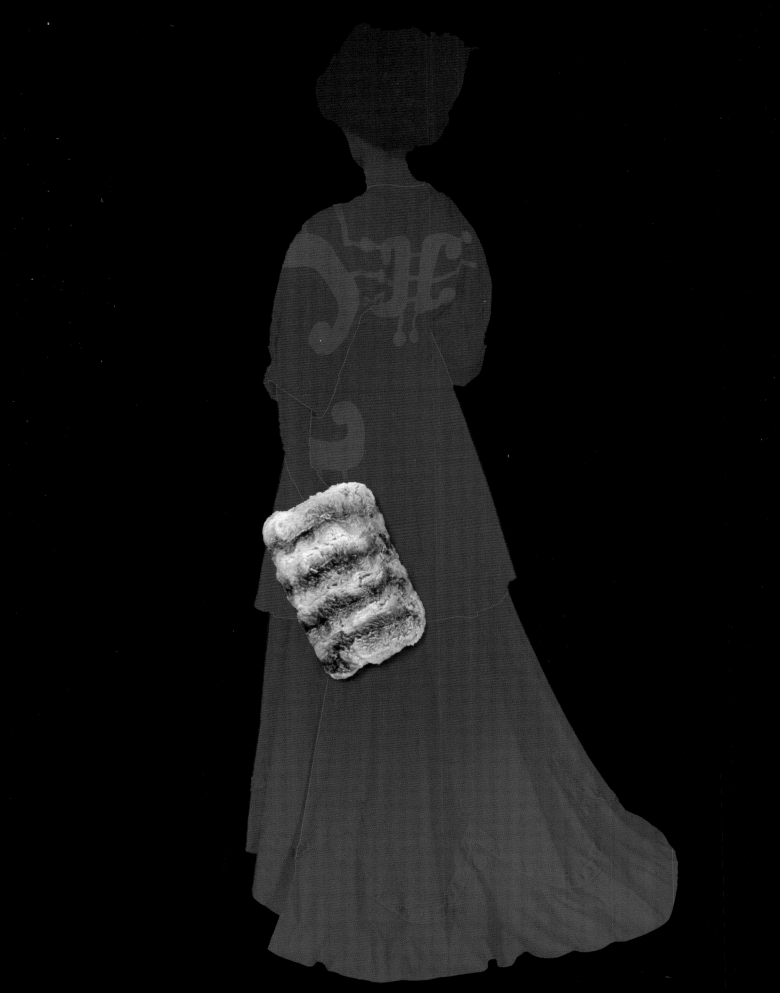

'net'). Heavily tasselled, beaded and embroidered, and made from materials very similar to those of her dress – such as satin and velvet, and in summer, lightweight muslins and lawn – the Edwardian woman's reticule hung from her wrist and accompanied her on afternoon visits and balls, and nights at the opera.

The Dorothy bag was used for more intimate occasions, such as at home in the drawing room or for evening wear. Made from a circle of dress fabric gathered together by a drawstring at the top to create a frilled opening, they were pretty concoctions of sequinned net with a lace insertion, decorated with beadwork or embroidered flowers. The bags were related in type and construction to the nineteenth-century needlework bag, and named after *Dorothy*, the eponymous heroine of A J Munby's play of the 1880s.

Fine sewing was a customary activity of the house-bound housewife, and this often included the making of a needlework bag, finished off with a pair of store-bought handles. However, the more complex and sophisticated needlework bags were manufactured in Austria, well known for the production of fine needlepoint and petit-point evening bags. Professional embroiderers would transfer images from classical paintings and prints onto a gauze backing by the means of a cardboard grid. More than 500 shades of silk thread and several thousand stitches per inch went into the making of the bag, which would then be attached to a jewelled or enamelled frame.

Equally minuscule mesh bags, constructed of circles like chainmail in silver or base metal, were also carried. During the winter, the all-purpose muff both protected the hands from the cold and served as a handbag of sorts, holding everything that might be put into a bag. With its origins in sixteenth-century Venice, the muff was generally made of fur, and had even been known to carry a small dog.

The period before the First World War was also the golden age of travel. With the introduction of the motor car, the expansion of the railways and the opening of the Cunard Line shipping company, the modern Grand Tour had never been easier. With summers in Biarritz or Deauville, autumn in New York and spring in Florence, the society year included travelling abroad for long periods, and this required fashionable luggage as well as fashionable clothes. Special trunks were needed, large enough to allow clothes to lie full length without creasing. Boxes were crafted for specific items such as hats, shoes and make-up. In an era of servants and porters, weight was not a consideration, and nor was space. It was from these products that the first true handbag was developed, created by leather goods companies such as Vuitton, Gucci and Prada (founded in 1913) and Hermès. Like miniature suitcases, these tiny leather handbags, often with silver corners and shaped handles, contained many compartments for specific items such as calling cards and notebook, and later, cigarettes and make-up.

OPPOSITE The muff was a roll of fur and served a dual purpose – it incorporated hidden compartments and kept hands warm. This version is French and dates from 1907.

BELOW LEFT The practical hard-framed handbag replaced the Dorothy bag and the reticule at the same time that the opportunities for social mobility of women increased. The influence of Art Nouveau can be seen in the patterning of the reinforced metal mounts on the corners of this crocodile-effect bag from France, dating from 1900.

BELOW RIGHT This 1910 leather opera bag by Lemière incorporates everything a woman needed for an evening at the opera: opera glasses, a fan, notebook and pen.

The Lean Silhouette

In 1909, the great Russian impresario Sergei Diaghilev brought the Ballets Russes to Paris and presented it to a startled and enraptured audience. With the dancers' exotic costumes and outrageous sets by Léon Bakst, the shock effect was instant. The ballet was seen as an instrument of change in all aspects of culture, from music and theatre to art, and its influence was seen in fashion with the work of French couturier Paul Poiret.

The Edwardian feminine ideal of bosomy curves swathed in pastels and delicate fabrics, and constrained by the tyrannous corset and boned collars, was suddenly out of date and old-fashioned. The longer, leaner silhouette by Poiret was the result of discarding the corset for garments that were cut to hang from the shoulders with a raised waist and a shorter skirt. He challenged the vision of the dainty, fragile Edwardian beauty with his loose Empire-line dresses, which were vibrant with colour and exotic patterning borrowed from other cultures: the Far and Middle East, India and Eastern Europe. He replaced mousseline and voile in sweet pea colours with embroidered velvets, silk and satin turbans, and richly woven jacquard fabrics and brocades in colours that shocked the world. Diana Vreeland, one-time editor of American *Vogue*, wrote of the influence of Diaghilev in her autobiography:

> The flavor, the extravagance, the allure, the excitement, the passion, the smash, the clash, the crash … this man smashed the atom … The colors! Before then, red had never been red and violet had never been violet. But these women's clothes in the Bois were of colors sharp as a knife: red red, violent violet, orange – when I say 'orange' I mean red orange, not yellow orange – jade green and cobalt blue. And the fabrics – the silks, the satins, the brocades, embroidered with seed pearls and braid, shot with silver and gold and trimmed with fur and lace – were of an Oriental splendor.

This dazzling new silhouette gave greater freedom of movement, and with different foundation garments came a different posture. The reticule was still used as the primary type of handbag, but it now had a curved jewel frame that hung from a long tasselled cord that swung from newly liberated shoulders. The design of the bag reflected the richly textured and decorated aesthetic of the clothes. The Liberty store in London's Regent Street began to sell 'Oriental' bags that were inspired by the colours and exoticism of Poiret. The fabric was gathered, ruched, tucked and pleated,

Les Sacs de Fourrures seront à la mode cet Hiver Ruge, 23 B^d Haussmann, en même temps que des modèles de fourrures en fait une Exposition du 5 au 8 Octobre et espère, Madame, recevoir votre visite.

THIS PAGE A 1910 advertisement for *'Ruge'* (fur) bags, replicating the style of the eighteenth-century reticule in shape and embellishment.

and patterned with embroidery, beading, fringing and tassels. Shapes, too, were more innovative, with deep ovals or long pointed triangles finishing with a tassel that swept to the ground.

Beaded Bags

The glass bead, a tiny molten drop of colour, has its origins in the skilled workshops of the Italian glass foundries. In the thirteenth century, the Venetians perfected the art of bead-making, their beads' tiny size, pure colour, transparency and perfection of shape being far superior to the Bohemian beads made in Czechoslovakia from the early 1800s to the 1920s. The latter, however, were larger and coarser, and more suitable for bold patterning than the Venetian glass beads, which were slightly iridescent. Beaded bags were imported from France, Germany and Czechoslovakia and featured designs based on Persian carpets or the curvilinear flowers and foliage of the Art Nouveau movement. In the 1920s, very expensive

'scenery' bags were inspired by Renaissance landscapes and fairy-tale castles.

Knitting with beads became popular at the beginning of the century. It was a time-consuming exercise, as more than 50,000 beads had to be strung in the correct order according to the pattern before the bag could be knitted. Commercially made bags realized a high price, though most knitted bags were constructed by housewives in the home. Patterns were sold in almanacs and women's magazines and featured romantic scenes such as temples, picturesque landscapes, floral designs and even hunting scenes. In the early decades of the twentieth century, the drawstring was replaced with decorative frames made of metal, tortoiseshell or plastic, and the design included Cubist and Art Deco motifs. Cut-steel beads, popular during the Victorian period in gold, silver and bronze, now came in a range of colours, though very few survive today owing to the weight of the cut steel. The best examples were made in France.

The New Seriousness

Edward VII died four years before the outbreak of the First World War, to be succeeded by his son, George V. George had none of his father's love of flamboyant society; his stalwart values, of duty before pleasure and a sense of responsibility, were appropriate for the sombre days that lay ahead.
The suffragettes had sewn the first seeds of feminism before the war, but it was only as the young men departed for the trenches of Flanders, many never to return, that women were not only allowed but encouraged to take their place in the workforce. Their jobs, as volunteer nurses, in the land army, in industry and at the munitions factories, meant that women were, for the first time, earning their own money.

After the First World War, having experienced the autonomy of the workplace, many women were no longer prepared to work in service to the aristocracy or to be content with merely running a household. The war had given even aristocratic women a taste of the satisfaction to be had in working outside the home, as they assisted the war effort with their previously untapped organizational skills they had accrued from running a large household. The increasing mechanization of cooking and housework also freed women to spend more time outside the home: going to work, lunching with friends, attending a matinee or visiting the local lending library.

Fashion responded to the practicalities and informality of women's new status. Women were literally much more visible on the city streets as hemlines rose, stockings became flesh-coloured and blouses were allowed to be open-necked. The tailor-made costume became the uniform of the modern woman, constructed in a sensible fabric, such as serge or tweed, or linen in summer, with a shorter, fuller skirt for ease of movement. This more utilitarian way of dressing required a more practical bag, and the long drawstrings of the Dorothy bag were shortened to accommodate its plumper, more commodious shape.

OPPOSITE The rigid Edwardian 'S' shape is relinquished in favour of a longer, looser silhouette as seen with these women strolling in the Bois de Bolougne, Paris, in 1912. The handbags, however, remain rooted in the past, with the soft folds of the reticule gathered into an embellished frame and clasp.

THIS PAGE Leather purses with handmade gilding crafted by the skilled artisans of the Wiener Werkstätte in 1911. The Institute was originally established by Josef Hoffmann and Koloman Moser in Austria in 1903 to produce artist-designed furniture and furnishings. Their remit came to include all aspects of the decorative arts, including fashion and textiles.

Bag Production and Retail

The beginning of the twentieth century saw an economy transformed by the mass manufacture and retailing of products, through industrial progress and invention. Mass-produced bags were created by leather goods manufacturers and not by couturiers. Saddlery skills were used on a diverse range of available skins: crocodile skin, snakeskin, glacé-grained kid leather, dyed and tooled leather, and reverse skins. Construction rather than ornamentation was the prevalent characteristic of the practical bag. Many of the early bag frames were made of 'German silver', an alloy of zinc, copper and nickel, which was more robust than pure silver.

The improved standard of living for the many rather than the few was a reflection of mass industrialization. It resulted in the rise of the American and European department store, from which these bags could also be purchased. Although stores had been established during the Victorian period (in London, John Lewis opened in 1864 and Liberty in 1875), it was only with women's greater social freedom and a more efficient transport system that, for the first time, shopping became a leisure activity, pursued for its own sake and out of want, not necessity. The first British *Vogue* appeared in 1916 (following the American edition, which first appeared in 1909) and added to the desire of the consumer to buy what was in its pages. Pioneers such as Gordon Selfridge added to the shopping experience with the introduction of musical performances and fashion shows, as well as incorporating restaurants, cafés and lavatories into the building when he opened his store in London in 1909. This meant that women could stay out longer without returning home to fulfil bodily needs.

A department store was a place of safety where a woman could meet friends, rest, repair her make-up, and survey a wealth of luxury commodities for herself and her home, as well as an opportunity to show off her latest purchases from previous visits. Thus, a practical handbag, usually unbranded and purchased from a specialist shop or department store, was required to carry whatever she needed to see her through the day. It was a useful addition to her collection of reticules, Dorothy bags and mesh bags, which continued to be used for evenings at the opera or for afternoon visiting.

LEFT A sturdy framed bag with a heavy metal clasp dating from 1910 from the Ledermuseum, Germany. The leather is tooled in a design depicting various styles of fan.

OPPOSITE The influence of the couturier Paul Poiret can be seen in the vibrant patterning and befurred figures of two women visiting a dress salon in 1917. The mesh bags they are carrying became an affordable accessory once A C Pratt's mesh machine was patented in 1908.

LEFT The ruched and folded design of this small bag is reflected in the loose drapes of this young French woman's outfit from 1915.

BELOW A leather handbag from the period 1900–20 in brown Moroccan leather with a metal frame, snap closure and decorative chain handle.

PARTS OF A HANDBAG

There are a number of components that make up a handbag, which can include the following:

★ **Outer covering:** this can be made of various materials, such as animal skins, straw, or some sort of durable fabric that may cover the frame or be used on bags without a frame.

★ **Frame:** a heavy-gauge steel or brass structure to give the bag its shape.

★ **Padding:** used to cover the hard edges of the frame and to protect the outer covering from the metal frame.

★ **Lining:** covers up the inside seams and frame of the bag, and is usually made of suede or leather, though cheaper bags will have fabric linings such as silk or rayon. The logo of the brand may well be woven into the fabric lining, and the interior of the bag may have the *griffe* or a designer label displayed.

★ **Interlining:** a stiffening product that provides additional support between the outer lining and the bag.

★ **Handle:** depending on the style, this is made of either the same material as the bag or a hard substance such as metal chain. The handle should be strong enough to support the bag.

★ **Fastenings:** devices used to close the bag may range from zips and buckles to clasps, depending on the style. They can be decorative, and may incorporate the brand logo.

★ **Gusset:** this provides expansion on the base and sides of the bag.

★ **Style details:** everything from novelties to luxurious decoration.

The Properties of Leather

The majority of handbags made throughout the twentieth century were of leather. The term 'leather' includes all of the processed skins and hides with the fur removed from land animals, reptiles, and fish, and from birds with their feathers removed. Generally, an animal skin is referred to as a 'hide' when it is derived from a larger animal, such as a cow, and as a 'skin' when it comes from a smaller animal, such as a sheep. The grain of the skin is the uppermost surface from which the hair grows, and this will have the characteristic markings of the animal. Layers beneath it are called splits and produce an inferior product. Leather is usually a by-product of the meat, dairy and wool industries, which is why bovine leather is one of the cheapest. Animals that are slaughtered specifically for their skins are more expensive. Vintage bags will have a *patina*, which is a result of the natural ageing and use of the bag and only enhances its desirability.

BELOW Women required their handbags to have volume and structure once they became more socially mobile. This Edwardian portmanteau in black leather is fastened with a square brass frame with a key lock and slide closure. The bag is lined in red Moroccan leather and has a small internal pocket. Good-quality bags always had studs on the base to protect the leather from wet or dirty surfaces.

LEFT The Gladstone bag, as it came to be known, was a small portmanteau constructed over a rigid frame, which could be separated into two equal sections. It was given its name after the British Prime Minister William E Gladstone (1809–98), who was noted for the amount of travelling he did. Although thought of as a British invention, it is actually based on earlier French models. This Edwardian black leather Gladstone has a single leather handle, a press closure with lock, and a brass pull tab on the frame.

Mesh Bags

The mesh bag, in spite of its military origins and metallic substance, has a fluidity, drape and soft handle that come from its basically knitted construction. Whiting & Davis, who are most closely associated with the design and manufacture of the mesh bag, are still in business today. The company originated in 1876 in Plainville, Massachusetts, when William H Wade and Edward P Davis founded the Wade Davis Company to manufacture small items of jewellery. Charles A Whiting joined the company in 1892, and it was he who was responsible for the design and development of the first mesh handbag.

Mesh had previously been used for military purposes, with chainmail mesh being the obvious example: the metal rings provided some protection from the piercing thrusts of knives and swords in hand-to-hand combat. During the eighteenth century, the technique was appropriated for gun-metal mesh purses, but it was only with the patenting of an automatic mesh-making machine, invented in 1909 by A C Pratt, that mesh purses achieved their highly visible ubiquity. Prior to this invention, mesh assembly was laborious as each completed mesh bag could contain up to 100,000 links, individually wound, split and then joined by hand.

Once the patent had been acquired by Whiting & Davis, mesh bag production combined quantity with quality. The machine process could join together 400 mesh rings per minute. The first stage of the process cut the wire to the length required for the ring, then these pieces were individually knitted into the mesh fabric, which was then hand cut, split and sized. A total of 24 hand operations were also required in the finishing process, including attaching the mesh to the frame, and adding the lining material.

The earliest Whiting & Davis mesh bags were made of ring mesh in gold or sterling silver wire; soldered ring mesh was the most expensive as every join was soldered by hand. With the onset of mass production, cheaper alternatives were used: silver plate, gold plate, platinum plate, gun metal, nickel-plated brass, copper and vermeil (gold plate over sterling silver). Baby-ring mesh appeared when Dresden, a German mesh-maker, developed an extremely fine ring mesh using early A C Pratt patents. The company co-opted the techniques and, in 1918, began offering the Whiting & Davis line of 'Dresden' mesh.

BURKHARDT & CIE., PFORZHEIM.

OPPOSITE ABOVE Mesh bags sustained their popularity for more than a century from the initial handcrafted bags of the 1820s to the machine-made bags of Whiting & Davis, who continue their production to the present day. This example of a chain purse set with semiprecious stones is dated 1908, and from Moscow.

OPPOSITE BELOW A Viennese mesh bag with a decorative edge and embellished clasp, dating from the early twentieth century.

RIGHT The German firm Burkhardt & Company made this luxurious mesh bag with a jewelled clasp of semiprecious stones in 1906. The bag is presented in the advert as a piece of fine jewellery.

Louis Vuitton Luggage

A name now synonymous with the luxury goods market and the high-profile fashion label, Louis Vuitton began his career as a box maker and an apprentice layetier, or luggage packer, to prominent households. The term *layetier* is derived from 'thin layer', describing a small trunk where valuable jewels or documents were preserved, and it came to be synonymous with the process of packing. However, the packer did not merely put items into cases; he actually measured the dimensions of everything to be transported before creating the cases or boxes, and choosing the appropriate filling to put between the layers, to keep clothes dry and protected, for instance. Vuitton's expertise at these tasks soon earned him an appointment as layetier to Empress Eugénie de Montijo, the wife of Napoleon III of France, propelling him into the service of the European *haut monde*.

Vuitton opened his own store in 1854, the Maison Louis Vuitton on the rue Neuve-des-Capucines in Paris, where he began to design his own luggage. His first innovation was the flat-topped trunk to replace the round-topped trunks known as humpback or camelback trunks, which had been constructed to allow water to run down the sides. Water penetration was not a concern with the Vuitton design; he added canvas to the outside of the wooden trunk, which was then coated with shellac to protect the wood and render it waterproof. Staves, trim and hardware were then added. Round-topped trunks had also been used as furniture; in contrast, the new flat trunk was unequivocally a piece of luggage, designed for easier stacking and mobility, and it was the foundation for Louis Vuitton's success.

Vuitton's reputation was such that many other luggage-makers began to copy his design; in 1888, the Damier Canvas chessboard (checkerboard) pattern (which was reintroduced in 1996) was created by Vuitton bearing a logo that read '*marque L Vuitton déposée*' or 'L Vuitton trademark'. In 1892, Louis Vuitton died and the company's management passed on to his son George. In 1896, the legendary Monogram Canvas was launched, and is still familiar today. It consisted of the intersecting LV initials, and a curved beige diamond with quatrefoils and its negative, a beige circle with a four-leafed flower inset. In 1901, the Steamer bag was introduced. The forerunner of the soft bags, it was a smaller piece of luggage designed to be rolled up and kept inside the Vuitton luggage trunks. Its tiny handle was designed to hang on the back of a cabin door as a sort of laundry bag.

In 1914, the Louis Vuitton building opened on the Champs Élysées, the largest travel goods store in the world at the time. Other stores opened in Bombay,

ABOVE At the turn of the twentieth century, transatlantic travel proved popular among the upper classes of Europe and America. In 1901 Louis Vuitton created the Steamer bag and cabin trunk in their distinctive monogrammed canvas, which were designed to fit neatly under the beds on board.

RIGHT An advertisement for a collection of Louis Vuitton luggage on the inside cover of a book entitled *Folie en Fleurs*, presented by M Paul Derval. The insouciance of the model's wave conveys the effortless ease of travel once supplied with enough of the right suitcases and trunks.

Washington, Alexandria and Buenos Aires. In 1885, the company opened its first store in London's Oxford Street. The Vuitton Company produced the Valise bag in 1923, followed by the Car bag in 1925. Throughout the twentieth century, the company produced many distinguished and memorable bags such as the Keepall in 1930, the forerunner of weekend totes, and the Noe bag, created in 1932 and originally designed to hold five bottles of champagne (four in a circle and one placed upside down between the others).

The Hermès Saddlery

The bespoke craft skills of saddle-makers are naturally affiliated to the making of fine handbags. The French couture house Hermès elevated these artisan skills to high art, producing coveted bags of an iconic status and hand-stitched perfection throughout the twentieth century in their Parisian atelier. One of the oldest family-owned and -controlled companies in France, it was established in 1837 by Thierry Hermès, who opened a workshop in the Grands Boulevards quarter of Paris supplying horse harnesses for carriages. It was a business founded on the principles of excellent craftsmanship, particularly in the execution of the saddle stitch, a process whereby two needles worked two waxed linen threads in tensile opposition.

Thierry's son, Charles-Émile, moved the company to their current home at 24, rue du Faubourg Saint-Honoré, where he began retailing saddlery. With a global reputation for excellence, in 1892, the company offered the Haut à Courroies (literally 'High Belts') bag especially designed to transport riding gear: saddle, boots and hunting equipment. The dynasty continued as Adolphe and Émile-Maurice, grandsons of the original Hermès, renamed the company Hermès Frères. At the turn of the century, the horse gave way to the automobile as the major means of transport, and Émile-Maurice anticipated that the company would need to diversify from its equestrian roots, a conviction that was reinforced by a meeting with Henry Ford on a visit to the United States.

While in Canada, Émile-Maurice foresaw the potential of a kind of zip used on the canvas roof of cars, and obtained an exclusive two-year European patent on its use. The 'Hermès fastener' revolutionized clothing design and appeared on their first leather garment, a zipped golf jacket for the Prince of Wales. In 1922, the first leather handbags were introduced at the request of Émile-Maurice's wife, and in 1923, the Bolide bag (initially called the Bugatti bag after the racing car) was the first in history to feature a zip.

In 1930, the Plume appeared, a more practical and pliable version of the horse blanket bag and the first that could double as both a day bag and an overnight tote. The saddle bag, the 'little tall bag with two handles' from 1892, was redesigned as a handbag in 1935, and was eventually named the Kelly when Grace Kelly appeared with it on her arm in a photograph on the cover of *Time* magazine in 1956 (see also pages 102–3). In 1958, a bucket-shaped feed bag with a gusset and a narrow strap, christened the Trim, was popularized by Jackie Onassis on her much-publicized sojourn on Capri in the late 1960s, and the Birkin bag was introduced in 1984. The basic style of these four bags has underpinned the design of the modern classic handbag.

▶ Fabric evening bags
Here an evening bag of furnishing damask in purple is edged with metallic gold braid with a matching handle. The bag is trimmed with four netted gold tassels, and contains a small internal coin purse attached with a gold cord.

▶ Tooled leather
The Arts and Crafts Movement wa born out of a reaction against the mass industrialization of the Victor era. This hand-tooled bag dates f the turn of the twentieth century ar an example of the beauty inherent the craft-made object.

Key looks of the decades
1900– 19

▼ The Dorothy bag
A Dorothy bag is one gathered into drawstring at the top. This 1900–10 bag is richly embellished with glass beads, the upper section having ro on an off-white bead ground, the lo section with multicoloured flowers a bright blue ground. The cream si cord handles are attached to two ri on each side of an expanding meta trellis opening.

◀ Beads and chains
Beaded bags were often imported from Czechoslovakia, France, and Germany. Here a black silk bag from 1901–8 is embellished with an all-over design in glass beads depicting stylized pink flowers and leaves. The frame is black plastic and the single chain handle is of the same material.

▼ **Tapestry and needlework**

A woven tapestry bag dating from 1910–20 in a stylized floral design within a geometric grid, redolent of a Turkish carpet design. The bag has a faux tortoiseshell frame. The narrow strap is constructed from a matching tapestry, and the bag is lined with peach ribbed moiré.

▲ **Fur muffs**

A practical and popular alternative to the handbag in the winter months was the fur muff, which could vary in size. This muff, dating from 1914, is large enough to incorporate internal pockets to hold daily necessities.

1920s:
Movement and Modernism

The 1920s were all about movement, from the flying fringes of the Charleston dress to the streamlined silhouette of the new automobiles; both were symbols of the new modernity that came to define the age and signified a break from the past.

Handbags reflected this desire for the new and the modern. The drawstring bag, drooping from a languid wrist, was finally out of style, and the emergence of the clutch propelled the handbag towards the future. Made of Bakelite and Perspex, in the clashing colours and vibrant patterns of the Art Deco movement and the decade's obsession with all things Egyptian, the clutch represented the aesthetic preoccupations of the age.

Aspects of modernism had existed since 1914, in Cubism, Expressionism, Futurism, and abstraction in painting, but it was not until after the war that modernism made its mark on everyday life, from Marcel Breuer's tubular chair, designed in 1925, to the architecture of the Bauhaus, founded in 1919. The post-war world had seen a seismic shift away from the discredited attitudes, hierarchies and prejudices of the prewar world. Manifestos of cultural revolution appeared; the arts influenced fashion and the avant-garde became mainstream. With the advent of modernism, the twentieth century was about to really begin.

Just as stuffy, heavily decorated Victorian interiors and restrictive corsets were rejected, so, too, was the impractical reticule with its dainty flounces and drawstring opening. This was the era when bags became a vital fashion accessory to a total look, rather than merely a useful adjunct. The new bags were streamlined exercises in restraint when decoration was perceived as 'feminine' and trivial, an attitude influenced by the writings of the Austrian architect Adolf Loos. 'Freedom from ornament is a sign of spiritual strength,' he wrote in his defining essay 'Ornament and Crime' in 1908, and he anticipated that with female economic independence, 'velvet and silk, flowers and ribbons, feathers and paint will fail to have their effect.' Certainly, there was an element of androgyny about the rangy, elongated silhouette of a new phenomenon, the 1920s flapper girl.

THIS PAGE The neat cloche hat, a popular style of the 1920s, frames a face of immaculate maquillage, reflected in the vanity mirror attached to a hard-framed handbag from 1924.

Flapper Style

In her short skirts and skimpy tubular dresses with only a flimsy combination of camisole and knickers, known as camiknickers, replacing the whalebone corsets, her breasts flattened and concealed, the flapper represented freedom from all the constraints of the previous century. No lady's maid was required to dress hair that was newly shingled or cropped into an Eton bob. The close-fitting cloche hat replaced towering confections of tulle and flowers, and no reticule dangled from her wrist; rather, a clutch bag was securely tucked between her upper arm and body, or carried in the hand to be opened with a decisive snap as she reached for her lipstick or powder.

The clean, pared-down silhouette of the body was also reflected in the simplicity of the face; the plucked, high-arched eyebrows, almond-shaped eyes, the small rosebud mouth and the flat, head-hugging shingle bob all reflected the influence of the Romanian sculptor Brancusi, whose works included 'Sleeping Muse'. This visage appeared repeatedly on the cover of *Vogue* throughout the decade, illustrated by great artists such as Georges Barbier, Georges Lepape and Benito.

Known collectively as the 'bright young things', this new generation of women was perceived as decadent and hedonistic, pursuing pleasure with a single-mindedness that went hand in hand with social emancipation. The flapper embodied the spirit of the Jazz Age and moved to the syncopated, rhythmic dance music that originated in black America and was yet another symbol of modernity. When hemlines are raised, the waistline changes; in 1925 it dropped to below the hips. This streamlined style gave the flapper the freedom of movement to embrace her partner for the Turkey Trot or to enjoy the uninhibited Charleston, a show dance first performed by the Ziegfeld Follies in 1923. As the flapper frolicked energetically around the dance floor, her bag had to fulfil certain requirements. It needed a secure clasp, and to be lightweight and small, often no more than palm-sized, as she needed to be able to grasp it securely. For this reason, the tango purse was sometimes fitted with finger rings or lengths of cord that could be wrapped around the wrist. The wit and poet Dorothy Parker, commenting on the new generation's provocative attitudes, wrote in her poem 'The Flapper':

The playful flapper here we see,
The fairest of the fair.
She's not what Grandma used to be,—
You might say, au contraire.
Her girlish ways may make a stir,
Her manners cause a scene,
But there is no more harm in her
Than in a submarine.

PAGE 30 In the fashions of the 1920s, the simplicity of cut that allowed ease of movement required simple, streamlined accessories, as in this envelope clutch. Muriel Finley models a crepe de chine dress and matching hat, both by Parisian couturier Lanvin. The understated jewellery is a pin by Black, Starr and Frost.

ABOVE During the 1920s hemlines reached unprecedented heights, heels got higher and bags got smaller. Laura La Plante, the blonde leading lady of Universal Studios, is standing with her sister, Violet, in a photograph taken in 1928; the bag takes centre stage.

ABOVE American film star Joan Crawford in a publicity shot at the beginning of her long career. The original caption reads: 'Joan Crawford, the lovely Metro Goldwyn Mayer player has at last found a very handy device for carrying one's lipstick and perfume vial without losing or breaking them. The handle of her purse is a hollow tube into one end of which the lipstick is held and in the other the perfume vial.'

BELOW As it became increasingly acceptable for women to apply cosmetics in public, the handbag was replaced by the vanity case. Like its counterpart, the powder compact, it was richly embellished. This one by Lacloche Frères, 1926, is gold, with black jadeite and black-backed chalcedony; the lid is set with diamonds, lapis lazuli, turquoise, malachite, rhodonite, mother-of-pearl and pearl.

RIGHT Founded in 1781 as a silk-printing business, Asprey moved to their current premises in New Bond Street, London, in 1847. An early speciality was dressing cases, creating portable designs suitable for the new style of travel. This advertisement for new wares, such as the Mulberry crocodile pochette and a flat-based handbag, appeared in *Tatler* magazine in 1926.

Vanity Cases

The use of cosmetics was perceived as dangerously provocative; 'decent' women wore no make-up, and even dabbing the nose with a French device called a *poudre-papier* was done surreptitiously by Edwardian matrons. In contrast, the flapper brazenly outlined her lips in public and rouged even her earlobes. This daily maquillage required constant refreshment, and handbags took over the role of vanity cases to transport powder, rouge, lipstick and perfume. The shape of the vanity case was attributed to the Japanese *inro*, a small box with compartments for medicinal herbs and perfumed water. Exclusive vanity cases were made by jewellers such as Cartier and Van Cleef & Arpels in silver or gold, enamel, mother of pearl, jade and lapis lazuli. Cheaper versions were made from coloured plastic and decorated with glass stones. Miniature vanity cases often had mini lipstick containers that swung on a length of tassel or were fixed to a Bakelite bangle worn on the lower arm.

The mesh bag manufacturers Whiting & Davis produced vanity or 'function' bags of a dazzling complexity, including the amphora-shaped Delysia, in which the powder puff, rouge puff and mirror were carried in the central hinged section, while the mesh pockets and top and bottom of the bag provided storage. A centre-mounted top strap and an elaborate hanging tassel completed the design, which at that time retailed at $500.

A further novelty was added to the vanity case when the British company Dunhill produced the Lytup bag, which lit up on opening. According to *Tatler* magazine in May 1922, it was 'invaluable in a taxi, or wherever the lights were dim'.

ASPREY
BOND STREET,
LONDON.

Bronze and Gilt Metal
Cartridge Placefinder.
1 . 10 . 0

Metal-gilt 8-day Clock, with
hand-painted Ivory Dial.
Size 4 inches square.
9 . 10 . 0

Shagreen Hair Brush, with Ivory Comb.
3 . 7 . 6

Gold ½ - Hunter
Watch, in Patent
Swing Opening
Dustproof case.
12 . 10 . 0

Combined Vanity and Cigarette
Case, with Silver-gilt and
Glass Fittings.
7 . 17 . 6

Revolving
Mahogany
Poker Chip
Stand.
Fitted with
Paranoid
Chips.
Small
9 . 0 . 0
Large
10 . 15 . 0

Race
Companion,
Silver-gilt mounts.
Crocodile, 7 . 12 . 6
Pigskin, 6 . 5 . 0

Silver-gilt and Enamel 8-day Minute
Repeating Clock.
Size 3½ × 2⅝ × 1½ ins.   28 . 10 . 0

Hide Leather
Flat base Handbag.
Size 9 × 6 ins.,   2 . 17 . 6
In various colours.

Mulberry Crocodile Handbag Pochette
Size 8 × 5¾ ins.   6 . 0 . 0

Combined Vanity and Jewel Case,
with Enamelled Silver-gilt Fittings.
13 . 17 . 6

SUITABLE
CHRISTMAS
PRESENTS.

WRITE FOR
CATALOGUE.

Shagreen
Cigarette Box, Ivory
angled, elevator action.
From 3 . 12 . 6

Crocodile Attaché
Case.
From 10 . 5 . 0

Style Influences

Dresses that were mere slips of fabric, in a neutral palette of various shades of shimmering pastels, were the perfect backdrop for the dramatic accessory. Boldly abstract jewellery, long cigarette holders, fans, feather boas and the clutch bag all brought fashion to life. The clutch bag was the ideal canvas on which to showcase the decorative styles of the decade; its streamlined modernism made other bags appear over-designed and fussy. Fashioned from new materials such as Bakelite and Perspex, the long narrow rectangular shape had softened corners, replicating the aerodynamic design of the age of speed.

As the decade progressed, the clutch bag evolved into the 'pochette'. While still retaining the rectangular shape of the clutch, some now had the addition of a small handle at the top or back, through which the fingers could slip. Others closed with an envelope flap, either angled to one side or covering the whole bag, which provided a perfect space for the fractional, faceted shapes and sweeping curves of the Cubist-inspired Art Deco movement.

The Art Deco style began in Europe in the early years of the twentieth century, though it was not universally popular until the 1925 Exposition Internationale des Arts Décoratifs et Industriels Modernes (International Exposition of Modern Industrial and Decorative Arts), and fell out of favour in the late 1930s and 1940s. It was a confluence of many trends, from the arts of Africa, Egypt and Mexico to the streamlined technology and materials of the 'speed age' – from modern aviation and the growing ubiquity of the motorcar. These design influences were expressed in the fractional forms of Cubism and Futurism. The popular motifs of the period – stepped forms, sun-ray motifs, chevron patterns and zigzags – were easily translated into leather, suede or embroidered and appliquéd fabric designs. Exotic materials, such as sharkskin (shagreen) and zebraskin were also favoured.

The discovery of Tutankhamun's tomb in 1922 provoked a craze for ancient Egyptian styles of ornament that endured well into the 1930s. It was an event that held a fascination with the public, fuelled by newsreel footage of archaeological digs and press reports. Howard Carter's remark on peering into the tomb for the first time, that he could see 'marvellous things', heralded an obsession with all things Egyptian, from scarabs, snakes and pyramids to hieroglyphs and sphinxes. The French jeweller Cartier relished the opportunity for Art Deco decadence, with their handbag clasps of pavé diamonds, lapis lazuli and gold scarabs mounted on plain black bags.

OPPOSITE A gold felt bag with hieroglyphic motifs from 1920. A craze for Egyptian-style ornamentation was a feature that carried on into the 1930s. It was sparked by the excavations into the pharaohs' tombs, particularly Tutankhamun's in 1922.

TOP The simplicity of shape of these two rectangular embroidered purses by the Austrian Hilde Wagner-Ascher in 1925 makes them a perfect canvas to express the geometric forms and patterning of modern art.

ABOVE Animal skins, such as the snakeskin used to make up this afternoon bag, were popular during the 1920s. The size and scale of the skin is perfectly balanced against the finesse of the chain and the cornelian clasp.

Art and the Artisan

The applied arts flourished in the late nineteenth century and first decades of the twentieth century. The Wiener Werkstätte, the Vienna Workshop of 1903–32, was a huge influence on pattern design during this period. With its roots in the Arts and Crafts Movement, the studio progressed from producing exclusive furnishing fabrics to gradually introducing a broader range of products, including bags. Usually created from dark hand-crafted leather with gold tooled patterns, their designs eventually shifted away from the curvilinear forms of Art Nouveau to embrace the more formal stylization of Art Deco, described in embossed and coloured leathers.

Fashion and art were inextricably linked for the Ukrainian artist Sonia Delauney. Together with her husband, Robert Delauney, she was a significant pioneer of abstraction. Through her 'colour rhythm' paintings, first shown in 1921, the artist endeavoured to provoke a simultaneous response to form, colour and movement. She produced 'simultaneous' dresses printed with patterns of loosely painted geometric blocks of contrasting colours, which she described as 'colour scales'. In 1927, Sonia Delauney spoke of 'The Influence of Painting on the Art of Clothes' at the Sorbonne in Paris:

> *A movement is now influencing fashion, just as it influences interior decoration, the cinema, and all the visual arts … we are only at the beginning of the study of these new colour relationships, still full of mystery to unravel, which are at the base of a modern vision.*

The angular abstraction and solid blocks of colour of her work provided an ideal way to decorate the flat planes and angles of a clutch bag: it was a perfect synthesis of form and decoration, and it was perfectly in tune with the era.

A more spontaneous approach to colour was to be found in the work of the avant-garde artists of the time, including a group of French painters called the Fauves ('Wild Beasts'), known for their uncontrolled use of violent, brilliant colour. One of these artists, Raoul Dufy, was introduced to a career in textile design by the couturier Paul Poiret, and from 1912 to 1928, he created more than 2,000 textile designs for the French silk-weaving company Bianchini-Férier. Dufy's strong graphic style, which was evidence of his earlier practice of wood engraving, encompassed a wide range of design genres including narrative, figurative and abstract. His textiles found their way into handbags that had a particular appeal to the 1930s bohemian set.

BELOW Intimations of the Art Deco movement in this green tooled-leather handbag from 1929.

ABOVE 'Fine art' bags with subjects such as romantic rural landscapes in woven tapestry panels were attractive to the Bohemian, together with craft-based jewellery and beaded and embroidered garments, as seen in the two women modelling drop-waisted dresses and suits in 1924.

RIGHT An advertisement for Asprey handbags that appeared in *Tatler* magazine in 1926. It features popular styles of the day, including Aubusson tapestry pieces depicting floral arrangements and scenes, a black embroidered silk purse, a leather bag with marcasite and onyx mount and one with a green enamel mount.

Black Silk Embroidered
1. 1. O.

8. 15. O.

Morocco Leather Pochette-Handbag
in all colours. Regd. design 1. 1. O.

7. 15. O.

5. 7. 6.

9. 5. O.

7. 15. O.

Aubusson Tapestry
can be obtained only at Asprey's
12. 12. O.

6. 15. O.

Bead purse
16. 6.

Petit-Point Silver Frame
18. 12. 6.

Steel beads with
any colour border
1. 5. O.

Hide Leather all colours
2. 17. 6.

Embroidered Pochette
4. 17. 6.

Marcassite and Onyx Mounts
15. 5. O.

Hide "Rip" Handbag all colours
Ripped open in a moment. 2. 9. 6.

WRITE FOR CATALOGUE

Green Enamel Mounts
4. 7. 6.

Coco Chanel

The understated clothes of the Parisian couturier Coco Chanel (1883–1971) revolutionized modern 1920s fashion. The inventor of the little black dress, she also brought a new, relaxed elegance to informal clothes. Influenced by the sporting garb of her aristocratic English lover, the Duke of Westminster, she popularized the cardigan and the use of wool jersey in a subtle colour palette of navy, taupe and cream, and introduced trousers into her collections. This relaxed, informal approach to fashion also applied to the handbag. She reportedly told her friend Claude Delay that because she was 'sick and tired of holding my handbags and losing them, I stuck a strap on them and wore them across my shoulder'. She was inspired by the military satchel to produce a version of the shoulder bag. Her first styles in 1929 were made from black or navy jersey, and lined in red or blue grosgrain.

This design evolved into one of the most significant fashion items of the twentieth century, the 2.55 bag, named for the month and the year of its creation, and requiring 180 different processes in its manufacture (see also pages 100–1). Inspired by the checked shirts of racetrack stable boys, the quilted jersey or leather bag hung from a long gold chain interlaced with leather, and featured a rectangular gold-plated lock. The interlocked-Cs logo was stitched onto the lining. Three flap pockets made up its solid, rectangular shape: the first in the shape of a tube for lipstick, the second zipped and the third for papers and letters.

During the 1920s, Coco Chanel was one of the first couturiers to realize the potential of accessories as a way to increase sales, and opened a boutique in her Paris salon dedicated to accessories and jewellery. Couturiers such as Jean Patou, Jeanne Lanvin and Mainbocher, while not specializing in handbag design, added to the total look of an outfit by designing matching clutches.

RIGHT Versions of the most iconic bag ever, the Chanel 2.55, so named for the month and year of its inception. The 2.55 had its provenance in the quilted jersey shoulder bag that was inspired by the military satchel of the First World War, which Chanel first devised in 1929.

OPPOSITE French couturier Coco Chanel revolutionized women's dress with the introduction of easy tailoring and knitted jersey separates that acknowledged the importance of healthy pursuits such as sea bathing and sport, activities previously confined to men. For the first time it was fashionable to have a suntan and pursue outdoor activities such as golf. Here golfing accessories, including a black-and-white plaid golf bag and a small 'zipper' bag to match, dating from 1929.

RIGHT Dressing the modern woman. At last freed from the corset and the hobble skirt Chanel designed clothes in 1929 of wearable simplicity to a formula that has contemporary resonances in the simple edge-to-edge jacket and knee-length skirt. The handbag seen here is equally timeless.

New Materials and Technology

The machine age brought innovation and the invention of new materials. It was inevitable that these would infiltrate fashion from their architectural or product-design origins. Plastics were one of the most significant cultural phenomena of the twentieth century. They changed the way objects were designed, produced and used; their chief quality was their ability to be moulded or shaped into different forms under pressure or by heat. Plastics revolutionized the injection-moulding process, which remains one of the primary ways to manufacture them.

After the arrival of the first plastics, such as celluloid in 1868, casein in 1897 and cellulose acetate in 1926, it became possible to imitate expensive natural raw materials, such as horn, tortoiseshell and ivory. The plastic simulation of these substances enabled bag manufacturers to produce more affordable ranges for the average woman. Eventually, plastics came to be used for their own properties rather than as faux animal products; one example is the fluorescent cellulose acetate that went under the trade name Rhodoid.

Bakelite was invented by the Belgian chemist Leo Baekeland in 1905. Once the patents on the product had expired in 1927, it pervaded all aspects of product design, and was embraced enthusiastically by handbag designers who loved its malleability and bright colours. It was formed by the reaction under heat and pressure of phenol (a toxic, colourless crystalline solid) and formaldehyde (a simple organic compound), and was the first plastic to be made from synthetic components. Initially, Bakelite was used for its electrically nonconductive and heat-resistant properties in electrical insulators, hence its connotations with old-fashioned brown radios and household electrical goods. However, its properties made Bakelite an excellent bearer of the stylized forms found in Art Deco, and it soon came to be associated with lively and colourful handbag design. Bandalasta, also known as Lingalonga, was a colourful marbled version of Bakelite that appeared in 1925.

Shagreen, a type of untanned leather, was also typical of the era, and used for many designed objects as well as handbags. Made from sharkskin, its distinctive surface comes from the shark's round, calcified papillae (called placoid scales), which were ground down to give a roughened surface of rounded protrusions; the dye, which is typically green vegetable dye, shows between these protrusions when the skin is coloured from the other side. Although the process was invented during the eighteenth century by Jean-Claude Galluchat, it was the British artisan John Paul Cooper who developed the technique in his London studio between 1899 and 1933.

BELOW Moulded plastic was frequently used for handbag 'hardware' during the 1920s and '30s. This clutch bag, quilted and corded in a geometric design in black satin, has a covered brass frame with an Art Deco bar clasp of moulded plastic sections in light green and black. The bag features an internal silk coin purse with a twist knob closure on a central pivot.

BELOW An ornate French evening bag dating from 1920–30, constructed in ribbed shot silk in gold and black. The plastic frame is embossed with coloured flowers and foliage, and inscribed 'Depose'. The press closure is also decorated with an embossed and coloured floral knob, with a matching single chain handle, and the edge is trimmed with leaf-shaped pendants. The front plaque has a round mirror on the underside and is positioned to cover a small pocket opening.

OPPOSITE A 1928 selection of handbags from the Revelation Suitcase Company. Although the products are described as 'not necessarily expensive', the antelope bag cost £21.0.0 – a month's wages for an office worker.

NOT NECESSARILY EXPENSIVE—

BUT CERTAINLY EXCLUSIVE—

8233. Pebble Calf. Silk lining, inner pocket. In navy, brown, beige, red, grey and saxe.
39/6

280. Aubusson tapestry bag, silk lining.
£6.15.0

5677/22. Calf pochette, leather lining. Real shagreen buckle. In brown and beige.
£4.4.0

1285. Morocco pochette, silk lining, 2 fittings. In tan, navy, beige, red, black, green.
21/-
Initial 3/6 extra.

296. Tinsel evening bag, silk lining, inner pocket. In gold and in silver.
25/-

4009. Crocodile handbag, marcassite and cornelian mount, silk lining, inner division. In cedar, beige, green, navy, red.
£5.12.6

4002. Plaited leather thumb bag, silk lining, inner pocket, three fittings. Also in brown/beige, beige/mastic.
£3.17.6

507. Beauvais embroidery on black, beige, green, red, blue or brown silk.
21/-

750. Antelope bag, marcassite mount, silk lining, inner pocket, two fittings.
£21.0.0
Other models from £5.5.0

902. Model evening bag, Broderie ancienne, silk lining.
£5.5.0

239. Finest morocco, inner pocket. In snuff, chocolate, navy, blue, beige, black, green, red.
21/-

THESE AND MANY OTHERS MAY BE OBTAINED FROM 170 PICCADILLY W.I THE HOUSE OF THE

REVELATION

SUITCASE CO LTD

Men ofttimes feel the need of advice when it comes to the selection of a Handbag. Such advice is, on these occasions, always available at "Revelation."

When ordering by post, quote the Reference number and colour desired.

1264/10. Crocodile Zip bag, fitted purse, mirror, powder case and passport pocket.
£8.8.0
In brown, navy, beige and black morocco.
£2.10.0

Seal note case.
27/6

Wallet in pigskin or brown morocco, with any school or college crest.
30/-

Crocodile key case.
13/6

Flask, lizard covered.
42/6

Collectable Mesh Bags

'Truly, a Whiting & Davis Mesh bag is the very embodiment of queenly beauty, refinement and utility,' said the *Ladies' Home Journal* in December 1923. The popularity of the ring mesh bag increased during the 1920s and 1930s with the introduction of Armor (armour) mesh, a flat surface formed by four-armed mesh cells or 'spiders' linked by rings at each corner. Previously, the mesh bag had been restricted to the use of silver and golden threads, but this new construction was ideal for the technique of enamelling, which enabled the application of the vibrant colour palette that was such an essential element of the handbag during this period. Paul Poiret was one of the designers commissioned to work for the company, his rainbow palette and distinctive Oriental patterning adding interest to the lustrous folds of the mesh bag. The American version of Art Deco, which was cleaner and more streamlined than the European style, lent itself to the medium of mesh; it provided vortices of blazing colour, interspersed with heavy black lines typical of the era. In contrast, the extremely fine Dresden mesh or baby-ring mesh was ideal for the gauzy, multicoloured pictorial imagery of abstract design, which was stencilled to the surface in muted colours in a form of screen printing.

Manufacturing processes dictated the parameters of the mesh bag and the squared-off, boxy shape; 12.5 x 25 cm (5 x 10 inches) was deemed appropriate for optimum practicality. Variety was introduced by cutting the base of the bag into various shapes, the most popular being the Vandyke, with triangular points repeated in various scales and lengths. Novelty also came from the diverse trimmings deployed. Fringing was the most popular, and sometimes incorporated metal drops, which came in various shapes: the round teardrop, the ovoid and the bullet. One style of fringing was the Venetian fringe, containing a central rosette, patented in 1923. Clasps, too, were an opportunity to change the style of the bag, and variations included the standard ball and socket, twist-knob clasps, and side-mounted latches. The 1920s also saw the popularity of 'dome' or 'cathedral' frames, which were decorated with jewels, embossed or enamelled. Vermeil was a gold-tone mesh of silver gilt.

Beadlite was a variation of Armor mesh: a raised dot in the centre of each 'spider' was enamelled, creating the tromp l'oeil effect of a beaded bag. The mesh could also be coated with an iridescent glaze, called Fishscale. Aluminium was used in the 1930s under the name Alu-mesh.

Whiting & Davis Handbags

The Whiting & Davis logo was first used in 1921, and became a registered trademark in 1922, first appearing on shield-shaped paper tags (blue for soldered mesh, white for all other mesh). This was followed by a metal tag attached to the bag frame. Finally, the logo was stamped on the inner side of the metal frame.

It is important for the collector to make sure that the mesh and the fringing are intact, and that there is no damage to either the frame or any embellishment. Torn linings are less of a problem, as these can be replaced without reducing

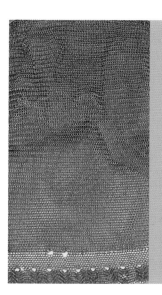

FEATURES THAT MAKE MESH BAGS MORE COLLECTABLE

* Bags with a fringe and drops, or indeed both, as they are more expensive.
* Bags made of finer mesh, such as baby-ring mesh.
* Any additional decoration on the clasp, particularly those of precious metals or jewels used in the bag's construction.
* Clear and unfaded images, especially on the Dresden type.
* Multipurpose bags such as vanity or 'function' bags.
* Bags that have retained their packaging, receipt and original labels.
* Pure silver bags tend to be lighter for their size, with smaller rings, than those made of base metal. American silver bags are usually marked 'sterling'; European ones are stamped 'silver' or have a hallmark.

the value of the bag. Original bags should be cleaned with a fine, soft brush and stored separately from each other, away from bright, strong sunlight. It is important to remember when buying a Whiting & Davis vintage bag that their bags are still being produced.

Mandalian Bags

The main competitor of Whiting & Davis for the mesh bag market was the Mandalian Manufacturing Company, founded in 1915 by Turkish-born Sahatiel G Mandalian. His Eastern aesthetic influenced the design of the bags, in contrast with those of the rival company. Whereas Whiting & Davis exploited the abstract geometric forms of Art Deco, Mandalian bags featured exotic, intricate patterning reminiscent of Persian carpets, ornate gardens, luscious roses, peacocks and feathers in rich, deep colours. These details were enhanced with a shimmering surface, the result of the Lustro-Pearl effect, a process of coating the enamel with a solution of 'essence of pearl' that gave an iridescent finish to the bags. Trimmings were equally lush and ornate, incorporating bejewelled frames and clasps, and Byzantine-like tiers of drops and fringing. Mandalian bags differed from their competitor's because the mesh cells were set on the diagonal, whereas the majority of Whiting & Davis bags had the mesh placed on horizontal and vertical lines. The company also developed the use of smaller 'spiders' to create a finer mesh surface. Mandalian specialities included the Gloria bag, featuring a bracelet frame; its spring-joined links formed a roomy, box-like opening. In 1944, the Mandalian Manufacturing Company was absorbed by Whiting & Davis.

TOP A form of screen printing allowed for the application of surface decoration on mesh bags in the 1920s, as is the case with this fine metal mesh bag printed in shades of green, yellow, lilac and coral pink. The base of the bag has an indented fringe trim. The square gilt frame is engraved with scrolling foliage to which a gilt chain handle is attached. The twist knob closure is tipped in black plastic or glass.

LEFT The look of needlework is recreated in mesh on this ornate and highly coloured bag with stepped fringe and decorative metal frame by French company Breville, dating from the 1920s.

◀ **Small bags**
Miniature hand-held purses and bags were a feature of the flapper style of the 1920s. Here a simple circular envelope style with small handles, dating from 1923, reflects the circular rings in contrasting colour appliquéd onto the sleeves of the coat.

Key looks of the decade

1920s

▶ Metal mesh
The mesh bag reached the height of its popularity during the 1920s. This fine steel example is attached to a shaped copper alloy frame and trimmed with square-cut imitation sapphires. The single chain handle is constructed of rectangular links and the front has a geometric design in soft shades of copper and grey mesh. The base of the bag is trimmed with a dentate fringe.

▲ Matching accessories
The vogue for matching accessories to the outfit was a feature of 1920s fashion. This ensemble from 1929 was illustrated by Gordon Conway for *Tatler* magazine. The spring evening frock of figured chiffon is embroidered with the same design as the envelope-style evening bag and the satin slippers.

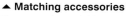

▼ Tango bags

The energetic and popular dances of the 1920s, such as the Charleston and the Tango, required a small bag that could either fit into the palm of the hand or wrap around the wrist so the bag was secure during the exertions of the dance. This finely corded version has a gilt metal frame, a snap closure and a handle of matching black silk. The bag is gathered at the base into a silk-covered button.

▼ Tapestry and embroidery

Embroidered and needleworked bags featured florals and landscape scenes. Here an embroidered bag with an embellished clasp detracts from the severity of the outfit on the left, lending a .feminine note to the strict tailoring. 'Tailor-mades', such as the suits here made in 1926 by Bernard, were worn for country pursuits and a feature of most women's wardrobes.

◄ Geometrics and Art Deco

Influences from ancient civilizations in the form of geometric stepped designs, chevrons and sunray patterns became stylized decorative features. Here a rectangular beaded evening bag dating from the 1920s is constructed from black and metallic glass beads worked into a Greek key pattern.

1930s:
Decoration and Surrealism

New York's Wall Street crash of 1929 introduced a new sobriety into fashion. The subsequent Great Depression shifted the spotlight away from the indulged 'bright young things' of the 1920s as the world witnessed the rise of Hitler in Germany, the steadily approaching war and the dispossessed poor on the streets of America and Europe. A population suffering the trials and tribulations of everyday life found escape at the cinema, and were easily seduced by the Hollywood glamour they saw on the movie screen.

Fashion matured as the silhouette emphasized form and cut. Women no longer appeared androgynous, the waist returned to its rightful place, and hemlines fell to mid-calf. However, a slightly more masculine silhouette emerged towards the end of the decade as the war grew closer, with squarer shoulders and narrower hips. This silhouette was emphasized by the fashion photography of the day, whereby the model turned her lower half away from the camera but faced it full on with her torso.

Ordinary life required practical daywear as increasing numbers of women entered the marketplace and cultivated a life outside the home. Even if not in employment, women might be expected to participate in cultural, charitable and community activities. Fabrics became more practical, too. Gone were the fragile insubstantial materials and the exaggerated accessories of the 1920s; they were replaced by sensible day dresses and the tailor-made suit, invariably worn with a hat, gloves and a handbag, usually matching in colour and materials. There was a new interest in the art of pattern cutting. The waist-hugging dresses in fine wools and crepe de chine now had cleverly concealed darts and seams; these were integrated into ruching, cowl necklines and draped bodices. Hips were defined with shaped seaming and belts became all-important.

The Dressed-Up Look

Although the silhouette was crisp and unfussy, there was a vogue for outsized, and exaggerated 'trimmings'. Large sculptural buttons, crafted from the new plastics, innovative belt buckles and cleverly constructed collars all added interest to the simplicity of the cut. This desire for decorative additions to an outfit could also embrace the novelty handbag. Women continued to enjoy aspects of needlework, and although a dressmaker would be employed for making up garments, sewing was considered a suitable occupation for women of all classes. *The Schoolgirls' Own Annual* of 1931 had some suggestions for homemade handbags, and included instructions for making an 'awfully dainty diamond-shaped bag surmounted by a doll's head with a cute little bonnet; it has a loop at the top to hang from the wrist'.

Costume jewellery was also an important element of the dressed-up look. It was the era of the brooch, and most women had a variety of these in their jewellery box. Stylized flower baskets and Art Deco-inspired Bakelite motifs might adorn the lapel of a tweed suit, or a dramatic large-scale piece might enhance the collar of a dress. This wardrobe of costume jewellery prompted the popularity of the box bag. Larger than the 1920s vanity case, the box bag was similarly used to carry cosmetics, but was now freestanding and doubled as both a decorative storage unit on a dressing table or vanity unit, as well as functioning as an evening bag. A popular choice were those made in black suede with gilt trimmings.

The clutch bag was still in evidence, although for daywear it was beginning to be replaced with a roomier, more three-dimensional bag that could hold the necessities of the office worker. Daily use required the bag to have the stalwart qualities of some sort of leather, and usually a zip fastening and chrome fittings with practical, short, over-the-arm handles. Reptile skins were widely used and worn without any squeamishness. A crocodilian bag would complement fur trimmings, and the pelts of dead mammals were often draped around women's shoulders, with the heads of foxes and ermines holding their own tails between their teeth.

PAGE 48 After the informal excesses of the 1920s, fashion for daywear again regained some of its decorum, with the emphasis on smart tailoring. Master of the art of cutting, Cristobal Balenciaga designed this suit in 1938 to follow the line of the body but reveal nothing. The black patent leather box-shaped handbag with short double straps exactly expresses the new ladylike proportions of the suit.

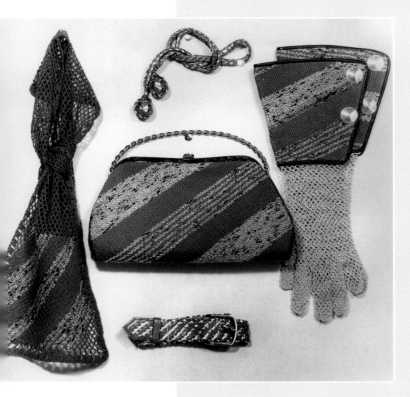

ABOVE AND RIGHT A set
of woven stranded cotton
and silk accessories cut
on the bias that includes
a handbag, gloves, scarf,
leather necklet and belt; a
similar version of the bag
as worn by the model
Mercia Swinburne, with a
matching fez, right, in 1933.

OPPOSITE Fashion in the
1930s propounded a
longer, leaner silhouette.
Daywear included cleverly
cut dresses that featured
interesting shaping and
draping of the cloth
and oversized details
such as novelty buttons.
Accessories mirrored this
trend, as can be seen in
this trio of handbags by
German company Goldpfeil
dating from 1936–9, and
manufactured in Offenbach.

Animal Skins

Skins such as snake, ostrich, crocodile and alligator skin are known as 'exotics' in the handbag trade. Now usually associated with the luxury goods market, during the 1920s, 1930s and 1940s, they were hugely popular and widely used by the mass-market bag manufacturers such as the French designer Germaine Guerin. This fashion was driven partly by supply: leather had become a rarity during the First World War, so designers had to turn to other sources, and reptile skins were readily available. All types of handbags were made from skins, including large, practical, box-shaped bags with double handles and solid brass fittings, and the envelope clutch, which was now squarer in shape with a flap that covered the whole of the front. Taxidermy was often included: gruesome little alligator clawed paws and even the animal's features, such as the tail or the head, were often incorporated into the bag as decorative features. The size and texture of the scales depended on which part of the animal they had come from, the osteoderms (back scales) providing the largest scales. Python skin is identifiable by a characteristic two-tone patterning, which was usually left in its natural state. Other species of snakeskin were often dyed in a range of colours, and lizard skin is identifiable by the dense pattern of tiny scales.

ABOVE An Hermès crocodile clutch bag with an envelope flap, secured with a silver clasp, dating from 1931. The silk scarf bears the signatures of contemporary Hollywood film stars such as Charlie Chaplin, in blue, orange, navy and purple.

BELOW A simple elongated clutch bag dating from the 1930s is carefully fashioned from undyed crocodile skin, which optimizes the patterning of the scales. A matching gilded metal clasp is fashioned in the shape of acorns.

Koret, Incorporated

Mass-production techniques meant that better-quality handbags were more available to all; the advice was always to buy the best leather bag you could afford and to look on it as an investment. Bags were still purchased from leather specialists, but branded bags from a particular label, such as those from Koret, Incorporated, were more commonly bought from a department store. Founded by Richard Koret in 1929, Koret is a major American handbag brand. The design, manufacturing and distribution operation produced high-quality handbags of understated elegance that were also 'fashion aware'. At this time handbags were beginning to conform to the softer 1930s silhouette, with detailing similar to the draped and ruched bodices of the dresses, as this advert in the 1936 issue of *Luggage & Leather Goods* makes clear:

The advance Fall handbag line at Koret, Inc. emphasizes a new trend in accessories towards femininity and elegance. They show soft, shirred manipulations and are entirely away from the hard, tailored handbag. They are made on fine polished gold finish frames, which are simple in character, having usually their own locks for ornamentation. Top handles are frequent. Black is the prevailing colour. A few of the bags are decorated with large script initials and monograms.

The company's Gazelle logo has appeared on handbags throughout the twentieth century, including the famous silk clutches carried by First Lady Jackie Kennedy during the White House years. In addition to their own brand handbags, Koret, Inc. was a licensee for both Christian Dior and Hubert de Givenchy.

LEFT A fashion illustration from 1930 by Gordon Conway for *Tatler* magazine features a morning frock of blue crepella with a matching bolero and scarf decorated with carved wooden beads in blue and white. The crisp, no-nonsense silhouette and clean lines of the outfit are echoed in the geometry of the antelope bag, which is decorated with crystals to match those on the belt.

BELOW LEFT During the 1930s couturiers were beginning to realize the marketing power of the *griffe*, or designers' mark, the precursor of the logo. The jacket, hat, gloves and handbag here are all the work of French designer Jeanne Lanvin in 1935.

OPPOSITE The heavily ruched and textured surface of this handbag dating from 1939 has a short handle and knotted leather loop attached to the zip for ease of opening. It combines practicality with the understated elegance of the era.

BELOW RIGHT During the 1930s the clutch bag became more three dimensional – both chunkier and longer to accommodate the modern woman's busy life. Black was the most popular colour for daytime handbags.

Evening Elegance

The more functional dressing of 1930s daywear did not apply to evening attire, when the Hollywood effect meant that glamour took centre stage. It was the era of the silver fox movie queen, when stars such as Mae West and Carole Lombard appeared larger than life on the screen in backless or halter-neck dresses, their bare shoulders draped in fur capes and stoles. At Paramount studios, the costume designer Travis Banton added to film star Marlene Dietrich's allure with his glorious confections of fur and feathers.

Hollywood replaced Paris as the arbiter of style. The American designer Gilbert Adrian translated the revolutionary new cutting technique invented by the Parisian couturier Madeleine Vionnet onto the cinema screen. In the film *Dinner at Eight* (1933), Adrian's bias-cut backless dress and ostrich cape for Jean Harlow introduced Parisian couture to the American mass market. The innovatory technique of cutting the fabric on the bias (across the grain, rather than with the weave of the cloth) allowed the fabric to cling to the body with an unadorned fluidity and a minimum of seaming. Vionnet's aesthetic has influenced pattern cutting to the present day; both the work of the 1960s designer Ossie Clark and the slip dresses

of John Galliano are reminders of her craft. However, glamour was not the prerogative of the screen idols, as the British couturier Norman Hartnell recalls in his autobiography, *The Silver and the Gold*, dressing one of his models, Avril, in the late 1930s:

> I have never loaded so many jewels and silver fox as I have done on the vibrant Avril. Inch-square sapphires would be stuck like Eastern mosaic all over a lemon evening coat. Prussian blue cloth would become stiff with magenta spangles, cherries and rubies. An innocent enough mustard velvet jacket was no good to Miss Avril unless it clanked with turquoise cabochons, zircons and scarabs.

Handbag design and production was now undertaken by couturiers who offered a total look from head to toe. British-born Edward Mainbocher, and Parisian couturiers Lucienne Lelong, Madeleine Vionnet, Marcel Rochas, Jeanne Lanvin and Molyneaux, all used the opportunity to advertise their products with a discreet monogram embroidered on the flap of the clutch or stamped on the metal clasp of a handbag.

RIGHT The French couturier Jeanne Lanvin designed this elegant, understated ensemble in 1933. The yoke of the dress and the waistband are decorated with metallic discs, demanding a simple leather clutch with a metal clasp.

BELOW A glamorous vanity case for evening use by French jeweller Boucheron dating from 1935. The gilded metal is engine-turned, and the clasp, set with rubies, epitomizes the geometric severity of Art Deco styling.

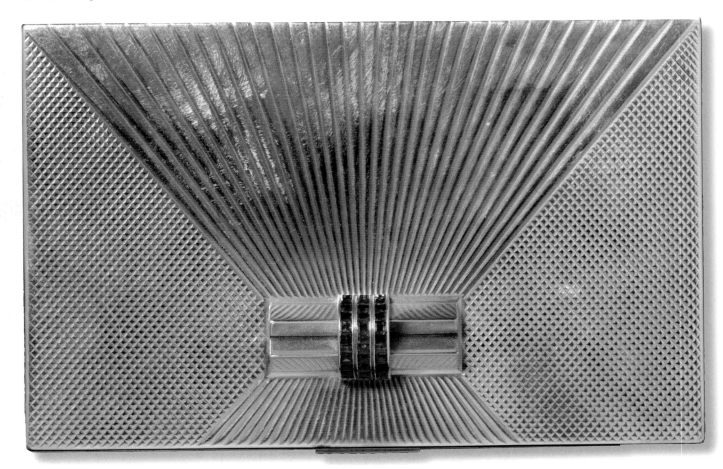

RIGHT Bias-cut silk satin worn with an envelope-style clutch epitomizes the glamour of 1930s Hollywood fashion. Although daywear remained ladylike and practical, evening dresses went to extremes of feminine sensuality, represented here by American actress Brenda Marshall, starring in *Espionage Agent* in 1939.

The Evening Bag

Evening bags are always more subject to whimsy, decoration and novelty than their daytime counterparts. Although times were hard in the 1930s, the evening bag continued to hold a fascination for women, and very few used the same bag from day to night. Film stars were seen to ritualize the application of make-up, and such activities became commonplace off-screen. Indeed, in contrast to the Edwardian distaste for public 'painting', this practice was even perceived as elegant, and handbags began to include mirrors and even lights to facilitate public repairs to the face. The bag became a mobile boudoir as women sashayed from the dance floor to the cocktail lounge. Evening bags were customarily small, with just enough room for a lipstick and powder compact, as it was assumed that the gentlemen escort would provide the cigarettes and account for any expenses incurred.

Evening bags utilized similar materials to the slippery silk and satin crepe de chine dresses then in vogue. Fabrics would be dyed to match a particular dress, and often incorporated luxurious detail, such as beading. Evening bags were designed to be held either in the hand or, if a clutch, under the arm. Some had a strap like a bracelet so that the bag dangled from the wrist. The very wealthy carried bags made of precious metals; all the big jewellery names of the era – Asprey, Cartier and Boucheron – produced evening bags that were closely related to jewellery. Frames and clasps, the 'hardware' of a handbag, reached a peak of craftsmanship in expensive materials, as they provided plenty of opportunity to deploy traditional jewellery-making techniques and the incorporation of semiprecious stones.

ABOVE CENTRE A 1930s Art Deco handbag with marcasite clasp.

TOP RIGHT An outfit comprising a Cartier clip of diamonds pinned to a black satin tricorne hat by Mary Manners, and turquoise earrings, is completed by an Art Deco black enamel vanity case set with bands of diamonds dating from 1931. The model on the left wears a blue crepe de laine hat with a rolled halo brim revealing a skullcap that matches a peach tricot pullover by Madelon Chaumet. The cap has a modernistic arrow in platinum and lapis lazuli with rose diamond points; the necklace is by Garrard.

SPARKLING SUBSTITUTES

Hollywood stars could afford real diamonds, semiprecious stones and expensive glass beads on their jewelled evening bags, but there were plenty of substitutes for the mass-market manufacturers.

⋆ **Marcasite** (the mineral pyrite) was an extremely popular alternative to diamonds as it could be cut and set in mountings just like the real thing. It is darker than rhinestone and paste and a deep grey colour. As it is not transparent, it did not require backing with foil or tin to increase its sparkle.

⋆ **Strass** were artificial glass diamonds that could be coloured to imitate precious stones, and were named after the Strasbourg jeweller G F Strass, who invented them in 1730.

⋆ **Paste** was another substitute product that was used to imitate diamonds. Made from glass, a high content of lead oxide was added to render it more refractive. This increased its sparkle but made the product softer, meaning that it became more easily scratched.

⋆ **Rhinestone** has become a generic term and tends to be applied to anything artificial that sparkles. It can be made of glass, paste or quartz crystal. Rhinestones were sometimes backed with tin or gold- or silver-tinted foil, though usually only on more expensive products. Occasionally, bags might be decorated with a combination of rhinestone and paste, or rhinestone and marcasite.

Together with sequins, these substitutes could provide the necessary glamorous glitter of an evening bag. When used to decorate a bag's frames and clasps, these products looked particularly effective against the 1930s propensity for black suede or silk handbags.

Whiting & Davis, in response to the Depression, began manufacturing their mesh bags in base metals such as copper.

OPPOSITE European bags in a variety of 1930s styles and materials: crepe de chine, beaded embroidery and quilted and ruched pastel satins. The foxgloves, shown on the centre bag from 1933, were a ubiquitous flower of the era.

TOP A luxurious silk damask evening bag dating from the 1930s based on the design of the reticule. The figured fabric is gathered into a decorated frame, which features baroque pearls that match those on the clasp and the chain.

ABOVE A typical 1930s evening bag displaying many of the elements of Art Deco: the pyramid of embroidered flowers set in the centre of a sunray of satin quilting and the ornate gilt metal lever trimmed with pearl beads.

Decorative Elements

'Odeon' style, the result of Bauhaus modernism meeting Art Deco and Hollywood, permeated every aspect of decoration, from handbags to architecture. The Bauhaus principle of 'truth to materials' meant that the new plastics ceased to be used to imitate animal products such as ivory and tortoiseshell, but were now valued for their own properties of malleability, transparency and colour. Bakelite continued to beguile handbag designers, particularly in aiding their interpretation of the still popular aesthetic of Art Deco. This design movement continued to be used throughout the 1930s as an inspiration for textile print design for clothes and for handbag decoration. The distinctive patterning and utilization of motifs such as the fan and sun ray could be seen on the clutch and pochette. Hand-tooled leather bags were also a popular means of exhibiting these various decorative trends.

Claudette Colbert's starring role in Cecil B DeMille's 1934 epic *Cleopatra* consolidated the desire for all things Egyptian. 'History's most seductive woman', according to the film's tagline, started the trend for Egyptian-themed furniture, household goods, clothing and accessories. Ornate and gilded bags decorated with printed or embossed hieroglyphics and featuring gilt or moulded clasps of the heads of Pharaohs and scarabs became popular.

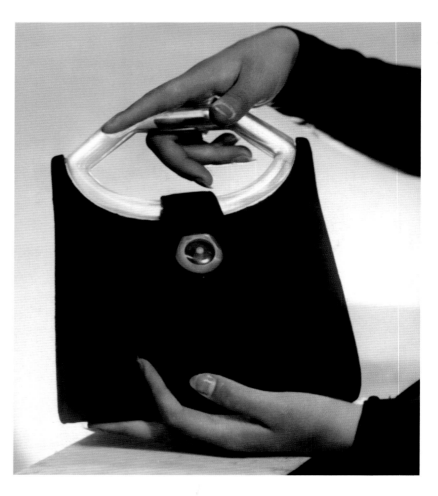

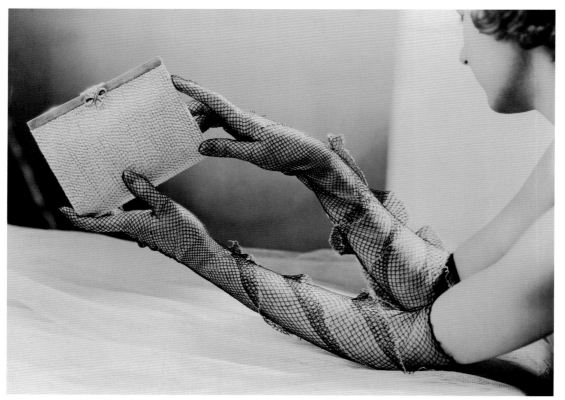

ABOVE Form follows function in the simple geometric shape of this 1935 black evening bag with a sculptured crystal handle.

LEFT A delicate 1934 silver cord evening bag with decorative bow clasp is worn with long mesh gloves; these were the perfect accessories for the decade's body-skimming silk and satin bias-cut evening dresses.

OPPOSITE Handbags became multipurpose in the 1930s, incorporating novelty additions such as cameras, cigarette lighters or watches. This elegant black clutch from 1935 features a clockface set into a diamond-shaped clasp.

The Minaudière

A minaudière is a small case that combines both handbag and powder compact. The first minaudière was reportedly invented in 1933 by the Paris jeweller Charles Arpel, of Van Cleef & Arpels, after noting that the socialite Florence Jay Gould carried her make-up and lighter in a metal Lucky Strike cigarette case. According to the fashion historian Claire Wilcox, Alfred Van Cleef patented the name as a tribute to his wife, Estelle, who had a tendency to *minauder*, or simper and charm. The small, usually rectangular metal box of the minaudière was designed to be held in the hand, with compartments for powder, rouge, lipstick and mirror, and cigarettes and lighter. The cases were exquisitely crafted in silver or gold and set with precious stones, or were a perfect example of the enameller's art. The device was at first only available from Asprey's in England, but as its popularity increased, other jewellers were quick to copy the idea. Many designers since have explored the concept, but one in particular is associated with whimsical, very luxurious minaudières: Judith Leiber, who produced her glitzy evening bags from the late 1960s. As a style icon and First Lady of America during her husband's presidency, Jackie Kennedy popularized the use of the minaudière once again when she took to using it as an evening bag, holding the small square box in the palm of her hand on formal occasions.

Jewellers, bag manufacturers and cosmetic companies, eager to tap into the flourishing make-up market and influenced by the encroaching power of Surrealism, also sold novelty items such as special powder boxes and lipstick holders hidden in a bracelet, or containers in the form of a gramophone record or telephone.

OPPOSITE Cosmetic houses such as Elizabeth Arden capitalized on the increasingly popular use of make-up, as with this crocodile-effect handbag dating from 1939, which contains a mirror, powder case and lipstick.

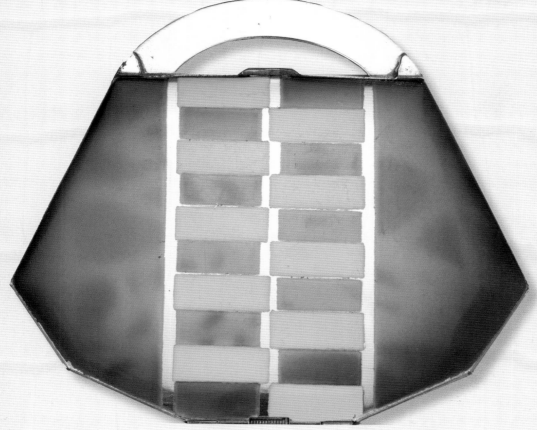

ABOVE This single-strap handbag dating from 1935 is resolutely Art Deco in style, featuring textured leather encased in a bold brass frame and a geometric clasp.

LEFT A 'Princess' handbag powder compact, Czech in origin and dating from the 1930s. The front has a stepped decoration in keeping with the geometric devices that were part of the Modernist movement.

THIS PAGE Elsa Schiaparelli wittily transformed the practicality of handbags into whimsical, exquisitely produced, highly decorated pieces of art.

Elsa Schiaparelli

'Beauty will be convulsive or not at all,' proclaimed the poet and polemicist André Breton, the French leader of the Surrealist movement. Art entered fashion via the society pages of magazines and newspapers which recorded the high jinks of the Surrealist and self-publicist Salvador Dalí and his associates. The flame of Surrealism and the acceptance of the avant-garde in *haute couture* were fuelled by private views of Dalí's work, when models arrived wearing sausages in their hair, and Dalí himself appeared in a diving suit.

The Surrealistic object was an exercise in displacement, and the simple form of the clutch was superseded by the radical handbag designs of the Italian couturier Elsa Schiaparelli (1890–1973). A friend and collaborator with the artist, Schiaparelli brought the handbag centre stage with her designs of surreal imagery and unexpected juxtapositions of subject matter. Her reputation was made with the use of trompe l'oeil (literally, tricking the eye) in her striking knitted garments, such as her 'bow' sweaters of 1927. She launched her first collection in 1929, from her boutique in the rue de la Paix, Paris. Born in Rome, with a privileged, intellectual background, Schiaparelli insisted that for her, fashion design was simply a different means of artistic expression; she did not sew and barely sketched. The Parisian couturier Christian Dior accused her of creating couture that catered only for painters and poets, and she was certainly at the centre of the artistic avant-garde.

Schiaparelli was friends with the Dadaists Marcel Duchamp, Francis Picabia, Alfred Stieglitz and Man Ray, and shared with them their subversive appropriation of the ordinary to place it within a new, usually unexpected context. As the Surrealists succeeded the Dadaists, she collaborated with their most famous exponent, Dalí, a painter of exquisitely executed dreamscapes of hypnagogic imagery. This connection with her own penchant for tromp l'oeil resulted in a series of witty excursions into bag design that included bags constructed around commonplace objects, such as the piano, the telephone, a Chinese lantern and, in 1936, a Birdcage bag reminiscent of René Magritte's painting *Le Modèle Rouge*.

In 1934, she pre-empted John Galliano's excursion into specially printed newspaper text with her cotton newsprint bag, bearing press cuttings of herself. It was the first-ever customized designer fabric; from a distance the bag looked exactly like a folded-up newspaper. Ever practical, Schiaparelli invented the Lite-On in 1938, again in collaboration with Dalí. This bag featured two internal light bulbs that backlit a hinged mirror, with a compartment for lipstick, alongside a Dalí engraving.

At the height of her powers, at the end of the decade, Schiaparelli presented four astonishing collections: the 'Circus' show included performing horses, acrobats

RIGHT The conventional lines of the knitted jersey two-piece suit, dating from 1935, are subverted in characteristic Schiaparelli style by the idiosyncratic knitted skullcap with a pointed halo. The suit is accessorized with matching gloves and handbag.

and elephants; the 'Pagan' collection was based on the paintings of the Italian artist Botticelli; and her third show explored the signs of the zodiac. The theatrical theme surfaced again with her fourth collection, an interpretation of the characters from the *commedia dell'arte*, a form of popular comedy from sixteenth-century Italy that included the player Arlecchino, or Harlequin.

Schiaparelli's idiosyncratic and eclectic approach influenced other handbag designers; suddenly everyone wanted a 'talking point' rather than just a handbag. Roger Modal, a skilled bag designer and craftsman, executed Schiaparelli's ideas for sculptural leather bags, and went on to work with the couturiers Jacques Fath and Hubert de Givenchy. Anne Marie of France produced handbags that combined witty, subversive design with innovative fastenings, such as a mandolin-shaped bag presented in a box decorated with an opera programme, and a black suede ice-bucket bag that contained Lucite ice cubes.

Travel Trends

In spite of the approaching war, the 1930s was an era of new access to mass travel. Handbag design reflected this trend, and bags were produced in the shape of cars and aeroplanes. Cruising became particularly popular, and influenced handbag design not only in terms of practicality, but also in the vogue for the souvenir – a bag that was a memento of the journey and something to impress the folks back home. A prime example was the clutch bag in the shape of the luxurious French cruise ship the *Normandie* – during the ship's maiden voyage from France to the United States in 1935, all the first-class passengers received the bag as a gift to commemorate the journey.

However, this cosmopolitan way of life was soon to come to an end. In his autobiography, Christian Dior wrote that '1937 had danced in the ospreys and furbelows of Schiaparelli, on top of a grumbling volcano'. The volcano was about to erupt.

LEFT Elsa Schiaparelli's Harlequin bag dating from 1939 is from her fourth handbag collection. It is based on characters from the *commedia dell'arte*, a form of theatrical comedy from sixteenth-century Italy.

RIGHT The complete travel companion, dating from 1939, and targeted to World's Fair visitors. Made of natural pigskin or reptile grained calf, it had three zipped sections that opened like a 'W'. It was fitted with a billfold and chained coin purse, a case for railroad tickets or passports, a cigarette case, key case, mirror, comb and compact and umbrella.

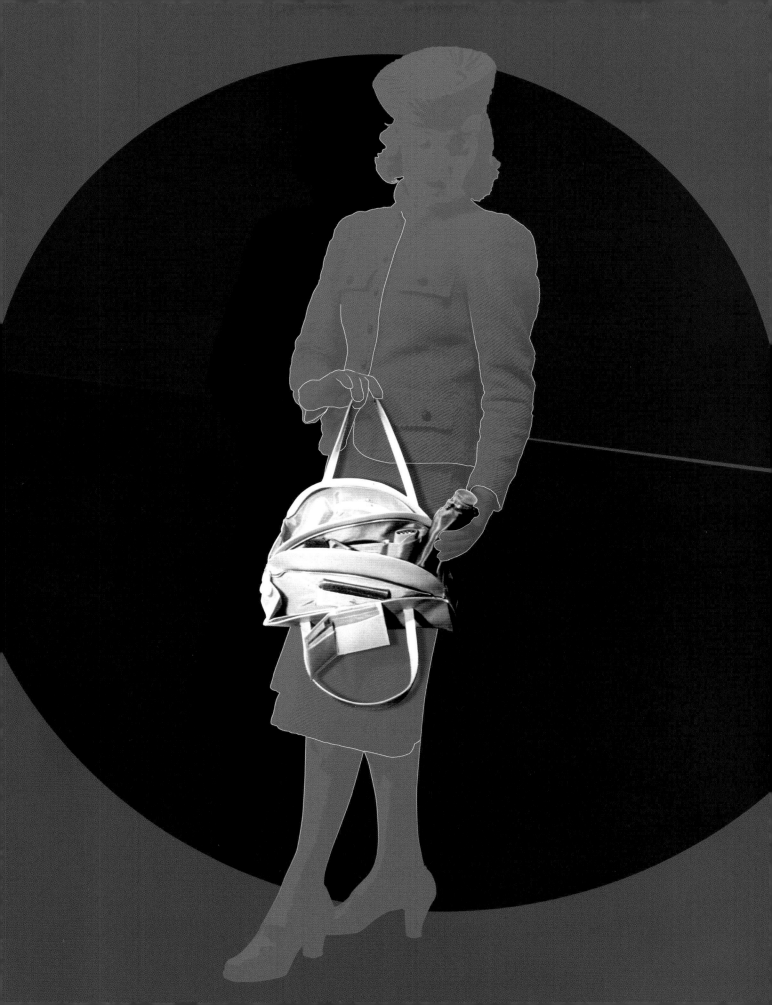

▼ Art Deco

A black leather handbag dating from 1930–5 epitomizes popular Art Deco features, including the geometric metal frame in chrome and black leather, the black plastic and silver ball clasp and the stamped chequerboard pattern on the front of the bag.

Key looks of the decade

1930s

▲ The envelope clutch

The streamlined clutch of the 1920s segued into a larger geometric and more substantial version in the 1930s. This version is by manufacturer Bienen-Davis and dates from 1937; it is worn with a knitted dress by Lampl, accessorized with gloves and a felt, feathered hat.

◀ Sequinned evening bags

Evening bags retained their whimsy and luxuriousness, even throughout the exigencies of the Depression. An envelope-style clutch bag with a front closure is closely covered all over with sequins in shades of gold. The bag contains a bevel-edged vanity mirror with a fabric-covered back.

▼ Novelty themes

Handbags took on novelty themes, such as aviation and cruiseship travel. The large lapels of this cruise suit are wittily echoed in the replication of the collar in a reverse colourway on the front of the handbag. Designed by Tinling and dating from 1937, the suit comprises a Harris Tweed coat, lined with blue suede, with matching blue suede trousers.

◆ Knitted and crocheted bags

Homemade accessories were popular in an era when it was customary for many women to make their own clothes, and women's magazines often offered knitting and crochet patterns to their readers. This 1930s matching set of crocheted accessories is made in red wool.

▼ Animal skins

The influence of Hollywood 'Odeon' style can be seen in this dyed crocodile 1930s handbag. The circular bag is bifurcated with solid brass fittings and contains a matching purse.

◀ Matching gloves and bags

Matching gloves to handbag was indicative of good grooming and a ladylike demeanour in the 1930s. Here, a timeless classic box-shape handbag by French company Hermès dates from 1937.

1940s:
Austerity and Innovation

The austerity of wartime imposed a necessary no-nonsense attitude towards fashion. The conscription of women in Europe and America made the look of the military uniform a familiar daily sight on the streets, and even civilians' daywear retained the practical features of clothes worn by the armed services. This included the handbag. The embellished clutch and the exquisite minaudières of the 1930s were surplus to requirements in war-torn Europe. A military-influenced satchel, with a sturdy strap and a buckled over-the-top flap, was worn with the sensible woollen suits of the day. These comprised a short, neatly fitted tailored jacket with a squared-off shoulder line and narrow reveres, and a straight skirt to just below the knee, with a pleat at the back for ease of movement. Such a silhouette was refined, even elegant, and when the suit was worn with an unadorned blouse and a felt hat tipped over a victory roll hairdo, the day look was complete.

The British Board of Trade issued a Civilian Clothing Order in 1942, forbidding the use of any extraneous detailing on garments, including fancy trimmings, decorative stitching, and pleats. No more than three buttons were allowed on a jacket. Foremost designers of the day, including Norman Hartnell, Hardy Amies and Digby Morton, lent their expertise to the project and formed the Incorporated Society of London Fashion Designers. As well as designing the uniforms for the Women's Royal Army Corps, Women's Royal Naval Service and Women's Royal Air Force, the society produced a collection of basic items for the general public, including a coat, a suit, and various day dresses for the working woman.

Norman Hartnell, then holding a warrant of 'Dressmaker by Appointment to Her Majesty the Queen', feared for his reputation in being associated with the production of clothes for women outside his normal clientele of actresses and the aristocracy. In his autobiography, *Silver and Gold* (1955) he reports that on expressing his reservations, the Queen replied, 'You have made so many charming things for me, that if you can do likewise for my countrywomen, I think it would be an excellent thing to do.' This collaboration between leading couturiers and the manufacturers of clothes for the mass market resulted in a populace probably better dressed than ever before.

Wartime Restrictions

In addition to the formal tailored suit, women needed other garments that could withstand the wear and tear of their daily life during the war. Ease of movement was essential, hence the popularity of casual slacks and trousers. The utility 'siren suit' was an all-in-one garment with a zipped front and large slouch pockets, which was worn over nightwear in case of bombing raids that required a dash to the air raid shelter. The 'kangaroo cloak' worn on top also had capacious pockets to store any necessary items. Elsa Schiaparelli contributed to the war effort with her version of the utility suit: an easy-to-wear siren suit with large, pouched zipped pockets that also did away with the need for a bag.

When handbags were essential for life on the move, the shoulder bag provided hands-free storage for those women who rode bicycles, drove ambulances and fought fires. After its first brief outing by the suffragettes before the First World War, and introduced by Chanel and Schiaparelli in the late 1930s, the shoulder bag once more became popular. Usually made from military issue canvas, the bag had a long strap that was wide enough to be worn comfortably across the body. The shoulder bag increased in size and shape to accommodate the obligatory gas mask, which became compulsory luggage at all times in Britain. Bags made by the London company H Wald & Company had a zipped compartment at the base of the bag to hide the gas mask (see page 74). Those women without a Waldybag, as they were known, often customized their cardboard gas-mask box to match their outfits. As the diarist E M Delafield wrote in her 1940s book *The Provincial Lady in Wartime*.

Gas masks are absolutely universal and [I] perceive that my own cardboard, slung on a string, is quite démodé and must be supplied with more decorative case. Great variety of colour and material evidently obtainable. From white waterproof to gay red and blue checks.

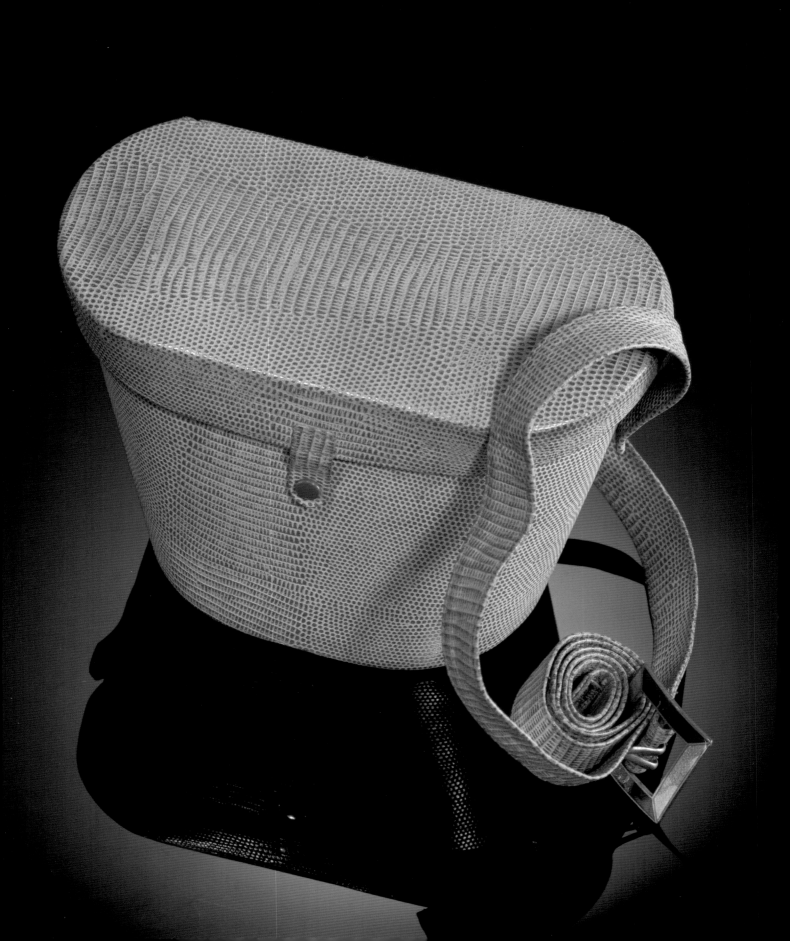

OPPOSITE Making a virtue of necessity, this elegant gas-mask bag in light brown reptile skin combines functionalism with style. It was designed by British manufacturer H Wald & Co., also known for their Waldybags (see page 72), from 1939–45. The company merged with Rayne in the 1950s.

LEFT Flying the flag in the form of a simple rectangular bag in felt appliqué, this 1940 design patriotically anticipates the subsequent entry of the United States into the Allied war effort.

ABOVE Bearing arms – with the wealth of military iconography available to designers of handbags, such as this attaché-case-style clutch, dating from 1940, they were able to create resonant motifs reflecting the patriotism of the population at large.

New Materials

In wartime Europe, accessories became less refined in terms of materials, though not in sheer creative innovation. Schiaparelli, undaunted by the restrictions on expensive materials, transmuted the French labourer's basket into an elegant accessory. She described her motives in her autobiography: 'As in Paris there was no more leather to be had for making women's handbags, I had taken some ordinary but pleasant-looking small baskets and lined them with cotton or chamois skins.'

It was no longer appropriate to be seen carrying an expensive bag in a luxurious animal skin. Leather was on the list of products to be kept for military use only, and commercial manufacturers had to utilize sturdier fabrics, such as tweed, instead. Just as the chunky wedge heel in wood and cork emerged as a response to the exigencies of the time, so the handbag became subject to the same restrictions of materials and practicality. As the constituent parts of the handbag became difficult to source and mirrors, zips and clasps became scarce, substitutes had to be found. Wood and plastic replaced metal, and the prevailing 'make-do-and-mend' ethos saw the utilization of found materials and fabrics. A version of the reticule reappeared, which was easy to make by hand: the fabric was ruched into a pouch with a drawstring top with fabric wrist loops, or gathered around bought plastic bracelet handles. Home dressmakers invented fastenings, created patchwork and looked to the sewing pages of the women's magazines for patterns and inspiration.

There were less stringent restrictions on materials in America, but even so, there was an element of do-it-yourself handbag production. Jack Frost Handbags, printed in 1945 by Gottlieb Bros, contained various patterns for crocheted handbags, including complicated fan-shaped bags, to be made up in cords of differing styles and thicknesses, depending on the use the bag was to be put to.

Simple enveloped-shaped bags were easy to 'run up' in whatever material lay to hand. Decorated with embroidery, stitching or appliqué, the bags were a triumph of the dressmaker's art. Old heirlooms were recycled; past handbags had their 'hardware' reincarnated with fresh fabric or recycled clothes. Fibrous materials such as straw and raffia were deployed, and even the metal discs from milk bottle tops were covered in raffia and constructed into bags. Bamboo was sectioned into half-foot pieces and given handles. Corde bags were made of a twine-like cord and were usually found as clutches or envelope-shaped pochettes. As metal was also scarce, Bakelite was often used in its place.

BELOW LEFT A multicoloured raffia crochet envelope clutch designed by Josef of Gold Seal Importers dates from 1940. It was imported through France to retail in America as a summer line at a price of around five dollars.

BELOW At the outer limits of austere invention, this red Goldpfeil bag made during the Second World War evades the strictures on the use of leather by converting cow stomach – tripe – to remarkable decorative effect.

RIGHT This tailored three-piece suit of jacket, skirt and handbag reflects the continuing impact of no-frills rationing in the adherence to the strictures laid down by the British Board of Trade's Civilian Clothing Order. The image was photographed by Norman Parkinson for *Vogue* magazine in 1946.

LEFT Actress Cyd Charisse's 1947 short-strapped shoulder holster resounds with the clipped realism of the post-war regeneration. Still in the grip of 'victory suit' directness and economy, this look was endorsed by a variety of Hollywood icons portraying strength in a man's world through reference to more 'manly' tailoring.

American Style

In 1940, the Occupation of Paris by the German army further undermined the capital's fashion leadership. The ideal female of the era was no longer the screen siren of the previous decade, in her white fox and undulating satin, but the brisk, capable woman epitomized by the stars of 'women's films'. These new Hollywood heroines, played by forceful stars such as Bette Davis and Barbara Stanwyck, fought the odds to become successful career women. Gilbert Adrian and Edith Head designed the costumes and deployed a structured approach to tailoring and accessories that was appropriate to women's new roles. Adrian's costumes for Joan Crawford in such star vehicles as the 1945 film Mildred Pierce – where a woman literally 'squares up' to the vicissitudes of creating a career in a man's world, yet is still a fool for love – featured a nipped-in waist and wide shoulders. (Rumour had it that the star did not need shoulder pads.)

Clothing restrictions similar to those in Britain also applied in America with regulation L85, the government's wartime order regulating various aspects of clothing manufacture. These included a maximum skirt length of 183 cm (72 inches), and limiting the trimming material in each dress to 46 cm (18 inches). The American version of the tailored suit was called the victory suit, and it was equally austere in terms of quality of cut, being much influenced by the designs of the Hollywood costumier Gilbert Adrian.

ABOVE American tailoring and a body-hugging handbag in a Hattie Carnegie ensemble from 1943. Carnegie's store in Manhattan was the destination for the aspiring business woman in the 1940s. Glamorous and expensive, the designer provided for all aspects of a woman's life in the city, from suits to handbags.

RIGHT A formal framed bag with double straps from 1948 is worn with a beige wool cape-coat by American designer Ken Whitmore, and accessorized with a navy blue hat by Mallory, the family-owned US milliner that was bought by Stetson in the 1950s.

LEFT Reptile skins once again became popular alternatives to leather due to the stringencies imposed by government agencies. This green snakeskin handbag is by Fassbender and dates from 1947–8.

OPPOSITE By 1946 the wartime silhouette began to soften, with greater emphasis on the waist and a fuller skirt, though it still retained the severe shoulder line, interpreted here by B H Wragge. The look is further feminized by the use of leopardskin for the large, practical handbag and the cloche hat.

The emphasis on streamlined structure for day-wear also applied to handbags. Although the leather shortage was global, in America, women who were not co-opted into the factories and who could afford such items accessorized their outfits with large, luxurious and yet understated handbags purchased from stores such as Hattie Carnegie's in Manhattan. That women required a bigger bag is evident in the article 'The Inside Story of a Handbag', which appeared in the *New York Times* on 21 January 1945: 'She wants it large. If she cannot get it in leather – now growing scarce – she will take it in fabric, fur or even plastic'.

The reporter, Anita Daniel, goes on to describe Mrs Roosevelt, then the First Lady:

In one hand she carried roses that had been presented to her; in another, her bag. What a bag! It was of dark leather and a tremendous dimension, practically bursting with invisible contents.'

The article concludes with a list of the contents of a typical woman's handbag in 1945:

One or two lipsticks, a compact, a fresh handkerchief, a package of letters, the laundry bill, 3 tickets from the cleaner, 1 nylon stocking to be repaired, 1 address book, 1 pack of cigarettes, 3 packets of matches, all ration books, 1 hairnet, 1 parcel of V-mail letters covering several months held by a rubber band, 1 bottle of vitamins, 1 fountain pen, and 1 hairnet.

Evening bags continued to contain elements of the earlier vanity case. Either box-shaped or circular with a central handle, they had a special section for cosmetics and a mirror. American cosmetics company Max Factor sent representatives into factories to give the workforce lessons in application, as the wearing of make-up by women was seen as almost a national duty to keep up morale. The softer-shaped evening bag or pochette had ruched, tucked or pleated fabric to add textural interest; this detail replaced the need for hard-to-get beads. Coloured sequins were not rationed, however, and evening bags were often appliquéd in a design similar to that of the sequinned bodice of the evening gown.

Mix 'n' Match

American fashion was developing a flourishing ready-to-wear industry of its own, and moving away from the influence of the European couturiers. Clare Potter, one of the first American designers to be known to the public, commented in the 1948 book *Fashion Is Our Business* by Beryl Williams Epstein:

> The Paris influence used to be too persuasive, I think – it affected everybody and they all turned out clothes that showed its mark. I don't think we should ever let that happen again. American designers know what sort of clothes American women want to wear and they can make them, too. Women used to think that they had to go to Paris for their clothes, but the war changed that. They discovered that they can be just as happy and just as well dressed without depending on Paris at all.

This developing confidence in an American aesthetic was fuelled by the popularity of the practical 'separates' offered by designers such as Norman Norell and Claire McCardell, and the Californian manufacturers Jantzen and Koret. It was a modern look that took into account the way ordinary women lived their lives. The designers and manufacturers provided comfortable classics such as the shirt dress, the gored skirt, the tailored blouse and high-waisted trousers. The concept of separates was born: a capsule wardrobe of pieces that could be put together in a variety of ways depending on the weather and the occasion. Fabrics were equally accommodating, including easy-wash cotton, chambray, and wool jersey in fresh-looking checks, stripes and plaids.

Practicality was paramount, which accounted for the burgeoning popularity of the boat tote bag, first introduced as a gardening tote by L L Bean in 1944. Founded in 1912 by Leon Leonwood Bean, the company built a brand on a newly relaxed style of dressing that was influenced by sportswear and the outdoors. The tote bag was the perfect expression of this principle, being a handbag in its simplest form. Sometimes called a shopper, it is based on a paper shopping bag, with handles at the top. The boat tote was made in canvas and was east-west style – that is, broader than it was high; a tall bag is known as north-south.

RIGHT In spite of the informality of this 1948 summer dress, fashion edicts still dictated white gloves. The casual look is accessorized with a bucket-shaped Glendale bag.

Homespun Handbags

In America, the homespun delights of gingham and denim were appropriated by the trend for 'peasant' clothes: blouses with drawstring necklines and puffed sleeves and dirndl skirts. Handbags reflected this use of simple materials, rustic charm and naive influences. The Sears catalogue of 1937 displayed brightly coloured ceramic and wood-beaded bags with the slogan: 'They're smart, they're practical, they're easily cleaned!'

The attraction of the homespun also embraced the exotic, particularly the naive arts south of the border, a look popularized by the American designer Louelle Ballerina. She was renowned for her 'adaptation of a rich variety of authentic native designs and influences which give her California-made play clothes a gay wear-ability'. Wood and cork not only appeared on shoes, but embellished her clothes and handbags. Her breakthrough design was a dress of rough hopsacking with a wide, turned-down collar embroidered in bright-coloured wool, and a wide skirt decorated with a broad band of yarn figures embellished with squares of wood sewn into the embroidery.

Straw, raffia and wicker baskets were also embellished with appliqué and embroidery. A design influence was the 'Bombshell from Brazil' Carmen Miranda. Part African, part Brazilian and known as the 'Woman in the Tutti Frutti Hat', the celebrated samba singer was at the time America's highest-paid entertainer. Her massive platform-soled shoes and fruit-embellished towering turbans introduced a Latin flamboyance into wartime fashion. Her multi-patterned sarongs and ruffled midriff-baring boleros provided a much-needed distraction from the austerity of the war.

LEFT A gored skirt utilizes the checked gingham of this ensemble from 1944. Although full-length, the dress echoes the simple sporty quality of much of American fashion during this period. A matching stole incorporates the same beadwork as the bag.

American Labels

The acceleration of fashion trends in post-war America was a direct outcome of an increased awareness of the importance of merchandising and marketing techniques, and an understanding that, in an increasingly consumer-driven society, choice was paramount. Together with new mass-production processes this resulted in a plethora of handbag styles to suit every occasion, from the beaded bags of Fre-Mor, to the understated elegance of Bienen-Davis.

Bienen-Davis

Featured on the front cover of the *Luggage & Leather Goods* newsletter in 1935, Edwin Davis of Bienen-Davis was described as a 'leading style authority'. The company produced classic urban designs in high-quality materials with gilt frames, such as the 'underarm skirt bag' in red Washette calf with a concealed zip and a gold ornamental pull tab, which appeared in 1942.

LEFT This photograph advertises a Bienen-Davis handbag for spring 1949. The original caption reads: 'Constant companion to the Springtime suit is the calfskin shoulder-strap pouch, a roomy carryall whose sleek lines lend themselves to sartorial perfection. This Bienen-Davis creation boasts a facile fastener, which opens wide with a slight pull and stays open until a gentle push snaps it back into place.'

The trend for personalization was also apparent in their advertising; monogrammed handbags were called the 'Personification of Elegance':

The new Fall handbags, highlighted by striking Monocraft Initials. Leading designers use initials for that smart accessory accent. Make your handbag displays appealing; feature them with initials.

Fre-Mor

The American manufacturers Fre-Mor were renowned for their range of beaded bags. Fashioned into hexagonal, round or rectangular shapes, the bags had gilt metal or Bakelite frames and were lined with silk. The round and rectangular bags are particularly collectable, and especially sought-after are those decorated with iridescent carnival beads. The owners of Fre-Mor Plastics later merged with Jewel Plastics Corporation to form Llewellyn, Inc., later famous for their Lucite handbags produced in the 1950s.

Delill Creations

The brand name Delill Creations was first used in 1941 and the trademark was registered to Desire and Lilly Rotkel in 1948; the label a combination of their two names. Situated in New York, the company produced fashion-led handbags with high production values, as evidenced in the swing ticket of 1942 inscribed 'the mark of creative handbag fashion'. In 1949 a posting in the trade paper *The Handbag Buyer* read:

Clear vinyl bags with laminated designs are big news at Delill Creations. Gold lamé or lace is laminated into dressier styles. Twisted ribbon makes smart all-over pattern on other vinyls. Handpainting and stone studding are other trims. Bag styles range from big totes to small clutches and pouches.

Delill were renowned for their 'trunk' style handbags, and for the transparent vinyl bags decorated with French poodles. From 1955 the handbags were subtitled 'Bags by Lily'. The last renewal of the trademark was made in 1968, and the trademark name is now unused.

OPPOSITE Lucite was used in the construction of an astonishing array of handbags; the injection-moulding process allowed for bizarre shapes and subject matter, from miniature chests of drawers to pagodas. These examples date from 1944.

RIGHT New York socialite Miss Sondra Ritter of New York arrives on the first day of Royal Ascot in Berkshire in June 1949. She carries a novelty transparent perspex vanity bag that discloses the contents, breaking the taboo that a woman's handbag is a private place.

The End of the Decade

Towards the end of the 1940s, handbag design was influenced by the processes and products of the burgeoning developments in industrial design and the new forms of architecture. Handbags became large and structurally complex, such as the brown leather, pleated collapsible bag by the American company Milch. Concertina shapes that opened on the diagonal, hardware clasps of sliding metal panels, and accordion-pleated bags led the way to the adoption of innovations in both materials and style that were to follow. In the book *Carrying On*, Olivier Saillard calls these items 'flying chests of drawers for the greedy decade' that was to come.

ABOVE RIGHT The post-war Marshall Plan provided aid, including modern materials, to boost the European economy; the German company Goldpfeil, a recipient of the funding, was thus inspired to name these pastel bags the 'Hollywood Series' in 1948–9.

RIGHT Although the shoulder pads are still in evidence in this flannel suit by Sacony, the more feminine silhouette is reflected in the pouched soft black leather drawstring bag, dating from 1946.

OPPOSITE LEFT The oversized envelope clutch, natural leather gloves and belt, and casually knotted silk scarf from 1944 presage the relaxed glamour and simple chic of the 1950s film actress Grace Kelly.

OPPOSITE RIGHT Fashion forward. In this 1949 photograph, all the details are in place for the 1950s – a perfect maquillage, a large, formal handbag, simple detailing and fur. A red calfskin handbag is worn with a skunk fur jacket by Christian Dior.

▼ Structure

Wartime utility gave way to ladylike formality in the later years of the decade. This 1948 red leather ba[g] Mademoiselle is a structured cho[ice] Etiquette demanded that shoes a[nd] bag should be a perfect match.

▲ Rucksacks and satchels

Wartime activities – such as responding to air raid sirens and riding bicycles – required a hands-free existence, hence the popularity of the shoulder bag, rucksack and satchel. This commodious unlined leather shoulder bag dating from 1945 is simple in shape with a gathered top that extends into a strap.

Key looks of the decade

1940s

▲ Raffia embroidery

A popular material during the 1940s, as it was available, easy to work and effective, raffia was often used for decoration as well as construction. Here an unlined fabric pochette from 1947 is embroidered with raffia flowers. The bag has a plain gilt frame with a cross-over snap closure.

◄ Messenger and shoulder bags
Sensible, sturdy satchel-inspired shapes with secure pockets and a long shoulder strap were typical of the wartime bag as practicality replaced decoration, providing surrogate homes for the dispossessed.

▼ Simple materials
Homespun and homemade, a young girl's red felt bag from America dates from 1945–50. A simple rouleau loop-and-button fastening secures the centre of the heart-shaped bag, which is decorated with appliquéd hearts.

▲ Waist-hung bags
A bag worn close to the body is the most practical accessory for a high-speed activity such as motoring. Here a yellow leather bag hangs from a belted pilot's coat from Carolyn Modes by Lo Balboa.

1950s:
Structure and Decorum

It was in the restrained and formal setting of the grand salon of No 30, avenue Montaigne in Paris, that a couture collection appeared and, in a single showing, changed the shape of fashion for a decade and defined the dominance of that city as the elite of the post-war fashion industry. When Christian Dior unveiled his 'Corolle' line in 1947, later dubbed by journalists as the 'New Look', it entered the annals of fashion as a defining moment. It received a tumultuous reception from an audience crowding the stairs of the salon, eager for a glimpse of the iconic silhouette. Named for the petals of a flower, the 'Corolle' collection emphasized the hourglass curves of a woman's body.

The sturdy, wide-strapped shoulder bag that had been worn with the austere, broad-shouldered tailored suits and narrow-hipped skirts of the Second World War era would have looked inappropriate with the new feminine silhouette. The softly rounded shoulders and tiny waist demanded that bags be small and dainty. It was a return to what Dior described as a more 'classical' style when he stated that 'in 1947 couture wanted to return to its true function, of clothing women and enhancing their beauty.' In defiance of post-war rationing, Dior's New Look presented a nostalgic form of femininity and was a celebration of luxury. Huge crinoline calf-length skirts were supported by layers of stiffened petticoats that used up to 23 metres (75 feet) of material.

Dior squeezed his models into 'waist cinches' or 'waspies', belt-like corsets that laced at the back and reduced the waist. Dior moved the padding that had resided in the shoulders to the hips. This exaggeratedly female silhouette, the result of cambric, taffeta, wire and whalebone, was seen by some critics as representative of a reactionary and idealized form of femininity, more suited to the home than the workplace. However, as Dior himself remarked, 'No one person can change fashion – a big fashion change imposes itself. It was because women wanted to look like women again that they adopted the New Look.'

Completing the New Look

The turn of the decade was an era when the fashion consumer was in thrall to the dictates of couturiers such as Christian Dior, Jacques Fath, Cristóbal Balenciaga, Pierre Balmain and Hubert de Givenchy. The twice-yearly fashion shows in Paris were reported by the press to eagerly awaiting consumers, as well as to a burgeoning mass-production industry. Manufacturers legitimately copied what was on the catwalk by purchasing the rights to individual garments, buying the *toile* (a calico version of the piece) so that they could copy it stitch for stitch in cheaper materials for the ready-to-wear market.

The new fashion and women's magazines reported the latest designs, and were keen to offer instructions on how these garments should be accessorized. Good grooming was paramount: hair had to be perfectly coiffed, a two-piece costume was *de rigueur*, and no lady left her home without coordinating hat, shoes, gloves and handbag. The American couturier Norman Norell stated:

> It always surprises me to see how little attention most women pay to the ensemble effect of their clothes. They may buy a dress that suits them well – and then spoil it completely by wearing the wrong shoes, or carrying the wrong bag. Every item a woman wears must be considered in its relation to every other item, and that's why we show our models as we do – complete to every accessory.

The quality of the handbag preoccupied the etiquette press. Edna Woolman Chase, editor of American *Vogue*, wrote in her autobiography in 1954:

> Although a good leather handbag costs money, it is a sound investment. Antelope or suede are usually desirable accessories for formal afternoon costumes, but they are expensive and spot and mat easily. Think twice about them; perhaps you can find some other good-looking, not so costly, fabric such as felt or a heavy, ribbed silk or straw.

Women not only returned to tightly tailored crinoline styles with the New Look, but attitudes and social mores also seemed to hark back to Victorian times. Women were encouraged to give up their autonomy and return to the confines of the home, and warned of the awful repercussions to their marriage if they 'let themselves go'. There was a more leisured way of life after the hectic pace and privations of the war, and yet the prescribed

activities of the middle-class housewife had their own demands, as she was expected to uphold standards of homemaking and her own appearance. These rigid attitudes as to what was deemed appropriate socially extended into the implementation of dress codes, including rules about what should and should not be worn with handbags. Edna Woolman Chase said: 'Never be guilty of wearing fancy shoes with a sports costume, an elaborate hat with a simple tailored suit. Do not wear long earrings for travelling or carry a business-like leather bag with a filmy summer frock.'

PAGE 90 The clutch bag continued to be an elegant staple throughout the 1950s, although larger in size than previously to match the new volume of the skirt. These ladylike proportions in 1952 included a girdle belt to cinch in the waist.

OPPOSITE The long, lean silhouette that was an adjunct to Dior's New Look gave an easy elegance to day clothes. The tweed coat is lined with red to match the red turban and worn over a tailored grey wool dress, accessorized with a classic hard-framed handbag with double straps dating from 1952.

THIS PAGE The batwing sleeves and the low-waisted knife-pleated skirt of the rayon dress by Majestic provides a more casual attitude to day dressing. The outfit is accessorized with a tan cowhide purse by Josef, from 1955.

Specialized Stores and Handbag Companies

After a decade when one handbag had to do for all occasions, 1950s decorum dictated that the elegant woman required several, and this was now possible as handbags became increasingly affordable. A proliferating number of specialist stores and handbag companies made a variety of handbags available to all, including well-known labels such as Jane Shilton and H Wald & Co. in Britain, Nettie Rosenstein, Hattie Carnegie and Koret, Inc. in America, and Roger Model in Paris. Handbags became cheaper with the increase in post-war mass production and the introduction of the new plastics, including vinyl, which soon ceased to be considered an inferior product to leather and became desirable in its own right. Vinyl could be wiped clean, which meant that lighter pastel shades became more practical, and its shiny surface lent itself to the almost futuristic streamlined shapes that appeared at the end of the decade and anticipated the space-age handbags to come.

A woman of fashion had a wardrobe of bags that might include a pigskin-framed box handbag to wear with tweeds, a framed balloon-style bag in leather with short handles for daywear, and for eveningwear an elongated envelope clutch by designers such as Gina and Neiman Marcus. The envelope clutch went particularly well with the long, lean lines of the designs of the Parisian couturier Jacques Fath. The clutch was now undecorated, unlike its 1930s counterpart, and the only trimming would be the brass or gilt clasp. The bags were redolent of the sleek stretch limousine increasingly seen on the streets of American cities.

LEFT AND FAR LEFT Norman Parkinson displays his signature style of photography for the April 1958 issue of *Vogue* magazine. Two young women carry the bags of the season – one white, one black – but both wearing pink, the colour of the decade.

OPPOSITE A beautifully crafted classic envelope clutch dating from 1958 is worn with a popular 'shirtwaist' dress of black-and-white stripes and white gloves.

Evening bags were generally considered at their smartest in black satin or suede, with a clasp and frame studded with rhinestones. More expensive evening bags had frames of gold, decorated with diamonds. For more formal occasions, a small cocktail bag of silver or gold brocade, kidskin or embroidered silk would be required to complement the rapier-slim silk sheath dress. The minaudière, the hand-held compact, once more became a vital accessory as the use of cosmetics returned after the wartime shortages. A perfect maquillage was an essential element of being well groomed.

The extensive range of bags on offer during the affluent 1950s even included special 'wedding bags', made in white satin or silk. Heavily embellished with Beauvais beadwork, involving a tiny chain stitch and equally tiny alabaster beads in a floral design, these bags had a slightly 'retro' look, harking back to the days of the reticule. One such example is by the American label, the Walborg Corporation, founded in New York City in the late 1940s. In Europe, summer day dresses needed bags with a lighter touch than the box-frame handbag. The London-based textile designer Zika Ascher commissioned the leading artists of the day to create designs for screen-printed fabrics that were made up into bags, and the London firm Liberty sold clutch bags made from their printed silks.

The decorum of the 1950s allowed no leeway for the idiosyncratic, and matched sets of shoes and handbags were an indication of perfect grooming. Companies such as the British label Edward Rayne even offered a personal service and would dye shoes and bags to match an outfit.

BELOW Model Anne Saint-Marie wears a cinnamon brown wool tweed evening coat, lined in black satin, over a matching black satin dress dating from 1959. The bag is richly encrusted with beads and gathered into a rounded frame with a ball-and-clasp fastening.

OPPOSITE The evening clutch was always smaller in size than the daytime version; this one dates from 1952 and is worn with a white strapless ballgown with a draped bodice, caught with a daffodil corsage, all by Christian Dior.

BELOW A luxurious evening bag in cream silk, heavily embroidered with beaded flower motifs, by British company H Wald & Co., dates from 1950–4. 'Waldybags' were also known as 'Sweetheart's purses' as they were popular with American GIs in the 1940s, who bought them as presents for their girlfriends back home.

ABOVE Fur was an important element of 1950s fashion and very much a status symbol; a fur handbag was the next best thing to a fur coat. Here miniature bags in six different fur forms date from 1959.

OPPOSITE A capacious fur bag by Greta dramatically sets off a red suit with brass buttons by Junior Sophisticates. The white gloves are by Superb, and the gold bracelet by Arpad. The black-and-white animal print of the handbag lends a touch of eccentricity to a conventional 1950s suit.

RIGHT American actress Jeanne Crain wears a leopardskin hat and bag dating from 1953. Although this leopardskin bag would have been too expensive for many women, fake fur began to be made in copious quantities during the decade and was used for both coats and handbags.

Chanel and the Birth of the Status Bag

Just as couture reached its apotheosis in the 1950s, so did the iconic handbag, which became an accessory that conferred status on the wearer. All the atelier skills utilized for the couture garment were extended to the production of the couture handbag. There was embroidery and beadwork by Lesage, and work by the most skilled *plumassiers* (feather workers), the best furriers (both Pierre Balmain and Christian Dior had a brief flirtation with the muff), artisan leather workers, and those who made the most exquisite *passimenterie* (trims including braids, tassels and knots). For those who could not afford the couture garment, there was always the possibility that a bag adorned with a designer label or *griffe* (a French word meaning claw or talon, and denoting a mark) would confer status and make up for any sartorial inadequacies. According to the fashion historian Valerie Steele, a cult bag must have the following three characteristics: '1, legitimacy within the fashion industry; 2, great advertising; 3, celebrity support'.

Legitimacy within the fashion industry required that the bag be allied to a respected name, such as that of Coco Chanel, whose reputation was consolidated during the 1920s and 1930s with her remarkable diversity into relaxed jersey dressing at a time when structured clothing dominated. Chanel's name or griffe certainly conferred prestige on the legendary 2.55 handbag, which she introduced in February 1955. Named after the month and year of its birth, the bag was a development of the shoulder bag that she first produced in 1929.

The couturier was 70 years old and had been in retirement for 14 years when she reopened her fashion house in 1954. Openly critical of Dior's structured and inhibiting clothing, she launched a fashion collection that took her casual signature style of the 1930s into the more formal 1950s with the understated classic Chanel suit. The edge-to-edge, short boxy jackets and the knee-length flared skirts were usually made in a luxurious textured tweed. The hem of the jacket was weighted with flattened chains so that the fabric hung without creasing. The suits were trimmed with a contrasting braid around the hem of the jacket, down the centre front and across the top of the pockets.

The square, padded and quilted 2.55 bag with its distinctive gilt shoulder chain, braided with leather, was the perfect accessory for the suit, being structured but with an element of informality. Evolved from Chanel's first handbag designs in the 1920s, the bag came in the couturier's favourite colours – beige, navy, black and brown – and was manufactured in leather or jersey. The three flap pockets remained: a tube-shaped pocket for lipstick, one with a zip for security, and a secret pocket for mementos. The bag had a gilt, rectangular revolving clasp and the double-C logo was discreetly stitched into the lining, which was originally a dark red. Colloquially known as the 'gilt and quilt bag', the 2.55 was adopted by the most famous stars of the 1950s and 1960s, such as Elizabeth Taylor, Jackie Kennedy and Catherine Deneuve. In the 1980s the designer Karl Lagerfeld, invited to put his signature on the label, made the bag larger, fattened the chain and flaunted the large interlocking double Cs on the front.

LEFT The 1950s was the era of the iconic handbag, and none was more prized than the Chanel 2.55, an undisputed classic. The quilted leather, long chain handle and the interlocking Cs (at this time discreetly placed in the lining of the bag) was instantly recognizable.

RIGHT Coco Chanel's favourite model, Marie-Hélène Arnaud, modelling a Chanel bag from 1959.

Paradigms of Perfection

Hollywood adopted Dior's New Look as its own, and called it the 'sweetheart line'. This look had particular longevity in the cinema where its popularity was prolonged by the costume designers Edith Head and Helen Rose. Both designed for Grace Kelly, who epitomized an ideal of feminine beauty and ladylike chic, but it was Edith Head who created the costumes for Hitchcock's favourite blonde in his film *Rear Window* in 1954. Head, who worked on all of Hitchcock's films, remarked on Kelly's faultless figure and carriage that needed none of the designer's customary disguises. The costumes for the film, the Hollywood version of Christian Dior's 1947 collection, showed off the actress's perfect figure. Kelly's first appearance in *Rear Window* shows her framed in a doorway, wearing a dress 'right off the Paris plane'. It has a tight-fitting black bodice, with a deep V-shape neckline, and sequinned panels on a froth of pale skirt that is wider than the doorway through which she steps. The actress is carrying an overnight case that had been especially created for the film by Max Holzman for the Mark Cross Company. She tempts the hero with the possibility that she might stay the night and, in an early example of product placement, mentions the maker of the bag as she opens it to reveal a negligee and a pair of slippers.

This was not the only bag that became famous by association with the elegant star. During filming in 1955 for Hitchcock's *To Catch a Thief*, Kelly met her future husband, Prince Rainier of Monaco, and they were married in 1956. Kelly became pregnant that same year, and famously appeared on the cover of American *Time* magazine hiding her pregnancy with a classic Hermès bag, after which the *sac haut à courroies* (tall bag with straps) travel bag became known as the Kelly bag.

How a Kelly Bag Is Made

In total, it takes 18 hours to construct a Kelly bag. Unlike manufacturing for the mass market, when each process is divided among the work force, the making of the Kelly bag is undertaken by one person, from start to finish. For the past 20 years, Hermès has even incorporated an embossed stamp inside the bag, denoting the name of the craft worker who made it, and the date. This is not only useful in case the bag needs to be returned for repairs, but is also helpful when checking whether or not the bag is fake.

The skins for the bag are selected according to personal requirements, and arrive at the atelier in hand-cut pieces. For a bag made of alligator, the skins from two alligators are required: skin from the belly is used for the body of the bag, and the neck

skin becomes the sides. The lining, made from goatskin, is constructed first, and the base of the bag is then hand stitched to the front and the back with a double saddle stitch; this involves a process of two needles working waxed linen threads in tensile opposition. Each bag requires more than 2,600 hand stitches, and every stitch requires that the skin is first perforated with an awl, the traditional artisan's tool, also used by saddle makers. The grain and density of the leather dictates the size of the stitch.

ABOVE The Noah Bag in seal-grained Moroccan leather is by American company Mark Cross from the 1950s. The drawstring pouch reputedly owes its name to being as roomy as the ark. It could be worn looped over the arm, or over the shoulder.

The handle is constructed from five pieces of leather and is shaped by hand using a special knife. The bevelled edges of the leather are then smoothed away with sandpaper and dyed to match the bag. Hot wax is used to seal this part of the bag to protect it from moisture.

The front flap is then stitched to the body of the bag, and the handles glued and stitched to the bag. The clasp and the four metal feet on the base are riveted to the skin, and four holes are punctured to secure the bag's locking belt hardware. The bag is then ironed to get rid of the crinkles in the calfskin, and the final stage is to stamp the 'Hermès Paris' name on each Kelly bag.

ABOVE Grace Kelly with her then-fiancé Prince Rainier III of Monaco in 1956. Kelly holds the style of Hermès handbag that was named after her. The *sac haut à courroies* (known as the HAC) first appeared in 1930, but the bag only achieved iconic status in the 1950s due to its association with the film star.

RIGHT The classic Kelly bag by Hermès. Each bag is handmade from start to finish and is even more covetable today than in previous decades.

Hepburn Elegance

Every era has an ideal to whom women aspire. In post-war Hollywood, glamour was all about the hourglass figure and Christian Dior's revival of the corset and crinoline. Hollywood's most celebrated film stars were Marilyn Monroe and Elizabeth Taylor, both voluptuous and brimming with sex appeal in wasp-waisted dresses that emphasized their provocative appeal. Audrey Hepburn offered an alternative to these stereotypical screen goddesses and was to influence a whole generation of women, including Jackie Kennedy. When she starred in *Roman Holiday*, her first American film, made in 1953, the actress appeared as a fresh-faced ingénue, swinging her large, straw tote bag around the Italian streets. She imparted a spirit of *la dolce vita* that was immensely appealing to a nation eager to discover the delights of 'abroad' once wartime restrictions had been lifted.

Hepburn embodied the appeal of a new decade. Although Hubert de Givenchy, an aristocratic French-born couturier, first opened his salon in 1952, Hepburn's adoption of his chemise line heralded the approach of 1960s minimalism. This body-skimming and simple line was the first innovation to come out of Paris since Dior's New Look in 1947. It liberated women from the torment of the waspie corset and cantilevered bosom, heralding a sophisticated look appropriate for life outside the home.

Givenchy's streamlined suits of solid blocks of bright colour, caught by a single button or fold of fabric, epitomized a clean-cut, unfussy glamour that necessitated a clean, streamlined handbag, hence the revival of the clutch bag. However, this time it was larger and longer. Breakfast at Tiffany's, made in 1961, conveys the difference between the decades in the fashion espoused by the two female leads. The character played by Patricia Neal wears structured, form-fitting and relentlessly matching outfits by the French-born American couturier Pauline Trigère, in sharp contrast to the modern, architectural style worn by Audrey Hepburn as Holly Golightly.

BELOW Parisian couturier Hubert Givenchy's pared-down aesthetic was the bridge between Dior's post-war New Look and the simply cut shifts of the 1960s. This short-sleeved sheath dress and bag date from 1955 and create an elegant and seamless look.

The Italian Influence

Iconic handbag brands such as Prada and Fendi became household names during the period between 1945 and 1965; this period was known as the _ricostruzione_ (reconstruction) in Italy, when the country began to develop a design industry that was to influence the world. The origins of these companies that went on to produce 'It' bags during the later decades of the twentieth century had their provenance in the years before the First World War as saddle makers and leather and luggage suppliers, including Gucci, established in 1906, and Prada, established in 1913. The economic aid from America during the _ricostruzione_ encouraged these family firms to consolidate their design and manufacturing activities in an era of post-war regeneration and creativity. During this period, 'Made in Italy' came to mean good design and superior craftsmanship, precepts which held true throughout the following decades.

Design innovation flourished: Salvatore Ferragamo invented the stiletto heel, Emilio Pucci started his fashion empire, and the Fendi family developed their fur and leather business. Aldo, the son of Guccio Gucci, produced the bamboo-handled handbag in 1957, a response to the post-war shortage of leather. Celebrity endorsement and thus its elevation to status bag (alongside the Chanel 2.55 and Hermès Kelly bag) came in the form of patronage by America's First Lady: Gucci's bag became known as the Jackie bag, after Jacqueline Kennedy Onassis. The scarcity of leather led the Gucci company to develop their trademark red and green striped webbing, which was derived from the saddle girth, and to print their distinctive

ABOVE Italian leather goods were widely imported. The March 1955 New York press release for this handbag read: 'Josef designed this smart swagger bag in lustrous leather, imported from Italy, with all-over domino-dot pattern.'

LEFT In 1957 Aldo Gucci put cane handles on his bags to circumvent leather shortages. Although the brand was selling luxury leather goods in 1938, it wasn't until the early 1960s that Gucci became internationally renowned for their handbags.

double-G motif on canvas. They also bedecked the front of their iconic suede moccasin loafer with a miniature horse's snaffle. These were the signature elements that defined the label for the next three decades, until the American designer Tom Ford was invited to rebrand the company in 1992.

There was nothing utilitarian about the luxurious Bagonghi handbag produced by the Venetian design company Roberta di Camerino, founded by the fashion designer Giuliana Coen Camerino. Also seen on the arm of Grace Kelly, the box-shaped bag had a centre panel of soprarizzo velvet manufactured by the same firm that produces velvet for the Vatican. The fabric is made in the dark to prevent the colour fading through exposure to light, and no more than 10 metres (33 feet) are produced a month. Giuliana defined the three qualities that go to make up the perfect bags: the precious materials from which they are made, their craftsmanship, and the beauty of their design.

ABOVE The geometric stripes of this oversized sweater in brown, black and white by Geist & Geist is echoed in the chrome detailing of the large square-framed handbag from 1955.

ABOVE As the decade progressed the elongated clutch gave way to larger, squarer shapes, which offered greater opportunities to show off various treated leathers, as in this unusual printed leather bag dating from 1956.

RIGHT Monochrome was a popular theme during the 1950s, particularly in the form of small all-over prints. This sleeveless dress, accessorized by a semicircular black patent bag, was designed by Mollie Parnis in 1953.

The American Fashion Industry

Claire McCardell, described as 'American as apple pie', began her professional life sketching Paris fashions for the American mass market, but eventually, in her own words, she translated them into 'American fabrics, making them a little easier, a little more casual, a little less self-conscious, and a little more American'. McCardell was the forerunner of American sportswear, known as casual wear in Europe. Hattie Carnegie had earlier seen the potential for lower-priced garments when, alongside her luxury brand, she had inaugurated a 'Spectator Sportsline' during the years of the American Depression.

McCardell knew that American women wanted clothes that worked; she understood that if there was something she herself needed that didn't already exist, then other women needed it too. When heating costs were high during the war, she produced long-sleeved evening dresses in wool. She introduced the dancer's leotard to daywear in vivid coloured jersey, and tailored suits in denim and striped linen, all of which responded to the modern need for practical clothes that appealed to a younger market, rather than the matron.

The designer's problem-solving clothes generally precluded the need for a handbag. Her coat dress, worn over a bathing suit, could be unbuttoned and spread out on the sand. It had a huge pocket to carry suncream and make-up items. Most of her garments contained capacious pockets that imitated the ease inherent in the get-up-and-go of menswear. The large-scale manufacturers of the newly industrialized American fashion industry responded to these fresh new ideas and began producing fashionable clothes for the burgeoning ready-to-wear market.

LEFT Although Pauline Trigère was one of the most popular American couturiers of the 1950s, she was born in France. This red leather handbag, designed in 1952, has all the hallmarks of her classic American style.

OPPOSITE American model and actress Suzy Parker (known as the 'face of Chanel') poses in casual clothes accessorized with flat shoes and a rustic tan leather-and-suede bag from the late 1950s.

Kitsch, Novelty and Whimsy

The boom time of the mid-1950s saw the parsimony of the Second World War finally come to end. Accessories needed to reflect a new carefree attitude, and the development of brightly coloured plastic and novelty bags certainly added to the general joie de vivre and spirit of optimism of the time. Bakelite was the forerunner of the plastic handbag. Once its patent expired in 1927, coloured plastic permeated all aspects of material culture, including household products and novelty items, as well as fashion accessories such as jewellery and handbags. The new translucent plastics, such as Lucite, placed Bakelite firmly in the past. Developed by chemical researchers at DuPont in 1931, for strictly utilitarian uses such as nose cones and windshields for bombers during the Second World War, Lucite was subsequently crafted into bizarre and eccentric handbags that turned the concept of 'good taste' on its head. One of the features of Lucite was that it could be transparent or opaque, so the owner could change the colour of her handbag to match her outfit by lining the bag with an offcut of material or a scarf. Others were studded with faux jewels, sculpted into mischievous shapes such as fans, baskets or caskets, or were resolutely three dimensional and hard-edged. Some even came with do-it-yourself decorating kits containing glitter or confetti. Handbags were no longer only crafted in the sober hues of leather, but were 'crystal clear' or coloured sapphire, jet, mink, marble, avocado, coffee frost or pink and blue pearl.

The majority of Lucite handbag manufacture took place in New York or Miami, Florida. Although the bags were very similar in styling, each company tended to offer specific features. Llewellyn, Inc. operated out of Madison Avenue in New York and was the result of a merger in 1951 between Jewel Plastics Corporation, manufacturers of carry-alls and frames, and Fre-Mor Manufacturing Corporation, who produced beaded bags. Their trademark was the Lewsid Jewel by Llewellyn. An edition of *Handbags & Accessories* describes in detail Llewellyn's 1954 spring line:

BELOW The developments in new technology had implications for handbag design. The invention of Lucite, a highly adaptable synthetic acrylic resin (polymethyl methacrylate) resulted in novelty handbags such as this rigid box-shaped structure by Rialto, New York, dating from the 1950s.

BELOW A 1950s transparent acrylic handbag, incised with stylized flower petals and in the form of a box with rounded ends, is labelled Maxin and made by Llewellyn.

A completely new design motif called 'Song of the Sea' is presented by Llewellyn, Inc., in a series of plastic boxes in all colors. Taking all the beauty and color of underwater life, this firm has a series of shaped plaques, which are recessed into bag lids. The plaques have tiny colorful shelves, in soft sea pastels, bits of real coral, tiny fake pearls nestling in shells, grains of silver as 'glamorized sand' set in a molten pearl base. The molten pearl is softly colored with an iridescent glazed quality, and acts as both a background and cement for the free-form shell designs. The plaques have the quality of jewelry, and in fact the same theme can be seen in a group of matching accessories.

Other well-known manufacturers in New York included Gilli Originals, owned by Associated Plastics, and Tyrolean, whose smoother, more sophisticated lines generally incorporated a metal frame. Myles Originals, based in Miami, produced glamorous bags with a three-ball metal clasp. Miami Handbags was headed by Morty Edelstein, who added another line, the better-known Patricia of Miami, named after his wife, Patricia Edelstein. Charles S Kahn was another Florida-based manufacturer whose signature styling was to produce bags in a solid metallic colour, particularly pink, with clear lids and handles, often featuring geometric or floral cut designs. The company used the same three-ball fastening favoured by Patricia of Miami and Myles Originals. Dorset Rex utilized a metal filigree for the body of their bags, usually in white or yellow, and combined this with a black, taupe or tortoiseshell base, lid and handle.

RIGHT Lucite was an expensive material to produce. To satisfy the urge for the new product, handbag manufacturers designed cheaper bags with Lucite features, such as this red woven bag with Lucite handles.

Wilardy

Will Hardy was a larger-than-life character who enjoyed all the consumer delights that the 1950s had to offer, including fast cars, silk suits and modern materials. Having studied industrial design in his late teens, the designer joined the family business, Handbag Specialties, in New York in 1948, when the Wilardy trademark was first used (he elided his name for commercial purposes). Always interested in the properties of plastic, Wilardy invented a form of Lucite that was both glossy and tough, which he developed into handbags of the most extraordinary and bizarre design. Although he claimed, 'I added two handles to a hard plastic jewellery box and it looked great as a bag', the shapes were far from simple. They included bags in the form of a bucket with a central single handle; bags shaped like 1950s dressing tables, complete with rhinestone-studded mirrors; miniature travelling trunks decorated with rhinestone travel stickers; and bags shaped like the Hollywood sirens of the day, Jane Russell and Marilyn Monroe.

Although plastic had always had connotations of the cheap and mass-produced when it imitated something finer and more expensive, the first Lucite handbags were hand-cast and heat-soldered together, making them as much a result of the artisan's skill as the finest leather handbags, and with a similar price tag. 'Hand-fabricated from the finest acrylic', declared an advertisement from the time. Wilardy excelled at innovative shaping: the bag that won him first prize from the International Fashion Institute in 1954 was a streamlined toffee-coloured box bag with barley-twist handles. Following the award, he was confident enough to hire 40 people for his New York factory and produced over 70 models a day. The 'handbag of the stars' was carried by all of Hollywood's leading ladies; a Wilardy rhinestone clutch featured alongside Ida Lupino in the 1954 film *Private Hell 36*.

The company went from strength to strength until the end of the 1950s, when plastic ceased to be a novelty product, and something more informal, less 'dressy' was in the air. The bags were copied by other manufacturers, who often produced almost identical designs, in spite of Wilardy's attempts to protect his patents. Wilardy Lucite bags have a paper label or the name in embossed lettering on the inside hinge of the handbag. The popularity of Lucite bags declined further with the introduction of the injection-moulding process, which allowed cheaper and more brittle plastics to be used.

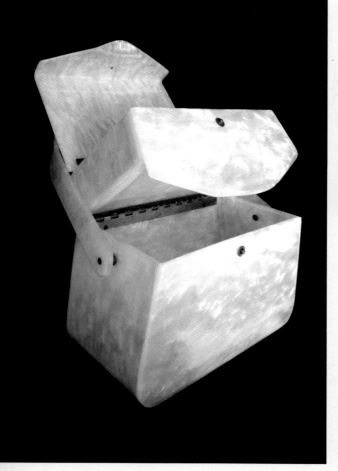

LEFT An early 1950s Lucite bag by Wilardy. The rigid box shape has an interior tray on a hinge, incised with the Wilardy logo. The bag resembles a small piece of furniture rather than a handbag.

BELOW CENTRE AND DETAIL OPPOSITE A 1950s American evening bag constructed from rigid transparent acrylic is decorated with an incised grid design on both sides, inset with imitation diamonds. The lever closure has a matching imitation diamond knob, a white metal frame and a single rigid acrylic handle.

OPPOSITE A delicately engraved Perspex box bag, dating from 1950–4, is an unexpected combination of new technology and traditional embroidery motifs of flowers and birds.

BELOW A grey Birdseye Lucite Wilardy bag dating from the 1950s has silver metal fittings and a high loop front-to-back mounted handle with a lid-mounted oval mirror. It is marked with incised lettering on the interior hinge.

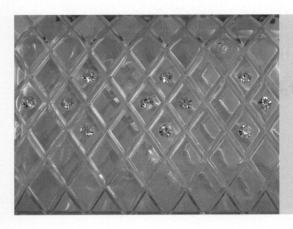

CARING FOR LUCITE HANDBAGS

✶ Keep the bags out of the sun, as heat causes them to warp
or to leak a toxic liquid.

✶ Toxic fumes can form when Lucite is exposed to heat, so dispose
of a bag if it exudes a strong chemical odour.

✶ Lucite is a fragile and brittle material, so if it is dropped, it is likely
to shatter.

✶ Store in a cool place away from direct sunlight and radiators.
Do not store them in a plastic bag, as this can cause discolouration.

THIS PAGE Vacation time at the airport in Kingston, Jamaica, 1957. The cheap and cheerful straw basket bag in the foreground has a cornucopia of fake fruit cascading down the front. Model Romaine Simenson, wearing a red shirtwaist dress by Anne Fogarty, carries a small case decorated with travel stickers. The bag in the background is an East-West tote bag, a roomy open-topped practical bag, perfect for holiday activities.

Fun in the Sun

Increased leisure and more money equalled excursions abroad and holidays by the sea, all of which required special versions of the handbag. Shore-side, cheap and cheerful prevailed, with washable embossed plastic replicating straw and linen, and painted wickerwork with plastic handles. Crocheted raffia embroidered with seashells and silk flowers proliferated, favourites being by Caron of Texas. Basket bags, the forerunner of the plastic throwaway supermarket bag, became highly decorative. They could be made of straw, wicker, rush or raffia, and personalized with collages of fruit or flowers.

The Nantucket Lightship basket and purse are the most valuable and sought-after of all vintage baskets. They originate from more than 150 years ago, when ships returned to Nantucket, Massachusetts, carrying rattan, a long vine-like plant from which the outer bark would be stripped off and used for basketry. In 1856, the first lightship was commissioned to warn ships of the dangerous waters surrounding Nantucket, and many sailors took basket-making materials to alleviate the boredom of being on watch, so the Lightship basket was born. In 1948, Jose Formosa Reyes, originally from the Philippines, introduced the use of a woven lid design on top of the basket. The baskets have a tightly woven straw body and a wooden lid often decorated with a carved ivory plaque. These carvings usually depict nautical subjects, such as seashells, lighthouses and whales.

As the 1950s progressed, adolescent girls ceased to want to dress like their mothers in watered-down versions of French couture or American ready-to-wear, and began to demand styles of their own. The sober virtues propounded by Dior – 'true luxury needs

LEFT Suzy Parker models a bucket-shaped Basket bag in 1954, a Josef design in natural marostica straw, imported from Italy. The lid is covered with a bouquet of pastel-tinted seashells, and closes with a simple raffia loop.

good materials and good workmanship; it will never succeed unless its roots are profoundly embedded in sober influences and honest traditions' – were about to be undermined by new products, innovations in manufacture and, above all, shifting attitudes as to what constituted a 'fashionable' handbag.

The sleek, sophisticated formal bag of the 1950s woman, which grew ever larger as the decade progressed, had no place on the arm of the teenager who wanted something that was fun and frivolous. Manufacturers were quick to exploit this new market, and special bags for bowling, records and make-up appeared. Novelty handbags included those made from wicker in the shape of animals. Bags flooded the market featuring printed or embroidered iconography of the female teenager, from musical notes and guitars to café scenes and ballerinas. Particularly popular were images of the poodle, which were supposed to imbue the bags with continental sophistication. In the late 1940s, the American manufacturer Walborg produced a range of highly collectable black poodle handbags that were hand-beaded in Belgium, to be followed in the 1950s with white poodles beaded in Japan. The British journalist Anne Scott-James was less than enthusiastic; she wrote in her book *In the Mink*:

My new merchandise editor had a miniature poodle with that indecent French clip. It looked like a chorus girl who wears boots, gloves and a hat and not much else. Hers was only one poodle among many around Bond Street; indeed there was soon quite a plague of them and I privately thought they were a bit vulgar.

LEFT Plastic was valued for its indestructible properties, making it particularly appropriate for use on the beach. Here the plastic imitates woven black leather and is constructed around a rigid frame. The bag has circular handles, a leather tab closure with a twist knob and metal stud feet on the base.

Lucite and plastic

Lucite lent itself to radical shapes such as this three-dimensional ellipse made by Florida Handbags. The transparent acrylic and grey pearlized plastic body of the bag is offset by the ornate grid of the lid, to which a single rigid loop handle is attached. The bag has the typical three-ball fastening, which was a feature of Florida Handbags.

Key looks of the decade

1950s

▲ Structured bags

Decorous dressing was a feature of 1950s fashion. The dress and jacket, a popular combination, is here accessorized in typical classic elegance with American manufacturer Koret's red calfskin bag dating from 1953.

▼ Elongated clutches

The clutch, found in more styles and shapes than ever before, w[as] a 1950s favourite. Here an even[ing] envelope-style in stiffened broca[de] made by Lederer exclusively for British retailers Russell & Bromle[y] has a pattern of flowering vines in gold lamé, red and light blue on a black ground. The bag is lined in black moiré.

▲ Mesh bags

Whiting & Davis continued to make mesh bags throughout the twentieth century. This 1950s envelope clutch is stamped 'After Schiaparelli' and is constructed from gold fish-scale mesh over cream satin. It has two internal pockets and a matching small coin purse and pocket mirror.

Raffia and straw

...day bags featured homespun ...erials, such raffia, plastic fruit and ...en basketry. This envelope-style ...ch bag in unstiffened woven ...a is decorated with three posies ...owers on the front, perfect as a ...mmery accessory.

▶ Imitation leather

Imitation leather and vinyl were valued for their 'wipe-clean' properties, and allowed paler colours to be introduced into handbag design. This shopping bag is in imitation cream leather, with a rigid, white metal frame, partly covered by plastic, a central lever closure with a pale grey translucent ball trim, narrow double strap handles, and a practical external purse section.

▲ Evening bags

Etiquette in the 1950s dictated that women dressed up for the cocktail hour and evenings at the theatre; every outfit required a matching bag. Here an evening bag in PVC with silver and gold discs is overlaid with an embroidered filigree pattern. The frame is white metal and the handle is a fine flexible golden metal chain.

1960s:
Youthquake

The advent of youth culture in the 1960s meant that old-fashioned notions of appropriate behaviour and dress were rendered obsolete. The post-war baby boom resulted in unparalleled numbers of teenagers reaching puberty in the early 1960s. At a time of unprecedented affluence and diminishing parental control, not least over appearance, they could look forward to an extended adolescence.

Buying a classic handbag from a stuffy department store held no attractions for these new teenagers. That was for their mothers. Handbags belonged on the arm of the Queen, or for old people over 30! They had no interest in status dressing, or longevity and quality of materials. At a time when clothing was minimal, so too were the daily necessities once deemed vital. British designer and master cutter Ossie Clark famously sewed a little pocket inside his dresses for emergency money, in case the evening hadn't turned out as planned. Make-up was applied lavishly at home so all that was needed was a 'top up' with a lip slave, carried in a pocket. If anything more was required, then the handbag became a matter of personal choice, not a branded appendage. Homemade tote bags in brightly printed furnishing fabrics, even a customized old school satchel would do, as long as it had a shoulder strap. In the 1963 film *Billy Liar*, the teenage icon Julie Christie represented freedom and a dread of conformity, swinging her shoulder bag as she flees a provincial town in the north of England for the bright lights of London.

In the mid-1960s, as hemlines rose ever higher, a new proportion evolved in fashion – the womanly curves of the hourglass figure were over. Only the 'blissful girls and crazy dollies' could wear the skimpy futuristic fashions of this era. These new clothes were not cut to conceal imperfections, but to reveal. Only the young could claim them for their own.

The New Order

In the early years of the 1960s the classic structured handbag with short handles remained popular, with the emphasis on good-quality materials and fine workmanship. Carried on the wrist, it was an accessory in keeping with the still lady-like fashions of the day epitomized by America's First Lady Jackie Kennedy. As the decade progressed, however, handbag design reflected the enormous changes taking place in Europe and America. As social hierarchies broke down with the emergence of 'Youthquake', and the subsequent counter-culture and the hippie movements, handbags reflected the informality of the new order, and became free-form, commodious and idiosyncratic.

The classic handbag with its snap closure, often constructed in patent leather or crocodile in black, navy or tan, never fell out of favour with the older, more conservative consumer. However, fashion during this decade was all about the young, and handbags became subject to the same speed of change as fashion itself. The miniature hatbox bag and the 'mod' pastel patent shoulder bag in orange, pink or turquoise gave way to the futuristic chainmail purses of Paco Rabanne, which were then superseded by the homemade patchwork or crocheted shoulder bag and the kelim carpet bag of the hippie. Materials ranged from stamped and decorated leather and suede, and natural fibres such as raffia and straw, to fashion fabrics such as velvet and embroidered silk. Decoration included the ubiquitous floral motifs of flower-power, the psychedelic imagery of Pucci and the embroidered box bags of American designer Enid Collins.

The advice of Genevieve Antoine Dariaux in her seminal etiquette book *A Guide to Elegance* published in 1964 probably went unheeded by the 1960s 'dolly bird' or hippie:

PAGE 118 Segueing from 1950s formality into the swinging '60s, a rice-paper shift dress from 1962 shows the rising hemline, yet the bag and hat coordinate.

BELOW LEFT Bold shapes in intense colours and unusual fastenings were representative of 1960s fashion, seen here in the geometric form and clever design of this 1967 bag.

BELOW RIGHT The subtle femininity of this bag by Christian Dior dating from 1967 lies in the symmetrical flat suede bow and the slender double handles.

THIS PAGE Shiny patent leather handbags in Pop Art colours from France date from 1966–7 and accessorize pastel skinny-rib sweaters and mini-kilts worn by British model icon Twiggy and friend.

It is indispensable to own a complete set of accessories in black, and, if possible, another in brown, plus a pair of beige shoes and a beige straw handbag for summer. With this basic minimum, almost any combination is attractive.

Of course, it would be ideal to have each set of accessories in two different versions: one for sport and the other for dressy. And in this regard I cannot restrain myself from expressing the dismay I feel when I see a woman carry an alligator handbag with a dressy ensemble merely because she has paid an enormous sum of money for it. Alligator is strictly for sports or travel, shoes as well as bags, and this respected reptile should be permitted to retire every evening at 5 pm.

And here, as in no other department, quality is essential. Be strict with yourself. Save. Economize on food if you must (believe me, it will do you good!) but not on your handbags or shoes. Refuse to be seduced by anything that isn't first-rate. The saying, 'I cannot afford to buy cheaply' was never so true. Although I am far from rich, I have bought my handbags for years from Hermès, Germaine Guerin and Roberta. And, without exception, I have ended by giving away all the cheap little novelty bags that I found irresistible at first. The same is true of shoes and gloves.

But change was afoot. A new freedom from the constraints of 1950s foundations – pointy bras and restricting girdles – was more to do with modernity than seduction. This liberating attitude towards fashion represented new social hierarchies; when youth triumphed over age, anything seemed possible. These new looks even infiltrated the ladylike pages of *Vogue*, through the endeavours of Marit Allen, editor of the 'Young Ideas' pages. She recalled:

> Things started to hot up, young people were finding a new personal voice; they didn't want to be like their parents. There was a universal movement afoot, that wasn't just about skirt lengths but a new social order.

This new social order included the democratization of fashion. Friends sold to friends in the boutiques that sprang up on the periphery of all the major cities. This occurred most tellingly in London where consumers no longer shopped on Bond Street, but sought out the new boutiques on the King's Road in Chelsea, and later Carnaby Street. Boutiques such as Mary Quant's Bazaar changed the nature of shopping, from being a peripheral activity to a social occasion; it was central to the experience of being young, attractive and cool. The entrepreneurial ethos of the 1960s that resulted in teenagers 'doing their own thing' meant that the young consumers could now also become the new producers.

BELOW Murray Resnick, the president of the company Gay Pauley and a founder of Julius Resnick (J R Handbags), is seen here surrounded with a vast array of handbags in the mid-1960s. Variety and choice exemplified the new freedom and youth in society. J R Handbags worked closely with Sommers Plastic Products into the 1960s, creating handbags worked in imitation leather and a vinyl patented as 'marshmallow'.

OPPOSITE A classic-shaped large white leather handbag by Nora Wiles dates from 1964.

RIGHT A 1960s green crocodile handbag with an envelope flap has long curving double straps attached to the base.

LEFT Among the older generation the classic handbag was never out of fashion. Here a red leather frame handbag with belt clasp dating from the early 1960s offers formality.

Op and Pop Art Influences

Bright new patterns, appropriated from the Op and Pop artists of the day, infiltrated all aspects of design and were used on products as diverse as paper dresses and plastic handbags. British artist Bridget Riley's first purely optical work appeared in 1961, though the term 'Op Art' wasn't used until 1964 when *Time* magazine used it to describe those optical illusions that utilized bizarre perspectives. Ossie Clark's graduation show from London's Royal College of Art in 1965 included a coat of swirling black and white Op Art patterns, reminiscent of the paintings of Victor Vasarely. Meanwhile, Mary Quant's self-confessed 'first crack at handbag design' comprised two monochromatic 'dolly' bags, both inspired by Op Art. One of them featured her stylized daisy logo and both had long, thin shoulder straps that could be worn across the body.

Quant's designs were labelled the 'Chelsea look', a mixture of the black stockings, elongated jumpers and skinny jeans of the Beat Generation allied to the sort of garments most often worn by children. These included pinafore dresses, knickerbockers, knee socks, shorts and pleated gym-slip-like tunics. As she remarked in her autobiography:

> The girls pranced down the stairs, one after the other, wearing little, high-waisted flannel dresses with white stockings, or alternatively, flannel tunics over red sweaters with red stockings to match… grown-ups wearing teenage fashions and looking like precocious little girls.

The designer played with scale, lowering the 'V' of a jumper to the waist, enlarging a football shirt so that it could be worn as a dress, and scaling-up cardigans into coats. Her 1963 Wet Collection included a classic trench coat in PVC (polyvinyl chloride). It was a fabric for the space age – modern, shiny, impermeable, and wipe-clean – and one of the many synthetic materials that 1960s fashion and handbag designers embraced enthusiastically.

Initially the fabric created manufacturing problems. British fashion designer John Bates recalled that it was a walk through Soho that sparked his interest in unusual materials: 'I saw an old shop with some black oilskin in the window, and I thought "I could do something with that" and had it made up into a dress. When the model moved, all the seams perforated like postage stamps.' It was the start of his experimentation with futuristic materials, such as PVC, transparent plastics and the new bonded jerseys made into clothes that pushed the boundaries of modesty.

ABOVE Actress Diana Rigg played feisty heroine Emma in the cult T.V. series *The Avengers*. British designer John Bates, who worked under the name Jean Varon, designed all the outfits and the accessories for the show, including this shoulder bag, in collaboration with Freedex.

The dramatic shift in the hemline changed the entire proportions of the garment. A shorter skirt demanded narrower shoulders and a higher waist. This streamlined silhouette emphasized the midriff, which in turn was accented with wide, low-slung belts, the insertion of a contrasting fabric, or cut-outs that left the midriff completely bare. When John Bates launched his Bikini dress, with a revealing mesh panel over the midriff, he might have caused shock waves in the national press, but it was designated 'Dress of the Year' by the fashion industry.

Having experimented widely with daring Op Art prints and bold shapes, Bates was the obvious choice to design a new wardrobe for Diana Rigg in the fast-paced, cult British television show *The Avengers*. Her outfits reflected the character she played. All-in-one jumpsuits, streamlined PVC and jersey and gabardine shift dresses featured motifs from Op and Pop Art, including targets, stripes and monochromatic patterning. Rigg was a new kind of heroine, modern, fearless under pressure, and provocative without being submissive. Her style influenced a nation of aspirational young girls. Fashion was no longer about the exclusive or the expensive; wearing the same thing as everyone else was proof that you were 'cool'. Bates also designed all the accessories for the show, including watches, furs, shoes and handbags, which were manufactured by British company Freedex.

The Space Age

Futuristic style in product design, interiors and inevitably fashion and handbags was prompted by the space age era, which began when Russia's Yuri Gagarin became the first man in space in 1961. A group of designers based in Paris, including Pierre Cardin, André Courrèges, Emanuel Ungaro and Paco Rabanne, reenergized French couture with space-age fashions that utilized the latest high tech synthetic sports fabrics. Cardin spearheaded the movement with his Space Age Collection in 1964. This included gabardine tabards in bright colours with deep-set armholes and cut-out midriffs, worn over skinny ribbed jumpers and tights. André Courrèges produced his Moon Girl range, thigh-high mini dresses that bypassed the curves of the body entirely. The densely woven fabrics formed a carapace of cloth that could famously 'stand up on its own', due to the rigid construction.

This 'alien warrior' mood was further emphasized by the astronaut helmets (bonnets that stood away from the contours of the head), outsize white sunglasses, and mid-calf boots with cut-out toes. Handbags became an extension of the body, Courrèges designed miniature bags to hang off the belt of the dress, but it was Paco Rabanne who exploited new materials to create the archetypal 1960s accessories of oversize plastic jewellery and chainmail handbags. An eager exponent of new materials and techniques, his first 'body jewellery' collection, in 1966, was constructed with a pair of metal cutters, pliers and a blowtorch, rather than a sewing machine and thread. This iconic chainmail bag reinvented the mesh bags of the 1920s for the space age. Copious copies in inferior materials soon flooded the market, alongside plastic, PVC and vinyl creations. Rabanne later constructed another type of chain mail formed from miniature triangles of aluminium and leather held together with flexible wire rings.

British fashion boutiques, such as Countdown in London's King's Road (named for the countdown to the rocket being fired into space), also offered their version of the future. Owned by fashion entrepreneurs Pat Booth and James Wedge, the Countdown boutique showcased young British talent such as Foale & Tuffin and later Ossie Clark. Handbags were rarely sold as part of a 'total look', or purchased because of the prestige of the label. Instead, handbags featuring comic-strip graphics, the British flag, dazzling Op and colourful Pop Art, and those made of metallic mesh and silver PVC became another way for the teenager to express 1960s style.

LEFT French fashion designer Paco Rabanne's coveted and much-copied chainmail version of the mesh bag from 1966.

OPPOSITE Twiggy as space warrior models a white jumpsuit in 1967 by Yves Saint Laurent, with chain-link belts by Bruce Rudow, Monet and Richard Monceau. Two faux animal-skin shoulder bags by Lucille de Paris are slung across her body as armour.

The London Look

London was the centre of 'Youthquake', the term coined by _Vogue_ editor and icon Diana Vreeland in 1963 for the spirited 1960s youth movement that sparked energetic changes in fashion, music and popular culture. Fashion boutiques flourished – in Carnaby Street, the King's Road and Camden – the most famous of them being Biba, the first British boutique to enter the popular consciousness, and change the way ordinary girls in the high street dressed. The first small shop opened on Abingdon Road in Kensington in 1964. It proved to be a phenomenon and grew until 'Big Biba' was launched in an Art Deco department store on Kensington High Street in 1975. Young women finally had access to high fashion at low cost. Unlike the preceding decade, status no longer lay in the price of something, but in the immediacy of the design. Barbara Hulanicki, along with her husband and partner Steven Fitz-Simon, had a vision that encompassed every aspect of the 'look'. Fashion was no longer just about garments, but about body shape, posture and attitudes. The clothes were cut high in the torso with narrow sleeves, which had the effect of elongating the body.

By the time the boutique moved to Kensington's Church Street in 1965, Biba was not only attracting the 'mods', but also pop singers, film stars and the aristocracy, all in pursuit of the unique Biba look. Hulanicki recalled: 'We must have been the only designers who were copied at twice the price'. Especially groundbreaking was their mail-order catalogue, introduced in 1968 with photographs by Hans Feurer and Sarah Moon.

Towards the end of the decade Hulanicki reprised the glamour of 1920s Art Deco using lush and seductive fabrics. Satin-backed crepe, knitted cotton jersey and jumbo cord were dyed in a unique colour palette of blackberry, maroon, amethyst, plum and 'dirty' pastels. Daywear was cut into feminine shapes that included high-waisted dresses with rows of covered buttons on the cuffs and drawstring necklines. The clothes were all colour matched to a range of accessories that included tights, hats and handbags. The bags featured Art Deco styling with ornate frames and clasps and exotic fabrics, the most popular being faux leopardskin. The store even sold leopardskin suitcases for 'the travelling man'.

There was some resistance to Britain's 'Youthquake' and the 'London Look' by the American fashion industry. During the 1940s and 1950s American fashion had been strongly influenced by Hollywood, but once the Second World War was over Sally Kirkland of _Life_ magazine, reputed to be the most influential woman in the business, led the move to resurrect the French and Italian fashion industries.

It took the opening of Paraphernalia on New York's Madison Avenue in 1965 to authenticate the 'London

Look'. Betsey Johnson was seen as the home-grown talent that could usurp the British stranglehold on the avant-garde. She was enormously influenced by Biba, whose shop she had visited while she was on a visit to London. She utilized found materials, such as plastic, paper, aluminium foil and vinyl, for her clothes and Edie Sedgewick, the Warhol muse, was her fittings model. Marylyn Bender recalls seeing Sedgewick at an exhibition of American paintings in 1965 at the Metropolitan Museum of Art:

> Among them were Andy Warhol in paint-splattered work pants, dinner jacket and sunglasses and, on his arm, Edie Sedgewick, a fragile creature with cropped, silver-rinsed hair. She wore a lilac jersey jumpsuit and furry shoulder bag.

In America, age still regulated the appearance of women and the fashion press continued to perceive British fashion as being the prerogative of teenagers. The American feminine ideal and style icon, meanwhile, was Jacqueline Lee Bouvier Kennedy.

ABOVE Jean Shrimpton in 1962 modelling a working girls outfit of classic easy-cut jacket and skirt, kitten heels and a capacious businesslike handbag.

OPPOSITE Schoolgirl white kneesocks and the short white smock are typical of the era in this 1964 photograph by Norman Parkinson; the hair, however, hasn't yet caught up with the 'mod' look. The chain-handled shoulder bag is impractically tiny and studded with metallic discs for space-age appeal.

Jackie Kennedy and the American Ideal

Jackie Kennedy was only 31 at the time of husband John Fitzgerald Kennedy's inauguration as the President of the United States. Together, they symbolized that youth and beauty were the future and that politics had entered the visual age. Eighty-eight per cent of American families owned a television set in 1960, which meant that for the first time they felt they could really participate in the lives that they watched on the screen. As the president stood at his 'New Frontier' of politics, Jackie was at his side. Almost immediately she became an international fashion icon, with every aspect of her appearance scrutinized by the press. Marilyn Bender wrote about the first lady's influence on American style in her book *The Beautiful People*:

Jacqueline Kennedy's achievement has been to translate the messages of the fashion industry for a mass audience without ever losing its rapt interest. Even such subtle details as the tucking of a three strand pearl necklace inside a boat neckline and the carrying of a handbag either over the arm but to the side of the body (never, never to the front and poised over the stomach) or with the fingers grasping the double handles were assimilated by her avid public.

According to Bender, Jackie Kennedy's adoring public also learned the importance of accessories from her:

…from Jacqueline Kennedy, American women absorbed the intelligence about chain handles, which, even before Chanel's quilted handbag version became a fad, had been appearing in the windows of Henri Betrix, a Madison Avenue shop of forbidding elegance, or in the collections of Martin Van Schaak, the most exclusive pocket-book salesman in New York. Mr. Van Schaak has no shop. He brings his wares to his gilt-edged clients at their homes.

RIGHT Jackie Kennedy and her son John Kennedy Jr photographed in 1965. The first lady is wearing Givenchy, her favourite couturier. The only jewellery she wears apart from her customary triple row of pearls and a discreet bangle is the gilt chain of her handbag.

Accusations of Jackie's excessive spending on European fashions were potentially damaging to the presidency, but easily dismissed by her. When Nan Robertson of the *The New York Times* asked her to verify the report in *Women's Wear Daily* that she and her mother-in-law had spent $30,000 a year on Paris couture, Jackie's tart reply was, 'I couldn't spend that much unless I wore sable underwear'. In Givenchy's architectural clothes Jackie Kennedy appeared inviolable. As *Women's Wear Daily* columnist William J Cunningham wrote: 'Those stiff, cut-out little Givenchy coats couldn't give a damn. The coat was so sharp and brittle and so positive it was right. Not that the women were arrogant. The clothes made them arrogant'.

ABOVE Quintessential Chanel style in 1961: the braided edge-to-edge jacket, the straight skirt to the knees, the two-tone shoes in beige and black and the iconic handbag.

However, as a way of deflecting criticism she enrolled the help of Hollywood designer, and Kennedy family friend, Oleg Cassini. He transmuted this inherently European look into what proved to be a uniquely American style, one of classic understated elegance that suited the new athleticism. This look was later confirmed by other American designers, such as Halston, James Galanos and Calvin Klein. As an ex-film designer, Cassini knew the importance of appealing to an audience, and incorporated into

Jackie's clothes the exaggerated detailing of a single large bow or an oversize button that could be seen from a distance. The clean lines and simple shapes preferred by Jackie Kennedy demanded understated handbags, and the streamlined clutch bag once again made an appearance for daywear. She continued her uncluttered look into the evening with Grecian-inspired gowns of stiff silks. The handbag of choice with eveningwear was the minaudière, which she also made popular (see also page 63).

Pucci and the Mediterranean Set

With the introduction of the jet plane into passenger service came the emergence of the 'jet set', the super-rich that flew to Europe to shop. Their destination was not only the couture houses of Paris, but also the flourishing fashion designers of Milan and Florence, among them the Marquis Emilio Pucci di Barsento (1914–92) who was famous for his designs made from brilliantly patterned fabric.

Emilio Pucci designed relaxed, glamorous leisurewear in marked contrast to the constructed artifice of Paris couture on offer at that time. He responded to women's increasingly active lives by being one the first designers to introduce stretch into his fabrics. In 1960 he invented 'Emilioform', elasticated silk shantung that he made into Capri pants, wide-legged palazzo pants and kaftan-like tunics.

Pucci trained as a pilot in the Italian air force and had no background in design, but in 1947 he was photographed skiing in St Moritz dressed in a ski suit he had designed himself. He opened his first shop in 1949 on Capri, and by the 1960s his clothes had become synonymous with the new jet age and an enduring status symbol worn by celebrities, such as Marilyn Monroe (who wanted to be buried in her favourite Pucci), Audrey Hepburn and Jacqueline Kennedy Onassis. His designs captured the post-war desire for travel – weighing less than 250 grams (9 ounces), the clothes were portable and required no ironing.

Immediately identifiable, and unfortunately too easily copied, the abstract, nonfigurative form and psychedelic swirls of colour of Pucci's prints defined the decade. He was inspired by his Italian heritage, including Renaissance paintings and the Palio race of Siena, and also the colours and patterns indigenous to exotic locations. His favourite hues – aqua, fuchsia, lilac, lime and orange – were incorporated into velvet printed bags with tangerine or turquoise leather trims and faux gold bamboo handles. The external fabric of the bag would always be printed with his signature, 'Emilio', in black script. The bags were also signed with his full name or 'Emilio Pucci Bags by Jana'.

RIGHT Matching beach dress and bag by the 'Prince of Prints' Emilio Pucci, dating from 1963. His colour range came straight from the Aegean horizon: turquoise and ultramarine set against sea green and lime, or fuchsia and yellow.

Aigner

'A German brand with an Italian soul', is the proclaimed aesthetic of luxury goods company Aigner. Combining German precision with Tuscan tradition, Aigner handbags define a finely crafted, sporty elegance. Distinctive features are the tanned calfskin leather in the company's signature rich burgundy red, purporting to be the colour of Chianti, and the discreet logo of the Aigner 'A' in the form of small inverted horseshoe. This betrays the company's association with equestrian matters: Aigner Racing Days held outside Munich are a fixture of the racing calendar.

The founder of the company, Etienne Aigner (1904–2000), was born in Hungary and moved to Paris in the 1930s to learn the craft of leather working. By the late 1940s he was designing exclusive bags for couture houses, such as Lanvin, Dior and Rochas. He eventually moved to New York in 1950, where he presented his first handbag collection under his own name. A meeting with businessman Heiner H Rankl led to the formation of the Aigner brand in Munich, Germany, in 1965. Munich was chosen not only as the best place to found a new leading fashion brand, but also because of its proximity to the Italian border. All the design and production of the label is undertaken in Florence, where the leather for the handbags is elaborately ground, tanned, sewn and polished by hand. As the company claims, 'Its heart beats in Munich, but its soul lives in Tuscany'.

The majority of bags are made from vegetable-tanned calf leather, which gains its patina from daily use, although the company also uses cowhide, elkhide, crocodile skin and ostrich. Sixty per cent of the output of the brand is devoted to a range of classic handbags regardless of season. These are produced in natural colours that remain constant in each collection, including red, black, brown, cognac and cream, and are supplemented by occasional fashion colours. Two of the company's most recognized bags are the Saddle bag and the Doctor's bag, both of which appeared in the 1970s. During the 1980s the label extended its product range to include watches, jewellery and eyewear. A clothing range for men and women was added in the 1990s.

ABOVE Psychedelic swirls of intense and vibrant colour decorate this printed fabric Box bag by Pucci dating from 1969.

RIGHT The textured surface of this shoulder bag with discreet intertwining of the brands initials is in typical Aigner style. The German company specializes in understated elegance.

THIS PAGE Model Twiggy carries a Louis Vuitton Papillon 30 in Monogram Canvas dating from 1967. With its round body and two medium-length handles evoking wings, it takes on the form and spirit of a *papillon* (butterfly). Twiggy wears a wool chenille jumpsuit by Pattie Tuttman for Silverworm accessorized by an Oster chain bracelet made for New York boutique Paraphernalia and a watch by Vacheron Constantin.

OPPOSITE Striding along the Champs-Élysées in culottes, the model wears boots by Parisian shoemaker Durer and carries a matching modular two-tone shoulder bag dating from 1968.

Bonnie Cashin and Coach

When influential American designer Bonnie Cashin (1907–2000) was asked to collaborate with the couple behind one of the country's most respected leather goods manufacturers for men, it was a marriage of quality with innovation. Coach started out as a wallet and billfold manufacturer run by Miles and Lilian Cahn in New York, established in 1941, and the company was famed for the clean uncluttered lines and the natural beauty of the products, the result of a very particular leather-tanning system.

Cashin, a pioneer of American casualwear, was obsessed with the relationship between use and form. In fashion this resulted in a pared-down look that incorporated unusual textures, such as leather-trimmed tweed and the 'layering' of separates in luxurious organic materials. She revolutionized the way leather was used in high fashion and in 1953 she teamed up with leather importer Philip Sills.

The invitation to work with the Cahns seemed a natural progression for the designer, and she joined them in 1962, applying her modern sensibilities to the design of handbags and becoming the sole designer for Coach bags. Cashin pioneered the use of industrial hardware on clothing and accessories, most famously the brass toggle that she incorporated into her handbag designs for Coach. She was notable in that she did not design within one price range; in the late 1950s and early 1960s, prices ranged from $12.95 to $2,000. Her bags were wittily christened 'Cashin Carry'.

The first bag she designed for the Coach company provided clear evidence of her delight in problem solving. Rather than having to rummage around the interior of a large bag to find a coin purse, the sling shaped pouch had a coin purse attached to the outside. Her practical aesthetic was further confirmed with the production of leather shopping bags in varying sizes that could be used separately or layered together. She had no interest in producing a formal black alligator bag; instead she designed handbags for women who led busy multitasking lives – deep square shoppers, tote bags that folded flat when not in use, a top-zippered bag like a portable filing cabinet for the office – all designed without fuss, but with wit and ebullience. The designer's utilitarian ethos did not preclude the use of colour. Cashin, who had developed her own shade of pink called Bonnie pink in the 1940s, had Coach make up specially dyed leathers in saturated colours to be worked and worn together – mustard and pink, olive green and lime, all lined with her signature striped madras.

BELOW LEFT Bonnie Cashin designed for American manufacturer Coach from 1962 to 1972; this Muff bag with external purse dating from 1963 was one of her first designs for the company.

BELOW RIGHT The designer Bonnie Cashin posing with her latest designs at the Coach factory in 1962.

BELOW An early Coach catalogue sketch by Bonnie Cashin from 1963.

ABOVE Pink Holster bag by Bonnie Cashin for Coach in 1967. The designer persuaded the company to undertake special limited-edition dye runs of her favourite bright colours.

BELOW The Coach Super Hero Lunchbox designed by Cashin dates from 1963. It features the toggle fastening she appropriated from her convertible sports car.

Hippie Chic

There was a time when every fashion-conscious teenage girl owned a pair of look-a-like Courrèges boots and hiked up her hemline. Once the mass-market manufacturers had rolled out the cheap replicas of 'mod' fashion, American and European youth were no longer concerned about what was 'fashionable', only with what was 'cool'. The emergence of the hippie movement began as a backlash to postwar consumerism and middle-class values. This teenage rebellion owed both its linguistic origins and its inspiration to the Beat movement in the US and combined a rejection of mainstream culture with questions about America's involvement in the Vietnam War. Hallucinogenic drugs such as LSD were perceived as the gateway to enlightenment and cosmic consciousness, and clothes reflected the bright colours and patterning of the resulting psychedelic experiences.

Vintage clothes replaced mass-produced items and included Victorian nightdresses, 1930s tea gowns, feather boas and Edwardian lace blouses that were sourced in attics, charity and thrift stores and boutiques, such as Granny Takes a Trip. These worn and faded garments were paired with patched jeans, kaftans, afghan coats, military greatcoats and cheap cheesecloth dresses. The plundering of Africa, the Americas and Asia for garments was part of a new aesthetic that drew from the increasing identification with marginalized cultures that the hippies felt. It also tied in with the desire of the counter-culture to be anti-consumer.

Bags were as eclectic as the clothes: a military satchel from an army surplus store, a little Victorian beaded bag, a crocodile clutch from the 1940s. Hippies did not buy their clothes and handbags; they found them in charity stores, attics and the new antique markets that were part of the Victorian revival. Increasingly they were also garnered from the souks and bazaars of the hippie trail through Greece, Northern Africa and India. Returning hippies brought home with them fringed and tasselled bags, carpet bags made from reworked kelims and bags

ABOVE The 1960s revival of interest in Art Deco is responsible for the vibrant colours and geometric patterning of this handbag with chain-linked strap and matching hat from 1967.

RIGHT An open-topped basketweave bucket bag modelled by Twiggy and photographed by Patrick Lichfield in 1965.

embroidered with mirrors. Those that didn't go on the hippie trail replicated the look with homemade crocheted or patchwork bags, or went to the local 'head' shop that had replaced boutique styles with imported ethnic items.

Handicrafts were part of the back-to-nature ethos. Bags were tie-dyed, macraméd, batiked or appliquéd, often with the ubiquitous flower motifs of the era. Commercial exploitation of this market included plastic transfers, or decals, that were a popular decoration for homemade handbags. Découpage, images cut out and pasted onto surfaces then sealed with a clear varnish, also provided a way to customize handbags.

While the 'Youthquake' and the hippie phenomenon were mainly the remit of the young, towards the end of the decade informality had extended to the older generation. Fashion had become younger and style

had become democratized. Nowhere was this more obvious than the wardrobe of Jackie Kennedy. While she was mourning the president she stayed out of the public eye. When she returned it was with a vigorous and lively eye for the new, the fresh and the different. Gone was the formal dignity of the Givenchy/Cassini era, the white gloves, the clutch handbag and the pearls. Captured on the streets of New York in a famous paparazzi shot by photographer Ron Galella in 1971, Jackie is almost unrecognizable from the iconic first lady (a title she resisted). She is turning her head on hearing her name, smiling, sexy, and striding freely in tight trousers that reveal the contours of her body. Her is hair blowing in the wind… and she is handbag free. She represents how the 1960s changed the role of women, and it was an indication of the freedom to come during the next decade.

Enid Collins

Sophistikits, complete do-it-yourself-kits by Enid Collins, also provided a means of customization. These were produced by the company in the late 1960s for those customers who wanted to create their own patterned bag. For many young American girls and women throughout the 1960s, the Enid Collins bag was a vital accessory. Combining whimsical subject matter with good-quality construction and materials, the bags represented the 'can-do' philosophy of the American dream.

Born Enid Roessler, the designer spent her youth in San Antonio, Texas, and in the 1940s she went on to study fashion design at the Texas Women's University. She married sculptor Frederic Collins and moved to a ranch outside Medina, Texas, where she started making canvas and leather bags to supplement the family income. Initially selling her bags in nearby tourist outlets, when the American department store Neiman Marcus placed an order Enid and her husband were able to open a factory in their hometown. By 1958 they had 80 employees and opened a retail outlet in Medina. They also started a plant to construct the wooden boxes for their latest product – the box bag.

BELOW CENTRE An alternative to the hippie fringed or patent leather shoulder bag carried by teenagers was the whimsical, somewhat homespun, wares of handbag designer Enid Collins. Appealing to an essentially American customer, the wooden box bags were youthful and charming. The People's Choice here, featuring a horse and foliage, is typical of Collin's subject matter.

BELOW DETAIL A section of a Spin Away bag by Enid Collins, showing the depth of detail and lavish use of beadwork.

FEATURES OF A COLLINS BAG:
* Handbags are marked 'e c' on the outside of the bag. Inside is the galloping horse logo and 'Enid Collins Original' and 'Collins of Texas'.
* Box bags were dated and some had Enid Collins' handwritten signature, which was often done on her frequent promotional trips during the 1960s.
* Bags made after the business was sold in 1970 have the design name on the bag or the horse logo, but not Enid's name.

The Collins company primarily made two types of bag: one was a small, rectangular box bag and the other was a stiffened linen bucket-style bag with a leather lid and handle and a wooden base. They were decorated with paint, sequins and rhinestones in themed designs, such as the signs of the Zodiac, Glitter Bugs bags and Sea Garden buckets. They were intended as good-quality fun bags for daytime use. The bags often featured a little tag reading 'Please don't drop me on a hard surface or handle me carelessly! I'm hand-painted and decorated for your pleasure. With a minimum of TLC you'll find me a lasting joy to carry. Love, Your Box Bag.'

The do-it-yourself Sophisticats were produced in the late 1960s and flooded the market with imitation Collins bags. In 1966 another factory was opened in Puerto Rico to manufacture the papier-mâché bags. This operation closed in 1968. In 1970 Enid Collins sold her business, together with the copyrights of her designs, to the Tandy Leather Corporation. She continued to work for Tandy for about a year before leaving the company. Tandy continued to produce Enid Collins designs through the early 1970s.

ABOVE LEFT AND RIGHT
A blonde wooden box handbag by Collins named the Pax, with painted and applied decoration portraying the dove of peace carrying the olive branch.

RIGHT A shoulder bag by Collins in a later, more casual style named the Cock o' the Walk. Collins initialled each bag to ensure authenticity, together with the bag's name.

BELOW LEFT AND RIGHT
A canvas Collins handbag with a leather strap named Night Watch, with a close-up detail of the beaded owl and acorns.

▲ Lamé and metallics

Traditionally associated with
eveningwear, lamé and metallics
were indicative of the space-age
influence in the 1960s. Here a go
lamé clutch bag dating from 196
has a retro feel. It features a cove
metal frame with twist knob closu
and is lined in cream ribbed ace

Key looks
of the decade

1960s

▲ Pastels and plastics

A wet-look plastic turquoise and
pink handbag dating from 1965
is accessorized with a pink pop-
beaded bracelet and belt; it reflects
the popularity of pastel colours
during the decade.

◀ Space-age effects

The space-age bag had enorm
influence on all aspects of fashi
fuelling an interest in metallic su
ingenious materials and innova
techniques used by designers
as André Courrèges and in this
handbag of linked metal discs
Paco Rabanne.

Op and Pop Art designs

Targets, flags and the eye-teasing tricks of Op Art were among the many devices featured on handbags during this era. This customer has hit the bull's-eye with her purchases from London's top boutique, Top Gear, owned by Pat Booth and James Wedge.

▶ Box bags

Many bags were hand-held rather than shoulder-slung, particularly box bags in straw and wood. Here kitten heels, bouffant hair and stiffened petticoats put this model on the cusp of the early 1960s. She is carrying a pastel straw basket with short handles based on a hatbox shape.

◀ Plastic beads

Plastic beaded bags were one of the most popular styles of the 1960s and varied in quality. Italian-made in 1967 this example epitomizes informal elegance. The handbag incorporates facetted turquoise ball beads on a plain crocheted base. The bag is lined in pale blue woven polypropylene with scarf-ended ties to the opening.

1970s:
Freedom, Fun and Fantasy

The 1970s were an era in fashion flux. The decade began with the commercialization of the hippie ethos by the ready-to-wear fashion industry in an attempt to exploit the market for ethnic-inspired fashion. It ended with a shop in London called World's End, a post-punk rock hangout owned by Vivienne Westwood and Malcolm McLaren and previously known simply as Sex, selling McLaren's appropriation of fetishwear incorporated into avant garde fashion.

The emergence of 'fun' clothes came between these two opposing aesthetics from British designer Tommy Roberts and his shop Mr Freedom. He sold scaled-up children's clothes; multicoloured striped wool socks, oversized dungarees and hot pants with bibs, straps decorated with rainbow stripes and appliquéd satin images such as hearts and stars. These were worn with primary-coloured clogs or platform boots and shoes and schoolgirl satchels in shiny patent. The 'pop' sensibility of Roberts also included handbags made in the shape of packets of Omo washing powder and Camel cigarettes. Also popular was the magazine clutch, a rigid plastic facsimile of a folded magazine with varying covers, often made in China. This kitsch overkill went on to inspire the excesses of glitter rock and disco later in the decade.

Handbags reflected the changes in style that occurred throughout the 1970s. To the embroidered, tasselled and fringed shoulder bags of the hippies and the sensible satchels of the newly emerging feminist movement could be added the jewelled clutches of British handbag designer Clive Shilton and the faux leopardskin bags of Biba. This eclectic mix of design styles at the beginning of the decade included a revival of interest in Art Deco. This was fuelled in part by Bernard Nevill; head of print design at London's Royal College of Art, and was consolidated by the opening of the biggest and final Biba store in 1973, a shopping emporium in Kensington, London, that exuded 1930s Hollywood glamour.

Feminism and Fantasy

This period of transition through various design aesthetics was interrupted by an increasing awareness of the rights of women. The feminist movement segued from the dungaree-wearing hardliners to the dress-for-success clothes of women at work. Feminists eschewed the accoutrements of fashion and wore dungarees, short-cropped hair and soft coloured-leather boots called Kickers. The pursuit of the latest trend was considered demeaning and trivial by feminists such as New Yorker Susan Brownmiller, who condemned any attire that wasn't 'trousered anonymity'. French writer and intellectual Simone de Beauvoir agreed that women's emancipation could only occur with the rejection of feminine clothing. However, feminism was instrumental in opening up a whole new world for women in the workplace and fashion became an important element of this drive to succeed.

As 1960s optimism yielded to the harsher realities of 1970s life, such as the 1973 oil crisis and the Watergate scandal, fashion designers tapped into the desire for an alternative way of life. In the UK Zandra Rhodes, Thea Porter and Bill Gibb all introduced a spirit of fantasy into a wardrobe made up of essentials suitable for the office. Zandra Rhodes based her ethnic-inspired printed dresses on her love of vernacular dress and print design. Thea Porter introduced the kaftan to eveningwear, and Scottish born designer Bill Gibb became the darling of the beautiful people such as Bianca Jagger, Elizabeth Taylor and later Princess Diana with his richly embellished fantasy ballgowns. He was named *Vogue* designer of the year in 1970. Gibb celebrated the demise of the miniskirt with opulent, intricately cut dresses made from yards of patterned silk and suede, leather and fur. His use of contrast braiding and appliqué and the incorporation of tassels applied to beaded, pleated and printed fabric deferred to the tradition of the early nineteenth-century Arts and Crafts movement with its interpretation of medievalism.

Bored with the mini and modernity, rich and beautiful women aspired to be the heroines of their own costume dramas, and needed handbags that were in keeping with the romantic ethos of the clothes. Small rectangular bags of exquisite craftsmanship were designed by British designer John Bates and produced in collaboration with John Williams, leather conservationist and craftworker at London's Victoria & Albert Museum. Reflecting both the aesthetic of the Arts and Crafts movement and the desire for the decorative, the leather bags were hand-tooled and coloured with images of birds, flowers and leaves. The designer sourced antique hardware for the fastenings and strap buckles. The bags were sold through Harrods and Liberty's, and their rarity makes them extremely collectable.

PAGE 146 An envelope clutch bag dating from 1973 from Italian luxury goods company Bottega Veneta. Established in 1966, the company merged with Gucci in 2001.

BELOW The informal suede shoulder bag by Marc Cross references the 'smart casual' rural-life outfit of crocheted vest and plum-coloured knickerbockers by American label Pandora.

THIS PAGE A homespun handbag of embroidered woollen flowers on felt dating from 1971 represents the back-to-nature ethos prevalent at the beginning of the decade.

Arts and Crafts Leatherwork

Tooling, stamping or embossing are terms that refer to the craft of impressing three-dimensional images onto leather. It is a process that has been deployed by skilled leather workers for centuries, but was a particularly popular technique during the Art Nouveau and Art Deco periods as way of introducing colour and pattern to leather (see page 19 for Wiener Werkstätte designs). The revival of interest in medievalism expressed in the Arts and Craft Movement resurfaced at the beginning of the 1970s and prompted an interest in this traditional skill.

The tooling and embossing process is only suitable for vegetable-tanned leather, which is also often called tooling leather. Tooling refers to the use of stamping tools, much like a sculptor might use a chisel, to create a detailed image on the leather. Once the design has been created it is transferred from the tracing film with a stylus onto dampened leather. The outline is then traced over with a swivel knife, which has to be kept upright at a 90-degree angle to the skin, deep enough to penetrate the grain. The leather is then placed on a marble slab and pressure from a wood or rawhide mallet is applied to various tools to add texture to the piece and to create depressions in the surface. The basic tools are a beveller, a pear shader and a camouflage tool. The wide edge of the beveller is placed into the cut made by the swivel knife and the end of the tool struck with a mallet. This process continues along the outside of the

design in order to give the design a raised appearance. The pear shader and the camouflage tool are used to add texture to the design and background. Other tools include a veiner, which is used to create the veining on a leaf design and a seed tool used to create a seedpod in the middle of a flower.

Stamping usually involves using very small metal stamps to make small images on the leather. Embossing leather is very like stamping but the embossing plates (also called embossing dies) are much larger. It is possible to emboss using a plate with a piece of metal and a hammer, but there are also embossing presses used in the manufacture of mass produced articles. Colour is then added to the leather in the form of water or oil-based dye or paint.

BELOW An exquisitely tooled handbag designed by fashion designer John Bates in collaboration with leatherwork artisan John Williams dates from the early 1970s.

OPPOSITE American designer Carlos Falchi set the style for huge pleated leather bags, as in this design photographed by Norman Parkinson in 1978.

Today's Woman

When youth culture exploded in the 1960s *haute couture* ceased to have any real influence on modern fashion. Balenciaga retired in 1968 and Schiaparelli and Chanel both died in the early 1970s. The couturiers' salon was perceived as the depositary of an ageing and ever-decreasing clientele. This was confirmed by the decision of Yves Saint Laurent to introduce the concept of *prêt-a-porter*, or ready-to-wear, with his show in 1968, followed by the opening of the first of his many Rive Gauche boutiques. Fashion in England now became street-led, an avant-garde proclamation of rebellion by the young and disaffected, fronted by Vivienne Westwood and Malcolm McLaren to the sound of the Sex Pistols.

It was the newly emerging American designers who filled the resulting gap in the market for fashionable, accessible clothes and handbags for the working woman. Calvin Klein, Ralph Lauren and Geoffrey Beene all offered their take on the relaxed tailoring and separates that made up the professional woman's capsule wardrobe and provided the popular suede slouch bag or duffel that reflected the ease of the clothes. However, it was a simple dress by Diane Von Furstenberg that defined the era. She designed her iconic wrap dress in 1973; among racks of flapping maxi-skirts and stiffly tailored trouser suits the dress was enthusiastically received by an army of professional women who wanted flattering, easy clothes. 'Feel like a woman, wear a dress' was written on every label. The body-hugging dress became a manifesto of the liberated woman. It wrapped in the front and tied at the waist and took seconds to put on and seconds to remove. In a busy woman's timetable it went from day to night, all she had to do was ditch the office briefcase and pick up an evening bag. The clutch returned in a diminutive form for evening and hung on long narrow straps, with larger, more practical bags carried during the day.

RIGHT An urban warrior is prepared for action with a pair of military-style shoulder bags in this 1976 photograph by Norman Parkinson.

Enny Leather Goods

Handbag designers were quick to pick up on the trend for business-like and practical handbags. Italian manufacturer Enny was one of the many labels to offer good-quality merchandise that was fashionable, reasonably priced and practical. Enny bags, alongside others for the mass market, were produced by hundreds of small craft enterprises around Florence which have been in existence since before the Renaissance. The Florentine craftsmen of the late Middle Ages were famed for their skills, and as a result their products were in demand all over Europe. The tanners and leather cutters amassed huge wealth, their success leading to the emergence of an affluent craftsman's class in Florence, still exploited by designers today.

Enny's marketing slogan of the period, 'Bags for Today's Women' acknowledged the desire of women for a handbag that was fashionable and functional. Made from soft calfskin and with a signature flapover and magnetic catch, the bags were often seen on the arm of professional women. The company ceased trading in 2003, and so the bags are highly collectable, particularly those by Alessandro Lunardi, one of the original designers.

ABOVE This all-purpose classic Enny bag is elegant and functional in finely crafted calfskin, suitable for a day at the office or a walk in the country.

RIGHT A circular shoulder bag dating from 1971 with the strap and flap printed with the double G logo of Italian luxury goods manufacturer Gucci.

British Country Style

This stylistically complex decade also featured nostalgia for a rural past. Unlike the back-to-nature ethos of the hippies, this was a more romanticized version of bucolic bliss and included the wearing of tweed hacking jackets, Fair Isle tank tops, jodhpurs, cord skirts and the floral milkmaid fantasies of British company Laura Ashley. Tweeds and rustic knits featured heavily in this look, the multistriped and patchworked knitted separates by Scottish designer Bill Gibb with his partner Kaffe Fassett enlivened the traditional sweater and popularized the art of knitting, kickstarting a home crafts revival. Natural fibres coloured with vegetable dyes and traditional materials such as canvas and leather reinforced the look.

Handbags had a utilitarian aspect rooted in the traditional working bags used during rural sports, such as the game bag. This was comprised of three pouches held together at the top, one of rope net to transport the game, a middle pocket of brown tarpaulin for personal possessions and a final pocket in grained leather with a gusset. The bag had a flap with rounded corners in vegetable tanned cowhide reinforced with a line of stitching following the edge. A shoulder strap with a square buckle with a fixed bar was attached to the narrow neck of the bag. This practical, many-pocketed bag provided the paradigm for the perfect rural handbag and inspired a raft of pastiches. One was the bag produced by Mulberry in 1975, the Musette, a string net bag (supplied by billiard-pocket-makers) on a long leather strap attached to a quilted cotton gabardine and pigskin shooting bag.

Mulberry

This traditional British look was espoused by accessory designer Roger Saul who established the Mulberry label in 1971. On the basis of a £50 gift from his mother the designer crafted snakeskin chokers and belts that were initially retailed through Biba. The suede and leather bags that followed these early successes were produced using traditional saddlery methods in an old forge in Saul's parent's garden in Chilcompton, Bath. From here he went on to build his empire, which remained under his directorship until 2003. Somerset continues to be

OPPOSITE Components of the rural idyll in a 1971 photograph by Norman Parkinson: a tweed waistcoat, trilby and a large satchel-inspired shoulder bag in hand-stitched leather made to last a lifetime.

RIGHT Rural style appears in the city. Though smaller and neater than the classic shoulder bag, this highly polished leather bag dating from 1974, with sturdy brass hardware, has connotations of the countryside.

the Mulberry Company's epicentre, producing seasonal ranges of 'It' bags that have gained cult status throughout the world. Many of the 206 highly skilled craftsworkers at the Rookery, a purpose-built site opened in 1989, have been with the brand since its inception, and the company now run an apprentice in Leather Goods Manufacture scheme to ensure a highly skilled workforce for the future. Mulberry is the only remaining UK factory making handbags in England at designer level.

While retaining traditional craft methods and materials Mulberry have pursued creative collaborations with various handbag designers. Nicholas Knightly, design director from 2002 to 2004, was responsible for the Bayswater, Roxanne and Elgin. Stripped of the excessive decoration of the 'Roxy', the Bayswater has proved to have the most enduring appeal, and continues to be manufactured in a variety of leathers, finishes and colours. Stuart Vevers, previously the creative force behind Bottega Veneta, joined Mulberry in 2004, where he remained until 2007 when he moved to Loewe. His designs included the Maggie, Mabel and the Emmy.

The majority of leather used for Mulberry bags is sourced from Europe, particularly Italy. The leather is subjected to 13 processes, the first of which is soaking, to reverse the curing process and to clean the pelt. The next stages are liming, to remove hair, and de-liming. Bating is when the skin is treated with enzymes to produce a smooth and clean pelt; this is followed by pickling to bring the pelt to an acid state ready for tanning. Tanning stabilizes the leather against the effects of acid, heat and water, and the pelt is then re-tanned to improve the feel and handling of the leather. Fat liquor/dye is applied to prevent cracking and hardening, and then the pelt is dried before finishing.

The company is renowned for its use of Darwin leather, which has been developed using a unique vegetable tanning process that allows the leather to soften and improve with use and age. Various finishes are deployed in the making of a bag: Congo is a printed finish and Glove has a heavier grain with a soft, tactile feel. Scotchgrain is a cotton-based PVC used for its durability and water resistance, trimmed with leather.

The American Equestrian Influence

Peter Dooney and Frederic Bourke started their eponymous accessories company in 1975 in South Norwalk, Connecticut. The brand also has its roots in rural pursuits, in this case, horse riding. Two products were instrumental in the company's initial success; a surcingle belt in vibrant colours and stripes, and a pair of classic braces, or suspenders as they are known in America. In 1981 the company launched the Tack Case and the Equestrian bag, both made from bridle leather. These were retailed from Nordstrom's Brooks Brothers and Saks Fifth Avenue, as well as from the company's store in their home town.

The first handbag to feature the company's duck logo and the signature russet leather trim was the All-Weather Leather. It was manufactured in waterproof cowhide – shedding water like 'rain off a duck's back'; the distinctive feature and unique selling point of the bag being the process by which the leather is shrunk to seal the pores of the skin, a technique that still remains secret today. The company catalogue explains:

The Essence of the All-Weather Leather: the secret lies in the tanning process. First, our hides are soaked in curing tannin oils and laid out to dry. As the leather shrinks, its pores tighten and close – this creates a natural barrier to moisture and gives All-Weather Leather its distinctive pebble-grain texture. The result is leather that's soft and supple to the touch, yet virtually impervious to the elements. There's no need to pamper it with wax or silicones. A simple solution of bar soap and water is sufficient to remove most dirt and water-soluble stains.

Dooney & Bourke continue to produce fashion accessories, including handbags, today.

OPPOSITE TOP LEFT A rigid brass rod holds this Mulberry bag in shape; a semicircular scoop in the leather forms the handle. Mulberry collaborated with various fashion designers over the years including, most recently, British designers Luella Bartley, Kim Jones and Giles Deacon, as well as illustrator Julie Verhoeven.

LEFT TOP AND BOTTOM The most collectable Dooney & Bourke designs are from the 1970s and 1980s. These vintage pieces are recognizable by the duck logo and the unique pebble texture of the leather. Dooney & Bourke produced classic equestrian-inspired handbags, often in canvas as well as in their famous All-Weather Leather.

FEATURES OF DOONEY & BOURKE VINTAGE HANDBAGS

* The original Dooney & Bourke brass fob had a stylized backward D and a B.
* Early bags have no sewn-in tags: the first sewn-in tags appeared from 1975 to 1979 and were large green rectangles sewn flat into the bag with 'Dooney & Bourke DB Made in USA' inscribed.
* Subsequent tags from the 1980s were red, white and blue, were sewn as tabs inside the seam, and featured the words 'Dooney & Bourke, Inc. Made in USA'. The tags have a registration number on the back, detailing the style, place of manufacture and year the bag was made.
* The duck leather seal or the brass duck fob only appeared after the production of the All-Weather Leather in 1983.
* From 1983 to the 1990s the bags featured an oval leather duck logo sewn onto the back or front of the bag, depending on the style.
* Bags subsequently had a solid brass duck fob hanging from a leather thong. The fob is inscribed Dooney & Bourke All-Weather Leather (with a registered trademark symbol). Authentic duck fobs show a sharp detailed eye and some space between the duck bill and his body and a textured background.
* All handbags were made with solid brass hardware including all buckles, rivets, D-rings and latches.
* More recent bags have been assembled in the US but manufactured elsewhere. These bags have a red, white and blue sewn-in tag that says Dooney & Bourke.
* Bags from the 1970s and 1980s are the most collectable.

Nylon and Sporting Bags

Nylon, for so many years considered the poor relation of materials and a cheap substitute for natural and more expensive products, began to be reappraised during the 1970s for its modern and industrial qualities. Brands such as LeSportsac, Longchamps, Hervé Chapelier and later Prada (relaunched by Miuccia Prada in 1978) elevated the material to designer status.

LeSportsac
The colourful and practical products of American company LeSportsac, founded in 1974, were a welcome alternative to the drab colour palette of the prevailing trend for brown, tan or beige. The handbags were typically American in their sporty styling, but also had connotations of French chic. Lightweight and functional, the fold-in pouch bags were made of ripstop parachute nylon in a wide assortment of colours and prints with a grosgrain ribbon and canvas trim. These became a must-have accessory with the habitués of Manhattan's disco scene in the early 1980s.

The label re-emerged as a brand frontrunner in 2003, when singer and style icon Gwen Stefani collaborated with the company to produce a line of '*roc sacs*' dubbed L A M B (the acronym also used for her fashion line), with the singer carrying a LeSportsac clutch of her own design to the 2004 Grammy Awards. The label continues its associations with designers to the present day. The list includes Diane von Furstenberg and Jonathan Adler, who in 2002 wittily incorporated the company's logo in his Le Cute bag. Tokidoki, a range of handbags influenced by Japanese *anime* of vibrant colours and kitsch iconography is designed by artist Simone Legno, and the LeSportsac range continues to include two of her designs every season. British designer Stella McCartney produced the Deer rucksack for the company in autumn 2008, complete with a printed deer head and padded antlers.

LeSportsac is the leading American brand of casual nylon bags in the US, Mexico, Asia and Europe. The handbag has a universal appeal, being an affordable alternative to the big-name bags and carried by everyone from students to suburbanites. The product line is a complete range of handbags, travel bags, totes, messenger bags, backpacks, attachés and accessories.

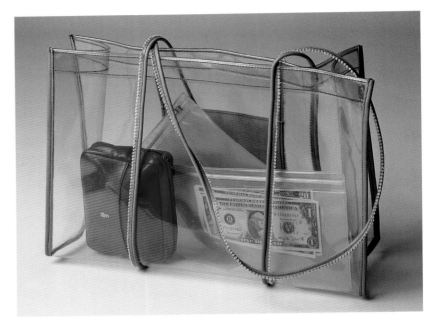

Hervé Chapelier

Intimations of the sporting bags of the era to come were evident in the forward-looking designs of Hervé Chapelier. Born in 1950 in the glamorous French resort of Biarritz and a keen surfer, Chapelier studied business before creating a nylon duffel bag in 1976 which achieved instant popularity with the young and active. This was followed by the 925N model, a waterproof nylon canvas bag for which the label became renowned. With its distinctive two-tone colouration and sturdy saddle-stitching, the lightweight trapeze-shaped bag consists of two contrasting but complementary shades, one for the bottom and interior, one for the outside. Chapelier was one of the first designers to recognize the design potential and the commercial and practical qualities of nylon, 15 years before Miuccia Prada.

All Hervé bags are made exclusively in France, and have a green brand tag sewed on the side of each item. The most popular bag is a large shoulder bag with black nylon straps, closed with a two-way zip on the top, and always in two colours. The designer introduces up to 15 new colours each season in single or multiple tones that complement the ready-to-wear seasonal trends. Practical and accommodating, the high-resistance nylon bags can be cleaned with a toothbrush, soap and water, and hung up to dry.

OPPOSITE TOP Plastic and nylon were easy-care materials for bags. Here a transparent plastic tote, a parody of the housewives' shopping bag, is by La Bagagerie from 1977.

RIGHT Distinguished by their interior and external colour combinations, these zip top totes by Hervé Chapelier are made of practical lightweight and weatherproof nylon.

OPPOSITE BOTTOM Founded in 1948 by Jean Cassegrain, the French company Longchamps originally specialized in leather-covered smoking accoutrements. By 1970 the company was producing a popular nylon-and-leather luggage line. The Pilage bag, seen here, a folding nylon shopper trimmed in cowhide, has sold over a million since its launch.

International Glamour

As the decade progressed a more sophisticated European sensibility replaced the bucolic aesthetic of the traditional British look. Continental designers such as Walter Albini and British designer Antony Price referenced a glamorous throwback to prewar Hollywood icons. British singer Bryan Ferry of art-rock band Roxy Music and his then-girlfriend model Jerry Hall were the leading exponents of this sophisticated mix of fashion and music. Accessories followed the trend for high-maintenance groomed perfection. Particularly evocative of the 1930s were the dyed snakeskin products such as shoes and handbags. The snakeskin revival was confirmed when Yves Saint Laurent showed python-printed dresses in his 1970 collection, as did British designer Jean Muir. Nigel Lofthouse designed clutch bags for the label, working exotic skins into appliquéd designs with leather and suede cut-outs.

As fashion became more focused there was an increasing awareness of the power of the label by the industry in marketing terms. Pierre Cardin was one of the first designers to exploit the financial potential of licensing his name, alongside Diane von Furstenberg. This was a process whereby the designer put his or her name to a variety of products without necessarily controlling the quality of either the design or the production. The subsequent lowering of standards meant that the exclusivity of the brand was diffused among a plethora of inferior products. This dilution of the brand image was a warning for those companies who were increasingly protective of their integrity in a decade when consumers were beginning to covet a label with genuine status. A combination of this desire, together with recognition by designers of targeting the right market, resulted in the rise of international brands such as Missoni and Gucci.

Yves Saint Laurent was one of the first designers to be influenced by what was being worn on the street. Initially appointed design director at Christian Dior after the couturier's sudden death, in 1960 he produced the 'Beat' collection featuring black turtlenecks and crocodile jackets. It was too youthful and modern for the traditional house of Dior, and Saint Laurent left the house to be conscripted into the French army to do his National Service, where he suffered a complete nervous breakdown. With the support of his lover and business partner Pierre Bergé he recovered, and went on to show his first acclaimed collection under his own name in 1961. By the 1970s his reputation was established as a radical designer, particularly in his consolidation of the relationship between art and fashion, an aesthetic that continued in his accessories line. In 1975 he produced a handbag in *homage* to a master colourist, painter Yves Klein.

One of the first labels to distance knitwear from its frumpy, artisanal image and place it at the forefront of 1970s glamour was that of Rosita and Tai Missoni, who founded their eponymous company in 1953. The company's warp-knitted multicoloured stripes and zigzags in effervescent space-dyed yarns were very much part of a return to European sophistication in the wake of the tattered remains of hippie culture. It was a look that required an elegant handbag, and Missoni also produced small bags in their signature polychromatic stripes, set within rigid frames and hanging from long, slender chains.

OPPOSITE The midi-skirt, initially rejected as dreary by consumers reluctant to discard the freedom of the mini, is enlivened by Victorian-style lace-up boots and a trio of handbags in this photograph from the 1970s. On the left is a python clutch bag; in the centre, a military-style shoulder bag with three outer pockets; and on the right, a patent leather shoulder bag.

ABOVE An elegant evening clutch bag from 1975 is engineered in silver and gold metalwork.

RIGHT Reappraising the elegance of the 1930s, with a cloche hat, button-through dress and a Deco-inspired clutch bag, all from Yves Saint Laurent's spring 1974 *haute couture* collection.

The Disco Era

With the opening of the New York's decadent nightclub, Studio 54, the Age of Aquarius was over. During the two-year period of the club's life, from 1977 to 1979, the 11,000 square-foot dance floor on West 54th Street was witness to the excesses of New York's demimonde. Andy Warhol, the catalyst of the New York social scene, together with his cohorts Lisa Minnelli, Cher and Bianca Jagger, cavorted under the strobe lights that reflected back the glitter and shine of disco fashion: Lurex knitted haltertops, boob tubes, body paint and glitter, and body-hugging spandex trousers. Equally light-catching were the gold and silver mesh bags by Whiting & Davis that now swung from the disco diva's wrist. Purveyors of chainmail purses since the beginning of the century, the metal mesh now appeared fittingly relevant. Fashion was about sex and shine, the androgynous hippie era was finally over, and lipgloss and leopardskin replaced crochet and cheesecloth. High-octane glamour was provided by New York designer Halston, creator of fluid bias-cut dresses for the new international celebrities frequenting the disco scene at Studio 54. It was time for the handbag to lose the constraints of practicality and respectability and get sexy. Carlos Falchi was the man to do it.

Carlos Falchi

The flamboyant decadence of the disco era was captured by handbag designer Carlos Falchi. His eye-catching handbags in vivid colour combinations and exotic textures had all the carnival aesthetic of his native Brazil. Falchi moved to New York City in 1964, and began working as a night manager at legendary rock-and-roll venue Max's Kansas City, a restaurant-cum-bar frequented by superstars Iggy Pop and David Bowie. Falchi's outrageous patchwork snakeskin trousers and other homemade sartorial excesses caught the attention of rock luminaries such as Mick Jagger, Elvis Presley, Cher and Tina Turner, who then asked the designer to make their stage costumes. Musician Herbie Hancock's wife encouraged Falchi to show samples of his work to Geraldine Stutz, then a buyer for Henri Bendel, the prestigious New York department store. Impressed by the satchel in which he carried his samples, she placed an order for a number of handbags for the store and the first Falchi accessories collection was conceived.

In 1974 Falchi designed the Buffalo, a full-bodied bag comprising swathes of luxurious leather caught into a curvaceous frame, the ideal laid-back accessory for denim-wearing hippies. Anna Johnson quotes Falchi in her book *Power of the Purse*; the designer recalls, 'bags were very stiff in the 1960s, more like weapons

ABOVE Brazilian designer Carlos Falchi was king of the disco scene, producing metallic leather handbags that reflected the strobe lights of New York's Studio 54. This shoulder bag designed in 1977 left the hands free for dancing on the disco floor.

OPPOSITE TOP Carlos Falchi produced the Buffalo bag in 1974, a sexy, pleated bag of soft-as-butter leather in vibrant colours that matched the ebullience of the era.

than accessories. I would take my leathers and dye them in the bathtub at home using crazy Analine colours. Nothing matched and they were very light [weight]. At a time when everybody was crying out for freedom, I made bags that swung, that moved and caressed the body.'

During the 1980s Falchi recognized that power dressing required an equally dramatic accessory. His range of striking leather clutch bags with multicoloured inserts of exotic skins were a perfect complement to the sharp-edged tailoring of the 'me' decade. Utilizing origami-like expertise, the designer created bags such as the folding box bag with a central opening of interlocking leather petals and, for Todd Oldham, a hexagonal three-colour bag inspired by a harlequin's cap.

Falchi's passionate involvement with the distinctive design of each skin, and the resulting unique textures of his bags are a result of sophisticated leather treatments. His aesthetic continues to exploit exotic materials to the full, hand-dying deerskin, alligator, crocodile, python and goatskin in his signature bright colours. In 1983 Falchi received a Coty Award for accessories design and in 2004 he was awarded accessory designer of the year by the Council of Fashion Designers of America (CFDA), the same year that he was granted his lifetime achievement award from the Accessories Council. Several of Falchi's designs have been placed in the permanent collection of the Costume Institute of the Metropolitan Museum of Art.

The designer still retains full creative of his brand, 'for me, there is something magical about the creative process… I blend art and design to produce a dramatic and fresh take on the leather product.'

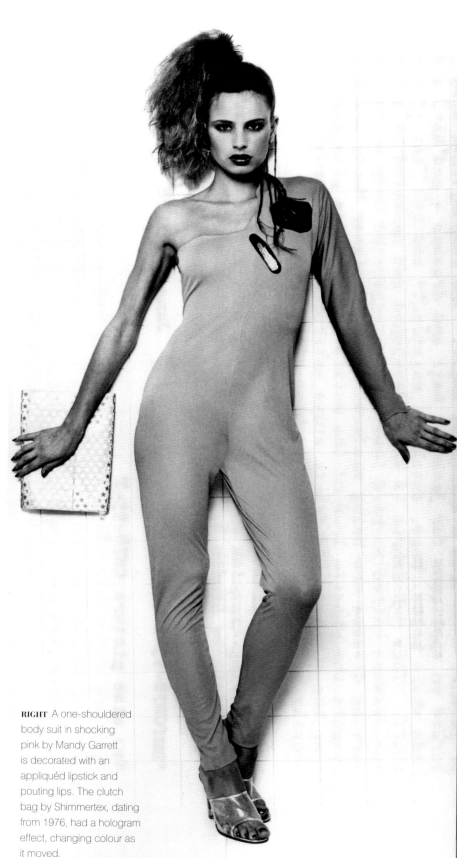

RIGHT A one-shouldered body suit in shocking pink by Mandy Garrett is decorated with an appliquéd lipstick and pouting lips. The clutch bag by Shimmertex, dating from 1976, had a hologram effect, changing colour as it moved.

▼ Rivets, studs and tooled leather
The early 1970s saw a renewed interest in the Arts and Crafts movement, recognized here in this leather handbag decorated with rivets and secured with a leather-covered peg and hasp closure. Dating from 1973, the bag has an internal central zipped section and is labelled Tête d'Or.

Key looks of the decade

1970s

▲ Wide-strap shoulder bags
Hand-held bags were out and shoulder bags, for ease and practicality, were in. These large, squarish shoulder bags with comfortable wide straps date fro 1971 and were a useful accesso the tailored trouser suits that bec popular leisurewear for women.

◀ Embroidery and appliqué
American film actress and political activist Jane Fonda acknowledges the trend for the highly decorated craft-inspired handbags of the early 1970s with this 'flower power' hand-painted, appliquéd and embroidered shoulder bag.

◀ Tote bags

Tote bags, often made in canvas and leather and by brands such as Dooney & Bourke, Coach, Laura Ashley and Mulberry, were influenced by rural and nautical traditions. Here a small dog – always a popular fashion accessory – is carried here inside a 1978 Gucci tote bag.

Suede and leather

The juxtaposition of suede and leather was a popular combination in the 1970s, seen here in a shoulder bag with adjustable strap and asymmetrical front flap with a matching leather-covered button press closure.

Animal skins and textures

Although this 1970s crocodile handbag is a formal classic, designers as Nigel Lofthouse, Yves St Laurent and Carlos Falchi experimented with animal skins such as leopard, crocodile and snake – often in brilliant hues and patchworks.

▲ Fringes and tassels

As the decade progressed hippie fashion went mainstream, as demonstrated in this 1971 ethnic-inspired printed midriff shirt and shorts by Jones of New York and knitted shoulder bag with tassels by Odyssey.

1980s:
The Designer Decade

From the outrageous fancy dress of the New Romantics to the ever-broadening shoulderpads of the woman's business suit, the 1980s was a decade that celebrated excess. The office glamazon, a new phenomenon of the era, hiked up her skirt, donned her stilettos and carried the biggest clutch bag she could find: the decade that celebrated big hair and big shoulders also demanded an oversized bag. The professional woman refused to make herself inconspicuous and flouted the advice of American author John T Molloy in his book *Women: Dress for Success* when he recommended wearing 'a blazer that should cover, not accentuate, the contours of your body, a below-the-knee skirt and a pair of low-heeled pumps, and a bra that completely obscures the nipples.'

This ball-breaking female executive, or the 'killer-bimbo' as Peter York describes her in his book *The Eighties*, had ambition that appeared to rival her sexuality. She could be recognized by the big-shouldered jacket, which ensured a woman had equal space to the men around a boardroom table. The stiletto spike of her shoes was representative of this new approach to working dress. Adding a good four inches to the length of the leg, the spike heel came to symbolize the power and sexuality of the 1980s woman, particularly when shod in Manolo Blahnik.

Status was the underlying theme of the era, embodied by the relaunching of classic fashion houses Chanel, Dior and Louis Vuitton, all of whom capitalized on the desire of the consumer for the latest 'must have' bag that represented their social standing among the American and European 'shiny set'.

The Power-Dressed Woman

Satirized by American journalist Tom Wolfe in his novel *Bonfire of the Vanities*, the young, upwardly mobile professionals of both sexes busy making hay in the financial capitals of the world were the 'baby boomers' who found themselves in well-paid jobs that required a sartorial concession to the new conservatism. The suit, for both men and women, became a requisite office uniform. However, for women the trouser suit was replaced by the skirt suit in bright look-at-me fuchsia pink or red. The jacket was fitted at the waist, sometimes with a peplum A-flared hem and worn with a matching miniskirt. Unlike the 1960s mini, which referenced the child-like look of the clothes, the 1980s version was all about power and freedom; worn with the spike heel, it represented domination.

A plethora of 'lifestyle' products on offer symbolized the aspirational nature of 1980s consumerism. The Filofax, first imported to the UK via the Philadelphia company Lefax and a sort of mobile office that required a briefcase to carry it around, became widespread,

in the UK thanks to British designer and retailer Paul Smith, who stocked them. Handbags were deemed to represent female fluffiness, and women were encouraged to leave them at home or to save them for the evening. As author John T Molloy said, 'Never carry a handbag when you can carry a briefcase'.

Such niceties were not observed by Britain's new and first female prime minister, Margaret Thatcher. The most powerful female politician in Britain could safely eschew such rules. Her 'trusty companion' was a black leather Ferragamo with a rigid frame, which exuded all the virtues she held most dear – conservative in style, functional and designed for longevity. Although renowned for the innovation of footwear design (Salvatore Ferragamo created the first wedge-heeled shoes during the exegeses of the Second World War), Ferragamo went on to produce handbags using the same innovative approach to materials, while upholding traditional craft skills, as they did with their shoes.

PAGE 166 The wide-shouldered garments of the 1980s demanded ever larger bags to balance the silhouette, as in this quilted briefcase-style bag worn with French designer Thierry Mugler's ivory silk dress dating from 1986.

BELOW Although a name more usually associated with innovatory shoe design, Salvatore Ferragamo also produces handbags and small leather goods, and was a favourite label of Prime Minister Margaret Thatcher during this period. This coloured crocodile bag, created by Fiamma Ferragamo and dating from 1988-9, has two rigid handles and a double fastening with gilt 'gancino' hardware details.

LEFT The clutch bag underwent a popular revival in the 1980s, though somewhat larger in format than its predecessors. This 1987 version in brown crocodile is by Ferragamo.

RIGHT Red was the colour of the decade, from eye-catching big-shouldered jackets to extravagant accessories, as in this 1985 envelope clutch in red nappa by Ferragamo.

FAR LEFT A 1988 ensemble by designer Anna Choi featuring a barrel-shaped leather handbag.

CENTRE French accessory designer Renaud Pellegrino opened his first workshop in 1970, and for the following eight years worked in collaboration with Parisian couturier Yves Saint Laurent. During the 1980s he was considered to be one of the *jeunes créateurs* of the French ready-to-wear scene. He remains one of the few independent luxury brands. This handbag dates from 1988.

LEFT Tunisian designer Azzedine Alaia was responsible for 1980s body-conscious dressing, and was referred to as the 'King of Cling.' Here he works against type with this 1988 highly decorated handbag in a style more commonly seen in a 'knitting bag', a base attached to two circular handles.

First Lady Style

The inauguration of Ronald Reagan as President of the United States with his society-loving wife Nancy as First Lady ensured that the 'big occasion' dress, accessorized with one of Judith Leiber's exquisite minaudieres, had plenty of outings in the 1980s. As designer Oscar de La Renta remarked after the dress-down informality of the Carter years, 'The Reagan's are going to bring back the kind of style the White House should have.' Washington became host to what became known as the 'shiny set', a group of fashion- and status-obsessed socialites dubbed by social satirist and journalist Tom Wolfe as the 'social X-rays' due to their extreme thinness. In his book *The Fashion Conspiracy* Nicolas Coleridge describes one of them: 'Hair teased into a diaphanous bombe glacée, shoulders projecting like sharks' fins from a backless Oscar de la Renta… her skin as taught across her face as surgeon's gloves … she glided. And you knew at a glance that she was vastly, astoundingly rich.'

The manager of the Gucci store in Beverly Hills, Carlo Celoni, witnessed one of Nancy Reagan's shopping splurges. According to *Nancy Reagan: The Unauthorized Biography* by Kitty Kelley, on one occasion in 1980 the store was closed to all other customers so that the president's wife could take her pick. Her booty included a black silk egg purse, a miniature calfskin bag with a bamboo handle, a black lizard day bag, and a white evening bag accented with the double G, which she intended to carry to the inaugural balls.

Television soap operas *Dallas* and *Dynasty* portrayed the lifestyle of the rich and famous, and Joan Collins' character Alexis provided the sumptuously dressed role model for the uber-bitch. Extreme bad behaviour was rewarded with ever-increasing viewing figures and even bigger shoulder pads, which had a starring role of their own. Clutch bags of vibrant colours and appliquéd exotic leathers played their part. Popular were matching shoes and bags by Gina featuring neon clashing colours, with added decoration in the form of bows or diamanté motifs for evening. Barbara Bolan provided more understated American-designed, Italian-made, handbags in glacé leathers. They often had an

TOP RIGHT Vibrantly coloured patent leather shoulder bags by Ferragamo from 1983.

RIGHT Colour blocking was an important aspect of the attention-grabbing fashions of the 1980s, as evidenced in this elongated yellow leather clutch bag by La Bagagerie from 1988.

RIGHT The 1980s saw the regeneration of French *haute couture*, exemplified by the opening of a new fashion house headed by Christian Lacroix, renowned for the riotous layering of intense colour and patterns. Lacroix's turquoise blue handbag with baroque metal handles, seen here, was designed for his 1987–8 autumn/winter collection.

asymmetric flap with a ruched base that reflected the tailoring details of the time. They were sold with an optional long thin strap that could be tucked inside the bag. Bolan's bags, immensely collectable, are also part of the Metropolitan Museum of Art's Costume Institute in New York City.

A different sort of fantasy was propounded by American designer Donna Karan, who featured a female US president in one of her advertisements. Karan launched her first independent collection in 1985, targeted at the urban professional woman. Her demographic was the New York business scene, and as a designer she was entirely in tune with the requirements of the aspirational working woman. Karan's body-conscious, classless basics included the all-in-one body, wrapped skirts and tubular dresses in stretch fabrics. These ruled the boardrooms of Manhattan and signified material success. In 1988 Karan's solution to the 'day for night' dilemma of the busy professional woman was to introduce her handbag 'systems', a series of bags that included a small pochette to be kept inside a matching briefcase. A leather knapsack was also introduced into the range to evenly distribute the weight of an ever-increasing number of necessary accoutrements required by the busy woman: filofax, calculator and cosmetics.

The Leiber Minaudière

Judith Leiber is the foremost exponent of the art of the minaudière. A combination of high fashion and decadent luxury the bags represented the apotheosis of 1980s conspicuous consumption, and continue to be coveted today. Toy-like in their dimensions, witty and inspired by such diverse subjects as sleeping cats, polar bears and butterflies, the bags have been held by every First Lady of the United States since Jackie Kennedy in 1963, including Nancy Reagan, Barbara Bush and Hilary Clinton.

Born in 1921 to a family of jewellers in Budapest, Hungary, Judith Pietro Leiber managed to escape from the Nazi occupation to become the first-ever female apprentice in the Hungarian Handbag Guild. In 1945 she met and subsequently married an American GI, Gerson Leiber, and moved with him to New York. After spending several years working for different handbag manufactures such as Koret and Nettie Rosenstein, the designer launched her own label in 1963. In the same year she produced the Stingray handbag which was carried by Jackie Kennedy: this was subsequently reissued in the

BELOW The exquisite and unprecedentedly expensive minaudières of Judith Leiber conformed to the 1980s concept of luxury. Acknowledging the Russian jeweller Fabergé is the Egg bag dating from 1983 which, as with all her bags, contains a coin purse, mirror and comb.

early 1990s. Although Leiber initially produced elegant and finely finished handbags in rare materials that combined wit and innovation with high production values, including diamanté and hand-cast enamel clasps, the designer's reputation now resides in her exquisite and extraordinary minaudiere evening bags.

The origin of these rhinestone-covered evening bags is serendipitous. Judith Leiber ordered a gift for a friend, and when the polished metal box arrived in the post it was damaged. Inspired by the precious Art Deco minaudières of Van Cleef & Arpels, Leiber embellished the scratched area with rhinestones, and the result was the first Judith Leiber metal evening bag. Three hundred of these were produced in 1967, to be followed throughout the following decades by infinite variations on the theme. Each one requires three to seven days to make. Initially sculpted in wax, the design is then cast in metal, goldplated and bejewelled with anything up to 10,000 Austrian crystal rhinestones hand-set over a painted design. In each Leiber bag, there can be as many as seven interlinings of different materials including paper, muslin, flannel, horsehair, foam rubber, canvas and wadding. Each bag contains a miniature comb, purse and mirror and is lined with gold kid leather.

BELOW The 1980s revival of the minaudière by Judith Leiber provided the super-rich with yet another investment opportunity. This evening bag, formed in the shape of a many-petalled rose, required more than 10,000 rhinestones.

TOP Incorporating pieces of patterned cloth stitched together with decorative embroidery, this Judith Leiber bag subverts the homespun craft of patchwork into an extravagant and bejewelled purse.

ABOVE Leiber, although most well known for her jewelled evening bags, also includes alligator day bags in her range, such as this vintage clutch.

Lana Marks

American Lana J Marks counts among her clientele royalty, Hollywood celebrities and political figures. These include the late Diana, Princess of Wales, Princess Marie-Chantal of Greece, former First Lady Laura Bush, Oprah Winfrey, Julianna Moore, Angela Bassett, Reese Witherspoon and Chloë Sevigny. Now a member of the Council of Fashion Designers of America (CFDA), Marks claims her handbag career started in 1987, when she was invited aboard Queen Elizabeth's yacht, the Britannia, for the monarch's birthday celebrations. Frustrated in her search for a red alligator bag to match her suit, Marks realized that there was a niche in the market for 'high-end handbags in fine exotic leathers in fabulous colours'. The result two years later was the production of the red alligator Lunchbox handbag that launched her career as a handbag designer. The royalty connection turned full circle when Helen Mirren attended the Academy Awards ceremony in 2007 to collect her Oscar for her role in *The Queen* carrying a specially designed clutch by Marks. The bag was made from cream alligator leather with an 18-carat gold frame embellished with a tiny crown on the front, itself decorated with 776 fully cut, individually set, white diamonds.

Operating out of her international headquarters in Palm Beach, Florida, Lana Marks purports to create function in architectural form: 'When someone chooses one of my handbags, they are making an investment in fashion, quality and practicality… most important, my handbags succeed in fulfilling the specifics of my customers' lifestyles.' The brightly coloured and richly textured exotic leather bags are handcrafted in Italy, and the collections are available in 150 styles in 100 different colours in alligator, crocodile, ostrich and lizard skins.

Marks provides bespoke handbags for particular clients. Two of her well-known handbags include the Princess Diana handbag and the Farrah Fawcett tote, both the result of requests by their namesakes for personally designed handbags. For the inauguration of President George W Bush she designed a powder-grey rounded handbag, the Inauguration clutch, for his wife Laura to wear with an Oscar de la Renta suit. For the candlelight dinners, Marks created a seashell-pink satin baby bag, the Inauguration tote, to match Peggy Jennings' beaded evening gown creation.

RIGHT Calvin Klein, master of American minimalism, designed this gold dress Lurex sheath dress and purse, modelled by Yasmin Le Bon, in 1988, capturing the decade's trend for luxe styling and materials.

OPPOSITE Lana Marks began designing bags in the late 1980s, during a revival of the clutch. Known for her use of exotic animal skins, this narrow elongated clutch is in yellow snakeskin.

Redefining Luxury

The world's largest luxury conglomerate was founded in 1987 with the merger between Moët Hennessy and Louis Vuitton. This brought together the champagne, spirits and leather goods divisions, some of which had been established more than two centuries before. Moët & Chandon originated in 1743, Veuve Clicquot in 1772, Hennessy in 1765; Johan-Joseph Krug founded his establishment in 1843, while Chateau d'Yquem and its wines go as far back as 1593. The house of Louis Vuitton was founded in 1854. Subsequent mergers have resulted in a fashion and accessories industry that is now dominated by two conglomerates. The first, LVMH, which includes fashion labels Loewe, Celine, Givenchy, Marc Jacobs, Fendi, Pucci and Donna Karan. Their rivals for supremacy in the luxury market, the Gucci Group, have a whole or partial interest in Bottega Veneta, Yves Saint Laurent, Alexander McQueen, Balenciaga and Stella McCartney.

The French Houses

In the 1980s luxury was defined by wearing or using the right brand. The corporate world rejoiced in this idealization of the label, and as the decade progressed branding emerged as a tangible asset, vital to a company's success, particularly in the luxury goods market. Couture shifted away from the provision of bespoke clothing to the mass production (albeit on an elevated level) of branded items that upheld the financial position of the company. Nowhere was this truer than in the rebranding of the couture house of Chanel.

When German-born Karl Lagerfeld was invited to become the artistic director of Chanel in 1983 he rejuvenated the label and increased its appeal to a younger, edgier clientele. The house once again became hip with the introduction of unexpected colours, fabrics and textures into reworked classics such as the wool bouclé suit. The most significant contribution to sexing up the label was Lagerfeld's interpretation of the original 2.55 'gilt and quilt bag' (see pages 100–1). By exaggerating its distinctive features – enlarging the interlocking double Cs of the logo and shamelessly positioning them on the front of the bag – Lagerfeld created the most coveted status symbol of the decade.

RIGHT A version of the 'gilt and quilt' bag by Karl Lagerfeld for Chanel. Skirts are high and sleeves are batwing on the runway in 1985. The chain-link belt and camellia at the throat are signature touches of the label.

The success of the bag inspired many other major brands to revisit their archives in order to relaunch their products and exploit the desire for instantly identifiable status handbags. Christian Dior logo-patterned clothing and accessories first appeared in the 1950s, and this was one of the labels to be reinvented for the 1980s. The quilted bestselling Dior bag was first introduced in 1989, and was available in three sizes, 20 types of material and 53 colours. A cluster of logo letters dangle from the handle like a charm bracelet spelling D I O R. This presaged the trend for adding stand-alone bag charms, yet another opportunity for a luxury label to extend their signature style into accessories that upheld the quality of the brand while providing more affordable elements. The Dior bag was presented to Diana, Princess of Wales, during her visit to Paris in 1995 by the French president's wife Madame Chirac, from which date it became known as the Lady Dior.

While never losing its reputation for quality and elegance, the Hermès brand also updated the formality of the Kelly bag (see pages 102–3) and produced the larger, less structured Birkin for a younger, hipper audience in 1984. Various versions of its genesis include an account of the British actress and style icon Jane Birkin being seated on a plane next to the then-president of Hermès, Jean-Louis Dumas. As she rummaged in her straw tote the actress reputedly complained that it was too small for all her needs. She was subsequently asked to design her dream bag, which was then labelled the Birkin and which is still in production. Waiting times for the bag can be anything from eight months to six years, but original vintage Birkins from the 1980s are rare. Family heirlooms, they tend to be passed down from mother to daughter.

LEFT The Hermès Birkin bag, designed for British film actress Jane Birkin, was created in 1984 as a roomier variation of the Kelly. It is possibly the most famous and coveted bag in the world.

ABOVE The expensive statement bag, including this Miss Dior launched in 1989 and later renamed the Lady Dior in honour of the late Lady Diana, typified the new consumerism of the era.

The Italian Houses

Established in Milan in 1906 as a saddlery house, Italian luxury label Gucci thrived following the Second World War when the double-G motif became internationally recognized. However, overexpansion of licensing agreements during the 1980s to include clothing and household items became Gucci's temporary downfall, and internal conflicts within the family-owned company also took their toll. With the appointment in 1988 of an American retail executive, Dawn Mello, many of the licensing deals were rescinded; she eliminated more than 10,000 inferior products. It was not until 1992, however, and the instigation of Tom Ford as creative director, that the brand really entered the fashion stratosphere to become the most coveted label of the 1990s (see page 190).

The marketing strategy of reinvention was also fuelled in some cases by the necessity of the big names to recoup their reputation and loss of credibility from the disastrous result of overlicensing in the 1970s. There was no better way to re-establish credibility and the prestige of the brand than by introducing a high-end luxury product with restricted outlets. The reputation of the brand was subsequently rigorously observed and protected, particularly necessary in view of the plethora of counterfeit bags that began to appear. Globalization, that is, the movement of manufacturing around the world, and the new technologies, both played their part in disseminating fakes.

Handbags now began to be subject to seasonal changes, with ranges introduced twice yearly, as was already the case with fashion. Identified by the designer label or brand logo, bags came to be regarded as fashion items rather than as investment pieces. A burgeoning clientele for *haute couture* emerged,too; in addition to New York socialites and the new money from the oil-rich Middle-Eastern market, a younger, hipper customer now had money to spend.

ABOVE Italian fashion designer Roberto Gucci talks to one of his employees at a Gucci factory near Florence, Italy, in 1984.

In the 1980s Italian fashion was polarized between the discreet understated tailoring of Giorgio Armani and the flashy uber-glamour of Gianni Versace. Armani established his own label in 1974. Renowned for deconstructing the male business suit by removing its carapace-like infrastructure of padding and stiffened interlinings, women also appreciated the softer silhouette. For those who required a less aggressive working wardrobe, the Armani trouser suit was the perfect solution, combining understated elegance with practicality.

In contrast Gianni Versace, founded in 1978, represented the moneyed excesses of the era. Utilizing clinging metallic fabrics and opulent decoration allied to a garment slashed to the thigh or cut down to the buttock, his dresses always emphasized the sexuality of the wearer; his signature style pushed the look to the edge of vulgarity.

In 1984, at the height of logo-mania, the luxury leather company Bottega Veneta decided on a different approach to market their handbags. In response to the era's brazen branding, their advertising campaign underplayed the notion of overt status dressing with the slogan 'When your own initials are enough'. Recognizable not by a logo nor a signature print, but by their distinctive construction,

the bags utilize a method of hand-woven strips of leather called *intrecciato*, originally developed by the company to give the products their signature softness. The simplicity and sophistication of the Cabat, a square-shaped basket which incorporates a numbered plaque inside the interior pouch, exemplifies stealth luxury. Variations of these distinctive woven handbags are still a hallmark of the brand, as is the understated promotion.

The company was formed by the Moltedo family in 1966 in the Veneta region of the north-east of Italy (*bottega* means artisan workshop). One of the first handbags to be produced was the lozenge-shaped woven minaudière, popularly seen on the floor of Studio 54 in the 1970s – the current creative director, German designer Tomas Maier, remembers the 'woven bags in unusual colours' from the period. Manufacture of the prototype bags still takes place in Verona, Italy, where the wear and tear and flexibility of the skins are tested. Leather cutters use scalpels sharpened on stone rods to carve out the shape of the bag from responsibly farmed skins, bought from France, Spain and Italy. Seven crocodile hide skins make up a bucket bag with hides selected to match scale, size of scales and shade. In 2001 Bottega Veneta was acquired by the Gucci Group.

BELOW LEFT Italian luxury goods company Bottega Veneta is renowned for the *intrecciato* system of woven leather that makes up their luxurious products.

BELOW RIGHT The humble tote is elevated to classic status with this multicoloured Club Stripe duffel by Bottega Veneta.

RIGHT A drawstring pouch in silk velvet, designed by Jean Paul Gaultier in 1986, references the Dorothy bags of the Victorian era.

CENTRE British designer Zandra Rhodes created this pleated and gathered silk evening bag with a drawstring fastening in 1983.

FAR RIGHT Soft leather is gathered into a rigid handle in an informal, roomy bag designed by Il Bisonte in 1982.

New Romantics and the Avant-Garde

The avant-garde in fashion design rejects traditional categories and crosses boundaries between art, politics, history and gender. Vivienne Westwood's aesthetic of historical revivalism took its inspiration from a synthesis of ideas drawn from such diverse sources as English seventeenth- and eighteenth-century tailoring and African prints. Westwood's first fashion collection under her own name in 1981 was called Clothes for Heroes. This plundering of other cultures surfaced in further collections: Aztec and Mexican patterns and motifs provided inspiration for the Savage collection in 1981, and Appalachian folk culture in the Buffalo collection of 1982, sold from the London shop Nostalgia of Mud. This practice ultimately presaged the 'pirating' of ideas by the followers of the New Romantic movement, when students from Central Saint Martin's College of Art and Design in London elevated dressing up into a thriving fashion culture.

The London club scene was witness to these extravagant sartorial excesses and fuelled the impetus for ever-more extreme modes of dress, including the costumes of the cross-dressing singer of Culture Club, Boy George, and woven and stretch knits from Bodymap, a company set up by Stevie Stewart and David Holah in 1982. John Galliano, a graduate of Saint Martin's in 1984, made an immediate impact on the fashion world with his innovative cutting techniques, derived from past masters such as Madaleine Vionnet, allied to an innate theatricality and attention to historical detail. Following a period as an independent designer he was asked to become the principal designer at French fashion house Givenchy in 1995 before receiving the prestigious accolade of heading the House of Dior.

The relationship between art, rock music and fashion was also energizing New York. In 1984 Stephen Sprouse, after several years of experience with Halston, the designer darling of the 1970s disco era, introduced his first influential collection. This was inspired by a combination of the visual ephemera of contemporary urban life and 1960s and '80s pop and street culture, and a fascination with the underground New York scene. Graffiti, once the subversive activity of disaffected youth in the 1960s, became accepted as a legitimate art form, and alongside practitioners Jean-Michel Basquiat and Keith Haring, Sprouse appropriated the tags and stencils of the street and added Day-Glo colours in rayon, velvet and satin. He was noted for using custom-dyed and screen-printed fabrics, sequin embellishments and he personally designed the graffiti patterns in his early 1980s designs. In 2001 he was invited to design for Louis Vuitton by Marc Jacobs, producing the much-copied and iconic Louis Vuitton Graffiti bag.

Further contrast to the hard-edged flashiness of designers such as Thierry Mugler and Claude Montana was provided by the sober deconstruction of fashion by two Japanese designers, Rei Kawakubo of Comme des Garçons and Yohji Yamamoto, who established themselves in Paris in 1982. Dubbed damningly by the American press as 'bag lady chic' the clothes were unprepossessing on the hangers, but once worn the eccentric cutting and asymmetrical seams provided a new mysterious silhouette that questioned the attitude as to what constituted 'fashion'. In deepest black, indigo, with some white and the occasional touches of red, the Japanese designers provided a thoughtful contrast to the power suit and its accoutrements.

Feeling the Burn

Sportswear became integrated into the modern wardrobe during the 1980s as global labels and big brands began to exploit the growing preoccupation with health and fitness. Branded sports clothing manufacturers including Nike, Adidas and Puma produced a variety of bags in response to the desire of the fashionable for active sportswear that was also worn on the street. The body-conscious culture, popularized by film actress Jane Fonda in her work-out videos and by such films as *Fame* (1980) and *Flashdance* (1983), had introduced the notion of purposeful activity towards self-improvement. Supermodels bestrode the catwalk and represented a new feminine ideal of a body honed and toned to perfection by intensive exercise.

Gym ownership was a customary adjunct to the professional woman's busy schedule, and Lycra provided comfortable and contour-enhancing garments that allowed full movement while still retaining their shape. Garments designed specifically for exercise began to permeate into daywear, providing a marked contrast to the strict tailoring of the on-duty business suit. The foremost exponent of this aesthetic was American designer Norma Kamali, who produced cotton fleece sweats inspired by exercise and dance garments including oversized sweatshirts worn as dresses over leotards and legwarmers. Lycra was also an important element of the 'body' – a combination of the 1970s body stocking and the dance leotard worn as an alternative to the blouse under power suits and American designer Donna Karan's answer to a smoother silhouette.

The Prada Nylon Bag

Leisurewear demanded a different bag from the dramatic oversize clutch or the briefcase that accessorized the business suit. A backpack had been introduced by Jean-Charles de Castelbajac in 1984, but it was the Vela, a small and lightweight backpack in Pocono nylon, that became the first cult, as opposed to classic, bag. Designed by Miuccia Prada, granddaughter of the founder of the Milanese accessory house, this must-have accessory, with its connotations of youthful fitness and activity, appealed to both men and women. The discreet triangular logo and utilitarian performance sportswear fabric was in marked contrast to the conspicuous consumption of the decade, and presaged the minimalism of the 1990s. This luxury sportswear style was subsequently appropriated by Chanel, Donna Karan, Fendi and Gucci. With her post-modern aesthetic Miuccia Prada continues to revisit traditional bags from earlier eras, such as the 1950s-inspired bowling bag, and interprets them for contemporary sensibilities in innovative fabrics, textures and colours. Winifred Gallagher in her book *It's In the Bag* recounts a rare interview with the designer:

> I think the point was that these were fashion bags for the first time. Labels like Gucci and Hermès had always done the same bag for many years. I treated bags as if they were fashion. Also, this was something practical, but also very luxurious.

OPPOSITE FAR LEFT The *enfant terrible* of French fashion, John Paul Gaultier fused street style with spectacular couture and ready-to-wear, as in this collection from 1989.

OPPOSITE LEFT Model Caroline Ellen is wearing a black and dip-dyed chartreuse T-shirt over a matching mini-dress by American designer Stephen Sprouse in 1985. The Day-Glo colouring is a theme that would reappear on many of his creations, including the Louis Vuitton Graffiti bag.

LEFT A signature material for Prada, nylon has been reworked into a variety of styles since the debut of the Vela bag. This gold nylon handbag with leather straps is from Prada's autumn/winter 2003–4 collection.

BELOW The practical minimalism of Miuccia Prada is evident in the design of the backpack in Pocono nylon. Produced in 1985, the discreet triangular logo was an early example of 'stealth wealth' in contrast to the prevalent ethos of conspicuous consumption.

◀ Brand logos
Logo-mania, the desire to be seen with the latest must-have handbag, was endemic during the 1980s, resulting in consumers purchasing leading brands such as Chanel, Gucci and Louis Vuitton as evidence of their visible wealth and social status.

Key looks of the decade

1980s

▼ Canvas totes
Canvas shoppers and totes became the preppy must-have accessory in the 1980s, particularly those by American company L L Bean and British brand Barbour, who also made canvas-and-leather cartridge bags. This version in cream canvas with brown leather trim is by Laura Ashley.

◀ Belted bags and 'bumbags'
French designer Sonia Rykiel combines Parisian chic with hands-free practicality in this diminutive belt bag designed in 1984. The commercialism of sport and the integration of sports uniform into mainstream fashion was a feature of the 1980s.

◀ **Business bags**
The professional woman required a handbag commodious enough to carry all the accoutrements of the office, including the ubiquitous Filofax. This model, L'Aiglon (the Eaglet), by Victoire was designed in 1982.

▶ **Pared-down styles**
Accessories in simple, architectural shapes were the perfect accompaniment to power-dressing. German designer Jil Sander specialized in pared-down minimalism and austere shapes for the modern woman, as exemplified in this architectonic bag designed in 1989.

▲ **Wit and whimsy**
Idiosyncratic accessories and witty fashion were exemplified by Italian label Moschino and French label Sonia Rykiel, who designed these handbags based on sunflowers in 1989.

1990s to Now:
Future Collectables

Fashion in the 1990s was defined by an interest in all things spiritual. A seismic shift in attitudes saw the almost instant death of the 1980s shoulder pad as designers tapped into an interest in New Age philosophies, a concern with the environment, a rejection of conspicuous consumption and an awareness of global activities. A new urban grittiness demanded utility above all; for this reason the three basic handbag shapes for the majority of the decade were the messenger bag with the shoulder strap and the front flap, the satchel and the rucksack. These were often constructed from industrial materials such as nylon, steel mesh and canvas. The influential Prada rucksack was still in evidence; the understated logo and the bag's construction represented the fashionable version of minimalism, albeit of the most expensive sort, and reflected a rejection of unnecessary embellishment in all aspects of visual culture.

The arrival of the twenty-first century saw the acceleration of the handbag as a replaceable, disposable accessory, as bags began to follow fashion's seasonal trends and the major labels realized the power of the handbag in generating income for the brand. No longer only appreciated for its longevity or quality of craftsmanship, the bag was important for its endorsement by a celebrity and the lavish eccentricity of its hardware. Once the expensive handbag was the remit of the elite and the moneyed, but from the twenty-first century onwards it was seen on the arm of the average woman. Today prices seem to have no limit; the most ordinary bag often carries a hefty price tag, and the most esoteric and sought-after model, an even greater sum – but it's a price many are prepared to pay.

LEFT AND BELOW RIGHT Tom Ford subverts the Gucci signature bamboo handles and snaffle fastenings by introducing unexpected materials such as this highly coloured python skin, and by deconstructing the traditional handbag shape.

PAGE 188 Italian design duo Domenico Dolce & Stefano Gabbana, who started their label in 1985, are renowned for their use of animal prints, seen here in the handbag on the left. The handbag on the right is by La Bagagerie. Both date from 2008.

Luxury Goods Labels

As the 1990s progressed two significant events occurred that effected major changes in the fashion hierarchy. Tom Ford became creative director of Gucci in 1992. His take on high-octane glamour retained the classic elements of Gucci style: the bamboo handle and the bold striped canvas, the double Gs and the horse bits, but Ford interpreted them for a younger, sexier fashion tribe. In 1995 he restyled the bamboo-handled bag that was originally designed out of post-war shortages in 1957 in patent leather. The Jackie bag from 1950 was also reinterpreted in 1999 in gold metallic leather and neon-bright colours.

The second event was the invitation extended by luxury goods label Louis Vuitton in 1997 to Marc Jacobs to reinvigorate the brand. He accepted on the understanding that Vuitton would agree to back the designer's own eponymous line in New York. A graduate of the Parsons New School of Design in New York, Jacobs produced his landmark 'grunge' collection in 1993 under the Perry Ellis label. The multilayered look of silk shirts, printed to look like flannel, and distressed fabrics worn with Dr Martens footwear was inspired by Seattle rock bands, among them Nirvana and Pearl Jam. Although commercially unsuccessful, the collection was enormously influential and sounded the death-knell to the mature over-groomed look of the 1980s.

When applied to handbag design Jacobs' modern sensibility and eclectic style assured a plethora of 'must-haves'. The list of classic collectables such as the Vuitton Noe and the Hermès Kelly could now include the Vuitton Monogram Vernis, a 1998 reworking in pastels of the previously sacrosanct signature canvas. This resulted in sales of $40 million within the first nine months of production. The checkerboard pattern had already been subverted with the introduction of the Damier at the company's centennial in 1996 when a range of items were introduced especially for the commemoration. These were made with natural

BELOW LEFT The Monogram Collage Lutèce appeared in Louis Vuitton's autumn/winter 2008 collection. Lutèce is named after Lutetia Parisiorum, the ancient Roman city where Paris now stands. The collage lettering is made from different materials and finishings such as resin, brass and python with an engraved Louis Vuitton silver lock and a python strap. A true collector's item, the bag is made only on request.

BELOW RIGHT The popular and much-copied Louis Vuitton Speedy Multicolore was designed in collaboration with Japanese artist Takashi Murakami.

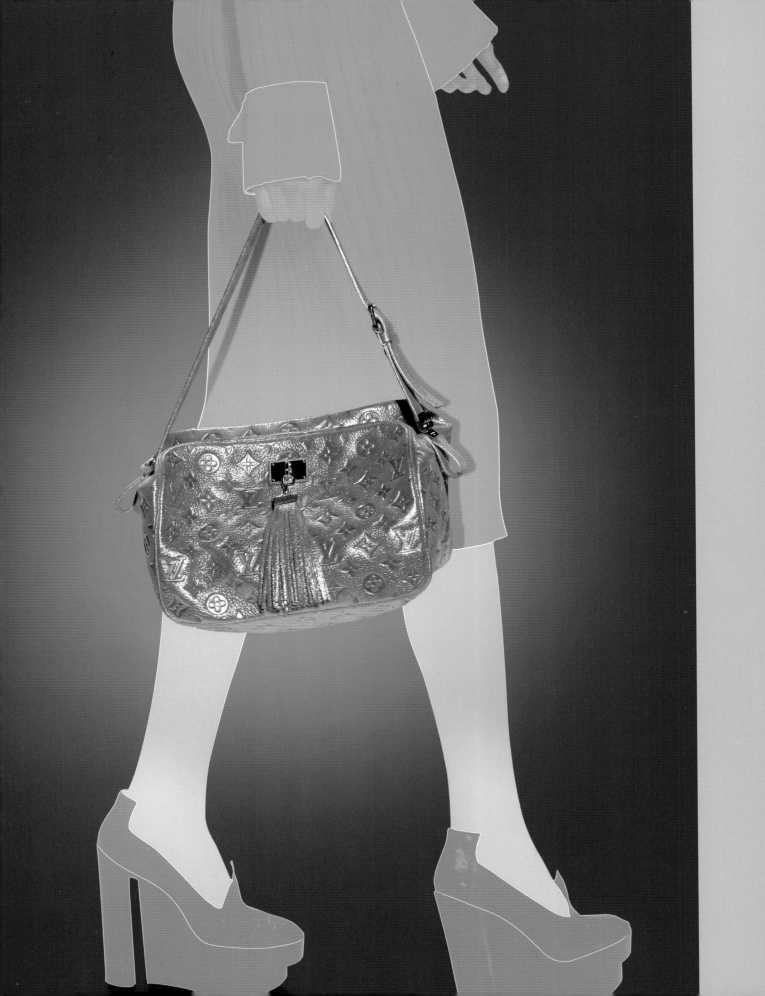

cowhide handles, straps and accents, whereas traditional Damier items are made in dark or ebony leather. Designers invited to collaborate with Vuitton included Isaac Mizrahi, Vivienne Westwood who designed a version of the bumbag, Romeo Gigli who produced an amphora-shaped bag, Manolo Blahnik, Azzedine Alaïa and Helmut Lang who created a case inspired by the dinner jacket.

The Speedy bag in Monogram Multicolore Franges (so called because it featured 33 shades) was the result of a collaboration between Takashi Murakami and Vuitton. A witty and satirical take on the power of the logo followed with the introduction of the Graffiti bag in 2000, a result of the collaboration between Marc Jacobs for Louis Vuitton and 1980s New York artist and designer Stephen Sprouse (see also page 184). The year 2002 saw the commercial success of the Murakami Monogram bag, an *anime* version.

Jacobs's eponymous line has also provided iconic handbags. His muse is the film director Sophia Coppola, for whom the Sophia is named, and the Stam, named after Jessica Stam, which is a quilted grained leather bag with a gusseted frame and gold brass hardware.

OPPOSITE The Louis Vuitton monogram of intersecting LV initials and curved diamonds with quatrefoils is recreated here in an embossed leather Monogram Vernis bag from 2008.

ABOVE AND RIGHT Two variations of Marc Jacobs' Stam bag – one in python and the other in peach leather. The bag has a kiss-lock clasp closure, double rolled leather handles, and a detachable chainlink strap. There is no blatant branding as the designer's name is inscribed on the small details – on one of the clasps and on the metal zip pull. The logo is stamped on the interior of the bag.

The Handbag As Art

Decorative bags that represent the skills of the artisan, crafted from esoteric, scarce or unexpected materials, are inevitably limited in number and therefore valued for their rarity. The definitive characteristic of the handbag as an art form is in the imagination of the designer, whether expressed in trompe l'oeil fantasies or as pieces of precious jewellery.

Nathalie Hambro

Connoisseur pieces are made by French-born handbag designer Nathalie Hambro. They are more likely to be found in galleries than on the arm of the owner, however. As a designer Hambro constructs a three-dimensional paper model of each bag to ascertain scale and proportion. Although treasured objects, the bags are often constructed in mundane materials; the designer cites artist Joseph Beuys as one of her influences and, like him, she subverts such substances as industrial felt and metal, straw, wire, nylon and horsehair to create something very precious. One of her first designs was the aluminium lunchbox, based on traditional Indian tiffin boxes.

The bags are made in limited editions, sometimes in as few as three, as was the case with the Cabat, produced in bronze gauze and hand-tied with a blue sapphire cord. The exquisite design detail of Hambro's bags often utilizes jewellery-making techniques, such as those deployed in the construction of the Japanese-style *inro* bags, far too precious to be practical. Hambro also designs for the couture house Balmain.

Jamin Puech

Predating the heavily embellished Fendi Baguette by three or four years was the romantic, folkloric appeal of the handbags designed by French label Jamin Puech. Isabelle Puech, one half of the duo, spent her childhood sailing around the world with her parents, which explains the eclectic nature of the designer's inspiration. She met her husband and partner Benoit Jamin as a student; they combined their talents in 1990 to create a collection of ceramic jewellery, followed by their first simple pocket-shaped bags created on a kitchen table in their Parisian apartment. By 1993 their bags were appearing on the runway at Chanel, Chloé, Lagerfeld and Balmain.

Their inspirations have ranged from America's Wild West to Britain's Bloomsbury Group, and research includes extensive watercolour studies that emphasize the importance of colour. Each collection features 82 designs in a minimum of five colour schemes, and the bags feature unexpected juxtapositions of textures and colours in a variety of materials from raffia to upholstery, cotton to wood, rope to leather, and canvas to cardboard. The designers list their global travels as providing inspiration, alongside flea market finds and bric-a-brac markets. This research is then adapted to current trends and influences.

The bags have become increasingly sophisticated while retaining the charm of novelty. Modern leather treatments such as Lycra leather, moiled leather, tattooed leather and thermo-changing leather are added to a mix of materials such as raffia, rattan, macramé, wood, nacre (mother-of-pearl), horn, plastic, rhodoid and silk. Processes include embroidery, plaiting and weaving, while patterns, ribbons, embossed motifs, silk-screen printing and reprographies are utilized. Production is limited to 50,000 hanbags a year.

OPPOSITE This Salvatore Ferragamo feather handbag is an exquisite example of the plumassier's art.

BELOW LEFT Nathalie Hambro transforms mundane materials such as industrial mesh tape and buttons to produce handbags that are works of art aimed at the specialist collector, as in this handbag dating from the 1990s.

BELOW RIGHT A richly dyed satin handbag encrusted with pearls from 2007 taps into the desire for the unusual and the handcrafted by the *haute* hippie, French designers Jamin Puech.

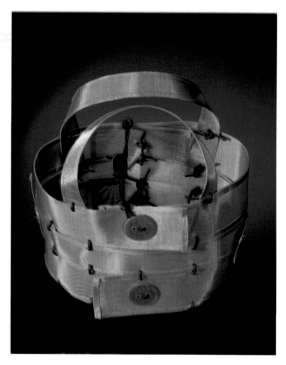

Lulu Guinness

Channelling the spirit of the surreal extravagances of Elsa Schiaparelli, together with a sensibility espousing 1950s glamour, accessories designer Lulu Guinness has retrieved femininity for the handbag. From initial production in the basement of the designer's house in West London she went on to open a shop in 1996 in Ledbury Road, Notting Hill, attracting a celebrity clientele. Produced in 1993 the Florist Basket was one of the designer's first successes, made of black satin with red suede roses. Together with the Violet Hanging Basket it resides in the permanent fashion collection at London's Victoria & Albert Museum. A series of trompe l'oeil House bags followed in 1995, which were whimsical handbags in the shape of houses, shops and theatres, often with the addition of witty directives such as 'Dare to be Different' in appliqué, print and embroidery.

The bucket-shaped bag lends itself to Guinness's subject matter, and forms the basis for diverse collections of containers from her range of flowerpot bags to a selection box of chocolates; the latter a limited-edition bag in lilac moiré, one of the designer's favourite colours. Each bag contains a card with the name of the woman who embroidered it. Clutch bags include the signature Daliesque pair of red satin lips and the open fan shape. Guinness produced the Flag Felicity purse, a sequinned Union Jack clutch, and the Stamp Frame bag in collaboration with artist Ann Carrington.

TOP A lipstick red evening bag dating from 2004 references the padded lip-shaped sofa of Salvador Dalí that first appeared in the 1930s. It has become a classic design, and is produced in different colours each season.

RIGHT The traditional shaped bucket bag transformed into a floral basket named 'Picnic rose' by British designer Lulu Guinness, an iconic design that is amongst the permanent fashion collection at Britain's Victoria & Albert Museum.

Fendi

The Fendi Baguette is not so much a handbag as a work of art, one of the reasons for its extortionate price. Developed by Silvia Venturini, the granddaughter of the founders of Fendi, and coveted by the *haute* hippie, the bag tapped into the New Age interest in craft and ethnic detailing. The bag offered a luxurious contrast to the sensible Kate Spade totes and Prada minimalism of the era.

Edoardo and Adele Fendi opened a leather and fur workshop on the Via del Plebiscito in Rome in 1925. Their five daughters joined the company after the First World War; one of their most far-reaching decisions was to hire Karl Lagerfeld to oversee the fur collections in 1965. The designer transformed the fur coat from its connotations of middle-aged frumpiness to edgy modernity, and the double F logo became instantly covetable. Reinvigoration of the leather goods business soon followed, culminating with the introduction of the Fendi Baguette in 1997.

The short shoulder strap requires that the bag fit high under the arm, as if carrying its namesake, a stick of French bread. It is impractically small, and features the interlocking double F logo on the clasp. Seasonal changes and limited numbers of each collection ensure that the bag remains at the top of the bagaholic's wish list. It is produced in a plethora of colours and in 600 different choices of materials, fabrics and skins, including velvet, fur and woven raffia, often patchworked together and embellished with precious metal thread and jewels. One example is the Lisio Baguette, made from silk velvet produced on traditional jacquard looms in collaboration with the Lisio Foundation, each of which can take up to a month to prepare for production, and with an output restricted to 20 centimetres (less than 8 inches) of fabric a day. The Baguette is always an appropriate accessory, the huge variety of materials in which it is made means that there is a version for casual daywear and the business meeting, as well as the special occasion or the formal evening. A smaller curved version, the Croissant, was launched with less success.

The Baguette was followed by Fendi's Salleria line, which revisited the company's hexagonal travel bags from the 1920s. Made from cowhide (*cuoio fiore*) and featuring Fendi's signature saddle-stitching, these were drip-fed onto the market and released in a limited edition with a serial number embossed on a silver plaque inside each bag. Venturini typically contrasts the styling of her bags from season to season. The structured Salleria line was followed by the relaxed slouchiness of the Fendi Spy, which preceded the structured B, originally produced in patent leather but later available in 40 fabric variations including embroidered straw and lace. In 1999 Fendi assumed partnership with LVMH.

BELOW LEFT One of the more subdued Fendi baguettes, which usually come in array of colours and textures. The bag is so called because the abbreviated strap demands that it is carried high under the arm, like a French bread stick. The clasp of the bag displays the interlocking double 'F' logo.

BELOW RIGHT Luxurious beadwork and fringing feature on this Fendi bag from 2008.

The Battle of the Bags

The millennium marked the 'battle of the bags', when every luxury brand and designer label endeavoured to produce the 'It' bag of the season. This resulted in an endless search for novelty in scale and decoration and the utilization of ever excessive and esoteric materials (collagen-injected snakeskin anyone?). The hierarchy of precious materials was relinquished as industrial fabrics such as nylon could be as costly as bespoke woven velvet.

A waiting list and celebrity endorsement became vital prerequisites of the commercial success of a bag. The notion of celebrity and headline-grabbing handbags became inextricably linked, and a marketing process known as 'seeding' gained popularity with the big brands and designer labels. This tactic was first deployed by Balenciaga in promoting Nicolas Ghesquière's Lariat in 2001. A squishy tote featuring tassels and rivets and with the signature leather strip on the zip, the bag was sent to 30 influential fashionistas and trendsetters, including Kate Moss, Sienna Miller, Chloë Sevigny and Charlotte Gainsbourg. Endlessly snapped by the paparazzi with the bag on their arm, it quickly achieved cult status with the commensurate waiting list.

An iconic handbag could also be used as a device to flag up the desirability of the brand as a whole. Alexander McQueen's black ostrich Novak bag in 2005 was limited to an edition of 200 and sold out even before reaching the waiting list. Named after Kim Novak, the actress in Alfred Hitchcock's film *Vertigo*, the formal design and upright stance of the bag reflected the repressed heroine of the 1958 drama.

Arguably one of the most famous bags of the decade, the Paddington bag, with its Victorian Gladstone bag shape and distinctive oversized lock, was designed by young British designer Phoebe Philo for French label Chloé. Credited with revving up the label for a younger, edgier demographic she joined Chloé in 1997, initially as assistant to Stella McCartney. In 2001 she succeeded McCartney as creative director of the luxury label until resigning from her role in 2006: during this time Philo designed various handbags including the Bracelet, the Camera, the Silverado, the Betty and the Edith. In 2008 Phoebe Philo was appointed creative director of Celine.

More than any other design house British designer John Galliano at Christian Dior has used the handbag to disseminate the seasonal trend of the catwalk to a wider audience. Inspired by a horse's tack – the saddle and bridle – the Dior Saddle incorporates a stirrup, buckle and bit. Launched in 2000 to mark the tenth anniversary of John Galliano's successful decade as the creative director of the couture house, the small, distinctively shaped bag heralded the trend for weighty embellishment. It is manufactured in a variety of materials, ranging from exotic skins to printed and patterned fabrics. In 2001 Dior's Trailer bag, complete with headlights and licence plates, introduced a note of novelty. When silver fox fur and bias-cut satin dresses hit the runway in 2004, inspired by 1930s Hollywood icon Marlene Dietrich, the fur D bag hit the shop floor.

French couture house Yves Saint Laurent produced the perennially popular Muse in 2005, to be followed by the recently launched Muse II. Seen on the arm of the usual fashion-led celebrities, the capacious oval design with its double zip referenced a piece of luggage rather than a handbag.

ABOVE The Muse by Yves Saint Laurent references the trend for the oversized handbag; as the size zero models got smaller the bags got bigger.

OPPOSITE Alexander McQueen's bags, like his fashion designs, are not for the faint-hearted. This 1992 model consists of luxurious studded burgundy leather.

BELOW Defining urban chic the Paraty bag was designed by the current creative director of Chloé, Hannah MacGibbon.

OPPOSITE A Diorita tote in twisted lambskin touting the D for Dior charm from the Christian Dior resort collection of 2009.

LEFT A natural wicker Ferragamo bag with a gilt metal 'gancino' fastening dates from 1996.

BELOW Aniline dyes produce the strong colours so typical of American designer Carlos Falchi in his 2008 bag featuring a patchwork of reptile skins.

ABOVE A 2003–4 design based on the Salvatore 'doctor's bag'. Produced in ponyskin printed in leopard motif and black calf, the unique construction has pocketed sides which form a double handle with a special convexity that gives the bag an anatomic grip. The model is named for the company's founder, Salvatore Ferragamo, and its shape was inspired by the big, burnt sienna ponyskin-and-leather bag that Salvatore used from 1950 for work and travel.

Modern Classics

What defines a classic handbag? It's not celebrity endorsement, the latest 'It' bag or the most expensive product. It is a bag that has enduring appeal and stands the test of time, reappearing season after season and immune to the transitory whims of fashion. Above all, it is a perfect marriage of form and function, resulting in beauty and practicality.

Burberry

With its origins rooted in practical clothes for the outdoors, including outfitting the polar expeditions of Roald Amundsen and Ernest Shackleton in 1914, Burberry continues to acknowledge the company's heritage while producing influential collections under the creative direction of Christopher Bailey. Thomas Burberry (1835–1926) opened his first shop in Basingstoke in 1856. He moved to London's Haymarket in 1881, which continues to be the site of Burberry's corporate headquarters. In 1901, the Burberry Equestrian Knight Logo was developed, containing the Latin word *prorsum* meaning 'forwards', and registered as a trademark.

In 1880 Burberry invented gabardine, a hard-wearing, water-resistant yet breathable fabric, and in 1895 created the Tielocken coat, adopted by officers in the Boer War. In 1914 he was commissioned by the war office to adapt its officer's coat for the army fighting in the First World War, resulting in the 'trench' coat. The trench subsequently went on to become a staple of traditional country outerwear, and the iconic Burberry white, beige, black and red check pattern, known as the Haymarket check or the Burberry classic check, was first used as a lining in 1924. It was not until 1967 that the check appeared on such accessories as scarves, umbrellas and luggage. The Novacheck followed, later used in an enlarged form and slanted in a diamond pattern. Christopher Bailey introduced the Housecheck, an even bigger version of the Novacheck, for spring/summer 2006.

ABOVE A plethora of buckles, straps and belts marries British heritage to high-end fashion in this Burberry Prorsum handbag with the traditional check, deconstructed for 2007.

OPPOSITE The minimalist 1990s was the perfect time to launch the 'anti-fashion' handbag. In 1998 Kate Spade, following the tradition of American designers such as Bonnie Cashin, designed a simply constructed, practical and strongly coloured nylon shopper that became one of the most successful bags of all time.

Kate Spade

In 1996 a new name appeared in handbag design that was neither affiliated to a traditional luxury leather goods house nor concerned with revitalizing a tired brand. The bag of the year was a simple, square satin-finished nylon shopper with an understated logo by the American designer Kate Spade. Born Kate Brosnahan of Kansas City, Missouri, the designer initially worked as an accessories editor on *Mademoiselle* from 1986 to 1991. Her experience on the magazine led Spade to spot a niche in the market for elegant handbags in bright colours that were not over-designed; bags that represented the personality of the owner rather than the designer. She invented a tote for her own use when on holiday in Provincetown in 1993 and together with her husband, Andy Spade, subsequently developed a line of six shoppers. Her first 'It' bag went on to win an accessories award from the Council of Fashion Designers of America (CFDA) in 1996. The company now also produces shoes, stationary and home furnishings.

Longchamp

French leather and luxury goods' company Longchamp was founded in 1948 by Jean Cassegrain, originally to create leather coverings for pipes and products geared towards smokers. By 1955 it had expanded to include small leather goods, opening its first factory in Segré, France. By the 1970s, Longchamp had opened boutiques in Hong Kong and Japan, and had became known for its lightweight travel goods (see also pages 158–9). In 1980, the founder's son, Philippe Cassegrain took the helm and expanded its retail and factory locations into Belgium and Germany.

Le Pliage, a collection of foldable travel bags made of vinyl and leather trim, was launched in 1993. In addition to its heritage as a luggage and accessories label, Longchamp has collaborated with notable designers and artists including London-based Thomas Heatherwick who designed a leather-and-canvas expandable bag constructed from a spiral zipper. Such was the success of the bag that Heatherwick was subsequently commissioned to design La Maison Unique Longchamp, the label's boutique in New York's Soho.

Orla Kiely

The leaf-and-stem design that forms the Orla Kiely logo represents the simplicity and love of pattern of the designer's aesthetic. With a master's degree in textiles, designer Kiely displays a profound understanding and graphic control of colour, pattern, texture and rhythm in her work.

The Orla Kiely label was launched in the 1990s with a collection of hats commissioned by London store Harrods, whose buyer had spotted Kiely's potential at the designer's graduation catwalk show at the Royal College of Art. Kiely then developed a collection of soft accessories, before designing a comprehensive collection of bags. In 1997 the Orla Kiely Partnership was formed with her husband Dermott Rowan and Orla showed as part of London Fashion Week for the first time, securing her first export orders. In 2005 flagship stores opened in London and Tokyo.

BELOW Dublin-born designer Orla Kiely extends her design aesthetic into all aspects of fashion and textiles, including accessories, distinguished by her controlled yet bold use of colour.

BELOW RIGHT One of Anya Hindmarch's coveted handbags, the Carker.

Anya Hindmarch

Identified by a discreet bow logo, British-born Anya Hindmarch produces luxury handbags designed to become heritage pieces. When the designer was only 16 her love of handbags was prompted by a gift of a Gucci handbag from her mother. Discarding the plans she had made for university Hindmarch decided to travel to Italy to learn the language, and while there was so inspired by the leather drawstring duffel bags carried by the Florentine woman that she imported them into England. She designed a bag for a reader's offer in British magazine *Harper's & Queen*, receiving 500 orders. After learning to produce her own bags, Hindmarch opened a small shop in Walton Street, London. In 2001 she was the innovator of the 'Be A Bag' idea; bags personalized with the customer's own photographs, which were sold to benefit the breast-cancer charity, the Lavender Trust. In 2007 Hindmarch, in collaboration with the global social change movement 'We Are What We Do' designed the global sell-out tote bag I'm Not A Plastic Bag. The limited edition canvas totes sold for £5, launching in four limited-edition colours around the world, and were selected by *Vanity Fair* to be included in their 'Oscars' goodie bags. Hindmarch has also produced the iconic Bespoke Ebury bag, handmade to order in calf or crocodile, and incorporating an inscription inside the bag in the owner or donor's handwriting.

In both 2006 and 2007 Hindmarch won Designer of the Year as awarded by *Glamour* magazine, and became the first winner of the Designer Brand of the Year at the 2007 British Fashion Awards. Hindmarch designs annually for three collections, which includes the core handbags plus shoes, luggage, small leather goods, a beach collection and a small range of ready-to-wear.

Smythson of Bond Street

Frank Smythson opened his first store in 1887 on 133 New Bond Street selling 'First class stationary leather goods and cabinetwork'. The current flagship store is opposite the original store on New Bond Street. An early example of their leather goods is the Monitor, described as being 'for the carriage or for travelling'. Lined with silk and in Moroccan leather, it was a vanity case for toiletry items. An original Monitor bag can be seen in the New Bond Street store museum. By 1910, the new age of motoring had arrived and Smythson had a number of products to meet the demand, including lucky motor mascots, travel cushions and Smythson's En Route writing pad, 'for use at home and abroad in a Motor, Steamboat, Railway or Aeroplane'. Today, Smythson continue to produce leather travel goods such as passport covers, luggage labels and wallets.

Early catalogues of the company date back to 1902 and show a variety of bags for day, evening and travel. In keeping with Smythson's heritage, the names of handbags, along with many other Smythson products, reveal a strong British connection, such as Bond Street, Mayfair, Bridgwater and Berkeley. Archive catalogues also illustrate a strong emphasis on novelty and innovation; for example, the 1909 Bridgwater is described as being 'Two bags in one… Utility and Elegance Combined'. Smythson entered the twenty-first century with the introduction of the Maze, so called because of the distinctive geometric maze pattern on the envelope pocket. Made in a combination of soft leather and suede with a brushed gold enamel clasp and an external pocket the bag has a magnetic closure. Another classic design from Smythson is the 2007 Nancy bag, in pleated leather, described by *Harper's Bazaar* as 'light on blingy hardware and heavy on effortless chic'.

BELOW The Nancy bag, designed by Samantha Cameron, creative director of the luxury goods company Smythson, was named after the Mitford sister, as well as Cameron's daughter. The bag is constructed from pleated calfskin and available in three colours.

Lambertson Truex

Producing handbags of chic styling and timeless elegance, Lambertson Truex designs and markets fine handbags and accessories collected by the world's connoisseurs of luxury merchandise. Founded ten years ago by Richard Lambertson and John Truex, the company quickly established itself as one of fashion's most original new voices. The products combine classic elegance with practicality; cell phone pockets and detachable key chains are discretely worked into bags' interiors, invariably lined in their signature sky-blue suede. Design is led by the unique properties of the leather, which in various finishes become the inspiration for new shapes.

Recognized for their expertise by the fashion industry, Lambertson Truex were awarded the accessory designer of the year by the Council of Fashion Designers of America (CFDA) in 2000. Following the success of its bags, Lambertson Truex launched a women's shoe line, then completed the collection by introducing small leather goods, gloves and belts, and then launched the same assortment of accessories for men. Collectors of handbags aspire to own one of the 200 signed limited edition handbags produced in conjunction with the Whitney Museum, the magazine *Vanity Fair* and American Express in collaboration with artist Donald Baechler. A signed edition of 1,000 was also produced of a canvas tote, the Gertrude.

TOP A Lambertson Truex specialty, this elegant clutch is styled from silver foil on linen and accented with aquamarine, moonstone, and crystal beading.

CENTRE The Box Car launched the Lambertson Truex legacy in 1998. This version is realized in premium South African crocodile, which has undergone a glazing process that results in a rich, high gloss.

RIGHT The Lambertson Truex Signature framed clutch is styled from luxurious, seamless crocodile with a signature LT clasp closure.

Tod's and Hogan

Renowned for the international success of the rubber-studded luxury driving shoe, the leather goods firm J P Tod may sound American, but is in fact based in Italy. The label is the invention of Diego Della Valle, the son of Dorino Della Valle who founded the company in the 1940s. The Gommini, a driving moccasin with 133 rubber pellets on the sole, was first produced in the 1970s, and it was not until 1997 that the first handbag collection was launched. The D-bag, a signature tote for Tod's, became an instant classic. Consisting of two pieces of leather joined down the middle, it is as simple and practical as the driving shoe. Marin Hopper, an ex-fashion director of British *Elle* magazine is now creative director to the company and was instrumental in launching the associated sportier Hogan line, one that produces younger, more relaxed designs, such as the popular fringed shopper. Lifestyle themes including international travel, aviation, motorcycling and surfing are reflected in the adventurous ad campaigns and channeled through the hardware, fabric and colour of the handbags. The Mini Eight is a small oval bucket bag constructed in eight pieces with metal studs for evening.

ABOVE A label and look that translates into instant prestige, this bag and coin purse are from Tod's 2009 collection.

Paul Smith

The 1990s was the era when successful fashion designers consolidated their label by producing handbag collections, and British fashion designer Paul Smith was no exception. Renowned for classic garments that also demonstrate a discreet eccentricity that is essentially British, Smith produces handbags that combine classic shapes in unexpected materials, often featuring imagery that display the designer's idiosyncratic sense of humour. The signature multicoloured swirls of stripes that identify the label have also been deployed on handbags.

Committed to the idea of creative independence Paul Smith is Britain's most commercially successful designer. Born in the city of Nottingham he left school at 15 and began his career running errands in a fashion warehouse. In 1970 he opened his first shop at the back of a tailor's shop; he then began manufacturing and retailing shirts, trousers and jackets under his own label, and in 1976 he showed for the first time in Paris.

The opening of the first Paul Smith store in London's Covent Garden in 1979 coincided with a resurgence in the money markets of the city, and subsequent changes in social attitudes. His suits for men became standard wear for the 1980s 'yuppie'. His amalgamation of traditional tailoring skills with a witty and subversive eye for detail together with his quirky use of colour and texture gave his customers the reassurance that it was permissible to be fashion-conscious without being outrageous. In 1993 he introduced a womenswear collection, including handbags, and in the year 2000 Queen Elizabeth II knighted him for his services to the British fashion industry.

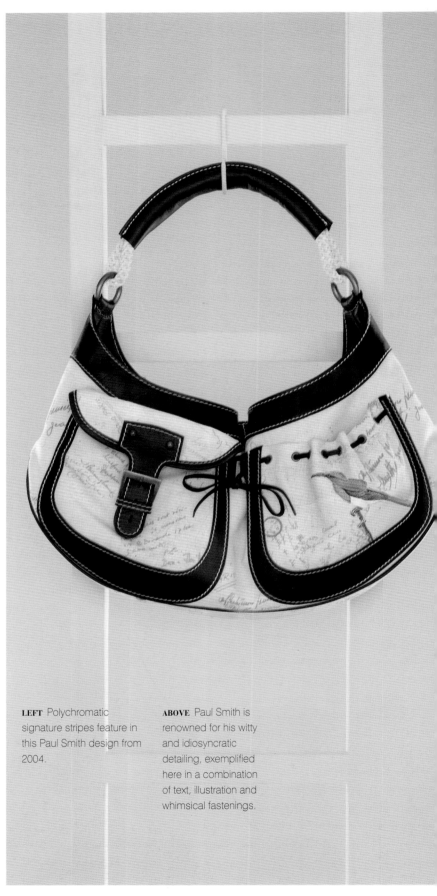

LEFT Polychromatic signature stripes feature in this Paul Smith design from 2004.

ABOVE Paul Smith is renowned for his witty and idiosyncratic detailing, exemplified here in a combination of text, illustration and whimsical fastenings.

Bill Amberg

Elements of traditional craftsmanship are combined with an understanding of the requirements of contemporary fashionable life in the work of Bill Amberg, hence the inclusion in his range of the leather baby papoose in 1998. Bill Amberg grew up in Northamptonshire, the home of the English leather trade, but it was not until the 1970s and a move to Australia that he began an apprenticeship under leather craftsmen that directed his career. Following his return to the UK he launched the Bill Amberg group of companies in 1984, working out of his own workshops and design studio in West London. The label incorporates an international fashion wholesale business, a specialist design consultancy, a bespoke architectural projects department, a store in London's Notting Hill and retail distribution. The Bill Amberg brand now embraces an expanding and diverse collection of bags, luggage, fashion and pet accessories, a shooting range, baby's collection and products for the home. He also designs ranges for Donna Karan, Margaret Howell and Coach Leather.

Bill Amberg collaborated with renowned British accessory designer Katie Hillier on the English Classics collection of canvas-and-leather day and travel bags, and a dedicated travel accessories line. Enlisted to create accessories for the young British designer Luella Bartley, Hillier also designed bags for Hogan in Italy and accessories for Marc by Marc Jacobs.

LEFT AND ABOVE Form and structure rather than extraneous decoration are the underlying concerns of British handbag designer Bill Amberg.

Shopping and Collecting

You are unlikely to find a piece of antique luggage or a vintage handbag from Hermès or Louis Vuitton at anywhere other than one of the major international auction houses such as Sotheby's or Christie's. A vintage Hermès bag can sell at auction for $10,000. Auction houses produce a catalogue that will list the provenance (history) of each item, including its designer, materials and construction. There is always a guide price and an opportunity to view the items before the sale. Luggage and suitcases from this period are too heavy to use, but often make interesting storage or can be used to style interiors.

Leather handbags from later periods, not necessarily those from a designer label or leading brand, are relatively easy to source, particularly from the 1930s onwards. Internet auction sites, dress agencies, vintage stores and charity shops are all good sources, though it would be unusual to find any bargains in the latter. Charity shop goods are now filtered through visiting experts and priced accordingly, but those sited in wealthy areas of a city, and particularly those supporting small or local one-off charities, will be more rewarding. Large antique centres with a collection of dealers displayed under one roof are a fruitful source, as are the big outdoor antique markets.

Buying Tips
- Always examine the inside of the bag, a good one will be as well finished as the exterior.

- Check the quality of the hardware. It should be solid and substantial, and cast rather then moulded. Make sure the clasp is still in working order, and that it closes with a satisfyingly heavy 'clunk.'

- Look at the hinges of the opening, as this is the first place a bag begins to show wear. If the bag has been overfilled in the past, the hinges will show signs of having been subject to strain.

- The leather should not be dried out or cracked, particularly on the straps. Check for real leather by smell, and the scratch test; it is possible to mark leather, but not plastic substitutes. Plastics were used for bags from the beginning of the century, but imitation leather was not used until after the 1960s, when a synthetic, breathable substance made from a plastic coating (polyurethane) was fused to a fibrous base layer (usually polyester) by DuPont in 1963.

- If the lining is torn or worn, it may not matter, as it is unseen, but be warned that biological stains are impossible to remove from suede or leather.

- Details such as straps and leather fastenings should be sewn, not glued, with even, unbroken stitches.

- Silk lining will mean a better quality bag than one lined with rayon or acetate.

- Check the rivets for signs of rust and the lining for signs of mould.

- The stiffer the suede and leather, the poorer the quality skin.

- Framed bags should have four metal 'rests' on the underside to protect the leather.

- Make sure the zip is the right weight for the bag, neither too flimsy nor too heavy.

Internet Auction Sites
Buying vintage handbags from a reputable auction house is relatively straightforward because of the absence of fakes but buying from an internet auction site is fraught with danger, owing to the multiplicity of fakes and the expertise of the fakers. Such is the volume of products on an internet site such as eBay that your search needs to be as specific as possible, and always remember to add 'purse' as well as 'bag' and 'handbag' at the end of the search. There are several points worth remembering.

- Sellers may not disclaim knowledge of, or responsibility for, the authenticity or legality of the items offered in their listings. If they cannot guarantee authenticity, it should not be on the site.

- Look not only at the total score of the feedback of the seller, but also the comments. See what they are currently selling, and what other items they have bought and sold in the previous 30 days. Also check for feedback that has been hidden.

- It is unlikely that one seller would have access to several authentic branded bags of the same type. Be wary if the seller offers multiples of the same items.

- Ask the seller questions as to the provenance of the bag; if you do not receive a reply, do not buy. It is also appropriate to ask for further photographs to be taken. Again, a refusal might signify that the item is fake.

- Check that the photograph has been taken by the seller and not downloaded from the designer's sales site.

OPPOSITE Maeve Brennan, a fashion writer at *Harper's Bazaar* in New York, examines purse fashions in 1944. An acclaimed short-story writer and journalist, Brennan was admired for her style, wit, beauty and intelligence. She joined *The New Yorker* in 1949.

- Make sure your payment is protected. Use a credit card and pay via PayPal. Through eBay, you will be given eBay's Buyer Protection to guard against items not received or significantly not as described (ie, fake when guaranteed authentic).

Identifying a Counterfeit Bag

There is a fine line between an homage to a designer handbag and a straightforward fake or 'knock-off.' An homage is an inevitable effect of the trickle-down of ideas, what is illegal is imitating the registered trademark. The duck emblem on Dooney & Bourke handbags and the LV symbol on Louis Vuitton bags have often been illegally pirated. Logo-patterned bags of plastic-coated canvas are very easy to copy.

Consult some of the many online sites that give detailed information and provide contrasting images of both real and fake handbags. My Poupette (www. mypoupette.com) is a US website which, for a fee, will check the authenticity of a designer bag. Here are some tips to help you authenticate a designer bag.

- Know what the bag should look like by checking online designer sales sites and, if possible, the actual handbags in the designer boutiques.

- Research the elements that make up the bag. What material should it be lined in, and what colour? Should it have feet? What does the base look like? Should it have a D-ring inside, and where? Does it have a date code?

- Examine the stitching. Stitching should be very even and regular. The same number of stitches should be found in similar locations on similar bags; for example, the leather tab that the handle attaches onto on any size of Louis Vuitton Monogram Speedy bag will always have five regular, even stitches across the top.

- Big brands do not sell 'seconds' and can only be purchased from registered outlets. They do not have discount outlets or sales.

- Some brands provide details that help authenticate the bag. Hermès have included discreet embossed stamps for the last 20 years inside their bags denoting when it was made and by whom. Louis Vuitton uses a production code inside its bags for the same purpose.

- Anything can be faked. Counterfeiters not only fake bags, but also fake the provenance details. These include receipts, boxes and dust bags.

Buying Bakelite

Bakelite has become a generic term used indiscriminately to describe almost any product made from thermosetting plastic materials. The trademark for Bakelite dates from 1926 and consists of three lobes containing the capital B. it was inspired by the amalgamation of three companies: Baekeland's general Bakelite company, Condensite and Redamanol. The logo was modernized in 1956, and the Bakelite era was from the 1920s to the 1950s. For care and storage, follow the tips for plastics opposite.

- Bakelite is heavier than other plastics such as celluloid and Lucite.

- Look for the brand name Rialto; this New York company produced an exquisite range of Bakelite, Lucite and plastic handbags in the mid twentieth century.

- If possible before buying, open and smell the bag; if you detect a chemical odour, the bag may deteriorate further. Bakelite does have a distinctive shellac-type odour.

- Bakelite items are subject to the oxidation discolouration – white becomes yellowed, blue darkens to green and pinks become more orange.

ABOVE This Ferragamo envelope clutch of over-sewn patchwork squares of coloured leather dates from 1989-90.

LEFT Referencing the classic handbags of the 1950s, with its box-like shape, plastic handle and poppy red colour, this handbag by Christian Dior dates from 1996.

Caring for Plastics and Other Polymers

When you buy, it is important to check the handbag for signs of chemical deterioration: distortion, odour, brittleness, stress crazing (fine cracks), an oily bloom on the surface or corrosion of metal fittings. If deterioration is evident later, isolate it from other items in your collection. It is better to acquire a product slightly physically damaged – with say a chip or a crack – than one that is chemically deteriorating. Try to ascertain whether or not the bag has been exposed to a harmful environment in the past.

- Do store plastics in the dark, in a cool, dust-free environment with some ventilation.

- Do inspect regularly for deterioration.

- Do wrap in acid-free paper, not newspaper, if packing away.

- Don't expose to strong sunlight.

- Don't keep in damp or stuffy places, sealed boxes or plastic bags.

- Don't clean plastic with solvents.

Caring for Leather Bags

Leather is known for its durability, versatility and strength and has been around for as long as humans have been hunters. Leather ages naturally, colours can change and darken with use – it will improve with age and with a bit of care and attention your leather bag will last a lifetime.

Traditional leather care is to apply saddle soap or a leather balm to restore suppleness, but always check with the manufacturer first. For example, aftercare for Louis Vuitton bags includes the advice to wipe only with a dry cloth and never use any kind of conditioner on Dooney & Bourke All-Weather Leather or patent leather. On no account use a silicone spray from an aerosol can. Handbag designer Ally Capellino recommends baby wipes for keeping leather clean, or you can try dampening a soft cloth with mild hand soap and warm water and wiping the surface. Don't scrub, but rub in a little conditioner after it's dry.

Be careful of pigment transfer from dark-coloured clothing; denim is a regular culprit. Oil, grease and ink are nearly impossible to remove. Fresh stains such as spilled liquids or food should be cleaned up immediately with a damp cloth or leather cleaner. Before using any products, always test a small, non-visible area, such as the base, first. Apply product to a cloth rather than directly onto the leather. Surface marking or scuffs that appears on some natural-finish leathers are often superficial and a result of the displacement of the oils in the leather. You can usually rub these out with a little bit of finger pressure.

ABOVE Discreet luxury in a classic handbag by American company Mark Cross, circa 1960s.

It is difficult to remove stains, so don't let pens and make-up loose in your bag. When using a bag lined with leather, suede or Alcantara put all sharp instruments and lotions inside another container inside the bag to protect the interior. Do not over-fill, as with time this will cause your bag to loose shape and the handles will weaken.

Leather isn't waterproof; if it's pouring rain, it might be better to use a different bag. However if it does get wet, blot with a paper towel, and then pack loosely with paper and allow it to dry naturally. Never place it in direct heat or sunlight for prolonged periods of time as this may cause the leather to crack or the colour to fade unevenly.

As a natural substance, leather must be kept clean and dry; if put away damp it will go mouldy. When you're not using your bag, store it in a cloth bag and stuff it with acid-free tissue paper, not bubble wrap as this can fuse to leather. For longer-term storage, undo strap buckles so that impressions are not created. If your bag has been in storage for some time, you can buff the leather with a cloth to restore lustre.

Waxed Cotton Handbags

Waxed cotton bags are proofed with a natural or synthetic wax and can be sponged clean with a damp cloth. If the oils have worn off, they can be reproofed professionally.

Crocodile and Other Skins

Most exotic skins, such as crocodile, python, lizard and ostrich, do not need any special cleaning. Real crocodile is supple and soft, and most skins are very resilient. The most important tips to care for all skin bags are to avoid exposure to sun or water. If it does get wet, air dry it away from any source of heat.

Museums and collections
UNITED KINGDOM
Gallery of Costume
Platt Hall,
Rusholme,
Manchester M14 5LL
+44 (0)161 224 5217
www.manchestergalleries.org
One of Britain's largest collections
of clothing, shoes and accessories,
dating from the seventeenth century
to the present day.

The Fashion Museum
Assembly Rooms
Bennett Street,
Bath BA1 2QH
+44 (0)1225 477 173
www.museumofcostume.co.uk
Iconic fashion designs, with a collection
of over 500 bags from the early
nineteenth century to the present day.

Victoria and Albert Museum
Cromwell Road,
London SW7 2RL
+44 (0)20 7942 2000
www.vam.ac.uk
Fashion and textile collection
dating from the seventeenth
century to the present day, with
an emphasis on influential
European design. Also
showcases accessories such
as shoes, gloves and jewellery.

EUROPE
Museum of Handbags and Purses
Herengracht 573
1017 CD Amsterdam
+31 (0)20 524 6452
www.museumofbagsandpurses.nl
Displays the history of the handbag
fom the late Middle Ages to the
present day. The museum shop has
a wide variety of bags for sale.

UNITED STATES
The Costume Institute
The Metropolitan Museum of Art,
1000 Fifth Avenue at 82nd Street,
New York, NY 10028–0198
+1 212 570 3828
www.metmuseum.org
Vast collection of 80,000 costumes,
including handbags and other
accessories.

The Museum at the Fashion Institute of Technology
Seventh Avenue at 27th Street
New York, NY 10001-5992
www.fitnyc.edu
Museum devoted to the art of
fashion, with an emphasis on the
avant-garde. Includes a collection
of luxury handbags. Tours must be
booked in advance.

Museum of the City of New York
1220 Fifth Avenue at 103rd Street
New York, NY 10029
+1 212 534 1672
www.mcny.org
Over 25,000 garments and
accessories dating from the mid-
eighteenth century.

CANADA
Costume Museum of Canada
109 Pacific Avenue,
Winnipeg, Manitoba
R3B OM1
+1 204 989 0072
www.costumemuseum.com
Intended as a national repository
for costume, accessories and textiles,
the collection includes pieces by
many international designers.

Stores and boutiques
UNITED KINGDOM
Absolute Vintage
15 Hanbury Street,
London E1 6QR
+44 (0)20 7247 3883
www.absolutevintage.co.uk

Armstrongs
83 The Grassmarket,
Edinburgh EH1 2HJ
+44 (0)131 220 5557
www.armstrongsvintage.co.uk

Beyond Retro
110–112 Cheshire Street
London E2 6EJ
+44 (0)20 7613 3636
58–59 Great Marlborough Street,
London W1 F7JY
+44 (0)20 7434 1406
www.beyondretro.com
One of the largest and most diverse
vintage stores in the UK.

Blackout II
51 Endell Street,
London WC2 9AJ
+44 (0)20 7240 5006
www.blackout2.com
A treasure trove, specializing in
the 1930s and 1940s.

Cenci
4 Nettlefold Place,
London SE27 0JW
+44 (0)20 8766 8564
www.cenci.co.uk

Frock Me!
+44 (0)20 7254 4054
www.frockmevintagefashion.com
Vintage fashion fairs in London
and Brighton.

The Girl Can't Help It
Shop G100, G90 and G80,
Alfie's Antique Market,
13–25 Church Street,
London NW8 8DT
+44 (0)20 7724 8984
www.sparklemoore.com

Kitt's Couture
51 Chapel Street,
Penzance TR18 4AF
+44 (0)1736 364 507
www.kittscouture.co.uk

Marshmallow Mountain
Kingly Court,
49 Carnaby Street,
London W1K 5AB
+44 (0)20 7434 9498
www.marshmallowmountain.com

One of a Kind
259 Portobello Road,
London W11 1LP
+44 (0)20 7792 5284

Palette London
21 Canonbury Lane,
London N1 2AS
+44 (0)20 7288 7428
www.palette-london.com

The Real McCoy
21 The Fore Street Centre,
Fore Street, Exeter EX4 3AN
+44 (0)1392 410 481
www.therealmccoy.co.uk

The Red Cross Shop
67 Old Church Street,
London SW3 5BS
+44 (0)845 054 7101

Rellik
8 Goldborne Road,
London W10 5NW
+44 (0)20 8962 0089
www.relliklondon.co.uk

Retro
8 Otago Street,
Kelvinbridge,
Glasgow G12 8JH
+44 (0)141 576 0165
www.retro-clothes.com

Rokit
101 Brick Lane,
London E1 6SE
+44 (0)20 7375 3864
107 Brick Lane,
London E1 6SE
+44 (0)20 7375 3777
225 Camden High Street,
London NW1 7BU
+44 (0)20 7267 3046
42 Shelton Street,
London WC2 9HZ
+44 (0)20 7836 6547
www.rokit.co.uk

Studio 66
Unit 205, Westbourne Studios,
242 Acklam Road,
London W10 5JJ
+44 (0)20 8964 4749
www.studio66.co.uk

TopShop Vintage
36–38 Great Castle Street,
Oxford Circus,
London W1W 8LG
0844 984 0264 (UK customers)
www.topshop.co.uk
Based in the Oxford Street branch
in London, the boutique contains
a large collection of vintage shoes,
handbags and clothing.

UNITED STATES

Atomic Passion
430 East 9th Street,
New York, NY 10009
+1 212 533 0718
An amazing array of vintage
and antique clothing and
accessories.

Cherry
17 Eighth Avenue,
New York, NY 10014
+1 212 924 1410
www.cherryboutique.com

Miami Twice
6562 Bird Road,
Miami, FL 33155–4830
+1 305 666 0127
www.miami-twice.com

New York Vintage
117 West 25th Street
New York, NY 10001
+1 212 647 1107
www.newyorkvintage.com

The Paper Bag Princess
8818 Olympic Boulevard,
Beverly Hills, CA 90211
+1 310 385 9036
www.thepaperbagprincess.com

Sasparilla
1630 Pennsylvania Avenue,
Miaimi Beach, FL 33139-7713
+1 305 532 6611

The Way We Wore
334 South La Brea Avenue,
Los Angeles, CA 90036
+1 323 937 0878
www.thewaywewore.com

CANADA

Divine Decadence Originals
136 Cumberland Street,
Upper Floor,
Toronto, Ontario M5R 1A6
+1 416 324 9759

Delux Junk Company
310 W Cordova Street,
Vancouver, BC V6B 1E8
+1 604 685 4871
www.deluxejunk.com

MaryAnn Harris
Ottawa Antique Market,
1179A Bank Street,
Ottawa, Ontario
+1 613 720 9242

The Paper Bag Princess
287 Davenport Road,
Toronto, Ontario
M5R 1J9
+1 416 925 2603
www.thepaperbagprincess.com

AUSTRALIA

The Vintage Clothing Shop
Shop 7 St James Arcade,
80 Castlereagh Street,
Sydney 2000
+61 (0)2 9238 0090
www.thevintageclothingshop.com

Online stores and resources

**1860–1960 One Hundred Years
of Fashion and Accessories**
www.1860–1960.com

Another Time Vintage Apparel
www.anothertimevintageapparel.com

Antique Lace & Fashion
www.antique-fashion.com

The Bag Lady Emporium
www.bagladyemporium.com

Ballyhoo Vintage
www.ballyhoovintage.com

Birdy Num Num
www.birdynumnum.com

Dandelion Vintage Clothing
www.dandelionvintage.com

Davenport and Company
www.davenportandco.com

eBay
www.ebay.com

Enokiworld
www.enokiworld.com

FashionDig.com
www.fashiondig.com

Heavenly Handbags
www.heavenlyhandbags.com

Incogneeto Vintage
www.neetstuff.com

It's Vintage Darling
www.itsvintagedarling.com

Kitty Girl Vintage
www.kittygirlvintage.com

Midnight Sparkle
www.midnightsparklevintageclothing.
com

Nelda's Vintage Clothing
www.neldasvintageclothing.com

Perfectly Vintage
www.perfectlyvintage.co.uk

Posh Vintage
www.poshvintage.com

Retrodress
www.retrodress.com

Retro Designer Deals
www.retrodesignerdeals.com

Rice and Beans Vintage
www.riceandbeansvintage.com

Sydneys Vintage Clothing
www.sydneysvintageclothing.com

Vintage Bag
www.vintage bag.com

Vintage Martini
www.vintagemartini.com

Designers' websites

Bill Amberg
www.billamberg.com

Botega Veneta
www.bottegaveneta.com

Celine
www.celine.com

Chanel
www.chanel.com

Christian Dior
www.dior.com

Coach
www.coach.com

Dooney & Bourke
www.dooney.com

Etienne Aigner
www.etienneaigner.com

Fendi
www.fendi.com

Gucci
www.gucci.com

Lulu Guinness
www.luluguinness.com

Hermès
www.hermes.com

Jamin Puech
www.jamin-puech.com

LeSportsac
www.lesportsac.com

Longchamp
www.longchamp.com

Marc Jacobs
www.marcjacobs.com

Lana Marks
www.lanamarks.com

Marni
www.marni.com

Mulberry
www.mulberry.com

Prada
www.prada.com

Jill Stuart
www.jillstuart.com

Louis Vuitton
www.louisvuitton.com

Vivienne Westwood
www.viviennewestwoodonline.
co.uk

Designer Glossary

Aigner, Etienne (1904–2000)

Hungarian-born designer, Etienne Aigner, presented his first collection in New York in 1950. In 1965 the company, Aigner, was founded in Munich. The equestrian-influenced style is characterized by rich red leather, fine craftsmanship, and the famous, horseshoe-shaped 'A' monogram.

Amberg, Bill

Bill Amberg launched his eponymous label in 1984, with traditional leather craftsmanship as a key element of his design. The brand is ever expanding and includes ranges of luggage, pet accessories, baby products and wares for the home.

Bonnie Cashin (1908–2000)

A significant pioneer of American sportswear, Cashin is famed for her use of a variety of organic materials, such as leather and wool, in her designs. In 1962 she was hired by the handbag and accessory firm Coach and is credited with applying her signature use of industrial hardware, in this case brass toggles, to bags.

Bottega Veneta

This Italian bag manufacturer was established in 1967 in Vincenza. Their highly fashionable bags are all handmade in soft leather, the most famous being the Intrecciato Bags that are made of woven leather. Bottega Veneta became part of the Gucci Group in 2001.

Burberry

Thomas Burberry (1835–1926) opened his first shop specializing in waterproof raincoats, in Basingstoke, England in 1856. In 1901 he was commissioned by the Department of War to deign a raincoat for military use, this led to his fortune. The company is still famous for its raincoats, but has also achieved worldwide acclaim for its traditional, yet cutting-edge, design of clothes and accessories that include a wide range of handbags, many of which sport the traditional Burberry check.

Cardin, Pierre (1922–)

Before establishing his own house in 1954, Cardin worked with designer Elsa Schiaparelli and was Christian Dior's *tailleure atelier*. In contrast with his former colleagues, he preferred unisex designs that were dominated by geometric shapes and patterns. He reached the height of his success during the 1960s, but his fashion house is still going strong today.

Cartier

This French jeweller and watch manufacturer has a long history of catering to royalty and affluent clientele. Creating high-quality jewellery and watches since 1847, the formidable company has also been involved with creating evening bags, cigarette cases and other fashionable accoutrements.

Celine

Celine opened its first boutique, designing and selling children's wear, in Paris in 1946. The boutique saw great success and the company expanded to include a women's shoe line in 1963 and leather collection, including handbags, in 1966. The 2003 Poulbot Bag, otherwise known as an 'urchin' or 'rascal' bag, is now an icon among bags.

Chanel

Established by Gabrielle 'Coco' Chanel (1883–1971) in 1914, this formidable fashion house is synonymous with modern sophistication. Chanel revolutionized *haute couture* by replacing the traditional corseted look with simple tailored suits and long clinging dresses. Chanel has produced some iconic pieces, including the 2.55 handbag.

Chapelier, Hervé (1950–)

A French business student with an eye for fashion, Hervé Chapelier created his first nylon duffel bag in 1976. The label has since branched out to include bags, backpacks and luggage, made primarily from nylon or leather.

Christian Dior (1905–1957)

The 1950s New Look is largely owed to the designs of Christian Dior, who established his fashion house in 1946. His designs heralded the return to a more feminine style and established Dior as one of the most important figures in French *haute couture*. He paid close attention to accessories, including shoes, hats, and of course handbags.

Coach

Established in 1941, this leather goods company is famous for its quality handbags. The famous 'Cashin Carry' bag was designed by Bonnie Cashin in 1962 and is marked, like many of the other bags Coach produces, by great innovation and quality.

Di Camerino, Roberta (1929–)

A Venetian handbag designer who was widely popular in the 1950s for her Surrealist and trompe-l'oeil influenced designs. She uses a wide range of fine materials to produce her creations. She won the Neiman Marcus Award in 1956 for her high quality, ultra creative handbags. Her most famous bags include the Bagonghi and the Caravel.

Dooney & Bourke

Peter Dooney and Frederic Bourke established this Connecticut-based accessories company in 1974. They began by producing just two products, a surcingle belt and classic suspenders, but in 1981 they branched out into bags. In 1983 they launched their highly successful All Weather leather bags that are still popular today.

Enny

A company that catered to the needs of the modern working woman, Enny created both functional and fashionable bags for the mass market without compromising the quality of their product. They used traditional Florentine craftsman, who are famed for their leatherwork skills, and super soft leather in their creations. The company ceased trading in 2003.

Fendi

Established in Rome in 1925, this Italian house specializing in furs and leather has become one of the most renowned accessory labels in the world, known especially for its Baguette handbag. It currently produces a series of luxury goods such as eyeglasses, fragrances, furs and handbags, as well as apparel.

Ferragamo, Salvatore (1898–1960)

Salvatore Ferragamo was an innovative shoemaker who created legendary women's footwear designs during the first half of the twentieth century. Having made his name making shoes for the stars in Hollywood, he returned to his native Italy in 1927 to set up his business there. The Ferragamo brand now produces other luxury items, including handbags.

Furla

This Italian leather company was established in Bologna, Italy in the 1930s. It initially dealt purely with distribution, but later began to manufacture bags, shoes and other leather accessories. It is now a venerable label known for its high-quality wares.

de Givenchy, Hubert (1927–)

A French designer, Givenchy is known for his classic, feminine cuts. He made his couture debut in 1952 during the New Look era and his house remains prominent on the fashion scene.

Goldpfeil

Established in 1856, this German company is renowned for the sophistication and craftsmanship of their wallets, briefcases, luggage, handbags and other leather accessories.

Gucci

In 1921 Guccio Gucci (1869–1953) set up a small workshop in Italy that specialized in handcrafted leather goods. The famous bamboo-handled handbag, which is still a company mainstay, was introduced in 1947, and the iconic green-red-green webbing was introduced in the 1950s. Over the years the Gucci's range has expanded and the company is now a formidable, popular and thriving fashion house.

Guinness, Lulu (1960–)

Known for her eccentric and imaginative styles, Lulu Guinness is a highly successful English handbag designer.

H Wald & Company

Popular in the 1940s and 1950s, H Wald & Company are well known for designing practical yet stylish daytime handbags, that carried gas masks during the wartime era, and luxurious 'Waldybags' for evening occasions.

Hambro, Nathalie

Handbags created by this London-based designer are considered to be more inventive than utilitarian. Her work is more likely to be found in museums than in boutiques, but designs such as her famous metal lunchbox ranks her as one of the most imaginative and expressive designers.

Hindmarch, Anya (1968–)

A self-taught English designer, Hindmarch primarily designs handbags, but her line has recently broadened to include shoes, small leather goods and luggage. She has boutiques in London and Hong Kong.

Hermès

Like many other European handbag manufacturers and designers, Hermès started out, in 1837, as a saddler. Hermès capitalized on the demand for high-quality leather accessories that emerged at the turn of the century and today sells a range of luxury products. Hermès bags are beautifully handcrafted and include the iconic Birkin and Kelly.

Jacobs, Marc (1963–)

Born and raised in New York City, Marc Jacobs teamed up with Robert Duffy in 1984 (the year he graduated) to set up the Jacobs Duffy Design label. In 1993 he established the Marc Jacobs International Company. He is noted for both elegant and whimsical apparel and accessories that are inspired by a range of influences, from grunge to classic chic.

Jamin Peuch

An accessories brand established by designers Benoît Jamin and Isabelle Puech, the label produces over 20,000 bags per year. Inspired by flea market finds and global travels, the pair produce vivid, well-crafted bags and accessories.

Karan, Donna (1948–)

American designer Donna Karan is known for her clean and modern style. She started her magnificent career working with Anne Klein, becoming stylistic director in the mid-1970s. She began designing under her own name in 1984, since then her fashion empire has grown to include the more casual DKNY label, accessories, cosmetics and interior decor.

Koret

This fashionable label was founded in 1929 by Richard Koret and became well known for selling good-quality, mass-produced bags at reasonable prices, mainly at department stores. Koret bags were especially popular in the 1950s and 1960s.

Kors, Michael (1961–)

Born and raised in New York, Michael Kors began a successful line of apparel in 1981. His minimalist approach is highly respected and he is considered to be a pioneer of clean, simplistic style.

Lagerfeld, Karl (1933–)

A German-born designer, Lagerfeld began his career in fashion in Paris at the age of 16. In the 1960s he became an independent designer, collaborating with the likes of Fendi, Valentino and Charles Jourdan. He became creative director for Chanel in 1983, but now concentrates on Fendi and running his own label.

Lambertson Truex

An American brand manufacturing handbags and accessories, the label, established in 1998 by Richard Lambertson and John Truex, is known for creating new bag shapes inspired by the creative use of textiles, colours and materials.

LeSportsac

Established in America in 1974, LeSportsac introduced colourful, sporty, practical and fun handbags into the 1970s fashion scene. Their most notable and recognizable design is their fold-in pouch, ripstop nylon bags and luggage, which are available in an assortment of bright colours.

Leiber, Judith (1921–)
Born in Budapest, Judith Lieber formally studied the handbag-making at the Hungarian Bag Association during the Second World War. She moved to America in 1947 and established her own label in 1963. Her work is widely appreciated for its sophistication and craftsmanship.

Loewe
Loewe was established in 1846 by the German craftsman, Heinrich Loewe Rossberg, in Madrid, creating and distributing quality leather goods from its inception. It is now focused on producing a wide range of accessories.

Longchamp
Frenchman Jean Cassegrain began to produce leather goods in 1948, after he was inspired to wrap one of the pipes he sold in his smoking shop in leather. Ten years later he opened his first factory producing leather cases. In 1993 the company introduced the popular Le Pliage bag, which is made of washable nylon, has leather handles and comes in a variety of colours.

L L Bean
A privately owned American mail-order and clothing company, based in Maine. It was established in 1912 and is still extraordinarily popular today. Their famous Boat and Tote bag was originally introduced as a gardening bag in 1944, and is still in production today.

Marks, Lana
Bags by the British-born designer Lana Marks are marked by their exotic materials, such as crocodile, alligator and lizard. She caters to the affluent and famous, and was the official handbag and accessories consultant for the 2002 and 2003 Academy Awards.

Marni
Consuelo Castiglioni, a Swiss designer, has been designing under this label since 1991. Marni specializes in furs, transforming them from a status symbol for old ladies to fashionable items. The collection has recently been expanded to include accessories and bags.

McQueen, Alexander (1969–)
A British designer, noted for his innovative and controversial designs, McQueen was appointed artistic director of Givenchy in 1997. He continues to create controversial designs and collaborate with other couture houses.

Mulberry
Established by Robert Saul as an accessories brand in 1971, Mulberry uses quality materials in its designs. Based in the English countryside, the company aims to combine both the beauty of the outdoors and the excitement of the city in its handbag designs. Although it now produces clothing and housewares, it is best known for its well-designed bags.

Prada
Craftsman Mario Prada established his company in 1913 in Milan. He made trunks, handbags and accessories of the utmost quality, and designed to never go out of fashion. His granddaughter, Miuccia Prada Bianchi, took over in 1978 and transformed the family business into an international producer of luxury goods.

Schiaparelli, Elsa (1890–1973)
Known for her Surrealist designs and creative genius, Schiaparelli is certainly one of the most important fashion designers of the twentieth century. Her work was trompe l'oeil-inspired, and she collaborated with some of the most esteemed artists and designers of the day, including Salvador Dalí.

Smythson
In 1887, Frank Smythson established a shop on New Bond Street in London that specialized in leather goods, stationary and cabinetwork. The brand continues to create and manufacture leather products for the luxury market.

Stuart, Jill (1965–)
While still a teenager, Stuart launched her first handbag collection with Bloomingdales. She now has two labels (the Jill Stuart Collection and Jill by Jill Stuart) and a range of handbags and accessories. Her style is soft and feminine.

Tod's
This company began as a family affair, being established at the turn of the last century in Italy by the Della Valle family. For some time they produced only shoes, achieving worldwide fame with the driving shoe, but diversification into other luxury leather goods has also led to the famous D-bag.

Valentino (1933–)
When this famous Italian fashion designer first debuted his own collection in the late 1950s, he failed to sell a single item. Undeterred, he presented another collection in 1962 to great critical acclaim. His designs are renowned for their elegant femininity and he counts celebrities and royals among his many clients.

Vuitton, Louis (1821–1892)
Louis Vuitton established his eponymous company in 1835 in Paris, where he specialized in selling bags and travelling trunks to the wealthy. He crafted tailor-made trunks with designs suitable for modern travellers, and also created one of the first logos to guarantee a product's originality. Since 1959, the product range has expanded to include bags, small leather goods, shoes and other accessories.

Westwood, Vivienne (1941–)
English designer who emerged on the fashion scene in the 1970s as a stylist and designer for bands like the Sex Pistols. In introducing outrageous punk and new wave fashion to the mainstream Westwood changed the face of fashion. Her style is fresh and innovative and she remains a leading figurehead on the fashion scene.

Wilardy
After studying industrial design in his teens, Will Hardy joined his family's company Handbag Specialties in 1948, and created the Wilardy trademark. His handmade Lucite handbags are among the most sought-after vintage pieces; the innovative designs often featured rhinestones, jewelled lettering, netting inserts and crystal-cutting effects.

Index

Further Reading

Age of Extremes: The Short Twentieth Century 1914–1991, Eric Hobsbawn, Abacus, 1995.

Bags, Claire Wilcox, V&A Publications, 2008.

Bags: A Lexicon of Style, Valerie Steele and Laird Borrelli, Scriptum, 2005.

Bags: An Illustrated History, Caroline Cox, Aurum Press, 2007.

The Beautiful People, Marylin Bender, Coward-McCann, 1967.

Boutique, a 1960s Cultural Phenomenon, Marnie Fogg, Mitchell Beazley, 2003.

Carried Away: All About Bags, Farid Chenoune (ed), The Vendome Press, 2005.

Costume and Fashion: A Concise History, James Laver, Thames & Hudson, 2002.

Dior by Dior, Christian Dior, V&A Publications, 2007.

Fashion, Christopher Breward, Oxford University Press, 2003.

The Fashion Conspiracy: A Remarkable Journey Through the Empires of Fashion, Nicholas Coleridge, Mandarin, 1989.

Fashion V. Sport, Salazar Ligaya (ed), V&A Publishing, 2008.

Handbags (Pocket Collectors), Judith Miller, Dorling Kindersley, 2006.

Handbags: What Every Woman Should Know, Stephanie Pedersen, David & Charles, 2006.

It's In the Bag, What Purses Reveal and Conceal, Winifred Gallagher, Harper Collins 2006.

Know your Fashion Accessories, Celia Stall-Meadows, Fairchild Books, 2004.

The Life and Times of Hollywood's Celebrated Costume Designer Edith Head, David Chierichetti, Harper Perennial, 2003.

Louis Vuitton Icons, Stephane Gerschel and Marc Jacobs, Assouline Publishing, 2007.

Pierre Cardin, Rishard Morais, Bantam Press, 1991.

Plastic Handbags, Sculpture to Wear, Kate E Dooner, Schiffer Publishing Ltd, 1993.

Silver and Gold, Norman Hartnell, Evans Brothers Ltd., 1955.

Whiting and Davis Purses: The Perfect Mesh, Leslie Pina and Donald-Brian Johnson, Schiffer Publishing Ltd, 2002.

Picture Credits

The publishers would like to thank the following sources for their kind permission to reproduce the pictures in this book.

Key: t=Top, b=Bottom, c=Centre, l=Left and r=Right

Front & Back Endpapers: ©Carlton Books

The Advertising Archives (Image Courtesy of): 153l ©**Aigner:** 135 akg-images: 84b **Alinari Archives:** /Fratelli Alinari Museum of the History of Photography-Favrod Collection, Florence: 8l, 22l ©**Anya Hindmarch:** 6r, 7l, 7tr, 7br, 204r, /Ben Knight: 6l **Art Archive:** /Alfredo Dagli Orti: 37b, 52b, 59t, 69c, 125t, 125b, /Eileen Tweedy: 58c **Bag Lady Emporium. com:** /Courtesy Marion Spitzley: 112l, 112r, 143c ©**Bill Amberg:** 209l, 209r **Bridgeman Art Library:** /Bibliotheque des Arts Decoratifs, Paris, France/Archives Charmet: 17, 25, /Hermitage, S. Petersburg, Russia: 24b, /Kremlin Museums, Moscow, Russia: 24t, /Private Collection: 63b, 161l **Camera Press:** /Andre Carrara/HQ: 155, /Richard Dormer/HQ: 153r, /Keystone/Eyedea: 8cr, 78, 127, 137, 160, /Madame Figaro/Roberto Badin: 195, /Madame Figaro/Isabelle Bonjean: 199, /Madame Figaro/Andrea Klarin: 188, /Madame Figaro/Jerome Laurent: 191l, 197r, /Madame Figaro/Renauld Wald: 181r, 194r, /Marie Claire/L'Harmeroult: 187tl, /Marie Claire/Assenat: 172b, /Marie Claire/Carrara: 9cr, 170l, 170r, 171, /Marie Claire/Feurer: 182, /Marie Clarie/Moser: 183r, /Marie Claire/Schmid: 186bl, /Marie Claire/Yurek: 133 **Carlos Falchi:** 163l, 201b ©**Carlton Books:** 111t, 111b, /Alvaro Canovas: 186tl, /Laurent Herail: 41b /Patricede Villier: 103b, 197l, 203l ©**Chanel:** 101t, /Photo All Rights Reserved: 101b ©**Chloe:** 198b ©**Christian Dior Couture:** 179t **Constance Howard Resource & Research Centre in Textiles:** /David Ramkalawon/VADS (www.vads.

ac.uk): 47bl **Corbis:** /Bettmann: 20-21, 67, 72l, 76l, 84t, 102, 103t, 105t, 115t, 122, 162, /©Condé Nast Archive: 4, 10, 30, 53, 60b, 68tr, 70, 72r, 73, 79t, 79b, 81, 82-83, 86b, 87l, 88br, 89br, 90, 92, 93, 96, 97r, 98, 99l, 104, 106l, 107, 114, 116tl, 118, 123, 129, 136, 146, 148, 158l, 165c, 166, 184r, /©Condé Nast/WWD: 1, 9r, 161r 192, 200, 207, /©Robert Eric/Corbis Sygma: 212l, /©Todd France/Corbis OutlineLive: 203r, /©Hulton-Deutsch Collection: 38t, 61, 69cr, 99r, 14l, /©David Lees: 180, /©Genevieve Naylor: 87r, 108, /©Underwood & Underwood: 34l, 40, 60t, /©Pierre Vauthey/Sygma: 173, 184l, 187r **Denna Jones (from the collection of):** 142t, 143tl, 143tr, 213 **DLM Deutsches Ledermuseum Schuhmuseum Offenbach:** 12l, 19b, 20, 29tl, 38b, 50, 63t, 76r, 86t, 120l, 120r, 187bl **Getty:** 57r, 100, 124, 177, 178, 181l, 202, /Hulton Archive: 8cl, 9cl, 13l, 32, 33, 85, 100, 109, 145t, 165t, /Imagno: 19t, /Lichfield: 140b, /Lipnitzki/Roger Viollet Collection: 54bl, 57l, 69bl, 121, /Popperfoto: 2-3, 8r, 9l, 95, 131, 140t, /Sasha: 51t & main, /Seeberger Freres/General Photographic Agency: 46tl, 47r, /Time & Life Pictures: 8c, 54br, 55, 75l, 75r, 83, 88t, 89t, 106r, 210 ©**Gucci/Raymond Meier:** 190t, 190b **Hampshire Museums Service:** /Caroline Littlewood: 16b, 22r, 23t, 23b, 28t, 28bl, 28br, 29b, 42l, 42r, 44, 45t, 46b, 47tl, 59b, 68tl, 68b, 88bl, 110l, 112c, 113t, 115b, 116tr, 116c, 116br, 117t, 117c, 117b, 144t, 145bl, 164tl, 164br, 165b, 186r ©**Hermés:** /Frederic Dumas: 179b ©**Hervé Chapelier:** 159t, 159b **Iain Davies Photography:** 150l, 150r **Jackie Perry:** /Image Courtesy easyontheeyes.etsy.com: 156tr **Janet Gersh:** 175c **Jodie Haffa-Iovarevolutionary.etsy.com:** 156b ©**Judith Leiber:** 175t, 175b ©**Lambertson Truex, LLC:** 206t, 206c, 206b ©**Longchamps:** 158b ©**Louis Vuitton:** 191r, /Malletier A Paris: 26 ©**Lulu Guinness:** 196t, 196b ©**Marc Jacobs:** 193t, 193b **Mary Evans Picture Library:** 12r, 13r, 16t, 29tr, 58b, 69t, 145br, /Illustrated London News: 35, 39, 43, 46tr, 54t, /National Magazines: 58t **Mirrorpix:** 163r ©**Mulberry:** 156tl **Museo Salvatore Ferragamo:** 168, 169t, 169b, 172t, 201t, 201c, 212r ©**Museum at F.I.T:** /Photographs by Irving Solero: 64, 66, 128, 135t ©**Norman Parkinson Archive:** 77, 94l, 94r, 130, 149, 151, 152, 154, 224 ©**Orla Kiely:** 204l **Pam Hawk:** /www.passitonplates.com: 142b, 143bl, 143br ©**Paul Smith:** 208l, 208r **Rex Features:** 185l, /Everett Collection: 164bl, /Kaius Hedenstrom: 164tr, /David Magnus: 132, /News (UK) Ltd: 176, /Roger-Viollet: 144c ©**Smythson:** 205 **All images, Courtesy Stephanie Lake Collection:** 138–139 topfoto.co.uk: 126, 144b, /AP: 134, /Roger-Viollet: 18, 26-27, 41t, 48, 65 **Victoria & Albert Museum:** /V&A Images: 14, 15l, 15r, 34r, 36, 37t, 45b, 49, 52t, 56, 62, 74, 80, 89bl, 97l, 105b, 110r, 113b, 174, 183l, 194l ©**Yves Saint Laurent:** 198t

Every effort has been made to acknowledge correctly and contact the source and/or copyright holder of each picture and Carlton Books Limited apologises for any unintentional errors or omissions which will be corrected in future editions of this book.

Author Acknowledgements

Many thanks to Lisa Dyer and all at Carlton Books, Dr Philippa Woodcock, John Bates, Iain Davies, Caroline Cox, Joby Jackson, Stephanie Green, Ruth Eley, Pam Hemmings, Phoebe Collier, George Collier, and to my daughter, Emily Angus.